Praise for *The Oxford History of Witchcraft and Magic*

'As well as a masterly summary of Voltaires life, the reader gains a much better understanding of 18th-century France and Europe.'

David Lorimer, *Network Review*

'Another quality book from Oxford University Press ... a goldmine for anyone looking for information on witchcraft and magic and perhaps those looking for inspiration and some unusual little fact or nugget if they want to dabble in some fiction involving witches or magicians, dark or otherwise.'

Ian Hunter, *Concatenation*

'The breadth of knowledge shown here is impressive ... It informs, shocks, repulses and entertains ... a scholarly and impressive work'

On Magazine (Yorkshire)

'comprehensive and impeccably researched, but also well written and fascinating to read ...'

Bad Witch

'readable and compelling ... this ambitious project presents a helpful ... contribution that should find a home as supplemental reading material in relevant undergraduate courses'

Jodie Ann Vann, *Nova Religio*

T0049109

The Oxford History of Witchcraft and Magic

Owen Davies is Professor of Social History at the University of Hertford-shire. He has written extensively on the history of magic, witchcraft, ghosts, and popular medicine, including *The Haunted: A Social History of Ghosts* (2007), *Grimoires: A History of Magic Books* (2009), *Paganism: A Very Short Introduction* (2011), *Magic: A Very Short Introduction* (2012), *America Bewitched: The Story of Witchcraft after Salem* (2013), and *A Supernatural War: Magic, Divination, and Faith during the First World War* (2018).

The historians who contributed to *The Oxford History of Witchcraft and Magic* are all distinguished authorities in their field. They are:

OWEN DAVIES, University of Hertfordshire
WILLEM DE BLÉCOURT, Huizinga Institute / Meertens Institute, Amsterdam
PETER MAXWELL-STUART, University of St Andrews
SOPHIE PAGE, University College London
JAMES SHARPE, University of York
RITA VOLTMER, University of Trier
ROBERT J. WALLIS, Richmond University
CHARLES ZIKA, University of Melbourne

The Oxford History of Witchcraft and Magic

Edited by

OWEN DAVIES

OXFORD

UNIVERSITY PRESS

OXFORD
UNIVERSITY PRESS

Great Clarendon Street, Oxford, OX2 6DP,
United Kingdom

Oxford University Press is a department of the University of Oxford.
It furthers the University's objective of excellence in research, scholarship,
and education by publishing worldwide. Oxford is a registered trade mark of
Oxford University Press in the UK and in certain other countries

© Oxford University Press 2023
The text of this edition was first published in
The Oxford Illustrated History of Witchcraft and Magic in 2017

The moral rights of the author have been asserted

First published 2017
First published in paperback 2021
Impression: 1

All rights reserved. No part of this publication may be reproduced, stored in
a retrieval system, or transmitted, in any form or by any means, without the
prior permission in writing of Oxford University Press, or as expressly permitted
by law, by licence or under terms agreed with the appropriate reprographics
rights organization. Enquiries concerning reproduction outside the scope of the
above should be sent to the Rights Department, Oxford University Press, at the
address above

You must not circulate this work in any other form
and you must impose this same condition on any acquirer

Published in the United States of America by Oxford University Press
198 Madison Avenue, New York, NY 10016, United States of America

British Library Cataloguing in Publication Data
Data available

Library of Congress Control Number: 2022946834

ISBN 978-0-19-288405-3

DOI: 10.1093/oso/9780192884053.001.0001

Printed and bound in the UK by
Clays Ltd, Elcograf S.p.A.

Links to third party websites are provided by Oxford in good faith and
for information only. Oxford disclaims any responsibility for the materials
contained in any third party website referenced in this work.

Editor's Foreword

Many people are vaguely familiar with the history of witchcraft and magic. The topic attracts regular media interest. Yet it is also a subject around which swirls much misunderstanding, misinformed opinion, and dubious facts. One such perennial notion is that witches were burned in England, and likewise the erroneous belief that millions of people were executed during the era of the witch trials. Over the last two centuries this notorious episode in European history has repeatedly been portrayed as a stain on the medieval age. Yet the vast majority of the prosecutions and executions took place not in the Middle Ages at all, but in what historians refer to as the early modern period, an era which runs roughly from the mid-fifteenth century to the mid-eighteenth century. Words like 'hysteria' and 'craze' litter the older literature on the subject, and continue to be widely used to describe the trials. Yet as James Sharpe and Rita Voltmer show in their chapters, the causes and pattern of the European witch trials were not the result of mass delusion or credulity. The greatest minds of the era believed in the reality of witchcraft and magic. This was a time in Europe when the Reformation transformed religion and politics, legal systems were becoming more sophisticated, and science made great strides in understanding the natural world. The belief in witchcraft and magic was not some evolutionary stage that society passed through on the way to general enlightenment and scientific progress.

The intense academic and public focus on the early modern witch trials can, itself, be seen as problematic. Does the execution of tens of thousands of people, for example, make it more important and of more historic value to research and understand witchcraft and magic in this era rather than before or after? One of the aims of this *Oxford History* is to describe how witchcraft and magic have a history that stretches back to the beginning of writing 5,000 years ago, and remain with us today as relevant cultural phenomena that continue to reflect fundamental aspects of contemporary societies and individual psychologies. The last three chapters (by myself, Robert Wallis, and Willem de Blécourt) show that we continue to live in a world fascinated by the promise of magic.

The origins of magic were already being debated in antiquity, and histories of the witch trials were appearing in Europe before the last of the trials and executions had ended. The topic has excited the minds of artists, playwrights, novelists, and screen writers over the centuries. For some it is the details of magical practices in pursuit of wisdom, health, wealth, desire, and harm that are of most interest, or the fabulous stories of the seemingly impossible, such as flying, shape-changing, and conjuring demons and angels. For others it is the gruesome stories of torture, persecution, and execution that intrigue, provoking reflection on how otherwise reasonable human beings could allow and perform such tasks. The history of witchcraft and magic provides rare glimpses into the human psyche and the complexities of human relationships in the past in terms of gender, age, ethnicity, and social status.

Less exciting to some, perhaps, but equally fascinating is what the history of witchcraft and magic can tell us about how societies formed, developed, and changed over the centuries. It enables us to see the profound if often subtle interactions between different cultures that are obscured by studying the 'bigger picture' of war, conquest, and the political games between kings, queens, and emperors. Peter Maxwell-Stuart's chapter provides us with an overview of how magical knowledge and practices reveal the cultural and religious flows between successive empires and religions in the ancient world. Magic unites as well as divides ideologies and religions. Sophie Page's chapter on medieval magic examines the extraordinary but brief flowering of knowledge exchange between Christians, Muslims, and Jews in Spain.

The geography of witchcraft and magic is another important theme running through this book. As Rita Voltmer observes with regard to the witch trials, thinking in terms of modern state boundaries can hinder our understanding of why and how things happened in the past. The same issue applies to the ancient and medieval worlds as well. Maxwell-Stuart notes the problem of talking about 'Greece' as an entity, for example. A basic understanding of the Holy Roman Empire is hugely important for making sense of the pattern and nature of the witch trials. During the early modern period the Holy

Roman Empire had influence over a big swathe of central and western Europe, and yet this long-lived European dynastic state is little known to the general public today. Germany and Italy did not exist as countries until the mid-nineteenth century, and yet we understandably talk about Germany when discussing the heartland of the trials. As well as being aware of the political geographies of different eras, I highlight in my chapter on popular magic that we also need to be sensitive to local and regional beliefs, and traditions that were not defined by national, religious, or administrative boundaries.

This *Oxford History* follows a familiar path in concentrating primarily on telling the story of how witchcraft and magic were viewed, practised, and suppressed in the Mediterranean and European world. But, of course, witchcraft and magic are global concepts. Encapsulating the diversity and complex contexts of magical beliefs and practices across seven continents is beyond the scope of a volume such as this. Yet the European experience was not isolated from global influences. Through colonial conquest and expansion from the sixteenth century onwards, Christian conceptions of witchcraft and magic determined how indigenous religions and beliefs overseas were conceptualized and dealt with by Europeans. Indigenous magical practices filtered subtly into European traditions. From the late nineteenth century onwards, western spiritualists and ritual magicians drew inspiration from the mystical traditions and religions of India and the East. Meanwhile the early anthropologists busied themselves gathering data for magical practices from across the globe, searching for overarching theories of human development. And in the final chapter on screen representations of witches and wizards we see how, today, cinema presents certain stereotypes to a global audience.

We should not see different parts of the world as being in different stages of human development because they believed in witches or relied on magic in their daily lives. The chapters in this book reveal remarkable continuities in what, why, and how people performed magic in different cultures over the millennia. The reader will find, for instance, the practice of sticking pins into figurines in the chapter on the ancient world and in the one concerned with European folk magic. The books consulted and copied by the medieval magicians discussed by Sophie Page have been 'rediscovered' over the centuries and are now found on the internet and used by modern magicians. While some of the key concepts that underpin magic are thousands of years old, we must also be careful not to portray the myriad beliefs and practices encompassed by the term 'magic' as somehow ageless or unchanging, either globally or within different cultures. Magic both reflects and is shaped by changes in environment, religion, science, and social relations over time.

The writings of the demonologists explored by James Sharpe provide us with a direct line into the mind-set of influential individuals and what informed their ideas and convictions. But most of the sources for the history of witchcraft and magic are much less authorial, much less tangible, and concern a mix of emotions, thoughts, dreams, fantasies, insinuations, verbal accusations, and physical actions that, when recorded at all, usually come down to us through the distorting lenses of bureaucratic selection and interpretation. The written archive is not all we have, though. In a book that has the gift of numerous illustrations it would have been wasteful not to focus on the material expressions of magical practice and visual media. Whether with regard to antiquity, non-literary cultures overseas, or nineteenth-century European folk magic, we are fortunate to have numerous archaeological remains for the history of magical practices. In some instances, from all periods and places, the material remains are the only record we have of widespread popular practices and rituals.

As to the pictorial record of witchcraft and magic, the chapters by Peter Maxwell-Stuart and Sophie Page show how the diagrams and depictions on ancient vases, tablets, and amulets, and the illuminated illustrations in medieval manuscripts, are as important for our understanding of magic as the written inscriptions and instructions recorded on such materials. Charles Zika's survey of the artistic representation of witches from the sixteenth to the eighteenth centuries explores how developments in technique and representation created a new visual language for depicting what witches and magicians were thought to do. Photography enabled modern magicians to shape and control their public magical personae, while the moving image, as discussed by Willem de Blécourt, led to a further reformulation of historic notions, stories, and stereotypes for a mass audience.

The remit of the *Oxford History* series offers a great opportunity to provide a distinct approach that will focus on how the archives, imagery, and material culture shape our understanding of the history of witchcraft and magic, and how history shapes the sources we have. The contributors to this book have risen to this challenge. Let the magic begin.

Contents

List of Tables   xv

1. Magic in the Ancient World   1
   Peter Maxwell-Stuart

2. Medieval Magic   29
   Sophie Page

3. The Demonologists   62
   James Sharpe

4. The Witch Trials   93
   Rita Voltmer

5. The Witch and Magician in European Art   134
   Charles Zika

6. The World of Popular Magic   165
   Owen Davies

7. The Rise of Modern Magic   195
   Owen Davies

8. Witchcraft and Magic in the Age of Anthropology   227
   Robert J. Wallis

9. Witches on Screen   258
   Willem de Blécourt

Further Reading   287
Index   297

List of Tables

1. Witch trials in the European kingdoms/territories (selection)   98
2. Witch trials in the regions and territories in the borderlands
   between Spain, France, the Holy Roman Empire, and Denmark   100
3. Witch trials in the kingdoms and territories politically
   bound to the House of Habsburg   101
4. Witch trials in the Holy Roman Empire: persecuting
   territories and intense persecutions (selection)   102
5. The absence of witch-hunts in the Holy Roman Empire (selection)   132

1

Magic in the Ancient World

Peter Maxwell-Stuart

As always, when we try to discuss magic there are problems of definition. What do we mean by 'magic' in any given context, and how does it differ from religion on the one hand and 'science' on the other? To some extent those are non-questions. They depend on a debate stemming largely from the nineteenth century which was eager to see clear lines of demarcation between these concepts, and which was particularly responsible for trying to draw one or another of them into the specifically western European corrals of 'rationality' or 'irrationality'. If we think of magic as a peculiar kind of discourse on power between the members of a society, we can envisage it as a set of social exchanges, the definition of which is liable to change in accordance with the passage of time and shifting circumstances, and the categories 'religion', 'magic', 'science' can be seen as fluid rather than distinct and impenetrable. Thus, for example, the Roman naturalist and philosopher Pliny the Elder (23–79 AD) records practices such as eating a salamander preserved in honey to awaken sexual desire, and chanting spells intended to cure disease and other impairments, and while dismissing them as examples of popular nonsense, he still regards them as medical rather than magical. Even so, there still remain to us difficulties attendant upon any discussion of 'magic'. So, perhaps, the only practical way to cope with them in short compass is to cut the Gordian knot and say that for our purposes here, 'magic' refers to a constellation of what are officially regarded as deviant ritualistic or ritualized ways of dealing with an individual's immediate problems by achieving access to sacred power which demands or compels the assistance of non-human entities. It should also be said in this context that we must be prepared to regard magic as entirely rational within its frames of reference, and not to be equated with 'superstition' or 'irrational or non-rational behaviour'.

Mesopotamia

Some of the earliest examples of magical performance are to be found in the records of ancient Mesopotamia (modern Iraq). These records are written in cuneiform, a script imprinted on soft clay tablets with the slanted edge of a reed-pen. The clay was then baked to make the record permanent. Thousands of these tablets survive (some small, perhaps an inch square, others large, over one foot square), their contents embracing myth, theogonies (genealogies of the gods), laws, literature, economics, hymns, incantations, proverbs, prayers, omen observations, and magical texts of various, but always practical, kinds. Cuneiform was used by a number of different peoples including Sumerians, Babylonians, Hittites, and Assyrians, from about the fourth to the first millennium BC, and much of what survives of their texts is in Akkadian, the lingua franca of the whole region. But once it had fallen out of use, its records became unintelligible until the eighteenth century when thousands of tablets were rediscovered and brought back to Europe by travellers and scholars eager to find confirmatory proofs of the places and events contained in the Old Testament. Gradually, during the nineteenth century, several scholars managed to decipher the amalgamation of writing-systems which go to make up 'cuneiform' until by the mid-1850s the task was substantially, although not completely, done.

The nature of these magical texts can be seen in one from the second millennium BC which tells us what to do in case of dog-bite. 'Take some clay and rub the outside of the wound with it. Fashion a dog from clay and place it on the north wall directly in the sun. Recite [the following] incantation three times over it until the dog surrenders its moisture and the man's bite dries up.' If stung by a snake, 'Take snake-stone, crush it, and heap it on the head of the man who has been bitten. . . . Fill a yellow bowl with seawater. Let the bitten man drink it. Its venom will come out.' These practicalities clearly involve the concept of 'sympathy' which assumes that everything in the cosmos is linked in some way to everything else, and that if someone wants to cause a particular effect, good or bad, in relation to one thing, an object bearing some resemblance to that thing can have its resemblance exploited, magic providing the means for that exploitation. Hence, in the case of dog-bite, one makes the clay image of a dog, links it to the bite by smearing clay over the wound, and then waits for the image to disintegrate under the heat of the sun, by which time the wound will have healed by nature but by a nature materially assisted by sympathetic magic. Likewise, the powder used in a case of snakebite comes from pulverizing a stone such as an ammonite, which resembles a serpent, and by making the patient drink water which is bitter and may well cause him to vomit. The yellow colour of the bowl may be reminiscent of pus. Hence the constituent parts of the practice combine to form a consistent magical whole.

Certain incantations to quieten a crying baby are interesting for the light they shed on Mesopotamian beliefs about the intrusion of evil into everyday life. One addresses the child directly, asking it why it is crying. 'You have woken the god of the house', it is told, and therefore the parents have been obliged to seek the help of an exorcist (*āšipu*) who chants this adjuration and ends by wishing that sleep may fall upon the baby as it does upon 'drinkers of wine, the habitués of a bar'. Disturbing the household god is clearly a serious matter, for if he has gone away (presumably to get some peace and quiet), the house has no protection against demons such as Lamaštu, a bird-like creature that inflicts the evil eye. This we learn from another similar incantation which lists some of the harm such a demon can do. 'She passed by the babies' door and caused havoc among them. She passed by the door of the women in childbed and strangled their babies. She entered the storeroom and broke the seal.' The word for 'god' in these texts can also be used for the dead and so Lamaštu is causing a number of catastrophes: the death of the younger generation, the starvation of the adults, and the expulsion of the deceased, protecting ancestor. A whole family may thus be destroyed because of a baby's crying, and this is why such a simple occurrence requires the help of a professional magician to disperse its potentially evil effects and restore harmony not only to the living but between the living and the dead.

Such instances of harm, accidents, confrontation with frightening or deleterious entities, and disease itself, may well have been caused by a 'witch' (*kaššapu*, male; *kaššaptu*, female), that is to say, someone with a command of harmful magic. 'Because she performed evil against me', says one text, 'and has fabricated baseless charges against me, may she die, while I continue to live.' Examples of the harm these 'witches' might do are numerous. Magical figurines could be employed for malevolence as well as healing, and a complex ritual known as *Maqlû* (literally 'burning') was used to destroy their effect. In this, counter-images of the 'witch' were made from a variety of materials, presented to the gods, especially the god of fire, and then, after a catalogue of the wicked deeds performed by the witch, destroyed in a kiln, each stage of the ritual being accompanied by appropriate incantations.

Witchcraft was assumed to be at the root of a good many illnesses, mental as well as physical. Impotence and indigestion, strokes and facial palsy, childhood convulsions, fevers, and a variety of skin complaints are among afflictions described in terms which suggest the hand of a demon or god, or the utterance of a curse, or the malignity of a 'witch' is the precipitating cause of the problem. 'Witches' frequently introduced their evil into a person via food or water which had been bewitched—'If someone has pains between his shoulders and his teeth are bleeding, he has a disease of the lungs and has been given an enchanted drink', says a text from the first millennium BC—and such hostile magic might well also depend on the stars for its full effect. The names of certain illnesses or disabilities reflect their astral origins, such as 'sperm of Jupiter' and 'hand of *Šamaš* (the sun)'. So it was to these same stars or planets that the healer-magician would turn in order to bring about a cure, his ritual involving purification of both healer and ritual space, libations, and prayers to the star, so that 'the sorcery and machinations [of the witch] will be released'. The stars and planets, indeed, figure large in Mesopotamian magic. Their journeys through the sky, their risings and conjunctions, their changing colours, and their non-appearance at the expected time were all scrutinized and carefully noted. For they were signs from the gods, and their movements were divinely written messages, portents perhaps of harm to an individual or catastrophe to a region. Their baleful influence had to be countered by apotropaic magic, a form of magic which had the power to avert such evil influence. Apotropaic magic was also used in response to such simple everyday omens as the abnormal birth of humans or animals, an outbreak of fire, the sudden appearance of a certain fungus on the walls of a house, or even the squeaking of a water-pot—the latter requiring offerings of fresh water, herbs, and beads to the appropriate star.

Magic, then, allied to worship of the gods and exorcism of demons, permeated Mesopotamian society, along with an acute awareness of the spirits of the dead as major players, for good or ill, in the lives of the living, and an equally ardent need to watch the stars and planets, since their influences were both potent and potentially dire. Expelling harm in the form of illness, bad luck, witchcraft, or accident formed a major part of the exorcist's magic, although precaution against such mischiefs could also be essayed by wearing amulets on one's person, or hanging tablets inscribed with incantations on the wall or door of the house. Does this suggest, however, that Mesopotamian society tended to live in a state of constant fear or nervousness in the face of a cosmos envisaged as essentially hostile? At first it might seem so. The general aim of men and women to live a healthy and prosperous life was evidently hampered by the potentially constant hazards presented by ill-intentioned or ill-natured entities, human and non-human alike. Their harmful activities formed part of the warp and woof of the universe, but they could be faced and their effects overcome by prayer and magic which often worked together to achieve their protective ends. The skills of the *āšipu* and *bārû* (diviner) counterbalanced those of the *maš-maš* (worker of harmful magic), and while individual men and women could call upon their services, magical aid and protection was readily available to everyone. So, far from being neurotic civilizations, societies in Mesopotamia were able, in theory at least, to live more or less in a state of equilibrium with both their human and non-human neighbours, relying upon that mixture of religion and magic and what a later age would call 'natural philosophy' that constituted the intellectual, psychological, and emotional ambience of their existence.

Egypt

To the west and south of Mesopotamia, another civilization, that of Egypt, was developing its own writing-system at about the same time. This system consisted of hieroglyphs which in later times were misinterpreted as symbols for objects and allegorical ideas. But while ideal for stone monuments and highly formalized records, hieroglyphs do not lend themselves to quick and easy writing on papyrus, and so two simplified versions emerged over time: hieratic, used mainly by priests, and demotic, used by everyone else. The surviving literature of all three forms is varied, ranging from historical inscriptions to stories, poems, hymns, letters, decrees, books of instruction, and a magical corpus of spells and incantations; and yet the last hieroglyphic inscription, dated to 394 AD, signalled the end of people's ability to read and understand the system. Thereafter hieroglyphs would be largely neglected and misunderstood, and an explanatory work from around the fifth century AD, *Hieroglyphica* by 'Horapollo', displayed basic incomprehension of how the system worked: 'when they would symbolise a man that is fond of building, they delineate a man's hand, for it performs all works.' Arabic scholars of the ninth and tenth centuries, and the Jesuit Athanasius Kircher in the seventeenth, made similar mistakes, and it was not until the discovery of the Rosetta Stone in 1799 that a number of scholars began to make headway with decipherment, paving the way for Jean-François Champollion's personal success in 1822. The stone bears an inscription from Memphis, dated 196 BC, and records it in three forms: hieroglyphic, demotic, and Greek. The inclusion of a Greek translation thus offered an invaluable key to interpreting the Egyptian, and once the nature of hieroglyphics had been correctly understood, decipherment of the written language was able to stride rapidly ahead.

What the decipherment revealed, among much else, was the wealth of magical prescriptions intended to protect the individual both during his or her life and after death. The most famous of the latter type are the *Pyramid Texts* which in their earliest form date from the third millennium BC and contain spells to reanimate Pharaoh's body and assist him to ascend into the sky. A further development of these may be found in the *Coffin Texts* (late third millennium), which emphasize the judgement of the soul by Osiris, god of the underworld and afterlife. A final version, or rather set of versions, of this protective tradition, the so-called *Book of the Dead*, from the late second and then first millennium BC, contains spells to guide the soul through the many post-mortem trials and ultimate judgement that await it. These spells were meant to be recited, of course, although their existence in writing was considered to be just as effectual. For here we have one of the fundamental concepts of Egyptian magic—*heka*. Spell 261 from the *Coffin Texts* makes clear that *heka* was regarded as the magical vitality which infused the first creative utterance of the solar deity Ra at the birth of the world and which continues to do so at its re-creation every morning with each sunrise. The commonly found phrases 'magic of their mouths' and 'spells of their utterances' show the close relationship between speaking and magic, and one inscription also links a female accompaniment of a personified Heka with the spoken *and* written word: 'possessor of spells, carrying her writings which are in her mouth'. But Heka does more—exorcizing, cursing, enchanting, and protecting, including protection of the passage of the sun through the underworld each night, and Heka's extensive powers, we are told, put fear into the gods themselves. Magic thus permeated creation, and its association with the spoken word, in particular, meant that the two were treated as more or less equivalent: 'you say as magic', notes the *Papyrus Ebers* (a medical text from the mid-second millennium BC). Individuals as well as things might, therefore, be imbued with magic and consequently possess the ability to use its ever-present force. Thus Pharaoh himself was sometimes referred to as *wr-hekaw-pw*, 'someone great in magic', while the *Coffin Texts* speak of evil magic practised by sorcerers as well as demons, and elsewhere we are told that Ra fled from the earth to avoid magicians 'who do as they wish against the whole land, using the magic that is in their bodies'. As far as Egypt is concerned, then, it is sometimes difficult to distinguish (should we wish to do so) where religion ends and magic begins—spells and hymns, for example, frequently overlap—although it should be said that much of the evidence for this comes from magical texts and may not be altogether impartial or indifferent.

So if *heka* permeates creation, can its power be harnessed and used by anyone regardless of status; and if so, could there be such a person as a 'professional' magician in ancient Egypt, as there undoubtedly was in Mesopotamia? Literacy in ancient Egypt does not appear to have been widespread, so presumably ownership of books of magic would have been limited to the class of priests and scribes, although as neither group would have been immune from the magic of popular culture, a degree of common theology, common aims, and common methods must be assumed. If, therefore, there was a magician in ancient Egypt, he was almost certainly a priest—the term 'chief lector-priest' implies someone associated with magical practices, and in late Egyptian the title simply becomes the ordinary word for 'magician'—and one thinks of the *hartumîm* (the Hebrew rendering of the Egyptian title) who engaged in a magical contest with Moses and Aaron at Pharaoh's Court, as recorded in Exodus 6: 8–12.

One of Egypt's most common manifestations of magical practice is to be found in figurines and amulets made of various substances which have been uncovered by archaeology. These were the focus of spells intended to transfer hatred or bad luck, or to protect, or, in the case of statuettes which had been brought to life by magic, to serve their human owners. A magician's box dating from the late third or early second millennium BC, discovered in 1896, contained a variety of magical papyri, figurines, human hair, amuletic knives, and a staff in the form of a snake. These serpent-staffs appear frequently in paintings and statues, and were clearly used as wands in a number of magical actions, such as that of drawing a protective circle on the ground or in the air. Representations of bound prisoners, their race often identifiable from their moulded features, are found both as separate artefacts and as pictures drawn or painted upon the soles of wooden sandals. The act of treading them down unseen on the soles of the sandals combines elements of psychology as well as magic, a personal desire reinforced by the use of *heka* which will transform hope into reality. Execration texts are carved on model figures or inscribed on pottery, and in a particular rite intended to inflict terror on one's enemies, red pots were inscribed and then broken, red being associated with demons and the hostile god Seth. Other figurines were pierced with nails or shown bound hand and foot or made headless or blind, their mutilation or disfigurement intended to disable their human counterpart and thus protect the one who made them or had them made.

Such objects were often buried, and spell 37 of the *Coffin Texts* tells us to make a wax image of our enemy, inscribe its breast with a fish-bone, and then bury it in a graveyard. Now, the knowledge of how to inscribe magical words on an object may suggest that consultation of an expert would have been necessary to achieve the desired end of the magical act, but it is always possible that a very simple formula could have been learned by anyone and reproduced without literate under-standing, just as many people in the past could pen their signature without being able to write anything else. Whatever the case, amulets, which appear everywhere, needed no such expertise. The names, uses, and required materials from which amulets should be made appear in papyrus texts and, in one notable instance, on the walls of the Ptolemaic temple of Dendera on the west bank of the Nile. Some consist of pendants in the likeness of deities, or the *wedjet eye* (sometimes known as 'the eye of Horus', although it refers simply to a divine eye in general, not just that of a specific deity). Others look like a cylinder (the *djed* pillar), or take the form of pieces of jewellery such as a necklace or bracelet. A series of objects involving knots also constituted important amulets—a knot in a garment, worn over one shoulder, the so-called 'Isis knot'; or several knots in a cord, known as 'Anubis knots', an example of which has been found in a cord bracelet in the workmen's village at Tell el-Amarna, the capital city of Pharaoh Akhenaten (who reigned from the early 1350s to the mid-1330s BC). While these knots may be interpreted as ways of binding or blocking harmful powers or influences, it is also possible to see them as means of anchoring the power of spells recited over the cord while the knots were being tied. Indeed, the well-known Egyptian hieroglyph known as the *ankh* may originally have represented a circular knot of this kind.

Mummies as well as the living were protected by amulets of various sorts, which were slipped between the bandages during wrapping of the corpse, and several statues are depicted with chest-pouches which probably contained magical objects of one kind or another. Indeed, some such pouches, we know, contained a slip of papyrus on which was written a protective spell. These were worn by children, in very much the same way as *bullae* and *lunulae* (amuletic lockets and moon-shaped ornaments) were worn by Roman children centuries later, and their principal purpose can be seen from the Egyptian words for amulet: *mkt* ('protector') and *wedja* ('the thing which keeps safe'). Perhaps the most frequently found amulets, however, were scarabs in the shape of a dung-beetle, produced and surviving by the thousand. This beetle rolls a ball of dung with its hind legs, and thus typifies the journey of the sun across the sky: hence its association with Ra. Many of these scarabs are stamped with the words 'good luck' and were often used in complex magical rites to obtain love.

But protection, while constituting a large part of the magical work done by these special objects and the incantations which accompanied their creation, was not the only reason ancient Egyptians had recourse to incantations and rituals both complex and simple. Healing under the guidance and patronage of Thoth was almost as important. Thoth was revered in particular as the god of medicine and writing—again we see the connection between speech, script, and magic—and indeed the Egyptian word for remedy may be derived from a verb meaning 'encircle', an etymology suggestive of magic, since 'encircle' frequently appears in Egyptian texts with a clearly magical sense. It is also worth noting that the magician's serpent-wand which was used among other things to draw a magic circle is shown in a wall-painting at Dendur as the *was*-sceptre of Thoth, complete with climbing snake and scorpion, an image strongly reminiscent of the later Greek caduceus (staff) which was adopted as a symbol of medical practice and authority. One spell, addressed to disease-demons and bidding them stay away from the patient, gives instructions for the practitioner to take a stick made of *des*-wood and draw a protective circle with it round either the patient's house or the patient himself. Papyri such as the *London Medical Papyrus* (*c*.1300–1200 BC) also contain spells to be recited over the ingredients for use in medicine, and doctors often told patients to recite magical formulae while they took their prescribed remedies. Female magician-healers are recorded at Deir el-Medina. Their particular task may have been to diagnose spirit-possession, since magico-medical papyri frequently say that some illnesses were caused by ghosts or demons. 'Retreat enemy, demon, you who cause this distress to one who is not dead', says one text, for example, while another, the *Papyrus Brooklyn*, tells us that female ghosts are liable to be especially dangerous to the living. But whether ghost or demon be blamed for a patient's illness, the papyri leave us in no doubt that the ultimate cause of sickness, regardless of whether its immediate cause seemed to be an accident or stem from a natural source such as a scorpion, was actually the anger or hostility of a deity. The ghost or demon acted merely as his or her agent. So a line of cause and effect may here be traced from religion to magic to material practicalities, showing how intimately connected were all three in the Egyptian psychology.

Other related magic rituals sought to induce love or protect fertility in this life or the next—spell 576 of the *Coffin Texts*, for example, promises the wearer of a particular amulet enhanced sexual prowess in the afterlife—and figurines and paintings clearly protective of the womb or the pudenda were placed in tombs. These, however, were not only relevant to the dead, but show the kind of magic practised to aid the living, and written spells inform us that sex and childbirth were regularly attended by their appropriate forms of magic. Again we are fortunate enough to possess a box, dated to the second millennium BC, which contains magico-medical papyri specifically relating to women and children, while nearby were discovered amulets and other magical equipment including a wand like that used by magicians. But if this life were to continue after death, it had to be protected against the numerous hostile forces ranged against it, and such papyri as the *Coffin Texts* and the *Book of the Dead* provided the spells necessary to ensure that the individual survived the trials and dangers attendant upon its immediate passage into the next world and avoided the annihilation waiting for any who failed the final trial and judgement. Notice that the texts were buried with the dead so that the dead could read them aloud each step of the way. Again we have the intimate connection between the spoken word and the magical act which were combined in the concept of *heka*. 'I have enchanted by means of your words which you created by means of the magic which is in your mouth', says the inscription on a wooden statue of Horus. Hence, obliterating a person's written name was a devastating magical act, for if the name could not be spoken, the *heka* was drained from it and the person would die a second, irreversible death.

It may be a cliché to say that the Egyptians were deeply religious, but it is clear not only that they were, but that they were also profoundly in love with their earthly lives and therefore sought to prolong them after death. The gods might sometimes be hostile enough to send demons or ghosts to inflict illness or accident upon them, but the Egyptians had a wealth of accumulated knowledge which told them how to cure and protect themselves by means that even divinities were unable to resist. While the written magical tradition was largely in the hands of priests and scribes, its formulae, incantations, and spells were by no means exclusive to them, but were known to, learned, and used by everyone, literate or not. Like the Mesopotamians, then, ancient Egyptians lived in a world which might appear to be full of dangers from non-human sources, yet which did not make them neurotic or constantly fearful. Magical vitality permeated everything and its power could be harnessed, tapped, used, and exploited at a moment's notice. Writing, which could have created a more or less self-contained class of magical experts, in fact proved no bar to the use of magic in general and created no barrier between literate and non-literate magic. This is largely because magic was so firmly integrated with religion and Egyptian religion was catholic in its embrace. No distinct theology, no limited pantheon, declared that such and such was orthodox, and such and such was not. In consequence, literate and non-literate could operate according to the same or similar beliefs, or deviate in accordance with local practice as they chose without excluding themselves from the efficacy of the *heka* which ran through all the gods, and whose power they could be brought to acknowledge and obey.

Jewish Magic

Open to influences from both Mesopotamia and Egypt, Israel-Judaea-Palestine possessed and practised a wealth of magic which included not only the kinds of operation we have seen already in its neighbours but also divination and a kind of ocular influence usually called the 'evil eye' which were part of the other cultures too, but had a certain distinctiveness of their own in Jewish society. One of the more tantalizing riddles of the Old Testament, for example, is the exact nature and purpose of the Urim and Thummim, which were two 'means, apparently, of obtaining oracular responses to questions put by the priest, their official guardian. According to tradition, they had been left by Moses as a legacy to the priestly tribe of Levi and seem to have been used in circumstances which required a simple answer 'Yes' or 'No'. Thus, Numbers 27: 21 says, 'He [Joshua] shall stand before Eleazar the priest who shall inquire for him by the decision of the Urim before the Lord.' Different passages in the Old Testament give differing views on what these objects were and where they were kept when not in use. One suggestion is that they were precious stones inserted into the High Priest's ceremonial breast-piece (the 'ephod'); another is that they were small objects kept in a pouch attached to the ephod; another is that they were two sides of a single object. So if these suggestions are right in general, it seems that divination by casting lots—and by these lots entirely peculiar to Jewish practice—was available to at least a limited number of people, limited because not everyone was likely to have had access to a Levite or the High Priest himself. Still, we do have several other references to sortilege during these ancient times. God Himself, indeed, is spoken of more than once as casting lots to decide the fate of Israel (Isaiah 34: 17); we find the Israelites signing a covenant saying (among much else), 'we have also cast lots among the priests, the Levites, and the people' (Nehemiah 10: 34); Aaron cast lots to determine which of two goats belonged as a sacrifice to God and which should be used as a scapegoat and an offering to the demon of the desert (Leviticus 16: 8–10); and Jonah was cast overboard into the sea because the sailors had cast lots in order to know which person on board had angered God enough to provoke Him to send a storm (Jonah 1: 7). Clearly, therefore, it was a practice common to all sections of Jewish society.

Belief in the efficacy of the evil eye was also common not only in Israel-Judaea-Palestine but throughout the whole of the Middle East. In Mesopotamia it tended to work as an irritant rather than as a means of inflicting lethal or near-lethal harm, causing the breakage of pots or the spoiling of food, for example. In Judaism its associations were more sinister: 'Take heed lest your eye be evil against your needy brother ... His eye shall be evil towards his brother and towards the wife of his bosom ... Her eye shall be evil towards her husband ... Eat not the bread of him that has an evil eye' (Deuteronomy 15: 9, 28: 54, 56; Proverbs 23: 6). Rabbinic commentators claimed that nearly all deaths happened as a result of the evil eye and that this eye caused sicknesses such as plague and leprosy. Protection against the eye was therefore common. A blessing from someone else would disperse its influence, but the most prevalent form of protection was provided by amulets, some consisting of objects in the shape of a hand gesturing against the evil eye, others of small receptacles containing strips of parchment with the name of God or a verse from the Old Testament written on them, while small bells or objects coloured blue were also considered protective. Here we think of Exodus 39: 25, 'They also made bells of pure gold, and put the bells between the pomegranates on the lower hem of the [High Priest's] robe all round, between the pomegranates.' We may also think of the injunction of Numbers 15: 37–8, 'The Lord said to Moses, Speak to the Israelites and tell them to make [knotted] fringes on the corners of their garments ... and to put a blue cord on the fringe at each corner.'

During late antiquity and the Middle Ages, Jews were credited with a detailed knowledge of magic and this reputation obviously did not spring out of nothing or appear suddenly in the Christian era. I have already mentioned the magical battle between Moses and Aaron on the one hand and Pharaoh's magicians on the other, and we should recall the most famous incident of necromancy recorded in 1 Kings (or 1 Samuel) 28: 8–19, when King Saul consulted the so-called 'witch of Endor' who conjured up the spirit of Samuel to answer his questions. But Hebrew itself has many words for specialists in different forms of magic, all of which appear in the Old Testament—*khartum*, 'magician', *mekashef*, 'sorcerer', *khober*, 'caster of spells', *qosem*, 'diviner', *me'onen*, 'soothsayer', *shoel ob*, 'necromancer', *yid'on*, 'wizard', *ashaf*, 'exorcist', *holem*, 'interpreter of dreams'—and so this, in itself, tends to suggest that magic and divination were both widespread and well regarded in early Jewish society. Between them, these practitioners cursed and blessed, and exorcized illness by means of fumigations, as can be seen in Tobit 6: 8: 'As for the fish's heart and liver, you must burn them to make a smoke in the presence of a man or woman afflicted by a demon or evil spirit, and every affliction will flee away and never remain with that person any longer.' (Here we are reminded of both the Mesopotamian and Egyptian belief that illness was probably caused by the deliberate action of non-human entities.)

All this, of course, was potentially dangerous, for there was at least one prohibition against mediums and necromancers which threatened them with death by stoning if they were found guilty (Leviticus 20: 27), another against a long list of similar practitioners (Deuteronomy 18: 10–11), and the well-known condemnation of Exodus 22: 18, 'You will not allow a witch to live.' But while all this is firmly located in Old Testament times, and while we can see a resurgence of a good deal of information relating to later antiquity and the Rabbinic period, there is, apart from relatively few references in the New Testament, a peculiar gap between the sixth century BC and the first century AD. Neither archaeology nor written evidence provides us with more than a very little indication of the continuance of magical beliefs and practice. The implication must be that Jewish attitudes towards magic were undergoing radical change during that period—not oblivion, because the subsequent explosion of evidence shows that magic emerged as strongly supported and widely practised as before, but abeyance of some kind owed in part, at least, to the extraordinary upheavals and internal divisions afflicting Jewish society at this time. So it looks as though literate people had many other more pressing things to write about than magic, and that for the most part magical tradition was oral (and hence lost to us) rather than written.

Nevertheless, there are written indications that magic did survive. A tablet in both Hebrew and Aramaic, dating from about the sixth century BC, records a complex incantation directed against the wicked practices of magicians. It begins by quoting the Scriptures, then invokes the archangels Michael and Raphael, and calls upon God to destroy the magicians' enchantments. These include casting the evil eye, inscribing bones with curses, drawing magical pictures of horses in an attempt to fix chariot races, employing spittle or herbs for magical purposes, making wax images, and using thread to sew amulets to garments. Magic also appears in the first book of Enoch, the book of Jubilees, and the Dead Sea scrolls, but it is notable that the writers of these texts associate it with demons and the dubious uses of herbs. 'Make no herbal concoctions and keep away from books of magic', wrote pseudo-Phocylides, a Jewish writer of the first century BC (or perhaps AD). Hence it is perhaps not surprising to find that exorcism is the best-recorded occult practice of the period, whether performed by holy individuals such as Jesus or by others using the customary techniques of incantation and ritual. There is some evidence, too, that people were still wearing amulets. The second book of Maccabees (12: 39), for example, refers to rebels against Roman rule wearing under their clothes 'sacred images of the idols of Iamneia, which are forbidden to Jews by the Torah': in other words, figurines of pagan deities worn as protective amulets while their owners went into battle.

The Jews were surrounded by societies which did not hesitate to call upon magic as an aid to solving their practical problems and as a means whereby relations between themselves and a plurality of gods and goddesses, demons, ghosts, and other non-human entities might be controlled, regulated, and if necessary eased. Affected as they were by requirements, difficulties, and impulses similar to those of all their neighbours, Jews were by no means averse from immersing themselves in the same range of occult systems. They employed what similar traditions told them were the requisite magical techniques to render their lives at once more comfortable and more reassuring in a world thrumming with forces, powers, and personalities beyond the human.

The biggest and most marked difference between Jews and their neighbours was the Jews' adherence to a monotheistic concept of divinity. But that was subject every so often to uncertainty as Israel-Judaea-Palestine was conquered or overrun by alien armies. In any case, as the prophets kept reminding them, the Jews were subject to backsliding and adoption of practices both magical and non-magical that were discordant with their belief in a single god who had a particular interest in them as a people. Even Moses (admittedly under divine instruction) had erected a bronze snake on a pole to serve as a source of remedy for anyone suffering from snakebite, a magical instrument which remained in public use until the late eighth century BC when King Hezekiah destroyed it.

Once we come to late antiquity (say the third to the seventh centuries AD), popular Jewish willingness to accommodate magic into everyday life becomes even clearer from the number of amulets in the form of rings, engraved gemstones, metal strips, bowls, and clay sherds which have been recovered by archaeology. These are scarcely different from those of contemporary pagan or Christian society bearing Names of Power, 'characters' (that is, pseudo-letters from a pseudo-script addressed to and supposedly understood by the relevant demons or angels), and requests or demands for protection from illness or misfortune, curses directed against some individual, and pleas that X will fall in love with Y. Books of magic, too, appear to have been compiled during this period. *Sepher ha-Razim* (The Book of the Mysteries), for example, can be dated tentatively to the early fourth century AD, although the form in which we have it now was put together by a Jewish scholar between 1963 and 1966 from assorted fragments. Its main purpose is to describe seven firmaments and the angels who occupy each of them, and the first six descriptions add practical instructions on how one may constrain the angels to do one's bidding. The first firmament, then, is called *Shamayim* ('The heavens') and is filled with encampments of angels who are obedient to anyone practising magic, although these angels are obliged to wait for instructions from their own angelic overseers before actually leaving the heavens to engage in magical actions. The names of the seventy-two angels under the command of the first of these overseers are provided, and then instructions for the appropriate ritual to summon them.

If you want to perform an act of healing, get up in the first or second hour of the night and take with you myrrh and frankincense. These should be placed on burning coals while you recite the name of the angel who rules over the first encampment. He is called 'WRPNY'L. Recite seven times the names of the seventy-two angels who serve him, and then say as follows. 'I, N son of N, beseech you to give me success in healing X the son of Y', and anyone for whom you ask, whether in writing or verbally, will be healed.

Further rites deal with hostile magic—'if you want to send [angels] against your enemy or your creditor, or capsize a ship, or raze a fortified wall ... exile [your enemy], or make him bed-ridden, or blind him or lame him'—with divination, necromancy, inducing love, healing, expelling dangerous animals from a city, protecting a soldier in battle, putting out a fire, winning a horse-race, and predicting the date of your own death.

Sepher ha-Razim, then, was obviously composed by a well-educated person conversant with the magical literature of late antiquity. It is clear from the enormous number of manuscript fragments remaining to us that there existed an extensive corpus of magical manuals both sophisticated and callow which could serve the needs of the individual for whom magic was more or less one technique among others for achieving a personal religious experience, as well as those of someone who had less exalted desires and simply wanted the satisfaction of seeing those desires fulfilled. So 'disapproved of, forbidden, but practised' seems to summarize the picture of Jewish magic delineated by the Bible and later sources—disapproved of and forbidden because, in effect, magic was officially regarded as part of, or at best tainted by, foreign religious and esoteric behaviours; practised because it was essentially a lingua franca which transcended national or tribal boundaries, and satisfied practical and psychological needs which the strict ethics of the Jewish religion either refused or were reluctant to address.

Greeks

Since it is from Greek that we owe our word 'magic', it will be important for us to try to understand what the Greeks meant by the concepts underlying the term and, indeed, to be clear what we mean by 'Greeks' in the first place. Common talk of 'Greek' culture, for example, in practice usually means 'Athenian', so we must bear in mind that the 'Greeks' were actually a conglomeration of disparate societies living both in Greece itself and the islands of the Aegean, and on the western coast of what is now modern Turkey. These last in particular were thus open to cultural and religious influences from well beyond the mainland of Greece, as the Greek term *mageia*, 'magic', makes clear. *Magos* referred to fire-priests at the Court of Persia and, as far as we can tell, had nothing to do with magical practices. So the development of this word, and its abstract noun, into terms with negative connotations suggests they were reinterpreted or misinterpreted due to the dislike of foreigners, a sentiment fuelled partly by memory of how close Greece had once come to being absorbed by the Persian Empire, and partly by a fear that such an invasion might happen again. The root of this development, then, lies in religion, since the *magoi* were priests in a non-Greek religious system and we may therefore initially understand *mageia* as meaning a collection of unacceptable religious practices.

As we noted in connection with Jewish magic, however, the vocabulary of practices and practitioners is diverse. Apart from *magos* and *mageia*, Greek gives us *goēs* and *goēteia*. These refer to the use of incantations—the verb *goan* means 'lament'—especially at first in summoning up the dead. So if *magos* means 'ritual magician', *goēs* may be understood as 'necromancer'. Thirdly, *pharmakeus* (feminine, *pharmakides*) and *pharmakeia* refer to the use of herbs and other substances in the manufacture of such things as curative medicines, love potions, and poisons, although the word did later broaden its range considerably to include binding spells which did not involve herbs at all. Indeed these and other Greek terms for magical operations underwent change and, to some extent, amalgamation during the fifth century BC under the influence of Athenian writers who conflated them to form a generalized notion of foreign, unethical, illegitimate, and therefore undesirable activity. This conflation was clearly illustrated by Plato (429–347 BC) who condemned such practices as both anti-social trickery and destructive criminality.

But these magical terms, if taken separately, can give us some notion of what kind of thing was expected of magical practitioners: invocation of non-human entities; consultation of the dead; the manufacture of amulets, figurines, salves, simples, and cordials intended to answer an individual's immediate or future needs. *Goēteia* and *pharmakeia* are found in some of the earliest surviving Greek literature. Odysseus, in Homer's epic, summons up ghosts from the realm of the dead; the magician Circe uses a combination of *pharmakeia* and *mageia* to turn Odysseus' men into pigs; and Odysseus is given a magical root (*pharmakon*) to protect him from Circe's spells. A long-standing tradition held that women from Thessaly were able to draw down the moon by the force of their magic, and an anonymous epic from the seventh or sixth century BC, *Phoronis*, describes magicians (*goētes*) from Phrygia, who live in the mountains and produce wonderful things from metal. Add to these the Telchines who, according to later writers, were able to change shape, cast the evil eye, used *pharmakeia* to produce poisons, and employed *mageia* to render places infertile or summon up natural disasters. Medea, a woman from Colchis (the Black Sea coast near modern Georgia), who, along with Circe, is the best-known *pharmakides* in Greek literature, is depicted as being able to kill with her potions as well as to restore a man's fertility. Her divine patron is the goddess Hekate, a divinity who straddles the Olympian-chthonic divide amongst the Greek gods, since she is said by Hesiod to be an intermediary between the Olympians and humans, and between humans and the deities of the underworld. A late magical invocation turns her into a 'nether and nocturnal and infernal goddess of the dark, quiet and frightful, feeding amid the dead', or 'the goddess of three ways who, with your fire-breathing ghosts, has been allotted dreaded roads and harsh enchantments'.

Hekate, it seems, was a foreign importation, coming originally from Anatolia, and indeed most of these early literary references describe the use of magic as something done by foreigners—Odysseus is the exception, and he is a character from 'long, long ago', semi-mythical even to those who may have regarded the *Odyssey* as history rather than legend. Still, it would be foolish to suppose that magic, of whatever kind, was imported into Greek communities otherwise innocent of any such practices, and although it seems to have been regarded by officialdom and the literate elite as either undesirable and somewhat sinister, or near-criminal quackery designed to part the deluded and ignorant from their money, we have plenty of evidence that people made use of it, apparently without much qualm, whenever they felt the need. Inscribed tablets in the form of potsherds or squares of lead, for example, have been found in large numbers at the oracle of Zeus in Dodona. They carry questions from everyone—men, women, couples, slaves—and ask the god whether someone has worked a piece of magic (*pharmakon*) against so-and-so, whether X has cursed Y, whether the inquirer should make use of a named necromancer, and so forth. Other tablets from elsewhere curse 'whoever has put a binding spell on me', or beg Hermes of the Underworld to bind certain specified individuals. Curses are directed against those who might violate a grave—a form of magic found especially among Greeks on the Turkish seacoast—while 'professional' workers of magic could be asked either to raise the dead or to lay an unwanted ghost. Binding magic included the manufacture of figurines as well as the inscription of small artefacts, both being intended for burial to achieve swifter communication with the appropriate spirits. These we have come across before in Mesopotamia and Egypt, and they can be found in the various Greek communities from as early as the sixth century BC. One example from Athens consists of a little figurine, which was found next to the pelvis of a skeleton, and two inscribed lead tablets. On the right leg of the figure is inscribed the name of the target, Mnesimakhos, and on one of the tablets, the words of the curse. These make it clear that the spell was supposed to make it impossible for Mnesimakhos and his friends to speak on their own behalf in a court of law.

Such tablets and figures are by no means uncommon. Neither are texts directed towards inducing or punishing love, such as so-called 'apple spells' intended to enchant the fruit so that whoever eats or catches it will fall in love with the person who has given or thrown it. This was a long-standing tradition, perhaps derived from the myth of Atalanta, the virgin huntress with an aversion to marriage, who was caught by her admirer Hippomenes by virtue of three golden apples supplied by the goddess Aphrodite. Aristophanes describes the Athenian custom of throwing apples with erotic intent, and magical instructions dating from the first century BC tell the giver to recite their spell three times and then throw the apple to, or at, the object of his desire. Amulets (*periapta*, 'things tied on') had tasks similar to those of the Middle East and Egypt, namely, to protect or to cure. They were sometimes applied along with an incantation, as Plato reveals in his dialogue *Charmides*, and were sometimes engraved with an allusion to their purpose. Folded lead tablets known as *Ephesia grammata* could be worn round the neck in little leather pouches; finger-rings similarly inscribed were common; and small engraved objects might be worn to guarantee success in some kind of contest such as boxing. Strips of metal bearing magical formulae (*lamina* or *lamellae*), which were then rolled up and inserted into small cylinders to be placed in the grave with a corpse, or worn round the neck as we see in coffin-portraits from Graeco-Roman Egypt, acted as amulets for protection in this life or the next as circumstances demanded; while phylacteries could be worn for a while (for example, to drive away a headache), or permanently (to help the wearer cope with epilepsy).

For all its popularity, though, disapproval of magic was fostered by such things as the presence in Greece of itinerant magicians from Mesopotamia and healers who specialized in binding spells. The arrogant inwardness of Athenian intellectuals, who regarded non-Greeks as 'barbarians', disdaining, with a combination of fearfulness and contempt, the constellation of ritual practices observable among the Greeks themselves, dismissed them with the borrowed and negative term '*mageia*'. There seems to have been little or no legislation enacted against magic itself, however, as opposed to harmful actions attributed to it. The occasional prosecution for *pharmakeia*, actual laws from the island of Teos (fifth century BC), private regulations for a private cult from Philadelphia on the Turkish coast (first century BC), and legislative proposals from Plato's treatise on laws are really all we have. Interestingly enough, Plato's proposals arise out of his discussion of poisoning cases and he draws a distinction between simple poisoning—harm done to bodies by bodies in accordance with the way Nature operates, as he puts it—and that which works psychologically as well as physically:

> Distinct from [simple poisoning] is the type which, by means of 'sorceries' (*manganeiai*) and 'incantations' (*epōdai*), as they are called, not only convinces those who try to cause an injury that they really can do so, but also convinces their victims they really are being injured by those who possess the power of harmful magic (*goēteuein*). With regard to all such matters, it is neither easy to perceive what is the real truth nor, if one does perceive it, is it easy to convince other people. Moreover, it is futile to get near the souls of people who view one another with dark suspicion if they happen to see images made from moulded wax at

doorways, or at points where three roads meet, or perhaps at the tomb of some ancestor, and tell them to make light of all such portents, when we ourselves have no clear opinion about them. Consequently, we shall divide the law about poisoning under two heads, according to the manner in which the attempt is made ... [Those who poison the body with poisonous substances may be executed or made to pay a fine, in accordance with the circumstances of the case.] But if the decision is that someone is behaving as a criminal by the use of spells, incantations, or any such method of poisonous magic (*pharmakeīon*), and if he is a seer or diviner, he is to be put to death. If, on the other hand, he knows nothing about prophecy, he is to be dealt with in the same way as someone convicted of poisoning—that is, in his case the court will assess what they think it is right for him to suffer or to pay.

In the end, however, if the authorities wanted to control or even abolish the practice of magic and its allied occult disciplines, they would have to rely on public disapproval since that would have constituted a more effective control over instances of magical behaviour than any legislation. But, in fact, there does not seem to be much evidence that public attitudes in this regard actually did have much effect on people's behaviour. Like the Jews, then, 'Greeks' (that is, principally Athenian writers) mocked, complained, despised, and occasionally thundered, but to no lasting or effective avail other than to confirm intellectuals' prejudices in favour of their own opinions. Everyone else, while aware of these condemnations, continued more or less as before, since magic satisfied a range of needs in ways which neither philosophy nor the Olympian cult could manage.

Romans

Nevertheless, a tone had been set and this tone was somewhat more noticeable and more insidious in its effects among the Romans than it proved to be among the Greeks. Once again, however, we have to bear in mind that 'Romans' tends to be shorthand for an extraordinary range of peoples from an immensely diverse spread of the globe. Beginning with the city of Rome itself and its environs, 'Rome' grew into a combination of imperial idea and fact, stretching from the borders of Scotland to the Sudan, and from Portugal to the edge of the Persian Empire, in which eventually every free adult male became a 'Roman citizen'. Hence, although it was Roman policy to encourage a certain cultural uniformity throughout these vast regions, the natural diversity of peoples within them meant that adaptation, interplay, imitation, and adoption of non-Roman behaviours were, by and large, the commonest expressions of people's belonging to the empire, rather than surrender of their own ways and modes of thought to imperial cultural strategies.

References to early Roman magic tend to come from later authors. Two laws from the fifth-century BC legislation known as the Twelve Tables, for example, are recorded by Pliny the Elder in the first century AD. Both prohibit the use of incantations (*carmina*) for harmful purposes, and Pliny gives an example of a farmer using *veneficia* ('acts of poisonous magic', the equivalent of Greek *pharmakeia*) to make his farm prosper at the expense of his neighbours. Indeed, his encyclopedic *Naturalis Historia* is full of references to popular Roman practices of the kind we should call 'magical', although Pliny himself, while recording them, adopts a superior tone, as he does in his discussion of *magi* ('magicians') whom he dismisses as fools and quacks and largely foreigners. Magic, he fulminated, was the most fraudulent of the arts (*artes*, i.e. 'practical skills'), and had dominated the world for centuries:

> No one should be surprised at how great its influence is because it alone of all the arts has embraced three others which exercise supreme dominion over the human mind, and have made them subject to itself alone. No one will doubt that it arose first from medicine and that, while professing to promote health, it insidiously advanced under the guise of a higher and more sacred discipline; that to the most seductive and welcome promises it added the powers of religion ... and again, that as it met with success, it made a further addition of astrology, because there is no one who is not eager to learn his fate, or who does not believe that the most accurate account of it is the one derived from watching the stars. Consequently magic, by holding people's emotions in a triple bond, rose to such heights that even today it holds sway over a great part of humanity. (30.1.1–2)

In spite of all this irritation, however, it is clear from Pliny's work, as it is from that of the earlier statesman Cato, that, in company with the Greeks, Romans employed magical practices regularly and for much the same reasons and purposes as everyone else. Curse-tablets (*defixiones*), inscribed by both private individuals and professional magicians—for by this time there were such people available for hire and consultation—have been found in abundance, and they are invaluable sources of information about such disparate subjects as popular beliefs, standards of education, and local variations on standard Latin. People also wore or carried amulets. The most common Latin term for these was *remedium*, indicating their use as apotropaics against disease or the evil eye, though they were also attached to hunting-dogs for success in the chase. Their ingredients included tufts of badger-hair, mussel-shells, pieces of magnetite or coral, and enchanted herbs according to one first-century AD author.

Lamellae were common, too, their magical formulae often starting with an appeal to foreign deities or non-human entities— 'Iao, Abrasax', says one bilingual example in Greek and Latin, worn by a German soldier, 'give health and victory to Tiberius Claudius Similis'—and wax figurines, love-philtres, and necromantic sacrifices make their appearances in Latin literature both fictional and factual. Nor were these confined to the peasantry or urban poor. When an investigation was ordered of the house of Germanicus, the Emperor Tiberius' nephew who, it was alleged, had been the object of a murder-plot, the floors were taken up, the walls smashed open, and various interesting articles were found: 'the remains of human bodies, written incantations and curses, leaden tablets engraved with the name "Germanicus", charred and blood-smeared ashes, and other instruments of harmful magic by which it is believed that the living soul can be consecrated to the powers of the grace' (Tacitus, *Annals* 2.69).

But what we find increasingly in the literature of the early empire is identification of women in particular with many of the magical arts, especially those designed to do harm or enable adultery or even kill. This was a trend which had started to be noticeable in fifth-century Athens, as the corpus of Greek tragedies shows, but while the Greek emphasis tended to stress the foreignness of the magical worker, its Latin equivalent pointed to women, both upper-class and of the lowest ranks, as the principal practitioners of these lethal skills. This is new. Our sources from Mesopotamia, Egypt, and Israel-Judaea-Palestine, for example, suggest that magic was largely in the hands of men, and even in Greek literature there is much talk of priests, soothsayers, professional magicians, and itinerant healers and hucksters, all of whom are evidently male. With Rome, however (and *pace* such Greek female figures as Circe and Medea), we can discern the beginnings of that female magician who will in later times be designated 'witch'. She is at her most obvious in poetry, in the caricatures of Horace and Lucan. In his early works, *Satires* 1.8 and *Epodes* 5 and 17, Horace depicts a number of old, ugly women attended by snakes, ghostly dogs, and eventually the spirits of the dead, engaged in sacrificing to Hekate in a graveyard, wielding a couple of figurines, and murdering a boy so that they can make a love potion from his liver and bone marrow. This is satire. Lucan's portrait is pure Grand Guignol. In his *Pharsalia*, an epic poem on the civil war between Julius Caesar and Pompey, his overblown portrait of the witch Erictho describes her seeking ingredients for her magic in a graveyard, where she rips off parts from dead bodies with her nails and teeth. Where Horace's women are figures of fun, however, Lucan's 'witch' is a grotesque and her depiction is intended to make the audience shudder. So can we take either with any degree of seriousness and discern some reality underneath the theatrics? The satirist Juvenal frequently attacks women for being libidinous, uppity, and murderous, and condemns them for dealing in incantations and *veneficia*. The historian Tacitus tells us about noblewomen—Nero's mother, for example, and one of her close friends—who were prepared to use magic to further their schemes of political advancement or revenge; Cicero suggests that some women were particularly prone to using acts of poisonous magic to achieve their personal, hostile ends; and the agricultural expert Columella strongly advises farm-managers not to allow other employees to consult 'wise women' (*sagae*). The virulence of some of these portraits, suggesting a genuine nervousness in the face of an actual phenomenon, and the near-ubiquity of references to both male and female magical practitioners does, therefore, imply that such people were to be found quite commonly. Evidence relating or belonging to parts of the empire other than Italy makes it clear that the practice of magic, as traditionally understood, was prevalent everywhere.

One such collection of essentially non-Italian evidence belongs to the scattered Christian communities which quickly spread throughout the Mediterranean basin. Their sacred writings recorded wonders (*miracula*), principally of casting out demons, curing the sick, or raising the dead. These *miracula* were then commemorated as proofs that the power on which they rested was legitimate as opposed to that of other people which was, rather, magic and therefore illegitimate and probably demon-inspired. But if these early accounts of Christian wonder-working may be regarded as partial, we can still discern popular attitudes to magic which ring true, whether they belong to propaganda or not. Acts 19: 11–20, for example, tells us that when St Paul was in Ephesus he cured the sick and exorcized demons, and that others then used pieces of cloth which had come into contact with his body as though they were amulets, or objects imbued with more than human power which could effect the same results for other people. It also relates that some itinerant exorcists who tried to do the same were utterly unsuccessful, with the result that 'a number of those who practised magic collected their books and burned them publicly'. These books were, apparently, very expensive, perhaps because they included a lot of material and were therefore in several volumes. The collections of magical lore attributed to Bolos of Mendes and Nigidius Figulus, both of whom were referenced by Pliny the Elder, would have been of this kind and so too, perhaps, Anaxilaus of Larisa's compilation of conjuring-tricks. Nigidius and Anaxilaus belonged to the first century BC and may have seen copies of their works disappear in the year 13 when, according to the historian Suetonius, the Emperor Augustus ordered 2,000 magical scrolls to be committed to the fire.

Admiration of the Apostles' wonder-working abilities elsewhere also seems to have interpreted them much as the Ephesians did. When St Peter and St John went to Samaria, for example, they found 'a certain man named Simon [who] had previously practised magic in the city and amazed the people' (Acts 8: 9). This Simon then attempted to buy St Peter's power, assuming that it was some kind of magical commodity, perhaps consisting of secret words which could be traded. St Peter's indignant repudiation of this misunderstanding was developed by later Christian writers such as Justin Martyr and Irenaeus in the second century into condemnation of Simon himself as a magician who worked his wonders with the help of demons operating through him, an interpretation which further evolved into the sin especially associated with his name, simony. Turning accusations of sorcery away from themselves and directing them against their religious opponents, whether Jews or heretics, became, in fact, a common mode of defence by Christian authors. Nor was this tactic a relatively short-lived way of dealing with unorthodox or contumacious individuals, for even as late as 385 Priscillian, Bishop of Ávila in Spain, who had expressed in both written and spoken word religious opinions contrary to those approved by the Church, was condemned and executed, not on doctrinal grounds but on a charge of practising magic, a civil crime then punishable by death.

Not that such fearsome disapproval appears to have diminished popular enthusiasm for magic during the early Christian period. The second-century Acts of Andrew warns a woman to avoid her husband's evil acts of necromancy; Origen at the beginning of the third century preserves extensive extracts from an anti-Christian treatise by Celsus, which show clearly that pagans regarded Christian worship and beliefs as rife with magic and demonry; Tertullian, Origen's near-contemporary, explained that all the Greek and Roman deities were, in effect, demons and that, therefore, all their priests must be magicians. In fourth-century Palestine, a floor mosaic in a monastery includes biblical inscriptions in its design, obviously intended to protect both monks and visitors: 'The Lord will guard your coming in and going out, henceforth and for ever' (Psalm 121: 8). In one of his letters, St Basil (*c*.329–379) observes,

> Women frequently try to draw men to love them by incantations and magic knots, and give them herbs (*pharmaka*) which dull their intelligence. When such women cause death, although the result of their action may not be what they intended, nevertheless, because what they have done is magical and prohibited, they should be accounted as intentional murderesses.

In one of his catechetical instructions, St John Chrysostom (*c*.347–407) laments,

> What is one to say about those who use charms and amulets, and encircle their heads and feet with golden coins of Alexander of Macedon? ... You don't simply always have amulets in your possession, but incantations which bring drunken and half-witted old women into your house. Aren't you ashamed, don't you blush ... to be terrified at such things?

Little wonder, then, that in 553 the Council of Constantinople forbade the use of magic and amulets by the faithful.

The tone of both sides, Christian and pagan, is of course polemical: I work miracles, you work magic; I am enlightened, you are superstitious; my 'magic' is legitimate, yours is not and should be suppressed. But in a Roman world in which those traditionally calling upon magic for their solution continued to be as ubiquitous and persistent as ever, hostilities between intellectuals and the *polloi* (the many), or between leaders and adherents of the empire's multifarious religions, made little or no impact on popular behaviour. What did begin to seep into public perceptions of magic and magical practitioners was the Roman-inspired notion that harmful magic lay particularly in the hands of ill-disposed and aggressive women, and the Christian con- viction that magic, especially harmful magic, was made possible only by demons and that in consequence anyone who worked such magic did so under the instruction or with the assistance of evil spirits. Here, perhaps, is the source of some of those later theories which the late Middle Ages and early modern period used to justify their prosecution of witches both male and female.

Still, the Church's stance on magic did not stop people from absorb- ing Christ into their magical pantheon. Greek texts from Christian Egypt alone, for example, show how common this became. From the fourth and seventh centuries we have spells and amuletic invocations calling upon Jesus to protect the owner or wearer against demon- induced illness, especially fever, or to heal someone already sick. 'Jesus Christ heals the chill and the fever', promises one, 'and every disease of the body of Joseph who wears the amulet daily and intermittently.' This particular amulet hedges its bets, though, and also calls upon another, pagan power. 'Let the white wolf, the white wolf, the white wolf heal the shivering fever of Joseph.' Other spells call upon the Apostles, often mixing their names with those of Hebrew words for 'God' and with an almost infinite number of ill-remembered Egyp- tian, pseudo-Greek, and Coptic terms. But by this time the Roman Empire had long split into its western and eastern halves, the high sunshine of Roman cultural 'diversity-in-uniformity' had dimmed, and a newer set of traditions and variant practices was emerging to answer the needs of late antiquity.

2

Medieval Magic

Sophie Page

In the early Middle Ages people used and feared magic for the same reasons they used or feared any other sacred ritual: magic was thought to strengthen or sever relationships between people, to overcome material obstacles, and to spread good or evil by protecting a community or introducing sickness and death. But magic was the name given to a class of *inappropriate* sacred rituals, which were excluded from normative Christian practice. Magical activities used objects and language that were not obviously part of Christian material culture or the liturgy, or in ways, or for purposes, which made churchmen uneasy. An unauthorized sacred ritual was thought to express its practitioner's ignorance of appropriate sacred forms, adherence to heathen practice, or association with the Devil.

The heartlands of western Europe had been Christianized in the fifth and sixth centuries, and Christendom continued to expand into pagan lands in Europe. In these newly converted pagan lands the beliefs and practices of Christians were scrutinized constantly; as earlier beliefs and practices began to disappear in favour of Christianity, some fragments of their mythology and ritual survived in magical sources, detached from their belief systems but still ascribed some kind of power. In a tenth-century manuscript, a 'Nine-Herbs Charm' to combat poison and infection includes an invocation to Woden (Odin); its user may have known nothing about the pagan god, but may still have accepted that it was a powerful name to invoke. Practitioners also responded to the spread of Christianity by replacing pagan sources of power with Christian ones: an early medieval Germanic spell to heal a lame horse has Balder's horse being injured and the god Woden healing it, but in later versions it is Christ who heals his own horse. Similarly, most surviving copies of the popular fifth-century Pseudo-Apuleius *Herbarium*, a work on the powers of herbs, open with the Lord's Prayer rather than with the original invocation to 'Holy goddess Earth'.

The early medieval triumph of Christianity over paganism instilled confidence in the superiority of divine over demonic power. In early medieval hagiographies the magician was often the counterpoint to the saint: a figure who revealed the powers available to humans in the cosmos but against whom the merits of saints could be demonstrated. In the Christianized cosmos, certain key powers associated with magical practitioners were appropriated for the saints, such as control over the elements—a valuable ability in an agrarian community. The appropriation of positive supernatural powers for saints was accompanied by negative characterizations of magic as an antisocial and even demonic activity. Two categories of magic which become prominent in hostile sources in this period—*sortilegium* (sorcery) and *maleficium* (literally 'evil practice')—present it as a harmful force aimed at causing sickness, death, poverty, and material destruction. But in order to legislate against magical practices, secular and religious authorities needed to define and describe them. The most comprehensive early medieval attempt to do this is found in the eighth book of the *Etymologiae* of Isidore of Seville (*c.*560–636), which discussed religion and religious sects, thereby suggesting that magic was a deviant form of religion. Isidore described specific varieties of magical practitioners and diviners; these included the *malefici* (evildoers), who had power over the elements and people's minds, killed by the power of their incantations, and summoned demons to help them, and the *incantatores* (enchanters), who worked magic by the power of words. Throughout the medieval period secular rulers legislated harshly against magic in order to express their piety and emphasize their role as protectors of Christian communities, and as the Christian territories of Europe became stronger and more consolidated such legislation could have a broader impact. The Emperor Charlemagne, for example, made a sweeping legal condemnation of magic in 789 in his *Admonitio generali* (General Admonition), which required magicians and enchanters throughout his kingdom to repent or be condemned to death.

Early medieval sermons also condemned magic harshly and urged men and women to more appropriate Christian actions such as prayer. Condemned magical activities included the use of unorthodox words (often distinguished from prayer as invocations or diabolical charms), of images (such as metal talismans or amulets made from natural objects), of physical actions (for example picking herbs at a particular time, or putting a child in an oven to cure fever), of religious actions like invoking deities or sacrificing to demons, and of the body or body parts (such as hair or saliva but also the malevolent gaze of the evil eye), and making concoctions from natural ingredients in order to harm or inappropriately influence others. There could be more than one reason for a given practice attracting suspicion: an inappropriate practitioner, intention, or source of power, or the inappropriate use of orthodox religious power. Particularly suspicious was an adaptation of sacred ritual: adding to or subtracting from what had been established by the Church, even if (sometimes especially if) it was churchmen themselves who initiated the deviations.

Critics of magic did not accept that its practitioners drew on natural powers in the cosmos like those of herbs, stones, or stars, but assumed that their actions expressed an association with demons or the remnants of heathen religious practice. However, local church authorities seem to have had some sympathy with the motives that led people to perform magic in order to solve domestic crises (such as the sickness of a child) or to try to improve their lives by making their fields and animals more fertile. Men and women at all social levels would have known the difference between calling on the aid of God or the saints and calling on demons, but they may not have worried about the source of power when they performed a ritual that might save their child or their crops.

Penitentials—books of church rules in circulation from the sixth century, which described the penances that a priest should apply for a range of transgressions—assign harsher punishments for priests (who should know better) than lay people, and view some intentions as more worthy of condemnation than others. The Burgundian Penitential (*c.*700–25) prescribes seven years of subsisting only on bread and water for magic that had destroyed someone, but fewer if the practitioner had been motivated by love and no harm had resulted. The passage in this penitential and others on magical practitioners inspired by love refers specifically to clerics, deacons, and priests. This may imply that they were sometimes motivated by pastoral concerns to perform rituals that departed from normative sacred rituals in order to help their communities. For example, a long and complex Anglo-Saxon ritual for restoring fertility to fields ruined by a sorcerer or poisoner required a priest to sing masses in a church over four sods of earth from the field, alongside ritual actions, the invocation of sacred assistance from the mother of the earth and the ritual gathering and use of various fruits of the earth. Other prayers and remedies from this period surviving in monastic manuscripts reveal the popularity of unorthodox angel names for specific areas of concern, such as Panchiel for crop protection or Dormiel for stomach ache.

Many magical activities could be performed by anyone: early medieval sources describe how words or incantations were used to transform everyday objects like knots, bread, cloth, and even grass into magical tools. The Bishop Burchard of Worms claimed in his *Corrector* (*c*.1008–12), which drew on earlier writings about magic, that these activities were frequently performed by swineherds and ploughmen and sometimes by hunters. In penitentials magical activities tended to be treated as the foolish errors of uneducated people who were able to redeem themselves through relatively light penances. Exceptions to this general leniency occur in cases where the magical practitioner intended harm, since ignorance of appropriate ritual forms was not an excuse for violence. Magical experts were also singled out as they were more threatening to the Church than ordinary people engaged in magical activities, experts such as male enchanters who were thought to use incantations to arouse storms and female practitioners who specialized in inciting love and hatred. The strong association of magic and language was characteristic of a religion of the book, whose leaders believed strongly in the power of the sacred word but were afraid of its improper use.

In the late Middle Ages there was a dramatic rise in the number and complexity of magic texts in circulation, which had significant implications for how people thought about celestial and spiritual power in the medieval universe and how it could be manipulated. Nevertheless, this period saw the continuation of three significant aspects of early medieval magic. Rituals continued to be easily adaptable to changing circumstances; in the later Middle Ages this was expressed in the translation and adaptation of Jewish and Arabic magic texts.

The strong association of magical practices with churchmen remained: increasingly the evil of magic was thought to lie not in a resurgence of pagan practices but in learned clerics using their priestly powers to the wrong ends. Finally, the stereotype of the evil magician in league with demons continued to be significant, though the nature of the relationship between demons and humans, especially women, changed towards the end of this period with a new emphasis on the demonic pact.

From Arabic into Latin: Translating Activity and Learned Magic

In the eleventh century Europe entered a period of expansion, centralization, and creativity. One of the areas of political expansion was Spain, where Christian kingdoms began to gain territories from Muslim rulers. After the capture of Toledo in 1085 the Pope sent foreign clerics into Spain to impose ritual uniformity on churches that had spent a long period under Muslim rule. In the newly captured territories Christian clerics discovered an extraordinary wealth of Greek philosophy and science that had been preserved in the Arabic world, and Arabic texts whose authors had already wrestled with many of the difficulties of reconciling pagan ideas with monotheism. A great translation movement was instigated as scholars from across Europe flocked to centres in Spain, Sicily, and the Middle East to translate works from Arabic into Latin, often collaborating with local Jewish scholars who had linguistic expertise in Arabic, Latin, and Hebrew. The ensuing extraordinary influx into Europe of magic texts from the Greek, Arabic, and Jewish traditions transformed the status of late medieval magic from an illicit activity into a branch of knowledge.

The intellectuals involved in translating activity did not form a distinct community. They had disparate backgrounds and contacts but shared a common openness to the diverse offerings of the new learning, which included works of medicine, philosophy, cosmology, geometry, astronomy, mathematics, and the occult sciences. In Muslim Spain (al-Andalus) the exact sciences were inextricably mixed up with astrology and magic, and many Latin translators followed this pattern of interests. For example, the Arabist Adelard of Bath (*c.*1080–*c.*1152) translated Euclid's *Elements* (a mathematical and geometrical treatise), al-Khwārizmī's astronomical tables, and several works of astrology and magic. Altogether about twenty works of Arabic magic were translated into Latin in the twelfth century. The names of several of their translators are known, but many authors were pseudo-epigraphic (attached to such biblical or legendary authorities as Hermes, Adam, or Solomon) or anonymous. This was partly because rituals, invocations, and signs were not supposed to be mere human inventions, and partly because theological condemnation in both Islam and Christianity made authorship potentially dangerous. But Arabic magic's association with the prestigious and more acceptable arts of astronomy and astrology aided its reception in the Latin West.

In late medieval Europe Latin was a transnational language of scholarship, which enabled magic texts to be quickly and widely disseminated. By the end of the Middle Ages many had also been translated into vernacular languages like French, English, German, and Italian, thus reaching a wider audience that included lay people. An important centre for the compilation and translation of occult texts into vernacular languages was the scriptorium of Alfonso X of Castile and León (r.1252–84), which employed Jewish, Christian, and Muslim scholars to translate texts from Arabic and Hebrew into Latin and Castilian. Five magic works were composed or translated under Alfonso's patronage: the *Lapidario*, the *Picatrix*, the *Libro de las formas et las ymagenes*, the *Libro de astromagia*, and the *Liber Razielis*. These reveal Alfonso's particular interest in networks of natural forces in the universe and how to manipulate them, as well as in Hebrew angelology. The preface to the *Liber Razielis* negotiates Alfonso's collection of potentially suspect texts by drawing parallels between his quest for valuable knowledge in diverse traditions and Solomon's pursuit of wisdom from distant lands.

There was also, through the transmission of original texts in Greek and texts derived from Arabic sources, a significant Greek contribution to medieval Latin astrology and magic. This source of occult texts is much less studied than the translation movement in Spain, but at least two Greek works of magic reached the Latin West in the early Middle Ages: a lapidary (a work on the magical powers inherent in different stones) by Damigeron or Evax, and a book attributed to Thessalus von Tralles on the medicinal uses of plants assigned to the signs of the zodiac and the planets. In the twelfth century a further group of texts on the magical properties of animals, plants, and stones was translated—probably by Pascalis Romanus, a priest, medical expert, and compiler of a book on dream interpretation working in Constantinople—and proved popular with Latin readers. In the Byzantine world, as in the Latin West, magical activities were a common feature of daily existence, but they often took distinctive local forms. Although the Orthodox Church and secular authorities in Byzantium made an effort to define and describe magical practices and to legislate against them like their western counterparts, the boundaries with Christian practices were less precise than in the Latin West. The greater cultural continuity between the pagan and Christian periods of the Graeco-Roman world meant that non-Christian popular practices were less threatening, and there were far fewer cases of witchcraft in medieval Byzantium than there were in the West.

The occult sciences (alchemy, astrology, magic, and divination) were part of the learned culture of the medieval Byzantine world, as they were in late medieval Europe. They attracted a similar class of educated bureaucrat, but learned magic had a much more discreet profile: almost all surviving magical and divinatory texts are anonymous and undated. Nevertheless, Byzantium was geographically well situated to promote the transmission of treatises on the occult sciences from and into Greek, Latin, and Arabic. Travel, written and oral exchanges, and competence in foreign languages facilitated these exchanges, but also gave learned magic a bad reputation as something mainly practised by foreigners. In the twelfth century a Byzantine nobleman, Alexios Axouch, was accused of consulting a Latin sorcerer who summoned demons to ask them about the future and provided Axouch with potions that would deprive the Byzantine Emperor of a male heir. As we shall see, the same kinds of anxieties at courts, about factions, fertility, and the use of magic to further political goals, were common in the Latin West.

The arrival of Greek and Arabic science through these various routes influenced Christian conceptions of nature and the cosmos and provided scholars in the Latin West with a new technical vocabulary to describe their universe. These intellectual developments form part of a movement of cultural renewal in the Latin West, commonly labelled the 'twelfth-century renaissance', during which interest in learned magic grew, though intellectuals were cautious about defending any specific practice that looked like magic. The twelfth-century renaissance increased confidence in the power of human reason to comprehend the secrets of the universe, which in turn changed the way people thought about their relationship with nature. There was a rapidly growing awareness of the regularity of the natural order, incited by the study of Aristotle in particular, and a new interest in investigating particular aspects of the natural world, from comets and rainbows to animal behaviour and human anatomy. Learned magic texts attracted the serious interest of scholars because they were supported by theories familiar to readers of other genres and because they offered the tools to reveal and exploit the secrets of nature.

In the early Middle Ages people could be described as performing magical actions, but there was little or no sense of a 'magical art' as an organized body of knowledge. After the translation and dissemination of learned magic texts, magic began to be taken more seriously and even its critics engaged with its claims of offering knowledge of the cosmos, if only to condemn them. The Abbess of the Hohenburg Abbey in Alsace, Herrad of Landsberg (1130–95), included magic in an image of the seven Liberal Arts, which was part of her illustrated encyclopedia, the *Hortus deliciarum* (Garden of Delights). In this image Queen Philosophy is surrounded by personifications of the seven Liberal Arts and placed above Socrates and Plato, who are seated in conversation. She holds a scroll which proclaims the divine origins of her art: 'all philosophy comes from God, only the Wise are able to fulfil their wishes.' At the bottom of the folio are poets or magicians, excluded from true philosophy because they are guided by impure spirits and capable of producing only tales and fables, frivolous poetry, or magic formulas. The evil spirits perch behind the heads of the poets and magicians and whisper in mockery of the inspiration of the Holy Spirit.

Unsurprisingly, the relationships between philosophy, magic, and spiritual inspiration are presented differently in learned magic texts. One of the most complex works of learned magic circulating in late medieval Europe was the *Picatrix*, the Latin translation of the *Ghāyat al-Ḥakīm*, an Arabic compendium of magic composed in Spain in the eleventh century and falsely attributed to Maslama al Majrīṭi. For the author of the *Picatrix* the practitioner of magic was a perfect philosopher (*philosophus perfectus*) who had mastered natural philosophy, metaphysics, arithmetic, geometry, music, and astronomy. This exemplary magician had acquired his wisdom from a study of the cosmos and of books, but he derived his power from celestial spirits and from the planets dominant in his nativity (the astrological chart drawn up for the moment of his birth). In the *Picatrix* the art of magic and the art of spirits are of equal importance, even indistinguishable. The text describes the founder of magic, Caraphzebiz, as the first person to have a 'familiar' (a spirit who remained with him as his companion). This familiar spirit performed marvels for him, helped him understand the secrets of nature and the sciences, and came when invoked with sacrifices.

Twelfth-century thinkers who were involved in the translations movement were excited by the claims of learned magic to manipulate and provide insights into the cosmos. An unusually sympathetic interpretation of the place of magic within classifications of knowledge is found, for example, in the *De divisione philosophiae* (On the Division of Philosophy) of Dominicus Gundissalinus, an Archdeacon of Segovia who had played a prominent role in the translating activities in Toledo in the twelfth century. Under the general heading of 'natural science' Dominicus proposed two categories of magic: 'necromancy according to physics' and the 'science of images'. The idea that magic could be a part of natural science gained increasing credibility in the thirteenth century as a result of attempts by scholars to understand and classify the properties of natural objects and bodies that were difficult to explain using Aristotelian physics or logic.

Natural Magic

The category of 'natural magic' emerged as a branch of natural science that studied properties and processes that were extraordinary but natural marvels. It was articulated most clearly by the theologian and Bishop of Paris William of Auvergne (*c.*1180/90–1249), who suggested that natural magic included the spontaneous generation of such animals as frogs, lice, and worms, the actions some souls exercised on bodies outside themselves, and the *sensus naturae* or *estimativa* by which, for example, the sheep divined that the wolf was its enemy. William wanted to distinguish the marvels produced by occult properties in nature from the trickery of prestidigitators and the illusions of demons. The concept of occult properties—properties whose effects were not explained by the *complexion*, or elemental constitution of a natural object, body, or substance—was inherited from Graeco-Roman notions of occult powers in the natural order. William emphasized, however, that these virtues had been assigned by God. Today some of these properties are understood, such as magnetism, and others, such as the basilisk's power to kill with its gaze, are known to be fantastical.

Among the Arabic and Graeco-Roman magic texts translated into Latin were works which drew on the natural powers of stones, plants, parts of animals, and celestial bodies. The influential fifth-century philosopher and theologian Augustine had assumed that practices of this kind relied implicitly on the power of demons. But Arabic texts brought with them more sophisticated theories to defend their efficacy and licitness, such as cosmological theories of celestial influence, discussions of the placebo effect, and arguments using the magnet's ability to attract iron to demonstrate that some striking properties could be witnessed but were difficult to explain. Magical operations that made use of occult powers in nature could now be defended as licit on the grounds that their effects were observable, even if their processes were controversial or not understood. Natural magic also expressed the new post-Aristotelian relationship between humans and nature, since magical practitioners saw the harnessing of powers in the natural world as an expression of humans' rightful dominance over nature. Many medieval writers disapproved, however, of the use of natural objects to influence a person's personality or emotions, for example by giving them courage or causing them to fall in love. They argued that recipes for achieving goals like this would either be ineffective or could only be achieved with the assistance of demons. Nevertheless, such recipes are very common in natural magic texts. A fifteenth-century illustration of the herb *lunaria* (honesty), drawn on one of the final folios of a mid-thirteenth-century collection of herbals and other medical texts (Wellcome MS 573, fo. 149v), is accompanied by a description of its magical uses. These include how to find treasure guarded by demons, have sex without getting pregnant, and predict the time of death of a man or woman.

In fact, natural objects with occult properties were ubiquitous in medieval culture. They were incorporated into personal jewellery for daily protection, kept for specific purposes such as childbirth or a long journey, and even placed with the dead to protect them in the afterlife.

In the later Middle Ages the relationship between sacred and natural powers became less distinct. The number and complexity of personal prophylactic objects increased, and these often combined sacred sources of power—Christian relics, formulae, and images—with the natural virtues of precious stones and other materials. The treasuries of cathedrals and princes came to be repositories for all kinds of objects of power and value, mingling the relics of saints with exotic marvels like ostrich eggs and crocodile skeletons and objects with specific marvellous properties such as precious stones and fragments of unicorn horn.

St Albans Abbey, for example, possessed a large late Roman imperial cameo (now lost) called Kaadmau, which was part of a collection of gems catalogued by the monk Matthew Paris in 1250–4. The cameo was used to induce overdue childbirths; slowly lowering it on its chain down the woman's cleavage while saying a prayer to St Alban was believed to cause the infant to flee downwards. This gem derived its power from its exotic imagery (incomprehensible to Matthew Paris, who interpreted the Emperor in his military kilt as a man wearing rags), precious materials (chalcedony, sardonyx, and onyx), and the sacred invocation of the saint. It was also thought to be empowered by its sacred residence: although it might be lent by the abbey to favoured lay women, it would lose its power if taken by violence or fraud.

Image Magic

The combination of rare natural materials, engraved representations, and a supernatural source of power was central to image magic. Image magic was the most common genre of magic translated from Arabic into Latin and consisted of rituals to be performed over a three-dimensional object (an image or talisman) in order to induce a spirit or heavenly body to imbue it with power. The magical object could be created by sculpting metal or wax, inscribing a piece of parchment or cloth, or engraving an object like a ring, mirror, or knife. Rituals including the invocation of spirits and suffumigations (the ritual burning of incense) were then performed over the image. When the rituals were complete the image was placed somewhere appropriate to the operation, for example on a merchant's stall to increase trade or on the body to protect it from harm. In some cases God was also asked to help the practitioner achieve his goal, allowing the Christian practitioner to express his piety in the form of a prayer.

An example of such a petition to God can be found in the instructions for using the magic square of Mercury from the *Liber de septem figuris septem planetarum* (The Book of the Seven Figures of the Seven Planets). This Arabic magic text was translated into Latin in the twelfth century, surviving in Arabic, Latin, and Greek versions. A magic square is a set of numbers arranged in a square which give the same total when added in a straight line in any direction. In some magic texts this mathematical curiosity was assigned marvellous powers. The planet Mercury was associated with science, knowledge, and philosophy. According to this magic text the operator could increase his memory and make learning easier for himself by drawing the magic square of Mercury on a ring, dish, knife, white glass, or pewter bowl, then effacing the figure with water and drinking the liquid which he had used to rub it out. If he wished to give his enemy spasms and paralysis and make him lose his sight or mind he should engrave it on a steel mirror, which would then afflict all those who gazed in it. If the operator wanted to acquire knowledge, he was told to fast for one day or three days continuously, eating nothing except bread with honey and raisins. At the end of this period he should draw the square on a cloth of saffron or yellow silk and fumigate it with aloe wood saying: 'O God by the virtue of this figure, reveal this thing to me.' When he placed the cloth under his head before going to sleep everything he had asked for would be revealed in a dream.

Arabic magic texts began to attract increasing scrutiny from the mid-thirteenth century, with theologians such as William of Auvergne concerned about whether their goals were accomplished using natural or demonic powers, and whether the rituals addressed to magical objects constituted planetary idolatry. But not everyone condemned the texts. The curiosity about the natural sciences newly translated from Arabic, and an intellectual concern with the influence of occult powers, especially those of celestial origin, attracted thinkers of the stature of Thomas Aquinas and Albertus Magnus to defend and debate the licitness of image magic. Some translators of magic texts tried to escape censure by adjusting texts to fit the requirements of orthodoxy. John of Seville omitted prayers to spirits in his Latin translation of an Arabic image magic text, Thabit's *De imaginibus* (On Images), so that the magical rituals drew only on natural celestial influences, and his version of the text was subsequently viewed as licit. Another approach was to adapt the Islamic spirits to more recognizably Christian figures. An Arabic work of magic called the *Liber Almandal* was rewritten in a version which Christianized the djinns, while the fourteenth-century scribe of a Christian text strongly influenced by Arabic magic, the *Liber de essentia spirituum*, wrote 'angelus' (angel) in the margin beside the term 'spiritus' (spirit) so that the reader would interpret the spirits of this text as good angels.

As learned magic texts spread, it became more important to the authorities to determine which texts constituted legitimate knowledge and which were illicit. In the mid-thirteenth century, an influential work called the *Speculum astronomiae* (Mirror of Astronomy) tried to lay out some guidelines. The author of this text was motivated by the defence of astrology to condemn certain kinds of magic which, in his opinion, were besmirching its reputation and working 'against the honour of the Catholic faith'. He categorized two works of image magic as licit because they depended solely upon astronomical calculations, and identified two kinds of illicit image magic—'abominable' Hermetic magic texts, which explicitly invoked spirits, and 'detestable' Solomonic magic texts, which instructed the operator to inscribe characters on objects and exorcize them with certain names. Hermetic magic (also called 'astral magic' to include works not specifically attributed to Hermes) was considered more deplorable because the prayers, invocations, and suffumigations offered to planetary spirits seemed to express a cult of planetary idolatry.

Hermes Trismegistus ('the thrice-great Hermes') was a mythical authority originating in a fusion of Greek and Egyptian esoteric traditions. In the Greek and Arabic world he was believed to be the author of a large number of works of astrology, magic, alchemy, and philosophy. The Arabic occult texts had their origins in Persian and ultimately Indian sources, and, possibly, in the Sabaean community of star worshippers at Ḥarrān in northern Mesopotamia. An intellectual branch of the Sabaeans was set up in Baghdad in the ninth century and included Thābit ibn Qurra, the author of several image magic texts translated into Latin. Although medieval magic texts did not explicitly encourage the magician to worship the planets, it is not hard to see how this suspicion arose. The *Picatrix* provides prayers to the planets and describes which animals are appropriate to sacrifice to them. The ritual sacrifice of an animal before invoking the spirits of a planet also forms part of the instructions in a magic text produced at the court of Alfonso X, the *Libro de astromagia* (The Book of Astral Magic, *c.*1280–1). The format of the ritual varies according to the planet being invoked and the sign that it is passing through. The ritual to speak with a spirit of Mercury when this planet is in the sign of Cancer requires the practitioner to offer a sacrifice and to make a votive spear and horse using red copper. In the image accompanying this ritual (MS. Reg. lat. 1283a, folio 32, column b) the practitioner can be seen next to the horse and spear, the goat he has sacrificed, and two lit braziers that have been used for the burning of incense. The practitioner stands in an attitude of reverence speaking to the winged spirit who his ritual has summoned, a messenger from Mercury. The god himself is depicted in the smaller roundel riding a peacock above the zodiac sign of Cancer.

The esoteric characterization of Solomon became popular in some currents of late antique Judaism and Christianity. Solomonic magic texts claim to have been written by Solomon, who is said to have received a revelation of their contents directly from God. Magic rituals in this tradition included prayers to angels and instructions for using magic circles, characters, and sacrifices to compel spirits. The cosmologies of Solomonic and Hermetic magic appear superficially different. Hermetic magic texts presented the universe as integrated by a harmonious web of connections across the celestial and physical worlds and described how the practitioner should bring together things with corresponding natures in his ritual—spirits, names, images, prayers, times, locations, and materials—so that power could be transferred from higher to lower bodies and be intensified by the harmony of all the parts of the operation. The practitioner of Solomonic magic dominated spirits through knowledge of their names, which he used to invoke the spirits to be present and obey him. But both Hermetic and Solomonic texts emphasized that the success of magical operations depended on the will of God.

The appeal of magic texts undoubtedly lay in the accessibility of their cosmologies. Whereas for medieval theologians precise knowledge of celestial realms and spirits, and of the means for humans to harness their power, was inappropriate and dangerous, expressing what was beyond the reach of humans to know for certain, Arabic and Jewish magic texts extended and elaborated the Christian universe, populating it with a host of named spirits with particular cosmological roles, and spatial and temporal inhabitations. Although vast numbers of angels were believed to exist—Augustine had posited an angel for every visible thing in the world—most of these angels were deliberately unnamed in mainstream religious sources. But in magic texts spirits were assigned to the air, winds, sea, earth, and fire, and to the celestial bodies of various heavens and parts of the heavens. Similarly, the days and hours and seasons and their names, characteristics, and powers were described so that the magical practitioner could use this knowledge to persuade or command them to help him. For example, Ascymor, an angel of Mars, appears in several magic texts with mainly Jewish origins which were compiled under the patronage of Alfonso X, King of Castile. He was a useful angel to invoke when someone wanted to inspire love and passion between two people, obtain grace and love from all people, or speak with the moon and stars, the dead, and demons.

The dissemination of Arabic and Jewish magic texts across Europe encouraged Christian authors to write their own texts to better reflect their religious beliefs, desires, and prejudices. The Christianization of illicit rituals was often a subtle matter. For example, the author of the *Liber iuratus* (Sworn Book), a ritual magic text which was influenced by both Jewish and Islamic angelology, forestalled criticism of this appropriation by describing a magic seal which could be used against the 'sect of Mohammad', and by claiming that Jews were unable to use the magic arts to achieve a vision of God or gain truthful responses from spirits because they had rejected Christ. Most Christian-authored magic texts reflected the gulf between good angels and evil demons in Christian cosmology, and focused primarily on one or other group of spirits.

Angel Magic

Angel magic or theurgy was intended to persuade angels to confer knowledge and power as well as spiritual benefits on the practitioner. In order to be worthy of spiritual renewal the practitioner had to undergo demanding ascetic practices to purify his body and soul; the rituals to induce a spiritual experience could take several months to perform. If these were completed successfully some texts describe how he would receive a divine transmission of wisdom; others speak of the ascent of his soul while his living body remained on earth, and in others angels descended to speak to him and be his teachers or companions. Some aspects of angel magic relate very closely to mainstream Christianity. The idea that angels could confer spiritual benefits on ordinary humans was popularized in the late medieval cult of guardian angels, who watched over individual souls and after death presented the case for them to enter heaven. Angel magic texts also catered to the thirst for spiritual experience which had spread across society by the end of the Middle Ages; they used many of the same techniques as orthodox texts to achieve this goal, such as prayer, fasting, and meditation on images.

The most significant work of angel magic, surviving in over fifty medieval manuscript versions, was the *Ars notoria*. This complex treatise claimed to miraculously endow the practitioner with knowledge of all the liberal arts, philosophy, and theology, by means of angelic revelation and a divine infusion of wisdom. It was written by a Christian in northern Italy in the second half of the twelfth century and was popular with clerical and monastic readers because it incorporated prayers from the liturgy and largely avoided offending mainstream Christian religious sensibilities. The practitioner was required to recite prayers while 'inspecting' the *notae* (figures composed of words, shapes, and magical characters), which looked like mystical diagrams. But their exotic names, magical characters, and unusual shapes aroused the suspicion that they were actually tools for communicating with demons. In some manuscript copies angels were placed beside the *notae* to reassure readers and critics of the work's orthodoxy. Magical diagrams like this could have more than one function. They acted as blueprints for the construction of ritual spaces and magical objects, and they were carried on the body and placed under the sleeping head for revelatory dreams. They acted as conduits for supernatural communication and repositories of power, and occasionally they were placed on the flyleaf of manuscripts to preserve their potency.

The prefaces of angel magic texts tried to persuade the reader that they contained knowledge that came directly from God and had first been received and transmitted by such figures as Adam, Solomon, biblical patriarchs, or prophets. Angel magic texts gave hope to the practitioner that, like Solomon and Adam, he would receive the mercy of God. This redemptive theme is particularly prominent in the *Liber Sameyn*, one of seven magic texts of mainly Jewish origin that were brought together as the *Liber Razielis* by the scriptorium of Alfonso X. The *Liber Sameyn* opens with Adam weeping on the banks of the river Paraig having just been expelled from Paradise, but the text relates how God took pity on his creation and sent the angel Raziel to give him a book—the *Liber Razielis*—containing knowledge of the workings of heaven and earth. The owner of this magic text had to undergo his own redemptive ritual to be able to perform its rituals. After seven days of ritual cleansing, he was told to sacrifice two white doves and name the angels assigned to the appropriate month. Three days later, he had to sleep in the ashes of the burnt intestines of the doves inside a house which was lit with burning candles. Angels would then visit him in the night and teach him how to use the magic text.

In both the mystical and the magical traditions, achieving a vision of angels or God demanded a pure soul. In the *Liber munditie et abstinentie* (Book of Cleanliness and Abstinence, also part of the *Liber Razielis*) the practitioner is told to guard against dirtiness, evil, wine, eating anything with blood, feeling or expressing desire, touching someone or something dead, and speaking evil or unclean words. If he fulfils the requirements for internal and external purity he will ascend to a spiritual level, which is separated from earthly things, he will be loved by angels, and good spirits will associate with him. Angelic magic texts guided the practitioner towards achieving the love and friendship of angels, and benign spirits were asked or expected not just to appear in human form but as human companions. A famous experiment in the *Liber Razielis* which originates (via Hebrew sources) in a Greek prayer to Helios describes how to see the sun at night and ask him anything. The practitioner requests that 'he will speak to me as a man with his friend'.

Like saints and mystics, magical practitioners were spiritually transformed by their companionship with spirits. The author of the *Liber de essentia spirituum* claims to have lived with spirits in the desert for thirty years, and through them to have attained the ranks of the blessed. The *Almandel* states that angels of the first altitude will render a man perfect after he has spoken with them only once, so that 'he will not need to fear eternal damnation or death without the grace of the saviour'. It is likely that many practitioners of angel magic accepted the sacred origins claimed by these texts and performed their rituals with pious intentions. But orthodox visions required God's grace, while magic texts offered the practitioner the ability to generate visions himself. The devotion of the magical practitioner can, therefore, seem 'performative' (i.e. to be following a text) and lacking in interiority.

Late medieval enthusiasm for spiritual experience became an increasing concern for the Church. In the early fourteenth century a monk named John of Morigny wrote a book called the *Liber florum celestis doctrine* (The Book of the Flowers of Heavenly Teaching), which was a practical manual for achieving a visionary ascent to the presence of God and acquiring knowledge of all the arts and sciences. The *Liber florum* was a revised version of the *Ars notoria*, which John had tried to make more acceptable to ecclesiastical authorities. In effect, John offered a democratization of the vision of God, and his work was intended for women as well as men—his sister Bridget was one of its first users—although like other angel magic texts its users had to have the leisure and inclination to undergo ascetic training and recite lengthy sequences of prayers. John's claims to have had revelatory experiences were viewed with suspicion and his work was burnt at the University of Paris in 1323. Nevertheless, his pragmatic approach to such experiences was attractive to many readers, particularly monks whose vocation had instilled in them an expectation that they could be spiritually close to the orders of angels. The more than twenty surviving manuscripts of the *Liber florum* so far found suggest that its use was thriving after 1350, especially in monasteries.

Angelic magic texts were always open to the criticism that they were instructing the practitioner to invoke demons who had taken the guise of more benign spirits to trick him into giving up his soul. But there were also more subversive magic texts in circulation that directed their rituals explicitly to demons: necromantic (or nigromantic) texts. Necromancy originally meant 'divination by the dead'—from the Greek, *nekros* (dead) and *manteia* (divination). In the twelfth and early thirteenth centuries, however, the Latin *necromantia* was often used to translate the common Arabic word for magic (*sihr*), and from this route found its way into classifications of knowledge made by scholars linked to the translations movement like Daniel of Morley (*c.*1140–1210), who brought Arabic learning back to England. Later in the thirteenth century discussions of appropriate and inappropriate magic—for example, those by William of Auvergne and the author of the *Speculum astronomiae*—used necromancy as a critical label for all illicit rituals directed to spirits, in contrast to natural magic or 'astronomical' image magic. From this general association with 'illicitness', necromancy began to be more specifically applied to experiments, texts, or manuals which involved conjuring demons to do the operator's will.

Angels could elevate the practitioner's soul, but demons were consumed with a desire to drag human souls to Hell, a malevolence summed up in the title of a notorious (and possibly invented) lost magic text *Mors anime* (The Death of the Soul). Illustrated copies of the *Pèlerinage de la vie humaine* (1331, revised 1355) by the Cistercian monk Guillaume de Deguilleville depicted the personification of necromancy holding or even stabbing a book with this title. The *Pèlerinage de la vie humaine* is an allegory of the Christian life: a man dreams he is a pilgrim journeying to the Heavenly City, and Necromancy is one of the many hostile malefactors who try to disrupt his journey. She is an old and terrible woman with huge wings, seated in a tree (an allusion to the tree in the Garden of Eden and the disaster which follows the pursuit of forbidden knowledge) and holding a sword that she uses to slay her followers.

Because demons were unremittingly hostile to humans, necromantic rituals were designed to protect the practitioner as well as compel the demon to help him. Surviving necromantic experiments reveal that the practitioner would invoke the names of Christ and other holy beings to force demons to be compliant and truthful, construct magic circles to act as zones of safety, and offer animals such as cocks, black cats, and hoopoes as sacrifices to placate demons and coax them into his presence. But demons still needed to be handled with care. The author of the *Liber iuratus* describes the spirits of the earth as so full of wickedness and depravity that the practitioner is advised to write his request to them on a tile with a piece of charcoal and then leave it inside the magic circle rather than risk speaking to them directly. In spite of the dangers involved, summoning demons was attractive because of the great powers fallen angels were thought to possess, and because magic texts imagined the possibility of more beneficial relationships between humans and demons than mainstream orthodoxy accepted; even a fallen angel might use its power in service of a necromancer.

Demonic Magic

As with angel magic, many of the ideas and practices of demonic magic were shared with mainstream Christianity. First, the rituals were an extension of the valid and conventional ritual of exorcism through which a priest gained control of a spirit by commanding it by the names of Christ and the saints. The difference between exorcism and necromancy lay in the fact that necromancers aimed to summon and keep demons present rather than expel them. Secondly, the powers of demons which necromantic rituals described conformed to powers which were accepted by medieval theologians. This is significant because it increased the attractiveness of necromancy to practitioners while also making the alliance between humans and demons a frightening prospect to critics of magic. Theologians had to decide whether necromantic practices only caused violence to the practitioner's soul or whether the alliance of human and demon had wider implications for the safety of the Christian community. One of the most detailed discussions of demons occurs in the *Summa theologiae* of Thomas Aquinas (1265–74), the most important theologian of the late Middle Ages. Aquinas' *Summa theologiae* was intended to be a complete system of thought that encompassed all previous Christian learning and combined it with Aristotelian philosophy. It summarizes a body of existing literature on demons by authors such as Augustine, Rabanus Maurus, and Gratian, to explain how necromancy worked and why it was not permitted. Aquinas argues that the ability of demons to perform marvels derived from their superior knowledge of nature and natural causes: men could understand demonstrable truths of science, but the demonic mind was keener and able to exploit natural causes more effectively, even though demons also operated within the limits of created nature.

The most significant powers of demons accepted by theologians— to reveal knowledge, move bodies to different locations very rapidly, and to create illusions—were among the most common goals of necromantic experiments. Necromantic handbooks contained instructions to compel demons to reveal hidden treasure or future events, to bring the practitioner beautiful women or magic horses that could carry him to any destination in an instant, and to create extraordinary illusions of boats, castles, marvellous feasts, and fighting armies. Some necromantic experiments seem to push at the boundaries of the theologically accepted limits of demonic power, however. In rituals intended to fill women with burning desire or passionate love for the practitioner, it is not clear how the demon would inspire such emotions. But love was such a popular goal for magic experiments that this difficulty was ignored.

A manuscript of the *Cantigas de Santa Maria* (Canticles of Holy Mary), 420 religious songs honouring the Virgin that were commissioned and partly written by King Alfonso X of Castile, depicts the story of a priest of Auvergne who used necromancy to make a girl fall in love with him. The priest threatened to trap demons in a bottle if they did not help him. According to the *Cantigas*, the demons did succeed in causing the girl to feel an overwhelming desire for the priest, but the Virgin Mary miraculously intervened to save her virtue and the priest was carried off to Hell. The *Cantigas* reveal that King Alfonso, who had a great interest in learned magic, was concerned to distance himself from rituals for summoning demons. The magic circle became a familiar visual reference for necromancy in the thirteenth century, but in this case it proved to be insufficient protection against the swarming hordes of demons.

Theologians argued that it was foolish for a man to think that he could have the upper hand in any interaction with demons, because even when demons gave true responses or performed true marvels they only did so to make men and women more trusting and thus lead them towards damnation. Some magic texts subverted the theological emphasis on demonic malevolence, however, by requiring the demon to become the companion, teacher, or servant of the practitioner. A necromantic experiment attributed to the infamous astrologer and magician Michael Scot (1175–*c*.1232)—placed by Dante in Hell— describes how to acquire a demonic teacher of all the arts and sciences who will give the practitioner lessons for thirty nights in his sleep. The experiment requires the spirit teacher to teach his pupil with love and only chastise him gently, but nevertheless the spirit is kept under firm control: the magical practitioner can summon or dismiss him at will and he will only be freed when his services are no longer required.

Necromancers may have been just as enticed by the prospect of spiritual experience as the practitioners of angel magic were, but by choosing to summon demons rather than angels they expressed a bold and flamboyant disaffection with social and religious norms. Many practitioners of necromancy were clerics who had the knowledge of Latin and liturgical rituals needed to perform the rituals but were disaffected with the religious establishment and used magic to try to fulfil their thwarted ambitions. But how serious were their subversive activities? It has been argued that necromantic experiments were sometimes a vehicle of youthful rebellion in which describing one's magical activities could be seen as a kind of 'manly brag', where the danger and illicit nature of these activities was part of their appeal. It is equally arguable, however, that the typical goals of necromantic rituals were in fact socially conformist, expressing a longing to be part of the establishment. The beautiful women, magical horses, treasure, and spectacular (if illusory) castles with which necromantic experiments are filled reveal the insecurity of clerical masculinity and a longing for status, political influence, and recognition from secular peers.

Konrad Kyeser's *Bellifortis* (1405) was an illustrated manual of military and magical technology written to promote the writer's skills and get him employment at court. Some of Kyeser's designs mingle horror with playfulness, presumably in an attempt to combine the theatrical appeal of the creation of marvellous illusions with the use of occult powers (in this case clear allusions to sorcery) to intimidate an enemy. Of the three goblins depicted in an illustration of a magical castle (Gottingen, Univ. bibl., cod. Phil. 63, fo. 94), one is sounding a trumpet to attract spirits, another is riding a broomstick, and a third is carrying a torch made from a noose.

From a theological perspective, necromantic texts undermined the orthodox positions that there was a strong boundary between good and evil spirits, that detailed knowledge of the world of spirits was hidden from humans, and that most humans were unworthy to interact with angels and unable to control demons. Yet necromancy was valuable to theologians in one sense: it provided useful evidence for the existence of demons. These malevolent beings were an integral part of the ethical system of Christianity due to their role in testing human virtue during the lifetimes of men and women and the threat of the terrible punishments they would inflict on the wicked after death. When the Abbot Caesarius of Heisterbach wrote his work of instruction for novice monks, the *Dialogus miraculorum* (1220–35), he worried that the demonic presence on earth was not taken seriously enough and tried to make demons more vivid in the imagination of his contemporaries by telling stories in which hapless lay people and clerics dabbled in necromancy. In one story a knight called Henry, who doubts the existence of demons, urges a necromancer out of curiosity to summon some. The Devil appears, in a huge, shadowy, terrifying form and reveals to Henry that he has travelled a great distance from beyond the sea and has knowledge of all the sins committed in the world, including the knight's own. After he narrowly survives this encounter, Henry no longer doubts either the importance of virtuous living or the existence of demons. Through didactic tales such as this ecclesiastical authorities sought to control the narratives of spiritual experience while not denying to medieval people curious for interaction with spirits that such experiences were possible.

The lay elite who were fascinated by supernatural interactions could turn to chivalric romances, a literary genre popular from the twelfth century that described the adventures of legendary knights. Chivalric romances celebrated an idealized code of civilized behaviour which was often demonstrated in encounters with marvellous or supernatural objects and beings. In the early thirteenth-century *chanson de geste* entitled *Maugis d'Aigremont* (the story of the youth of Maugis) the enchanter Maugis is told by his fairy mother to prove his knightly qualities by capturing the marvellous horse Bayard. This progeny of a dragon and serpent is imprisoned on a volcanic island and Maugis succeeds by disguising himself as a demon and killing the serpent. In literary contexts the representation of magic and magical practitioners was often used to provide playful subversions of the normative world view. In this case the subversive image of a magician pretending to be a demon to battle his enemy, whose serpent-like form would have evoked the Devil to a medieval audience, is an ironic element in the narrative. The mingling of magic and poetry was intended to stimulate playful debate and conversation, and many literary representations of magic used it as a vehicle for a moral lesson; for example, as in Maugis's case, winning or being given a magical object might express the hero's worthiness.

In chivalric romances marvellous horses appear as worthy steeds and companions to the hero, as Bayard does, in spite of being of monstrous ancestry. The magical horses of necromantic experiments are a rather different kind of creature, demons in disguise who have to be subdued with sacred adjurations. In a surviving fifteenth-century manuscript (Wellcome MS 517) an experiment to conjure a magical horse advises the practitioner to go at dusk to a silent house where no one is living and write demonic names on the wall with bat's blood, then conjure four demons by the names of God and by Christ to bring him a horse: 'I command that the horse comes very quickly to me prepared for riding and without delay or deception to that safe place and it carries me with power and enjoyment and without deception, fear or terror.' Outside the house the practitioner will find a beautiful black horse prepared for riding. It will carry him wherever he wishes and back again, but just before he leaves on a journey he must conjure it by Christ, God, and the Virgin Mary to be sure that it will carry him safely and cheerfully.

In the early Middle Ages demonic powers were mostly limited to trickery, temptation, and deception, but popular fear of demons and their human allies grew as stories about the ways humans and spirits could be bound together through possession, invocation, and pact became more credible and significant. These three forms of bond had different implications. First, the openness of the human subject implicit in the idea of possession became a striking feature of the late Middle Ages. Men and women were thought to have the potential to undergo incorporation and inhabitation with the divine, but they were also thought to be vulnerable to possession by the Devil, sometimes merely by the utterance of an ill-judged wish. A second development was the new emphasis found in learned magic texts on the ability of humans to compel, persuade, and manipulate spirits. Finally, the theory of a strong and heretical pact between human and demon was developed by theologians and canonists, particularly during the papacy of John XXII (1316–34).

Heresy, Sorcery, and Witchcraft

The late medieval responses of ecclesiastical authorities to magic must be placed in the context of widespread and diverse heretical groups which emerged in the eleventh century and reached their medieval apogee in the Cathars and Waldensians. A variety of religious opinions could and did exist in late medieval Europe, and an opinion or doctrine at variance with religious authority only became heresy when it was declared to be intolerable and explicitly or implicitly condemned by the Pope. But the Cathar and Waldensian heresies spread widely and in such numbers from the second half of the twelfth century that they incited significant repression. A crusade was launched against Catharism in 1209, and in the 1230s the Inquisition (a group of decentralized institutions within the justice system of the Church) was founded to combat heresy. The Inquisition consisted of a system of investigation, accusation, trial, and punishment; its formidable and destructive powers derived from the fact that its personnel were responsible only to the Pope and often combined spiritual zeal with a blatant disregard for normative legal processes.

The practice of magic did not involve significant deviance from Christian doctrines and it was not publicly disseminated in the way that heretical ideas often were, but fear of heresy and its targeting by the Inquisition drew attention to magical activities in two significant ways. First, the rhetoric against heresy borrowed from—and influenced the rhetoric against magic. Heresy, like magic, was viewed as the work of the Devil and an expression of pride (heretics did not accept the opinion of the Church), ignorance (heretics were unable to understand their errors), and fraud (heretics pretended to be pious but were guilty of terrible sins). Heretics were often accused of practising sorcery, and magical practitioners were accused of not being true Christians.

Secondly, the founding of the Inquisition against heresy put magical activities under scrutiny as well. At first magic was not considered as dangerous as heresy: in 1258–60 Pope Alexander IV ordered inquisitors to pay attention to *sortilegium* and divination only when heresy was clearly involved. But in the fourteenth century fear of magic had become more widespread. Trials for sorcery increased especially at the French, English, and papal courts, where they often had a vicious political character. John XXII had to deal with multiple cases of sorcery in the early years of his papacy, including several in which defendants were accused of plotting to take his life. Perhaps unsurprisingly, he became particularly paranoid about sorcery. Although many of the papal trials for sorcery involved high-ranking individuals such as the Bishop of Cahors Hugues Géraud, and Galeazzo Visconti of Milan, the main impact of John XXII's aggressive stance towards magic was on popular magical activities. In 1326 John issued a decretal, *Super illius specula*, which assimilated magical practices (the making of images, rings, mirrors, phials, or other things for magical purposes) with heresy, asserting that magical practitioners 'who are Christians in name only' sacrificed to demons, worshipped them, bound themselves to them with a pact, and fulfilled their most depraved lusts. Magic—in the terrifying shape of idolatrous, licentious, demon-worshipping sorcerers—was now very much a focus of inquisitorial activity.

It is worth noting that the kinds of magical activities which John XXII's decretal condemned were ubiquitous at all levels of late medieval society, took similar forms in both learned and non-learned contexts, and were often part of rituals that combined orthodox and unorthodox elements. Both literate and illiterate practitioners made rings and talismans, inscribed knives and pieces of clothing, prepared ritual concoctions, and performed rituals which drew on the natural powers of celestial bodies, herbs, stones, and animal parts. Magical invocations, charms, and curses were collected by literate users into their manuscripts, circulated orally, and were inscribed onto parchment or objects where their power could be accessed by illiterate owners. Many magical activities should thus be viewed as belonging to a 'common magical tradition', which was accessible to different social groups and indeed transmitted between them. The prayers, images, and magical seals inscribed on 'prayer rolls' that were wrapped around a woman's body to protect her as she gave birth would probably have been commissioned from a cleric, but the transmission of magical knowledge was not all top-down. Adelard of Bath, the translator of several works of Arabic image magic, said that he had learned the craft of making talismans from a wise old woman skilled in this art.

Surviving examples of late medieval textual amulets (writings worn on the body for protection) show how people at all levels of society trusted in the power of sacred and magical words. An amulet to protect against the plague in a late fifteenth-century English medical manuscript (Wellcome MS 404, fo. 33v) has pleas for Christ to save the bearer of the amulet inscribed in its inner circle. The outer inscription gives the amulet pious authority by claiming that it was delivered into the hands of the Abbot of Corby by an angel on the order of Jesus Christ, and in the centre of the figure are signs of the cross and abbreviated symbols of Christ's names. An example of a more magical image is the 'Abraham's eye' experiment. The earliest known version of this experiment to reveal the identity of a thief comes from an early fourth-century Greek papyrus. An early fourteenth-century example recorded in a compilation of learned medical texts (Munich, CLM MS 13057, fo. 106r) depicts the eye in a circle inscribed with angel names, and a key, hammer, and knife are also represented. The operator is instructed to paint the eye on a piece of parchment and take it to a public place where he suspects the thief will be present. He prays to God for assistance, invokes the names of spirits, and drives the point of a knife (or bangs the key with the hammer) into the eye. At that moment the thief will cry out that he has been wounded and his identity will be discovered.

Activities in the common tradition of magic were brought into disrepute by being labelled *sortilegium*. This term originally meant the power to promote harm or prosperity, but its negative connotations dominate medieval sources, reflecting the ecclesiastical rhetoric against magic and (at the end of the Middle Ages) the motives for magical practice expressed by those tortured by the Inquisition. Guillaume de Deguilleville's *Pèlerinage de la vie humaine* has the personi-fication of Sorcery exclaim, 'I am beloved of all folk', to express the numerousness of her practitioners and that they come from all levels of society. According to Guillaume, Sorcery inflicted physical and devastating violence on the bodies and material wealth of her victims and caused ruin, illness, and death. Popular practitioners were usually illiterate women who had learned their trade through an apprentice-ship and worked closely with natural materials, especially herbs and animal parts. Conversely medieval sources suggest that the typical practitioner of learned magic was male, literate, and a cleric. He used complex rituals described in manuscripts to invoke spirits and needed to understand the workings of celestial bodies.

Before the fourteenth century it had been difficult for clerics to believe that women, who were deemed physically, mentally, and spiritually weaker than men and lacked clerical training and literacy, could control powerful, threatening demons. But this paradox was resolved by an increasing theological emphasis on the satanic pact, a formal written contract which involved the complete and explicit submission of the witch to demons. In exchange for surrendering their souls, witches could call on the assistance of demons using only simple gestures or spells. Late medieval trials of female magical practitioners reflect perceptions of the roles of demons in their rituals. For example, at the 1324 trial of Lady Alice Kyteler in Ireland she was accused of having sex with a demon called Robin Artisson, while in 1391 a French peasant woman called Jeanne de Brigue, who had acquired a reputation in her village for finding lost objects, identifying thieves, and healing the sick, confessed to invoking a demon called Haussibut and was burned at the stake.

The theology of witchcraft drew together ideas about demons, sorcery, and necromancy. A late fifteenth-century painting of love magic (*Liebezaube*, now at the Leipzig museum) reflects this new vision of the female practitioner. A young, naked, and beautiful woman is depicted in the act of shaking liquid concoctions onto a heart in a wooden chest. Some objects in the room evoke the practice of learned magic: the book, the mirror, the 'blank' incantation scrolls (perhaps the painter was afraid to fill them with real spells), and the fire lit ready for suffumigations. Others—the woven cloth, the fan, the carefully delineated flowers and vessels of oils and ointments everywhere—are more feminine tools of magic. The lapdog and parrot, elite women's pets, are more suitable to a female practitioner than the black cat and hoopoe of necromancy, and also suggest that this woman is from a higher social group than the village practitioner. There is no sign of a demonic helper in this painting, but the late medieval witch did not need one to be present for her operations because she had already pledged her soul to the Devil and been granted powers. Her boldness and capacity to dominate men is indicated by the man entering at the back of the room with the submissive air of being a client or servant; certainly she does not appear to be afraid of his scrutiny.

Another vivid portrayal of a female magical practitioner is found in the 1499 play *Celestina* by Fernando de Rojas, at the time of its publication a law student at the University of Salamanca. Celestina is a witch and procuress and a specialist in love magic, the arts of beautification, and the reconstruction of lost maidenhoods. Her remedies for 'invigorating passion' and 'mesmerising objects of affection', use herbs, animal parts (deer's hearts, vipers' tongues, pheasant heads, and so on), bread, cloth, and hair. She makes clay and lead images, paints letters on her clients' hands, and gives her clients wax hearts filled with broken needles. These magical activities are derided as 'all mockery and lies', yet Celestina's erotic magic is shown to be success-ful when she performs a necromantic ritual to conjure Pluto, lord of Hell, with incantations and magical signs written in bat's blood. The girl Melibea is subsequently filled with such uncontrollable love for the witch's client Calisto that she submits to his desires and later throws herself from a tower when she discovers he is dead. Celestina's ritual closely follows a necromantic format, except that it omits the invoca-tion of demons by the names of God, Christ, and other orthodox figures; witches did not need to command demons in this way because demons helped them willingly, according to the terms of their pact.

A high proportion of the people tried in medieval courts for using erotic magic—rituals to secure desirable partners for sex, love, or marriage or to destroy partnerships that were obstacles to passion or ambition—were women. Female sexual powers were considered more threatening than men's, particularly in relation to political and reli-gious concerns over the stability of marriage. There may occasionally have been tacit approval of a woman in a socially appropriate rela-tionship using love magic to prevent her husband from straying, but the use of magic to seduce someone outside marriage, make a man impotent, or reduce him to erotic dependence on a mistress was subversive of a stable, patriarchal Christian community. Clerics warn-ing against erotic magic suspected that women used their menstrual blood and their own hair in rituals, and the nakedness of the female practitioner in many contemporary depictions expresses a presumed alliance between seductive female bodies and malign demonic powers.

Some of the earliest prosecutions of magic took place in the royal and princely courts of Europe, where it was often condemned as a malicious practice used by relatives of the ruler, especially women, to gain improper advancement. Medieval courts were rife with succes-sion anxieties and intense competition between formal and informal sources of power, and it was not uncommon to use the services of an occult practitioner (or accuse a rival of doing so) to gain political advantage. As early as the twelfth century, works of political philoso-phy, such as John of Salisbury's *Policraticus* (1159), were warning that magicians, diviners, and soothsayers were particularly tempting to courtiers. Accusing someone of practising magic allowed a courtier to criticize those who were otherwise untouchable, and it could also help to explain political misfortune, inappropriate attachments, and the failure to provide an heir. At the same time, fear of sorcery was real and it was viewed as a point of vulnerability for the state, just as heresy was for the Church. The presence of magicians at court threatened the king personally, and even created a risk that God might bring his wrath down on his kingdom, which is why the crime of treason was often linked to the crime of political sorcery.

Practitioners offering occult services could be readily found in the *demi-monde* of court retinues and hangers-on. Elite women involved in political sorcery were often thought to draw on the magical expertise of male accomplices, and sometimes women of a lower social group. Eleanor Cobham, the Duchess of Gloucester (*c.*1400–52), was accused of commissioning predictions of King Henry VI's death so that her husband could take political advantage of this knowledge. She and her supposed accomplices, the clerics Thomas Southwell and Roger Bolingbroke and the 'witch of Eye' Margery Jourdemayne, were said to have conspired to kill the King with necromancy, and Bolingbroke and Margery Jourdemayne were executed. Clerics and members of religious orders were often among the accused in cases of political sorcery, which suggests that contemporaries recognized that these were the most likely groups to be practising learned magic.

At the end of the fourteenth century the frequency of political trials for magic had decreased slightly in France and England, but in Germany and Italy sorcery accusations began to spread to lower social groups in towns and rural areas. The threat of sorcery became further magnified around 1400 as the Pope and certain inquisitors and lay judges accepted the idea that a real sect of sorcerers and sorceresses existed who were participating in a vast plot against Christianity. Sorcerers were not implicated in the natural disasters of the fourteenth century but by the second quarter of the fifteenth they had become scapegoats for the misfortunes of their time. In this period various stereotypical features of witches, such as their night flights, also became fixed. Late medieval witchcraft persecutions were concentrated in France, Germany-Austria, and above all in Switzerland, partly because this was where the remnants of the Waldensian heresy lingered and partly because in these territories the temporal powers were seeking more control in legal areas including sorcery (which had previously been under the Church's remit), so that magical activities were increasingly coming under the scrutiny of both religious and secular authorities. Nevertheless, compared to the early modern period relatively few of the men and women found guilty of sorcery at this time were condemned to death.

The Defence of Magic

In the late Middle Ages, magic was condemned with increasing vigour and precision at universities and in legal codes. The development of the concept of the demonic pact and the involvement of the Inquisition in investigating magical practices widened the scope of persecution and contributed to the construction of an emergent theology of witchcraft. But the translation of learned magic texts from the Graeco-Roman, Arabic, and Jewish traditions, and the discovery of their intellectual resonances with Greek and Arabic philosophy and science, led also to a gradual shift towards more positive attitudes to magical texts and ideas in western Europe. By the end of the Middle Ages the number of defensible magic texts had grown and works of angel magic were being increasingly widely disseminated. Moreover, some magic texts had been written which had 'real' authors, whose ideas relied on philosophical justifications, and which even integrated necromancy within compendia of different kinds of ritual magic. Since theological condemnation made authorship dangerous, the fact that authors were becoming confident to put their real names to works of magic is a striking development. Unlike John of Morigny in the early fourteenth century, who had described his work as the product of personal revelations, later medieval authors took a more 'scholarly' approach to magic, providing general theories and philosophical justifications and producing summaries of texts and genres. This proved a successful strategy into the Renaissance.

The first half of the fourteenth century saw the burning at the stake of one author-magician but the unhindered emergence of others. Cecco d'Ascoli, who had incorporated necromancy into his commentary on a cosmological text, the *Sphere* of Sacrobosco, was burnt at the stake in the Florentine Inquisition in 1327. But those who followed him published with impunity: the Catalan scholar Berengario Ganell, author of a colossal compendium of magic, the *Summa sacre magice* (1346); the philosopher and physician Antonio da Montolmo, whose late fourteenth-century *De occultis et manifestis* drew on magic texts from the Hermetic and Solomonic traditions; and the physician and scholar Giorgio Anselme da Parma, whose *Opus de magia disciplina*, written in the first half of the fifteenth century, discussed theories of magic and divinatory techniques and gave detailed descriptions of the ceremonies of ritual magic. In fifteenth-century Italy a new intellectual climate allowed magical practitioners to confidently assert the human capacity to manipulate the forces of the universe. Learned magical practitioners like Marsilio Ficino (1433–99) successfully incorporated previously illicit images within the licit category of 'natural magic', thus providing them with philosophical validation.

How did learned magic survive and flourish in the difficult conditions of the late Middle Ages? Three factors are particularly important. The first is that the strategies with which the authors of learned magic texts appealed to the intellectual curiosity and the spiritual thirst of medieval men and women were to a large extent successful. Those who supported magic thought that it could be harnessed to pious goals, combined with orthodox rituals, and used to improve human understanding of the cosmos. The second, less positive reason was that the theology of witchcraft shifted the inquisitorial gaze onto female popular practitioners and away from the male practitioners of learned magic. And finally, censorship was difficult to enforce in the manuscript culture of the late Middle Ages.

Magic texts advocated the practitioner's secrecy in order to create a sense of their power and to conceal suspicious texts from scrutiny. They were kept and circulated in ways that were intended to avoid censorship. In medieval libraries they might be concealed in secret rooms to which only the owner had access, a tactic the cleric, surgeon, and writer Richard de Fournival (1201–*c.*1260) employed with his collection of occult texts at Amiens. Sometimes works of magic were simply concealed in plain sight in the licit subject areas of the library. This was the case with the collection of over thirty magic texts at St Augustine's, Canterbury, in the late Middle Ages, which were fairly typical in being compiled with more acceptable genres such as astronomy, medicine, devotional literature, and natural philosophy.

At this abbey the common tactic of encouraging donations to the library—offering annual prayers for the souls of donors—also gave the books a pious association that probably discouraged criticism of their contents. Monks could argue that their pious vocation enabled them to safely handle suspicious texts and even draw out useful things from them. Powerful secular rulers may not even have needed to conceal their occult interests, however. The Marquis of Mantua, Francesco Gonzaga, owned a magic text openly identified as necromancy in the 1407 inventory of his books.

In manuscripts, tactics to evade suspicion took the form of cautionary marginalia or even notices condemning magic, which allowed the piety of the owner to be expressed while the usability of a ritual was unaffected. An owner of the fifteenth-century necromantic handbook, Wellcome MS 517, noted that some magical operations were 'not worthy of the faith' but nevertheless did not destroy them. Some magical experiments were written in code, others were rendered useless to anyone except the owner and his preferred confidants by the erasure of a vital name. There were more significant interventions such as parts of rituals being cut out of manuscripts, or magical characters being altered to turn them into crosses, but these were often not so much acts of censorship as attempts to preserve the viability of other rituals in the manuscript. The ownership of occult texts could clearly cut both ways—the piety of an owner might diminish the suspiciousness of a magic text, but there was always a risk that the illicitness of a text would undermine its owner's reputation or safety. Since summoning spirits, especially demons, was itself a dangerous pastime, the practice of magic must have attracted the interest of specifically those men and women whose curiosity, quest for knowledge, power, and salvation, and perhaps even pleasure in risk-taking, made it too tempting to resist.

3

The Demonologists

James Sharpe

Taking a basic definition, 'demonology' implies the science of demons and what they do. For the historian of witchcraft, the term has acquired a wider resonance. By demonology most such historians would understand the intellectual system that expressed the framework within which educated Europeans between the fifteenth and eighteenth centuries understood and debated witchcraft, frequently with reference to related matters like magic more generally, popular superstitions and religious fallacies, prophecy and fortune-telling, and demonic possession. Although very alien from most modern ways of thinking, demonological works could be large, complex, sophisticated, and based on a wide and impressive scholarship. The people who wrote them were neither unintelligent nor obscure: they included the French lawyer and philosopher Jean Bodin (1529/30–96), one of the most important philosophers and political theorists of the late sixteenth century, and Bodin's contemporary, the English Protestant theologian William Perkins (1558–1602), writer of numerous theological works which were translated into Gaelic Irish, Hungarian, and most languages in between. Demonological writings, as they grew more complex, became entwined with, were informed by, and in turn helped inform areas of thought which will be more recognizable, and more acceptable, to modern preoccupations. As the historian Stuart Clark, author of the most important recent analysis of the subject, has put it, 'In effect, demonology was a composite subject consisting of discussions about the workings of nature, the processes of history, the maintenance of religious purity, and the nature of political authority and order.' These were central concerns for most thinking Europeans in the late Middle Ages and early modern periods.

Why was a science of demons necessary? The answer to this question lies in the widespread belief, current in the Christian world from an early date, that humans lived in a world that was also inhabited by a number of supernatural beings. These beings, as the centuries progressed and the concerns of theological writers both broadened and deepened, came to be increasingly identified as demonic. Reading medieval chronicles or chivalric literature, the *chansons de geste* which flourished from the twelfth century onwards, reveals a world where the intervention of demonic spirits or other supernatural beings in everyday life was commonplace. The presence of evil spirits, and the harmful consequences of this presence for humans, was also firmly established by the New Testament, with Christ as a powerful exorcist, casting devils out of suffering humans on a number of occasions. And as well as these lesser demons there was, of course, that incarnation of evil, the Devil. A fundamental dualism existed in Christian thinking between evil (which included the desires and temptations of the flesh, committing any of the seven deadly sins, or breaking any of the ten commandments, and such human qualities as ambition and despair), and good, which for medieval and later Christian thinkers involved primarily cleaving to the love of God, with consequent harmonious social relations on earth and eternal salvation in Heaven. The Devil was also, of course, the great tempter. He had tempted Christ in the wilderness, and Christ's ability to withstand that temptation ensured the salvation of human souls. Moreover, from the early fifteenth century, a new problem was identified which put the souls and salvation of Christians at risk: the satanic witch. Most historical societies, and many of those currently in existence, believed or believe in witches or something like witches. What was different about Europe at the end of the Middle Ages and during the early modern period was that witches, at least on an official level, were seen as members of an organized satanic sect, and had entered into a pact with the Devil in which they renounced Christianity and promised their allegiance to him. It is easy to see why understanding the Devil and his inferior demons, analysing and being able to recognize and possibly predict their actions—and working out what could be done about them—should achieve a fair degree of importance.

Although this rough and ready dualism might exist, dualism in its formal sense, allowing the Devil as much power as God, and thus allowing the forces of evil as much power as the forces of good, was *not* acceptable to orthodox Christian dogma. Groups adhering to dualism, such as adherents to Manichaeism in the early Christian period or Cathars in the high Middle Ages, would be regarded as heretical. As demonological tract after demonological tract was at pains to point out, for witchcraft to exist, three elements had to be present: the Devil, who provided temptation to commit evil, the human being who fell into temptation, and God, who permitted this to happen. The rejection of dualism implied that the Devil could only act with God's permission. This, of course, then encourages the question of why God allows the Devil to act thus, a question which leads us back to that basic problem for Christianity, explaining why evil exists in the world. The answer demonologists provided to this question was that witches themselves were clearly sinners destined for perdition, while the evil which they wrought on their fellow humans served to chastise the ungodly or test the faith of the godly, the Old Testament book of Job usually being referred to as an exemplar in this latter context.

One point that needs to be emphasized is that if demonology connects with a number of other intellectual concerns of the period, so the demonologists were often men whose thoughts on the issue were often only one aspect of a much broader *œuvre*. This is certainly true of Jean Bodin and William Perkins, to whom we have already referred. It would also be true, for example, of a number of the other English clerical writers who, like Perkins, authored demonological works in the late sixteenth and early seventeenth centuries. One such was Richard Bernard (1568–1641), who published his work on witchcraft, the *Guide to Grand Iury Men*, in 1627. Bernard, educated at that great school for Puritanism, Christ's College Cambridge, minister of Batcombe in Somerset, combined being an effective parish minister (Batcombe was to stay solidly Parliamentarian during the Civil War) with being a religious controversialist, and his tract on witchcraft was only one of the forty or so books he published.

It should also be stressed that demonological works were frequently written in reaction to a set of specific circumstances. This was certainly true, as we shall see, of that most celebrated of demonological works, the *Malleus maleficarum*, written after its main or sole author, Henry Institoris (*c*.1430–1505), had been frustrated by authorities in the Tyrol when he attempted to gain convictions in witch trials by employing irregular legal process. Much the same could be said of another work we will be touching on, the *Tableau de l'inconstancie des mauvais anges et demons* (Picture of the Inconstancy of Evil Angels and Demons), published by the French judge Pierre de Lancre in 1612. De Lancre (1553–1631), on the instructions of the *parlement* of Bourdeaux, had led an investigation into witchcraft in the French Basque country which had generated numerous convictions for witchcraft. But the *parlement*, insisting on the importance of due legal process, confirmed only a handful of these convictions. The continuing indifference of the Bordeaux judges to de Lancre's views led him to publish another work in 1622, *L'incrédulité et mécréance du sortilège* (The Incredulity and Non-Belief of Witchcraft), which focused on judicial disbelief. Neither this work nor another of 1627 managed to convince the Bordeaux judges to initiate witch-hunts, and across France as a whole at this time convictions for witchcraft were few.

As is suggested by de Lancre's failure to change the attitudes of the judges in the *parlement* of Bordeaux, the actual influence of demonological works on the running of trials or the intensity of witch-hunting is uncertain. Most of the trials that reached the courts originated in disputes and enmities between peasants who were extremely unlikely to have read works by Bodin, de Lancre, or any other demonologist. As I have argued elsewhere, the image of an Essex husbandman (the county experienced numerous witch trials) leafing through the *Malleus maleficarum* to sharpen his desire to launch a witchcraft accusation is, likewise, an unconvincing one. Some demonological works were set at a very theoretical level: the most intellectually accomplished demonological work produced by an English author in the Elizabethan or early Stuart periods, Henry Holland's *A Treatise against Witchcraft* of 1590, included almost no references to current witchcraft trials, and addressed a set of theological issues in a discussion which could not easily have been mobilized for a witch trial. Conversely, when the barrister Michael Dalton (1564–1644) rewrote the passages concerning witchcraft in his handbook for justices of the peace, he based his ideas on Richard Bernard's *Guide to Grand Iury Men* and a lengthy tract on the Lancashire trials of 1612, while Richard Hunt, a justice of the peace investigating witchcraft in Restoration Somerset, was clearly aware of demonological writings on the witches' sabbat. And when assessing the pervasiveness of demonological ideas it must, of course, be remembered that they were present not just in works that modern historians would label 'demonological' but in a much wider range of publications: theological works, tracts on medicine, legal treatises.

Another issue to be considered when discussing the influence of demonological writings is that, by the late sixteenth century, they could acquire a political aspect. 'Rebellion', so the King James Bible of 1611 assures us, 'is as the sin of witchcraft' (1 Samuel 15: 23), which meant, logically, that witchcraft could be a form of rebellion, against the state or the monarch as well as against the Christian Church. In some ways there was a considerable overlap between these entities. The sixteenth and seventeenth centuries were to witness the emergence of what modern historians would call the confessional state, and what Elizabethan Englishmen would have described as a godly commonwealth. In most European states, the good citizen had also to be a good Christian, and, moreover, a good Christian according to the Christian denomination which that state favoured. In early modern Europe, the witch, in the words of historian Christian Larner, 'was a transfigured creature who began her career in the farmyard as an enemy of her neighbour, and ended it in the courts as a public person, and enemy of God and the godly society'. This statement has a special resonance for Scotland, where James VI, as well as being an advocate of divine right monarchy, wrote a demonological tract, the short and completely conventional (within a Protestant model) *Daemonologie* of 1597. That year saw a major witch-hunt in Scotland, and it has been suggested that James was encouraged to publish it when a group of witches were found to be envisaging using their witchcraft against the monarch. But James is much better known for his involvement in the North Berwick trials of 1591, Scotland's first major witch trial, and it is probable that the book, although not published until a few years later, was written in the immediate aftermath of these trials. That must remain conjectural, but one publication which did come in 1591 was a short pamphlet entitled *Newes from Scotland*, a propagandist account of the North Berwick trials probably written with an English audience in mind. James's involvement in the North Berwick trials had been prompted by the discovery that the witches in question planned to kill the King, most notably by using magic to sink the ship in which he was returning to Scotland with his bride, Anne of Denmark.

According to the pamphlet, when the witches asked the Devil why he bore such ill will to the King, the Devil replied, because 'the king is the greatest enemy he hath in the world'. Obviously, targeting a divine right monarch was a worthwhile strategy for the Devil's minions. By the late sixteenth century the science of demonology had clearly acquired ramifications which went far beyond the theologian's study.

The Development of the Demonological System

By the fifteenth century the Devil was seen as the embodiment of evil. Curiously, the Devil does not figure much in the Old Testament, although the name Satan does appear, and, more particularly, and very relevantly for early modern demonologists, Satan is there to tempt and punish, as in the book of Job. The concept of the Devil seems to have been stronger in Jewish apocalyptic writings, and these were influential on the New Testament and other early Christian writings. In the New Testament the Devil figures more prominently, among other things tempting Christ, while in at least some strands of Christian thinking Satan was identified as the leader of the rebel angels who had been cast out of heaven. By the high Middle Ages the Devil and the inferior demons he controlled figured prominently in art (not least wall paintings and other decorations in churches), in literature, and in sermons. People developed a very clear idea of his powers, and he, his minions, and the fear of being cast into Hell were all engrained in both learned writings and popular culture. This situation was to remain largely unaltered by the Reformation and the Catholic Counter-Reformation of the sixteenth century, and for most Europeans the Devil was to remain a very real entity across the following century and beyond.

It took time, however, for the Devil to achieve this status, and for witches to become clearly associated with him. In the early Middle Ages there are, indeed, strong indications of a lack of interest in demonic witchcraft among theologians. The key document here is the *Canon episcopi*, a canon (or church ruling) recorded in the *Two Books of Synodal Causes* put together by Regino of Prüm (*c*.840–915) in 906. This was a handbook of canon law apparently requested by Regino's local archbishop, and intended for use by officials running ecclesiastical courts in the region of Trier in western Germany. Part of the book dealt with sorcerers and other occult practitioners, touching on such familiar matters as charms and love magic. These were identified as being of diabolic origin, with their practitioners liable to be thrown out of the archdiocese (not, it will be noted, at this time to be burned). But the *Canon* also touched on women who believed they flew at night with the goddess Diana. These women were not identified as witches: they were, rather, people who were deceived, but whose stories led others into the same error to the imperilling of their souls. In a world governed by God alone, there was no place for beliefs of this type. The *Canon episcopi* was to cause a number of problems for later demonological theorists. Most importantly, it became a very problematic text when ideas of the sabbat spread. Witches were meant to fly to the sabbat, and so an authoritative text denying that women could fly with the goddess Diana might also serve to challenge the belief that witches flew to their nocturnal meetings. And, more generally, it raised the problem of people who confessed to witchcraft in general being deluded. The Devil was, after all, a great deceiver, so how could one be certain whether a confessing witch had really done the things she claimed to have done or had been deceived into such beliefs by the Devil?

Despite the *Canon episcopi* and the attitudes which underpinned it, Catholic Europe gradually began to accept the reality of diabolic witches, and hence the science of demonology became more established and its arguments more complex. Certainly, the roots of demonology as an organized system of thought can be traced a long way back. Although they had little to say on witchcraft proper, late medieval demonologists wishing to base their ideas on impeccable sources could trace them back to the most prominent of the early church fathers, St Augustine of Hippo (354–430). Augustine, as an extremely well-educated man of his time, was aware of classical literature in which good and evil spirits, in one form or another, were familiar figures. In his major work, *The City of God*, published in various parts around 420, Augustine systematically employed Scripture to demonstrate that the gods of ancient Rome and the religious practices associated with them (as well as the religious practices of other Mediterranean pagan peoples) were of demonic origins. In developing these ideas, Augustine developed a notion of an antichristian hierarchy of demons, with the Devil at its apex, a hierarchy which was in a constant state of warfare with the Christian God, His Church, and His people. These demons were immortal, and hence as intelligent beings became very experienced in evil and in tempting humans to do evil. For it was also a central tenet of Augustine's that demons and human beings were in regular contact, which could include sexual intercourse and the conception of children (notably with the demigod Pan). From a general notion of contacts between demons and humans, Augustine developed another idea: that human beings seeking out demons were, either explicitly or implicitly, entering into a *pact* with them. And it was Augustine who first set out clearly the notion that demons only operated with divine permission. So if there was little by way of direct mention of witchcraft in Augustine's writings, he did provide later demonologists with an intellectual framework vital to their science.

This intellectual framework was developed and made even more secure by the writings of what was by far the most renowned of high medieval Christian thinkers, St Thomas Aquinas (1226–74). Aquinas was a key figure in the development of scholasticism, one of the most remarkable achievements of which was to achieve a rapprochement between Catholicism and Aristotelianism. But it was Aquinas' interest in the development of a systematic theology, another key element in scholasticism, which led him to develop his ideas on the role of demons and, albeit in a not yet fully developed form, their relationship with magic and, by extension, witches. Aquinas made an important contribution to later understandings of the nature of sexual relations between humans and demons and, in particular, the problematic issue, given scholasticism's attachment to Aristotelian science, of the possibilities of this sexual intercourse resulting in conception. According to Aristotelian science, a union between denizens of the spiritual world (demons) and the material world (human beings) could not happen. However, in his thinking on incubi and succubi (male and female demons), Aquinas saw a way around the problem. A demon could take female form and obtain male sperm through sexual intercourse, and then take the form of a man and impregnate a woman with it. Conversely, Aquinas also spent some time thinking about a matter which was to loom large in at least some European cultures, the ability of witches to hinder conception through *maleficium* (malevolent sorcery, literally 'evildoing').

Aquinas followed the *Canon episcopi* in arguing that humans could not fly or be made to fly by demons, and he reiterated the notion that harm could only be inflicted through occult or magical means with God's permission. Nevertheless, his ideas, particularly his insistence on the interaction between demons and humans, helped provide support for later demonological writers. Aquinas was to remain a massively important thinker until well into the seventeenth century, and as late as 1879 Pope Leo XIII could declare that he was the model theologian for Catholics. Perhaps more sinisterly, Aquinas became the theologian of choice for an institution which reached maturity during his lifetime, the Inquisition. It is, indeed, in the handbooks written by and for inquisitors that we can see demonological ideas developing. One of the most important of these was the *Practica inquisitionis heretice pravitatis*, written by Bernard Gui (1261–1331) in the mid-1320s. Gui was a Dominican, had studied theology at the Universities of Montpellier and Paris, and served as inquisitor of Toulouse between 1307 and 1324 (he was Bishop of Lodève between then and his death). As the title of Gui's book reminds us, the Inquisition had been founded to combat heresy, and Gui's work provided inquisitors with a comprehensive guide to existing heresies, real or imagined. Although magic and witchcraft were not a central concern of Gui's, he did devote sections to them, warning inquisitors of both the learned magic of clerical or upper-class occult practitioners, and the work of those popular folk practitioners who three centuries later in England were to be known as 'cunning-folk'. Although he did not deal explicitly with demonic witchcraft, his belief that all magic came from the Devil, enshrined as it was in the pages of an inquisitor's manual, became influential. Matters were taken further by another inquisitor's manual, the *Directorum Inquisitorum* of Nicholas Eymeric (*c*.1320–99). Eymeric was a Catalan, and another Dominican, and eventually served as Inquisitor General for Aragon, his career there being punctuated and eventually ended by being exiled from the kingdom by its rulers for a rather over-enthusiastic inquisitorial style. Eymeric's lifetime had seen a number of high-profile sorcery trials, and knowledge of these, as well as his theological training and experience as an inquisitor, fed into his ideas on demonic magic. He emphasized that divination and magic were diabolic practices, implying that those involved in them were apostates who had gone against the First Commandment. These ideas, stated in his widely circulated text, helped pave the way for the emergence of the demonic witch in the next century.

When Eymeric wrote, the focus of attention was on high-profile trials normally involving relatively highly placed men rather than the peasant women who were to become the archetypal witches of early modern Europe. These trials helped to develop the notion of diabolic input into occult practices. Perhaps the most famous of them was the trial of the Knights Templar. This order had been founded in 1119, and was essentially a military order of monks originally founded to protect pilgrims in the Holy Land (Jerusalem had fallen to crusaders a few years previously in the course of the First Crusade). In 1307, for reasons that are not altogether clear but may have included both a desire to get his hands on the Templars' now considerable wealth, and a desire to rid his land of what he saw as a corrupt organization, Philip IV of France arrested the 2,000 or so members of the order resident in his realm, and charged them with sacrilegious rites, apostasy, idolatry, sodomy, and worshipping an idol, Baphomet, who bore resemblance to the Devil. Trials were conducted with the application of torture, and accordingly lurid confessions were made. The period was marked by a number of what could be described as 'treason cum sorcery' trials, mainly directed against popes or monarchs. One ruler who seems to have been especially concerned over such matters was Pope John XXII (1316–34), again a Dominican by training. Like Philip IV with the Templars, Pope John brought accusations of sorcery and idolatry against his political opponents. He was also concerned with popular sorcery and demonic or potentially demonic magic, and ordered his inquisitors to root these practices out, issuing a papal bull entitled *Super illius specula* (Upon His Watchtower), a statement of his views on such matters which was to prove influential on later writers.

Thus by the early fifteenth century an extensive literature was in existence which stressed the reality of demons, accepted that they had regular contacts with humans including sexual intercourse, and which regarded a wide range of magical practices as both satanic in origin and heretical. Meanwhile, inquisitors and other clergymen working within this intellectual framework, in the years around 1400, became aware of a new phenomenon which clearly needed to be fitted into this framework: the demonic witch. As far as we can tell, the early trials in the Alpine lands were largely fuelled by popular pressure, but the Catholic Church swiftly situated these trials within its own intellectual framework. A number of works incorporating this new phenomenon into existing demonic ideas were produced in the early fifteenth century, perhaps the most noteworthy of these being the *Formicarius*, written in the late 1430s by yet another Dominican, Johannes Nider (*c.*1380–1438). A theologian, Nider was concerned with the reform of the Church and the reform of Europe's Christian population and the raising of its religious standards. The *Formicarius* was just one of a number of tracts he wrote, a work aimed generally to expose the sins of the day and to suggest ways of amending them. Among the sins and errors Nider concerned himself with in the work was witchcraft. Nider, writing a tract for the times, drew on recent examples of witch trials, especially those conducted by the secular judge Peter of Bern, and also those instigated by the Dominican inquisitor of Autun in Burgundy. Building on what these trials had revealed, Nider was able to give a vivid impression of peasant witches who caused harm in a number of ways that were later to become the staples of accusations against witches: causing infertility, causing illness, destroying crops, killing children by *maleficium*. The ability to do this harm was obtained through demonic assistance granted after the witches had renounced their faith and decided to worship the Devil. These witches worshipped the Devil in large numbers at nocturnal meetings which were the prototype of the later sabbats. At these meetings the witches desecrated the cross, ate the bodies of babies, and indulged in promiscuous sexual orgies. Nider also, in the course of a discussion of Joan of Arc, established another important point: women were more prone to demonic temptation than men, and hence more prone to witchcraft and perfectly capable of using demonic powers.

Over the fifteenth century sporadic trials continued, with malefic witchcraft, defined partly by what those trials revealed, becoming a subject regularly discussed in theological texts, and gradually the cumulative concept of the demonic witch emerged. This process culminated in the publication, either in late 1486 or in early 1487, of a massive work (524 pages of Latin in its most recent modern full edition) entitled the *Malleus maleficarum* (Hammer of Witches). This work, either mainly or wholly authored by a Dominican inquisitor Heinrich Institoris (a Latinized form of Kramer), is widely regarded as the most important work of demonology ever written. Its significance is threefold. First, it set out clearly both the theological bases for witch-hunting and the massively varied repertoire of *maleficium* employed by witches. These matters were discussed in parts one and two of the work. The first focused on the interactions of the three elements which were essential to this new model of satanic witchcraft: the demon or Devil, the sorcerer or witch, and the permission of God. Throughout, the book is organized into short chapters framed in response to questions, and the answers to these questions in parts one and two painted a picture of a disturbing world where demons were actively enticing humans into apostasy and the sins which would follow. Humans were all too willing to succumb to these enticements and induce other humans to join them, while a harsh God, who had, after all, given humans the free will which allowed them to enter into dealings with demons, punished them for so doing. Question one established that belief in witchcraft was a Catholic orthodoxy and that to disbelieve in that orthodoxy was heretical, and the logic of the book unfolded from that departure point. Secondly, enshrined in part three of the book were instructions on how to conduct a witch trial, an essential guide now that secular authorities needed to be persuaded of the need to punish witches. The *Malleus* followed Innocent VIII's papal bull *Summis desiderantes affectibus* of 1484 (the text of the bull was usually included in the various editions of the *Malleus*) whose main purpose was to convince apparently reluctant secular judges in Germany that they should cooperate with the Church's inquisitors in suppressing witchcraft. Now such judges had a clear guide on what to do. And thirdly, for the modern observer, the *Malleus* is appallingly misogynistic, demonstrating that most witches were female (*maleficarum* is, of course, a female form) and that the reasons for this lay in women's spiritual, moral, intellectual, and physical inferiority.

The *Malleus maleficarum* was much reprinted; twelve Latin editions were published in Germany and France between 1486 and 1523, and then, after a lull, numerous other editions (all in Latin) were published, for example two in Venice in the 1580s, four at Frankfurt between that decade and 1600, and nine at Lyons between 1584 and 1669. It is this frequent reprinting which has led to claims for the *Malleus*'s importance. Yet, despite some evidence that it may have encouraged a number of trials immediately after its publication, its long-term importance remains problematic. Although copies may have existed in most cathedral and university libraries in western and central Europe, it is uncertain how much it encouraged witch-hunting. In 1526, for example, we find the Spanish Inquisition instructing its judges not to believe everything they read in it. The only sustained discussion of the work in English came in 1584 when Reginald Scot, in an unrelentingly sceptical work, cited passages from it as evidence of Catholic wrongheadedness. Moreover, the uncovering of the circumstances under which it was composed has revealed that this was not a triumphalist manifesto for witch-hunting, but rather work thrown together in the face of official distrust. In 1485 Institoris had been involved in witch trials at Innsbruck where he had sought to obtain confessions through intimidation, physical maltreatment, and severe use of torture. There were complaints not just from the relatives of the accused witches but also from a broad spectrum of the public in Innsbruck, and the local bishop stepped in to stop the trials and freed the accused. It was reaction to this setback, and his growing fears of the heretical sect of witches, that led Institoris to write the *Malleus* in the first place. The input of the other person associated with the book, the prominent Dominican theologian Jacob Sprenger, remains problematic. There have been suggestions that Institoris was the sole author of the book, and simply added Sprenger's name to give weight to what was going to be a contentious work. It has also been proposed more recently that while most of the book was written by Institoris, Sprenger (given his area of expertise) contributed the sections dealing with theological niceties.

In the decades immediately after the publication of the *Malleus maleficarum* major works of demonology were scarce. A number of authors, however, many of them Dominicans, wrote works restating and elaborating the demonological conceptual framework established in the *Malleus*, a framework which was itself heavily derivative from earlier writers: thus Bartolomeo de Spina published *Quaestio de strigibus* (Inquiry into Witches) at Venice in 1523, the papal judge Paulus Grillandus the *Tractatus de hereticis et sortilegiis* (Treatise on Heretics and Witches), written in 1525, and the Dominican Silvestro Mazzolini da Prierio the *Strigimagarum demonumque mirandis* (On the Wonders of Witch-Sorceresses and Demons) published in Rome in 1521. Of these early sixteenth-century works perhaps the most important was that by

Grillandus. It helped establish the importance of the witches' sabbat, encouraged witch-hunting in Italy, was reprinted on at least four occasions, was frequently included or extracted in later miscellanies on witchcraft, and was widely cited by later authors. But, acting as a reminder that the writings of the demonologists never attained hegemonic authority, this period also saw a number of sceptical works. Of these, perhaps the most significant was Ulrich Molitor's treatise *De lamiis et phitonicis mulieribus* (On Witches and Female Oracles) which first appeared in 1489 in the immediate wake of the *Malleus* and was to be reprinted on numerous occasions, in both Latin and (unlike the *Malleus*) in German. Molitor (*c.*1442–1507) took the traditional Catholic position which can perhaps be traced back to the *Canon episcopi*: those who actually made a pact with the Devil or renounced Christ for him should be punished as apostates and idolaters, but much of what witches were supposed to do was either illusory or based on faulty intellectual premises. Thus in his book Molitor denied that witches could affect the weather, inflict illness or impotence, shape shift, fly to the sabbat, or conceive children through sexual intercourse with demons. Molitor was a canon lawyer, and it is possible that he wrote the work in response to a request from Sigismund, the Count of Tyrol and the local secular ruler, to explain the issues which lay at the root of the Innsbruck trials.

Generally, the period of the Reformation and the early years of the Counter-Reformation witnessed little by way of witch-hunting or the publication of major demonological treatises. This situation was to change from about 1580, when the uncertain stability achieved in Europe's religious affairs seemed to pave the way for witch-hunting and the renewed publication of elaborate demonological works. In terms of its author's reputation, one of the most significant of these was Jean Bodin's *De la démonomanie des sorciers* (Of the Demonomania of Witches), which appeared in 1580. Bodin was one of the leading intellectuals of his time, author of a major treatise on the nature of monarchy (printed in English as *The Six Books of the Commonwealth*) along with other important works, including an analysis of that major late sixteenth-century problem, inflation. He was also a judge. He received legal training at Toulouse, and then worked his way up the legal system so that, by 1580, he held important judicial office. Bodin drew on Scripture, the church fathers, earlier writers, and above all what he and his fellow judges had experienced while prosecuting witches, to reiterate that witchcraft was a heresy that struck at God and both the ecclesiastical and state hierarchies. Most of what he said regarding demonological concerns was conventional, although his emphasis on the witch as a threat to the state and the public tied in neatly with his views, expressed in *The Six Books of the Commonwealth,* on the need for a strong central monarchy. Thus with Bodin demonology took on a clear political aspect, with the body politic as much under threat from demons and their agents as the Christian community. Bodin's experience and training as a judge, moreover, allowed him to give credence to a tendency which can probably be traced back to Institoris's handling of the Innsbruck trials—the notion that witchcraft was an exceptional offence (a *crimen exceptum* to Bodin), and that judges should be able to use exceptional means to investigate witches and convict them. Accordingly Bodin advocated the use of a range of irregular techniques to judges charged with trying witches, as well as suggesting that the normal rules restricting the use of torture could be dropped.

It was another French judge, Pierre de Lancre, who was to write the major work on one of the phenomena which most exercised demonologists, the witches' sabbat. Probably harking back to beliefs about what happened at secret meetings of Jews in the Middle Ages and (ironically) of early Christians in Rome, the notion of the sabbat had appeared in the early fifteenth century and by the late sixteenth was regarded as one of the more significant activities of the heretical sect of witches—Bodin, for example, had much to say on this matter. In its classic form, witches flew to the sabbat, either physically or in spirit, sometimes after rubbing themselves with foul ointments to facilitate their magical flight. Once there, in their hundreds, sometimes thousands, they danced, they feasted off the flesh of newborn or dead babies, they indulged in promiscuous sexual intercourse, they profaned the host, and they gave homage to the Devil, gracing him with the 'obscene kiss' on his anus, and, more prosaically, reporting to him the acts of *maleficium* they had committed. De Lancre had been sent by the *parlement* of Bordeaux to investigate reports of witchcraft in the Pays de Labourd in the Basque country in the extreme south-west of France, and in 1612 published a large book based on his experiences of witch-hunting there, the *Tableau de l'inconstance des mauvais anges et demons.*

De Lancre was another demonological writer who was apparently driven by the notion that there was a sect of heretical witches and that the continued existence of both the secular state and religious life depended on their extermination. De Lancre's demonology was in most respects orthodox: he wrote, for example, that the Devil could not transform humans into animals, but that he could create illusions of such power. But what was different about his book was his lurid descriptions of the sabbat, based on the evidence of the suspected witches de Lancre had interrogated. A number of major works of demonology were published between Bodin's tract and that of de Lancre, notably by another French judge, Nicolas Rémy, in 1595, and Peter Binsfeld, suffragan Bishop of Trier, in 1589. But the major work of this period, and probably the summation of large-scale works of demonology, *Disquisitiones magicae libri sex* (Six Books on Investigations into Magic), was published in three parts in 1599–1600, its author a Jesuit theologian of Spanish origins but born at Antwerp, Martin Del Rio. Del Rio was a scholarly phenomenon. He taught at the universities of Douai, Liège, Louvain, Graz, and Mainz, mastered nine languages, and published numerous books, including, at the age of 19, an edition of the works of Seneca which cited 1,100 sources, his research being aided by the construction of a desk on wheels which allowed him to transport himself and his papers between different parts of great libraries. With the *Disquisitiones* we are confronted with a massive work of erudition, as widely cited by seventeenth-century writers as was Bodin's *Démonomanie*, one that was certainly cited more frequently in that century than was the *Malleus maleficarum*, for which Del Rio's work was hailed as a replacement.

Some Demonological Issues

To delve deeper into the science of demonology, let us consider Del Rio's *Disquisitiones* in more detail. This work, as its title suggests, is divided into six books, four of them describing to the reader the range of magical activities which existed, the remaining two giving advice about what to do about them. Book one discusses the various forms of magic, and considers whether they are licit or not (the answer is generally no). This section ranges over the efficacy and legitimacy of astrology, alchemy, the use of amulets, the use of incantations in healing, and such major topics as natural magic. Although Del Rio is generally hostile to all forms of magic, he is usually willing to weigh up rival opinions. Thus he discusses whether alchemy is a liberal or a mechanical art, whether it is a type of magic, whether or not it works, and whether it is illicit or licit. Book two focuses on magic involving evil spirits. Here again the reader is led through a range of subjects. As might be expected, such standard issues as the demonic pact, the sexual intercourse between human beings and spirits, and the sabbat are discussed, but Del Rio also considers such tangential problems as whether Elizabeth I's claim to be able to cure scrofula by the royal touch, an attribute commonly claimed by English monarchs, was valid. Book three covers two topics: harmful magic and superstition. The first half ranges over many of the matters which both earlier demonologists and the law courts commonly considered when dealing with maleficent witchcraft: the illnesses caused by the witch, her ability to induce abortion, to dry the mother's milk, to inhibit conception, and the use of image magic. Del Rio also discusses the types of people likely to fall into the Devil's temptation and become maleficent witches. The discussion of superstition again covers that wide range of popular beliefs which worried demonologists, and attempts to rank them according to their level of sinfulness.

The fourth book deals with divination and prophecy, two activities which attracted considerable attention from demonologists. Again, a wide range of topics is covered: Del Rio's discussion of divination incorporates astrological predictions, deriving prognostications from such unusual phenomena as meteors, as well as the interpretation of dreams. Interestingly, Del Rio, like most educated observers who commented on the practice, at this point rejected the water test used against witches, the notion that a suspected witch should be thrown into a river or lake and declared guilty if she floated. In book five, indeed, we move on to the trial of witches, with comprehensive instruction on how to carry out a witch trial properly and also on how to interpret suspects' behaviour. Judges were reminded of the procedures to be followed when applying torture, and also on what types of occult practices were heretical and what not. Del Rio takes a hard line against those who suggested that confessing witches were merely deluded old women, and also argues that convicted witches should be executed even if they had committed no maleficent act—they deserved to die for entering into a pact with the Devil. The sixth book gave advice to confessors in witchcraft cases, obviously centring on the possibilities of a witch being truly penitent and the relationship of the confessor to the legal system trying and executing the witches.

As this brief summary demonstrates clearly, demonology was not just concerned with maleficent witches. Del Rio's *Disquisitiones*, like other major demonological treatises (the *Malleus maleficarum* is another good example), attempts an encyclopedic analysis of erroneous practices, from maleficent witchcraft through to using charms to cure sick horses. What will strike the modern reader is that with Del Rio's work and the other major works of demonology, there is a remarkable eclecticism in the selection of sources. In book two, for example, Del Rio draws, as might be expected, on Scripture, but also on the church fathers, and a massive array of writers on magic and the occult which encompasses such major figures as Henry Cornelius Agrippa of Nettesheim and such minor ones as the Italian poet and astrologer Calcagnini. Demonological works cited include the *Malleus maleficarum*, Nicholas Rémy's *Daemonolatria*, and Peter Binsfeld's *Tractatus de confessionibus maleficorum et sagaram*. Classical works, for example by Seneca and Tertullian, are drawn upon, as is a selection of medical tracts (Del Rio draws heavily on these throughout the book), legal treatises, and a variety of other works such as writings by the twelfth-century Byzantine historian Michael Glycas. Further information is provided, here as elsewhere in the *Disquisitiones*, by reports from Jesuit missionaries sent overseas as Catholicism became a worldwide religion. Thus a discussion of magicians' supposed powers over nature includes a discussion of local rain-making ceremonies from 'our Jesuit brethren in Peru'. Anybody attempting to read this work in the original Latin will also be reminded by another feature of the demonological writings of the period: covering as they do a wide range of occult activities, they have a wide range of names for occult practitioners of various different kinds: *striges*, *sortilege* or *sortilegae*, *malefici* or *maleficae*, and so on, each with its own precise meaning.

Many of the practices castigated by Del Rio are regarded with hostility because they are thought to encourage people to obtain knowledge about the natural world which is really restricted to God; the use of astrology to predict events is a good example of this. People also needed to be warned against superstitious practices or elements of folk religion which were really of satanic origins, or might lead people participating in them to making an implicit pact with the Devil through their actions. Del Rio, like other demonological writers, was convinced that both God's enemies and their malicious intentions were multiplying. Writing a large book emphasizing this point and showing the dangers of one of their core activities, magic, was therefore essential. And Del Rio, good Jesuit that he was, made no bones about the connections between witchcraft and heresy. Heresy in its new and dangerous form, Protestantism, had gained a hold in England, Scotland, France, and 'Belgium' (which in this context probably means the Netherlands in general) and, according to Del Rio, it was therefore no surprise that magic should be flourishing in these regions. 'We see numbers of atheists and *politici* [moderate Catholics] increasing', wrote Del Rio towards the end of his prologue, 'while there are few fervent Catholics left. The heretics are strongly opposed by the Jesuits. This book is a weapon in that war.'

We have focused upon Del Rio's *Disquisitiones* not only because of its importance but also because, as we have suggested, the book is an elaborate and lengthy exemplar of demonological writing in general. 'Witchcraft' as understood by most modern readers (i.e. the type of maleficent magic that led to thousands of executions in the period of the witch-hunts) is a major theme, but it is considered along with analyses of an enormous variety of other occult or arguably occult practices and popular superstitions. Moreover, the modern reader might be confused by the kaleidoscopic use of sources: Scripture, church fathers, classical authors, legal treatises, medical treatises, earlier works of demonology, travel writings, information derived from witch trials, and tales of odd events, some of them anecdotes from the authors' own experience. Turning to witchcraft, however, we do find a number of areas which are generally discussed by all the writers above: the importance of the satanic pact; the way in which the Devil tempts people to witchcraft, and who is likely to be tempted; what witches actually do; the witches' sabbat; and how witches should be tried in the courts. All demonologists addressed these themes, and there was a broad consensus concerning them, although there was, of course, always room for disagreements, sometimes merely of emphasis, between different writers.

Before we turn to what was perhaps the major area of difference, that between Catholic and Protestant demonology, we need to consider briefly one theme, the much-vexed connection between women and witchcraft.

The *Malleus maleficarum* was a handy lucky-dip from which misogynistic quotations could be pulled. Despite the claims of some modern editors, the *Malleus* does come across as an explicitly misogynistic work. Being informed that it was typical in this respect and that it was, in fact, more restrained than some other late medieval writings on women does not entirely reassure. What is surprising, however, is that most other demonologists had very little to say about the connection between women and witchcraft. In contrast to the deserved attention this issue has attracted from modern historians, most early modern demonologists seem to have regarded the issue as a nonproblem: the connection was so axiomatic as to be virtually devoid of interest. William Perkins, in his *Discourse of the damned Art of Witchcraft*, published posthumously in 1608, was typical in this respect. The 257-page book contained two short passages dealing with the issue. Thus we find Perkins discussing the point that the Hebrew term for witch is feminine, and arguing that witches can in fact be male. But he opines that:

> the woman being the weaker sexe, is sooner intangled by the devill's delusions with this damnable art, than the man . . . his first temptation in the beginning, was with Eve a woman, and since he pursueth his practice accordingly, as making most for his advantage. For where he findeth easiest entrance, and best entertainment, thither will he oftenest resort.

The two tropes, the moral weakness of women and Eve's role in giving in to temptation, were regularly adduced by demonologists, while many added that the fact that most witches tried before the courts were women demonstrated the point. That the connection was taken for granted is, in a sense, more worrying than if it had attracted lengthy comment. But beyond that thought, and beyond the *Malleus maleficarum*, those seeking to understand why so many witches were women will find little detailed guidance in demonological tracts.

The acceptance that witches would tend to be women was shared by both Catholic and Protestant demonologists, and this was but one aspect of a widely shared set of attitudes about witches. Well into the seventeenth century clerics in both camps had been educated in a system which laid emphasis on Aristotelian science and the theology of St Thomas Aquinas. They shared common concerns about sin and salvation, and were equally qualified in knowledge of the Bible and the church fathers. A number of Protestant writers, among them the Puritan Richard Bernard, felt able to cite the Jesuit Del Rio and other Catholic authors. Indeed, this tendency is well illustrated by the Saxon jurist Benedict Carpzov (1595–1666). Carpzov held high judicial posts and was also professor of law at Leipzig University, and in 1635 published his *Practica nova imperialis saxonica verum criminaliam*, which, as its title suggests, sought to introduce new rules for trying criminal cases in Saxony, a Protestant state, and earned its writer a lasting reputation as the father of German criminal jurisprudence. Carpzov's rules included instructions, based on an earlier code, on how to try witches which came near to advocating that witchcraft be treated as a *crimen exceptum*. To support his views, Carpzov happily drew on the *Malleus maleficarum* and on other texts authored by Catholics, among them those of Jean Bodin, Peter Binsfeld, Nicolas Rémy, and Del Rio.

A number of differences did, however, exist between Protestant and Catholic demonologists. Perhaps the most clear-cut of these revolved around the issue of demonic possession. The idea that demons could inhabit the bodies of humans was well established, not least because, as we have seen, there are numerous references in the New Testament to Christ casting out demons, and Scripture also relates (Matthew 10: 1, 8) how Jesus instructed his disciples and, by extension, those who were to follow them, to cast out demons. The medieval Church, in the spirit of this text, had developed the rite of exorcism as a method of dealing with demonic possession. This rite was, however, one of a number of Catholic practices which were rejected by Protestants after the Reformation. Doubts had, in fact, been mounting over exorcism in the fifteenth century: it was something which had acquired magical overtones among the populace and which also was already beginning to open a pathway for what might be described as celebrity exorcists. Protestants rejected the rite as an incorrect practice which, like much Catholic ritual, seemed to have magical overtones and which could be seen as making unreasonable demands on the almighty. Protestants took as their text the biblical information that there were some spirits which could be conjured out by prayer and fasting, and used these means to attempt to aid the afflicted. Much of the population, however, would have presumably seen the Catholic solution as the more attractive option, a point demonstrated by the situation in Augsburg in Germany in the second half of the sixteenth century. This was a religiously divided city, with elaborate mechanisms for maintaining tolerance between its Lutheran and Catholic populations. Yet in the 1560s Counter-Reformation Catholicism made considerable advances in the town through the assistance of a number of well-publicized exorcisms. Likewise a tract published in 1603 by Samuel Harsnett, chaplain to the Bishop of London and himself a future Archbishop of York, aimed at discrediting the Jesuits in England through their use of exorcisms, had to admit that the practices he was decrying had pulled in 4,000 converts to Rome. But Protestant demonologists remained firm in their rejection of exorcism. To William Perkins, Catholic attempts to exorcize were 'mere conjuration', for although Christ had given these powers to his disciples, 'there is no such ordinarie gift left to the church of God'.

Another key divergence between Protestant and Catholic thinking lay in attitudes to the sabbat. Although some Protestant demonologists did discuss the sabbat, they generally did not afford the same centrality to it as did their Catholic equivalents. There was no scriptural basis for the sabbat, something which would be especially worrying for Protestants, and the concept had its origins as an imagined inversion of the Catholic mass, something which Protestant demonologists were obviously less likely to be concerned about. Protestant acceptance of the reality of the sabbat was further complicated by the rather problematic nature of how witches got there, and argument on this point leads us to one of the essentials of demonology. All demonologists, Catholic and Protestant, were convinced that the Devil or inferior demons could not actually cause changes in the physical world. To be able to do so would imply the ability to work miracles, something which only God could do. If then, for example, a devil assumed a human form he did so through a delusion worked through occult means, the act thus constituting a *mira* or wonder rather than a miracle proper. As William Perkins put it, only God could succeed in 'abolishing and changing nature': the Devil, a creature with massive knowledge of the natural world acquired over nearly six millennia, could 'doe extraordinarie works by the helpe of nature'. The problem was, of course, whether these 'extraordinarie workes' included enabling witches to fly to the sabbat, with the connected problem of whether witches flew to the sabbat in person or whether their spirits went alone, leaving their bodies besides their sleeping husbands. Although Del Rio listed a number of Catholic authorities who shared their reservations, it is noteworthy that he should begin his list of those who held that both the sabbat and flying there were delusions with the names of Protestants, notably Martin Luther and his collaborator Philip Melanchthon. We are speaking here of a difference in emphasis rather than a complete divergence of views, but here (and as we shall see elsewhere) Protestant demonologists were more likely to ascribe what witches confessed to doing to satanic deceptions than their Catholic counterparts, and were also a little less convinced of the Devil's ability to cause *mira*.

There are two other areas where, although it is not possible to see fully elaborated differences, there is nevertheless a variation in emphasis between Protestant and Catholic demonologists. The first revolves around that massive range of magical practices which Del Rio attacked: Protestant demonologists attacked these too, although possibly with more focus and severity than did their Catholic counterparts. Protestant churches, arguably more vehemently than their Catholic counterparts, wished to evangelize the populations they controlled, to bring them to what they regarded as a proper understanding of religion. To do this they had to wipe out many aspects of popular culture, including popular superstitions and popular magical practices. Thus Protestant demonological works more consistently than their Catholic counterparts attacked the village cunning-folk and charmers whom the population felt useful, the men and women who told their future, told girls whom they were going to marry, helped in finding stolen goods, provided folk medicine, and gave advice about what to do to persons who thought they were bewitched. The Puritan William Perkins and the Jesuit Del Rio agreed that these people derived their powers from the Devil, and should be extirpated. But it was Perkins who set a more strident tone. Towards the end of his *Discourse of the damned Art of Witchcraft* (1618) he reminded his readers that 'by witches we understand not those onely which kill and torment; but all diviners, charmers, jugglers, all wizards commonly called wise men and women'. Perkins went on to include under this heading 'all good witches, which do no hurt but good, which do not spoile and destroy, but save and deliver'. These, as surely as the maleficent witch, had derived their powers from a pact made with Satan; 'death therefore', Perkins wrote in the final sentence of his tract, 'is the just and deserved portion of the good witch'.

Mention of the satanic pact leads us to our final point in this section. Part of the task of educating the inhabitants of Protestant Europe into correct religious attitudes was to inculcate correct views about witchcraft. These views would include two related matters. The first of these was that it was the pact, not *maleficium*, which was the point at issue: the witch should die for apostasy, not because she used the powers the Devil had given her to kill cattle. The second was that many of the misfortunes which were attributed to witches were, in fact, the outcome of God's will, of the working of divine providence: if your cattle died, it was chastisement for your sins, rather than the outcome of an elderly female neighbour's malice. This line of argument was established in sermons as early as 1539 by the Lutheran pastor Johann Brenz, at that time pastor at the Free Imperial City of Schwäbish Hall. There had been severe hailstorms in the locality, which popular opinion attributed to witchcraft. In 1557 Brenz eventually published his *Homilia de grandine* (Sermon on Hailstorms) which argued that natural disasters and personal misfortunes were not caused by witches, but were the work of God, who used them to punish the sinful and test the faith of believers. Brenz's underlying position, probably shared by Martin Luther, was that although making the demonic pact was apostasy and thus worthy of being punished by death, witches were incapable of performing the harm attributed to them, and most popular ideas about witches were therefore groundless superstitions. And like Luther he shared a worry that attributing too much power to the Devil and to witches was in itself a form of apostasy, a putting of the First Commandment in jeopardy. One can perhaps sense in this extreme belief in divine providence and in the somewhat marginal role ascribed to the Devil that some sort of grounds were being established, however unwittingly, for the rejection of witchcraft beliefs altogether.

Demonology in Decline

There had always been, as the respective writings of Heinrich
Institoris and Ulrich Molitor demonstrated, a divergence of views on
witchcraft. As the seventeenth century progressed doubts about its
reality began to strengthen, and over much of western and central
Europe these doubts were dominant by the mid-eighteenth century.
In 1600 most educated Europeans, whatever their position on witchcraft, would have at least realized why the concerns worrying Martin
Del Rio were valid. By 1750 few would have done so: by that date
demonology as a science was on its way out. The reasons for this
process are complex and disputed. Among them would be a growing
scepticism among the senior judiciary about how to try witches, even
whether witches could or should be tried at all. By the 1630s the
parlement of Paris, hearing cases on appeal from the northern two-
thirds of France, was regularly quashing capital charges for witchcraft
on the grounds that provincial judges did not understand due legal
process in witchcraft cases. As we have seen, their equivalents at the
parlement of Bordeaux adopted the same attitude to the convictions for
witchcraft described by de Lancre.

There was also that bundle of intellectual changes which we know
as 'The Scientific Revolution of the seventeenth century', heralded by
the publication of René Descartes's *Discourse on Method* in 1643. The
mechanical philosophy of Descartes and later natural philosophers left
little room for the occult in general and witches in particular. Both the
nature and the impact of the Scientific Revolution have been questioned, but it remains apparent that, however partially and imper-
fectly, a new view of the cosmos was emerging. There was also a
similarly gradual and imperfect move towards a less fraught type of
Christianity, in which the Devil was thought to be less likely to
intervene in human affairs on a daily basis. And, more prosaically,
there was a wider gulf between popular and elite culture which would
make it increasingly possible for educated and better-off Europeans to
regard witchcraft accusations and witchcraft beliefs as something
associated with the ignorant peasantry. Snobbery may well have
been a powerful force for the end of witch beliefs among the elite.

Little of this was apparent when Del Rio wrote, and with the old
demonological framework not being displaced until the early

eighteenth century, it is clear that the forces of scepticism had an uphill struggle. Indeed, the two works which are generally interpreted as heralding the onset of scepticism were both working firmly inside the established system. The first of these was Johann Weyer's *De praestigiis daemonum* (On the Tricks of Demons), published in 1563. Weyer (1515–88) had been educated in medicine at Paris, and from 1550 served as physician to Duke William V of Cleves-Jülich. This was an area of low witchcraft prosecution, and apparently the Duke was a relatively tolerant man in religious matters and probably unlikely to encourage witch-hunting. Weyer shared the assumptions of many demonologists. He was very hostile to popular beliefs regarding magic, for example, and was fully convinced of the power of the Devil. Indeed, he probably attributed more power to the Devil than did many contemporary writers, and for Weyer only God's will kept the Devil's powers from becoming stronger. What Weyer derived from this point of view, however, was that witches, who were normally poor, physically weak, or suffering from what the period described as 'melancholia' (a mental condition akin to the modern concept of depression), had been deluded by the Devil into believing that they could perform impossible actions. He argued that such witches, who were normally women, should be acquitted. Weyer has been seen as a force for modernism: Freud saw him as a prototype modern psychiatrist, and others have followed that lead. It should be noted, however, that, as his views on the Devil demonstrate, he was working within the existing demonological framework while, interestingly, he argued that magicians should be punished because they had made a pact with the Devil. His book was much republished in the two decades after its appearance, with six editions in Latin, three in French, and two in German, as well as the publication of an abbreviated version for a popular audience, *De lamiis*, in 1577. Weyer routinely attracted odium from later demonological writers, who singled out his tolerant line on witchcraft for especial opprobrium.

Another writer who has been, wrongly, hailed as a prototype for modern rationalism was Reginald Scot. Scot (*c.*1538–99) was a gentleman living in the English county of Kent who in 1584 published an unrelentingly sceptical book entitled *The Discoverie of Witchcraft*. Witch-beliefs in general were attacked, the Catholic volumes on witchcraft (particularly the *Malleus maleficarum*) were excoriated as erroneous papist writings, and confessions of witches dismissed as the 'melancholic' fantasies of confused old women. Yet Scot was not some sort of 'modern' thinker misplaced by chance in Elizabethan England. His two main objections to witchcraft were firmly lodged within the parameters of the intellectual discourse of his time. First, he took an extreme Protestant view on the importance of divine providence and on the relative unimportance of the Devil in everyday affairs, and followed the line that most of the misfortunes attributed to witches were in fact the result of God's will. Secondly, Scot took another route open to sceptics of the period by arguing that scriptural references to witches and witchcraft used to justify witch-hunting were in fact mistranslations. Demonologists routinely considered the question of whether the witches described in the Bible were the same as modern ones, and Scot answered this question in the negative, thus challenging an important proof of the existence of witches. More extremely, in an appendix to the work entitled 'A Discourse upon Divels and Spirits', Scot, while accepting the existence of demons and other spirits, denied that they were capable of interacting with human beings. Given that the notion that such interaction was possible was the fundamental underpinning of the whole witchcraft paradigm, Scot was therefore denying the very essence of witchcraft. Scot's work was not much known on the Continent (English was not then a widely understood language) but it does demonstrate how sceptical positions could be reached and maintained long before the arrival of 'science'.

Sceptical tracts continued to be published, although they were rarely as radical as Scot's. In 1631 the Jesuit Friedrich Spee (1591–1635) published his *Cautio criminalis* (Precautions for Prosecutors), a book prompted by its author's recent experience of witnessing recent mass trials in Germany. Any general objections to witch-hunting Spee may have had were not stated, but his work was a powerful attack on the extreme use of torture and other irregularities in witch trials. Another German writer to express concern over witch trials and some demonological certainties was the Jesuit Adam Tanner (1572–1632). Although never devoting a full-scale tract to these issues, Tanner's doubts may well have been influential: certainly Spee drew on them. And in 1653 another Kentish gentleman produced a measured but insistent sceptical tract when Sir Robert Filmer, best known, through his *Patriarcha*, as an apologist for divine right monarchy, published his *An Advertisement to the Jury-Men of England touching Witches* in 1653. This book attacked the problem of the mistranslation of passages of Scripture, and also focused on the writings of William Perkins and Jean Bodin. Perkins was attacked over the notion of the demonic pact: as Filmer noted (and this was a continual problem for demonologists) there was no scriptural basis for this central component of demonological belief. As an experienced justice of the peace, he also attacked Bodin's proposals on how witchcraft could be proved in a court of law. Demolishing each proposal in turn, he arrived at the *reductio ad absurdum* that a witch could only be convicted if the Devil appeared in court and gave evidence against her.

Despite such sceptical works (and we should remember that scepticism over the demonological framework for witch-hunting had never really been absent), works advocating witch-hunting, and repeating the now fully established demonological theories, continued to be published. In the English-speaking world, indeed, a new synthesis was attempted between the need to preserve belief in witches and spirits and the new natural philosophy which has traditionally been seen as paving the way to the Scientific Revolution. The key figure here was Joseph Glanvill (1636–80), whose *Saducismus triumphatus: or, Full and plain evidence concerning witches and apparitions* (1681), and its earlier iterations, were intended to counter what its author considered as increasingly fashionable sceptical attitudes to witches and the spirit world, attitudes which were, in his view, threatening to encourage atheism. The work was a compendium of first-hand accounts of witches, poltergeists, and other occult phenomena. Glanvill, a member of the Royal Society and a man fully abreast with current scientific thinking, sought to harness this thinking and the experimental method to demonstrate the proof of the spirit world. That his book was to prove popular well into the eighteenth century was an indication that his views had considerable support. And perhaps rather unexpectedly, much the same connection can be made with the influential clergyman implicated in encouraging the Salem witchcraft trials of 1692, Cotton Mather. Mather was the author of about 400 works, although he is probably best remembered for his *Memorable Providences, relating to Witchcrafts and Possessions* of 1689, and his *Wonders of the Invisible World*, a defence of the Salem trials influenced, it should be noted, by the writings on witchcraft of William Perkins, Joseph Glanvill, and

Glanvill's associate Henry More. But Mather was no backward-look-ing bigot. He was *au fait* with the writings of Descartes and other materialist philosophers, was a member of the Royal Society, and in what was probably the most important of his scientific works, his *Christian Philosopher: a Collection of the Best Discoveries in Nature, with religious improvements* (1721), he praised the work of Isaac Newton. Demono-logical ideas were proving more durable and adaptable than any simple model of the decline in witchcraft beliefs might indicate.

Such beliefs were, nevertheless, being strongly challenged by the turn of the seventeenth and eighteenth centuries. Between 1691 and 1693, to take one of the more important sceptical works, a Dutch Reformed pastor named Balthasar Bekker published the various parts of his *De betoverde Weereld*. Bekker (1634–98) served as minister in a number of places before being called to Amsterdam in 1680. He was interested in witchcraft and related matters, and in particular in the reality of the Devil and the spirit world. Bekker was another thinker who became worried about translating and interpreting Scripture, while his theological concerns about contemporary learned witch beliefs were reinforced by his interest in Cartesian ideas, which were becoming increasingly influential in the Netherlands. Bekker's work, in four volumes, was complex, but perhaps the main conclusions he reached were coloured by Descartes's dismissal of the possibility of contact between the physical and the spiritual world. On this basis, the Devil could not affect humans, while, on Bekker's reading, there was no scriptural basis to believe that he did so. Bekker, in fact, attributed a metaphorical meaning to the Devil as referred to in the Bible, arguing that the term was a synonym for evil in general rather than an indication of a real entity: in effect we return to that Protestant view which regarded affording any real importance to the Devil as down-grading the importance of divine providence. Bekker also joined other writers in arguing that the 'witches' referred to in Scripture were fraudsters rather than agents of Satan. The publication brought heavy censure from the establishment of the Dutch Reformed Church, and Bekker was deprived of his clerical status and denied access to the Reformed communion. Yet the book was much reprinted in Dutch, and was translated into English and German.

Another major attack on demonology came from the German thinker Christian Thomasius (1655–1728). The son of a professor of philosophy and rhetoric, Thomasius became a lawyer and law professor, eventually gaining employment at what was then the new University of Halle. Writing in the context of his more general doubts about the use of torture and the type of evidence accepted in inquisitorial process, Thomasius published *De crimine magiae* (On the Vice of Sorcery) in 1701, a work that flatly denied the crime of witchcraft, and followed this in 1712 with another publication, his *Historische Untersuchung Vom Ursprung und Fortgang Des Inquisitions Processes Wieder die Hexen* (On the Origin and Progress of Inquisitorial Procedure against Witches), which mounted a full-scale attack on the demonological canon. By this time witch-hunting in the German-speaking lands was on the wane, but with Thomasius we have an important intellectual statement on the non-existence of witchcraft. Even so, witchcraft was to be a much debated subject well into the eighteenth century. To take one famous demonstration of this point, in 1749 a 71-year-old nun named Maria Renata was executed as a witch in Würzburg, and in a sermon preached at the execution a Jesuit named Georg Gaar attacked those progressive intellectuals who denied the existence of witches and magic on the familiar grounds that their arguments would lead to a denial of God. This incident troubled the Bavarian authorities, and attracted considerable attention throughout Europe, to the extent that it opened up a debate about the reality of witchcraft in Italy which then spread back to Germany and into France. The result of these debates was that, despite its strenuous advocates, the idea of witchcraft and the demonological framework supporting that idea was finally thrown out among enlightened Europeans. Those adhering to this framework, once so influential, were now regarded as the rump of a defeated and outdated intellectual movement.

Although perhaps a somewhat more rapid process than the creation of the demonic witch stereotype, the dismantling of demonology was a slower and more partial process than may have been expected. The crucial point was the difficulty of making a complete break with an acceptance of the reality of the spirit world and of the contact between humans and demons, of the direct intervention of the Devil in human affairs. To do this really was to make a major intellectual break, a break which, as we have seen, might leave those pursuing it open to accusations of atheism and, by extension, of subverting the social order. Like the development of the concept of the demonic witch, the destruction of that concept was a cumulative process: concerns grew over procedures in witch trials; Protestant pastors worried about how divine providence fitted in with the role demonologists gave to the Devil; scholars fretted over the translation of the Hebrew terms generally rendered as witch, and over the implications of the lack of a scriptural basis for either the demonic pact or the witches' sabbat. Slowly, in a context where Cartesian and Newtonian ideas were becoming fashionable, a more rational approach was being taken to Christianity, and judges were proving themselves unwilling to convict in witchcraft trials, these doubts could coalesce and the premises of demonology and of the demonologists could be rejected. But this system, we should remind ourselves, was durable, flexible, and—however foreign to the modern observer—complex and intellectually demanding. It needs to be understood on its own premises, rather than simply dismissed as some massive, and pernicious, intellectual 'wrong turn'.

4

The Witch Trials

Rita Voltmer

What was a witch trial? Simply stated, it was a legal punitive procedure against people of both sexes accused of practising criminal witchcraft, sorcery, and magic. But definitions are rarely simple in historical contexts. In the age of European witch-hunting from the early fifteenth century through to the late eighteenth century, one must distinguish, for example, between what were considered inherent magical abilities on the one hand and the occult power of *witchcraft* on the other, transferred to the witch by the Devil through a pact. Different languages throw up different definitions. In German trial records, tracts, and reports, the term *Zauberei* was used for all types of benevolent magic (*beneficia*) and malevolent magic (*maleficia*), with or without an overtly expressed Devil's pact. The German term *Hexerei* (witchcraft) is not found before the beginning of the fifteenth century. Even during the mass persecutions in the western parts of the Holy Roman Empire at the end of the sixteenth century, diabolic witchcraft was still referred to as *Zauberei*. The term 'sorcerer' is more akin to the German *Magier*, namely, a magician who practised learned ritual or natural magic.

Looking at terms for magic, sorcery, and witchcraft across European (and non-European) vernacular languages, similar problems of inconsistency occur; as a consequence, the 'witches' who stood trial throughout Europe and its colonies appeared in a variety of guises. Young children, teenagers, adults, the elderly, men and women, simple folk and members of the elite, magistrates, Catholic priests and Protestant ministers were all accused, charged, and executed as witches. Usually, a witch was imagined as the enemy *within* a community. It could be a wife or husband, child, family member, household servant, or neighbour. On the other hand, witches could also be the enemy *from outside*, a vagrant, beggar, or gypsy. Self-interest, insubordination, revenge, hatred, envy, greed, belligerence, and fornication were thought to drive these 'witches'—literally into the arms of Satan, from a demonologist's point of view. Generally speaking, a witch represented the disorderly 'other', a rebel against patriarchal, social, political, and religious order. This all-inclusive stereotyping of enemies from within and without was broad enough to label even the smallest conflicts within families and households, in rural as well as in urban neighbourhoods, as evidence of witchcraft. Likewise, the notion of witchcraft mixed with fears of rebellion and conspiracy, and provided labels for religious and political adversaries in confessional wars and turmoil.

Depending on the political, religious, social, and particularly the juridical context, the relevant indictments listed an assortment of suspected evil doings. This included such atrocities as committing malevolent witchcraft against people and livestock, suckling a demon in the shape of a pet (a 'familiar'), creating tempests and hailstorms by evil spells, shape shifting, night riding through the air, and gathering at sabbats to feast on human flesh and copulate with devils. At its core, the cumulative concept of diabolic witchcraft contained five elements: the Devil's pact, sexual intercourse with the Devil, the witches' flight, the attending of the sabbat, and *maleficium*.

Witch trials targeted women in greater numbers than men. The overall ratio for early modern Europe and New England is 75–80 per cent women to 20–5 per cent men. But this masks a lot of variation. The proportion of women amongst the victims of witch persecution ranged widely, both chronologically (from witch-hunt to witch-hunt), and geographically (from region to region). And men outnumbered women in certain areas, such as Normandy, the Pays de Vaud, Finland, Estonia, Iceland, and Russia. The reason why, on the whole, more women than men were suspected as witches is much debated. No obvious and simple answer offers itself.

The trials occurred in a range of differing formats, from single cases to mass prosecutions, and they were conducted under a range of quite diverse legal systems across continental Europe, Scandinavia, the British Isles, and in the transatlantic colonies. Moreover, witch trials were based upon a broad spectrum of regional and social systems of popular and learned witchcraft belief, and were linked to ideas stemming from political, theological, and social debates about authority, masculinity and femininity, the family, and motherhood. Witch trials were not predominantly a rural phenomenon. Great cities like Paris, London, or Madrid experienced few witch trials, and yet magical belief systems (including witchcraft), magical subcultures, and 'markets' for magical services were pervasive in the milieu of big cities. Small and middle-sized cities in the Holy Roman Empire, on the other hand, saw devastating witch-hunts (such as in Lemgo, Osnabrück, Minden, Rottweil). Urban witch trials took place in the context of wider struggles for political power, both within and beyond the city. No common standard of categories has been established as yet to differentiate between isolated trials, linked trials, and witch-hunts. The historian Brian P. Levack makes a distinction between individual prosecutions (so-called small witch-hunts with at most three victims at a time), medium-sized witch-hunts (linked trials charging between five and ten persons), and large witch-hunts (more than ten, up to hundreds of linked trials). Based on his study of Bavarian trials, Wolfgang Behringer, building on definitions proposed in earlier studies by William Monter on France and Switzerland, and H. C. Erik Midelfort on early modern Germany, suggested four categories: single witch trials (up to three executions); panic trials (four to nine executions); large witch-hunts (ten to nineteen executions within a short time span); and witch persecutions (more than twenty executions in one year and in one place). Whichever system of categorizing one chooses depends entirely upon individual preference.

The phrase 'witch craze', used widely in older histories of witchcraft, is now avoided by most historians. It implies that both the common and elite participants in the trials were, in labelling, excluding, denouncing, charging, sentencing, and executing witches, driven by panic and paranoia, by some temporary phase of inexplicable insanity. In the context of their respective policies against the threat of witchcraft, believers and hunters acted in a level-headed and logical manner. Belief in witchcraft, the acceptance not just of *maleficium* but also of the existence of diabolic witchcraft, the labelling of neighbours as devilish enemies of God, and forcing them to undergo life-threatening trials: all this was the result not only of fear but also of dogmatism, fanaticism, bigotry, and ignoble self-interest. Particularly in its German equivalent *Hexenwahn*, the term 'witch craze' was ideologically misused in the politically motivated conflict between Protestant and Catholic scholars in the nineteenth century, either to discredit the Catholic Church for promoting 'superstition', or to hold the Protestant Reformation responsible for the early modern witch persecutions. Likewise, the label 'witch panic' is problematic, since it insinuates that whole communities, territories, or even nations were driven by mental panics and panic-stricken actions against witches. Witch-hunts as part of so-called moral panics occurred, however, in the Franconian bishoprics, for example. In general, the term 'witch-hunt' points to the fact that all kinds of witch persecution, be it legally conducted trials or lynchings, included the active search for evildoers. 'Witch-hunt' should only really be applied to the prosecution of a larger group of suspects.

A global paradigm cannot cover the linguistic, religious, cultural, economic, and political influences on local, regional, and territorial witch trials. But purely national paradigms of distinctly English, French, Scottish, German, or Russian witch persecutions are not necessarily helpful either. Some Protestant lands like the northern Netherlands, England, and the Scandinavian kingdoms saw a rather moderate quota of witch trials, whilst it was in Protestant Scotland that the most severe witch-hunts in the northern peripheries of Europe occurred. Catholic Ireland was largely spared from the witch trials, whereas in the southern and western ecclesiastical territories of the Holy Roman Empire massive witch-hunts took place. Orthodox Russia prosecuted about 490 witches during the seventeenth century and approximately the same number again the following century. There were few executions, though, with the authorities preferring to mete out severe punishments (beating, severing a body part, exiling). The Islamic world of the Ottoman Empire and its European territory was not haunted by witch-hunts. Massive persecutions took place particularly in the politically fragmented border regions between France and Spain (the Basque land and Catalonia), between France and the Holy Roman Empire (Savoy, Alsace, Lorraine, Luxembourg, Flanders), and in Finnmark, a region between Norway and Finland. Witch-hunting was generally less intense in both the Mediterranean region and northern Europe. However, Catalonia (1618–20), lowland Scotland in general, eastern England (1645–7),

Finnmark (1621–63), and northern Sweden (1668–76) are notable exceptions. Even in highly affected regions with severe witch-hunts the geographical spread of trials was uneven. Some areas of Europe experienced endemic, others epidemic episodes of witch persecutions. People in many regions never witnessed a witch trial, but would have heard about the alleged horrible crimes perpetrated elsewhere in reports from pamphlets, newspapers, or sermons. To quote the historian Brian Levack once more: 'there was more than one world of the witches in early modern Europe.'

Witch Trials: The Causes of Prosecutions

Over the last century some historians have tried to seek fundamental, overarching causes for the rise of witch persecution. It has been argued, for instance, that extreme weather and crop failures during the cooling climatic period or 'Little Ice Age' of the sixteenth and seventeenth centuries generated widespread fear that Satan and his witch minions were to blame. This environmental crisis then led to brutal, linked witch trials condensed into a very few years where extensive torture and mass executions took place. Yet, not everywhere in Europe can a correlation be found between witch-hunts and the disasters created by bad weather, harvest failures, or economic crises—for example, the sparse pattern of large-scale witch-hunts in most European peripheries, like England, Finland, Hungary, and Russia, where single trials against magic and sorcery comprised the majority of incidences.

Witch trials had many different causes. Recent witchcraft scholarship acknowledges that no mono-causal explanation should be accepted. A one-dimensional view pays too little attention to the distinctive geographies and territories, the particular religions, languages, cultures, politics, and economies within Europe and its colonies. The belief in magic and witchcraft was not the only existing system of explaining and handling mischief or misery. We need to distinguish between single trials for sorcery, magic, and witchcraft on the one hand, and linked trials with witch-hunts, based primarily on the collective matrix of a secret coven of witches, which in the Catholic context was understood as a heretical sect, acting as the Devil's minions and meeting at the sabbat, on the other hand. The analysis

Table 1 Witch trials in the European kingdoms/territories (selection)

Kingdom/ territory	Affiliated kingdom/ territory	Trial period/ main phase	Trials (can include multiple defendants)	Executions
Denmark		1609–1687	494 (only Jutland)	
Iceland	Part of the Danish kingdom	1593–1720	128	22
Norway	See above	1601–1670	*c.*780	*c.*310
England		1563–1712		*c.*400–500
Ireland	Affiliated to England		9	4 at most
Scotland		1563–early 17th century		*c.*2,500
Estonia		1520–1725	205	55
France		1570–1670	total number unknown, numerous lynchingsin some parts of the kingdom	*c.*400–1,000
Dauphiné	Part of the French kingdom	1425–early 16th century	287	*c.*230
Burgundy, duchy	See above	1470–1664	Several hundred	Less than 50
Normandy	See above	16th–17th centuries	*c.*400	*c.*100
Livonia, Grand Duchy		15th–18th centuries		50
Netherlands (northern)		*c.*1500–1608		*c.*200
Poland		1511–1776		*c.*2,000

Russia		17th–18th centuries	*c.*650–1,000	few
Sweden		1550–1750		*c.*400
Finland	Part of the Swedish kingdom	1520–1750	*c.*2,000	75

Note: Clear statistics are missing about the total numbers of witch trials, the number of individuals prosecuted, and final verdicts. A single trial could include several defendants, and not every alleged witch was sentenced to execution. Since reliable statistical material is still missing, parts of southern Europe are not included in the following charts.

of isolated trials improves when considered within the entire local paradigm of criminal prosecution. Witchcraft slander suits are useful for gaining insight into popular witchcraft beliefs, for example, but should not be confused with criminal charges of diabolic witchcraft.

What factors established a witch-hunt? At the end of the sixteenth century, severe witch prosecution happened in the Imperial abbey of St Maximin near the city of Trier, which ranked among the very worst outbreaks anywhere in Europe (around 400 executions between 1586 and 1596, thus a death toll of roughly 20 per cent of inhabitants). In the electorate of Trier about 1,000 executions took place over this period. Both territories belonged to the archdiocese of Trier in western Germany. Likewise, in the first half of the seventeenth century, in the Franconian prince bishoprics of Bamberg, Eichstätt, and Würzburg, and in the Imperial abbey of Ellwangen, about 3,000 persons were killed as alleged witches. In the Moselle region as well as in Franconia, a persecuting environment was established, which left little chance for the accused to escape. In the electorate of Trier and in the Imperial abbey of Saint Maximin, organized groups of the populace were a dynamic force driving on the witch-hunts. In Franconia, responding to popular pressure, single men in authority orchestrated the persecutions. Nevertheless, we find similar structures: in both regions, diabolic witchcraft was defined as a *crimen exceptum*, which had to be fought with inquisitorial procedures including torture to extract a list of accomplices from the accused. Political interests played an additional vital role. The Franconian ecclesiastical territories were

Table 2 Witch trials in the regions and territories in the borderlands between Spain, France, the Holy Roman Empire, and Denmark

Territory/region	Changing affiliations over time	Period/main phase	Trials/charges	Executions
Basque lands/Navarre (region)	Divided between France and Spain	1610–1612		c.120
Bar, duchy	Holy Roman Empire / Duchy of Lorraine / France	1580–1630		c.250
Lorraine, duchy	Holy Roman Empire / France	1570–1630	c.2,000	c.1,400
Alsace (region)	Holy Roman Empire / France	1570–1630		c.1,000
Franche-Comté	Spanish Habsburgian provinces / France	1500–1680	c.870	c.480
Savoy, duchy	Holy Roman Empire / France	1560–1674	More than2,000	More than 800
Switzerland	Holy Roman Empire (until 1648)	1420–1782	c.5,000	c.3,500
Schleswig and Holstein, duchies	Denmark / Holy Roman Empire	1530–1735	852	More than 600

ruled by ardent Catholic lords, educated and backed by Jesuits and committed to post-Tridentine Catholicism. In purifying their realm to establish a godly state, battle was declared against the enemies of God—witches, adulterers, dissenters, and people seen as the disorderly 'others', all had to be disciplined to the fullest extent of the law. In both regions, the archdiocese of Trier and the Franconian lands, fanatic suffragan bishops such as Peter Binsfeld and Friedrich Förner wrote anti-witchcraft treatises that propagated notions of diabolic witchcraft and the idea of the witches' sabbat. In both regions, the witchcraft trials were conducted by secular courts run by ambitious

Table 3 Witch trials in the kingdoms and territories politically bound to the House of Habsburg

Territory/city	Kingdom/confederation/region	Period/main phase	Trials (can involve multiple defendants)	Executions
Artois, county	Netherlands (southern) / Spanish Habsburgian Provinces	1450–1685		c.47
Brabant, duchy	See above	1450–1685		88
Flanders, country	See above	1450–1685		202
Hainault, country	See above	1450–1685		28
Luxembourg, duchy	See above	1560–1683	c.3,000	c.2,000
Namur, county	See above	1450–1685		144
Roermond	See above	1450–1685		more than 64
Outer Austrian and Swabian Austria	Austrian hereditary lands	1479–1751	1,100	880
Tyrol, county	See above	1530–1720	c.250 (including 420 defendants)	72
Bohemia, kingdom		15th–18th centuries		c.800
Moravia, margravate	Land of the Bohemian Crown	1678–1696		c.300
Silesia (region)	See above			593
Hungary, kingdom (partly occupied by the Ottomans until c.1700)		1526–1800	c.4,000	c. 1,100

Table 4 Witch trials in the Holy Roman Empire: persecuting territories and intense persecutions (selection)

Territory/city state/prince-bishopric	Period	Main phases	Trials/charges	Known executions
Augsburg, prince-bishopric	1575–1745	1586–1592		c.200
Baden-Baden, margravate	1560–1631	1560–1580, 1625–1631		275
Bamberg, prince-bishopric	1595–1630	1626–1630		c.1,000
Bavaria, duchy	15th century–1756	1589–1591	c.1,500	Less than 200
Eichstätt, prince-bishopric	1590–1631	1590–1592 1603 1617–1631		279–400
Ellwangen, prince-abbey	1588–1618	1588, 1611–1618		c.450
Fulda, prince-abbey		1603–1606		239
Hesse (region)	16th century–1739	1626–1630		c.1,750

	15th century – 1650			More than 2,000
Cologne, electorate	15th century – 1650			More than 2,000
Lippe, county (inc. city of Lemgo)		1550–1686		More than 300
Mainz, electorate	1511–1684	1593–1630		c.2,000
Manderscheid (Kail, Blankenheim, Gerolstein) counties		1580–1638		More than 300
Mecklenburg (Schwerin, Güstrow) duchies	1560–1700	1599–1614 1661–1675	4,000	2,000
Mergentheim, territory of the Teutonic Knights		1590–1631	584	387
Pomerania (western), duchy	1570–1710		1,000	c.600
Saxony, electorate	1407–1766	1610–1630 1655–1665	c.900	c.300
Saint Maximin, imperial abbey		1586–1596		c.500
Trier, electorate	c.1480–c.1653	Around 1590		c.1,000
Würzburg, prince-bishopric		1616/1617 1625–1630		More than 1,200

men seeking social and financial profit and power in the name of godly zeal. Similar factors can also be found in Protestant witch-hunting regions, such as in the duchy of Mecklenburg-Schwerin.

One needs to look for a cluster of factors to explain witch-hunts, most of which needed to coincide to give rise to severe witch-hunts. In the background we often find social, economic, political, and/or religious crises, or the fear of imminent multiple crises to come, such as the impacts of the Little Ice Age, plague, religious fragility (fuelled by the Reformation and Counter-Reformation), or political conflicts and wars, such as the French Wars of Religion (1562–98), the Thirty Years War (1618–48), and the English Civil Wars (1642–51). Such factors created a climate of credibility for the existence of evildoing witches, responsible for single acts of *maleficium*, as well as the collective act of invoking tempests, or conspiracies against the establishment. Substantial numbers of the local populace and ruling elite, learned as well as unlearned, then accepted the perception of the forthcoming threat from witches as minions of Satan. To instigate witch-hunts it was necessary to envision malevolent witches organized into an under-cover criminal organization to wreak havoc, gathering in groups, sometimes at a sabbat. This collective element was strengthened by demonological theory.

Individuals and groups of inhabitants often took an active interest in detecting, denouncing, and bringing to court suspected witches from within their own community. Rural villagers as well as town dwellers were involved at all levels in selecting, excluding, and ultim-ately extirpating their accused neighbours. The most effective group of local witch-hunters were the witch-hunting committees in western territories of the Holy Roman Empire and in the duchy of Luxem-bourg. These committees had the job of gathering the evidence necessary to bring a suspect to trial for witchcraft. Only men—includ-ing local lay jurymen or court assessors, clerks, landlords, and parish priests—were appointed by their respective communities to join such committees. Villagers sometimes had to pay a 'witch tax' to fund the enterprise. Thus, the committee became a quasi-institutionalized instrument of witch-hunting, taking over administrative prerogatives. It was the committee who sought out suspects in the neighbourhood; it was they who travelled from one execution place to the other to hear confessions and listed names of alleged accomplices; it was they who paid notaries to get written copies of witchcraft denunciations and indictments; it was they who brought supposed witches to court; and it was they who helped as gaolers and in the torture room.

The administrators of local and regional jurisdictions such as bailiffs, district officers, and minor lords were often eager to accept the accusations from below. But they were perfectly capable of initiating severe witch-hunts even without strong pressure from below. Some, being ardent witch-hunters, thought themselves to be the first likely target of devilish mischief. To conduct witchcraft trials was useful to gain juridical and political power, autonomy, and reputation. Anti-witchcraft policies and witch burnings were striking spectacles of power. A number of abbots, counts, and lords gained a dubious reputation as witch-hunters. The exercise of high criminal justice via witch trials, as well as its documentation in trial records, affirmed their autonomy and authority. Minor rulers clung ever more tenaciously to their privileges of criminal justice the more this privilege was challenged by major territorial lords. In cities, magistrates could also adopt witch-hunts as a political instrument, when one or more members of the political-juridical elite attempted to advance their careers by demonstrating zeal in prosecuting witches. Witch-hunts became part of a rigorous programme of reform in religion, morals, and politics. Recent studies concerning Silesia, the bishopric of Münster, the cities of Lemgo, Osnabrück, and Minden, the numerous lordships in the Rhine–Meuse area, Alsace, Switzerland, northern Italy, Catalonia, even in Finnmark, support the idea that middle-sized and small jurisdictional units were the true core of European witch-hunts.

Control from the centre was either missing or not yet sufficiently effective. This allowed local lordships and jurisdictions a greater freedom to pursue their own witch-hunts. Working within the locally established system of bringing witches to justice, there were ambitious specialists, such as clerks, notaries, judges, witch finders, and executioners, who eagerly fulfilled their roles. Accordingly, they took a great personal and social concern in the witch-hunts, sometimes combined with economic interest, and thus pursued an 'anti-witchcraft' business model. Beyond a doubt, believing in magic, detecting witches, accusing them of witchcraft, excluding one's neighbours as minions of Satan, acting as a witness, scribe, minister, or father confessor, accepting charges, conducting witch trials, interrogating and torturing suspects were all *choices*. Such choices had a very decisive impact on whether single trials generated linked trials. The biographies, social status, and career of the scribes, being the main 'constructors' of the trial records, have received special interest. More generally, we have to look at the actors both in and out of the courtroom, their education, social background, and their networks, to understand their personal decisions pro or contra witch-hunting, and their individual struggles for honour, resources, prestige, power, and profit.

Last but not least, the dynamics of expanding communication in the era is important: geographical frameworks, political fragmentation, settlement density, travel and trade routes, networks of noble families and officials, ecclesiastical societies like the Dominicans and, most noteworthy, the Jesuits. Without such a widespread set of connections, the rapid movement of media (books, tracts, pamphlets, sermons) and ideas concerning witchcraft, witch trials, and witch-hunts would have been impossible.

Witchcraft: The Law and the Impact of Torture

Various early modern territories and states promulgated laws and Acts against witchcraft. In the Holy Roman Empire, Emperor Charles V enacted a criminal law code called the *Constitutio criminalis Carolina* (1532), which remained in use until 1806. For much of that time it included several clauses dealing with both the offence of witchcraft and how to conduct a proper criminal lawsuit against accused witches. In its procedural law, the Carolina code combined the accusatorial with the inquisitorial procedure. Torture was defined as a legal instrument necessary for extracting confessions. The type and duration of torture during a criminal procedure was not regulated, but was left to the arbitrary judgement of the courts. In dubious and difficult to decide cases, the Carolina code obliged the local courts and lay judges to consult the faculty of law at a university or a higher court with learned judges. Only after obtaining the written authorization of a legally trained, superior panel could the local court continue with the interrogation under torture. In the same way, the verdict of the local court had to be confirmed by the superior courts or law faculties. Thus, with its decision in favour of the *processus ordinarius* (a criminal procedure, wherein the ordinary rules of the law were applied), the Carolina code established an organized, authoritative legal system that could have prevented massive witch-hunts. Most noteworthy of all, the Carolina code punished only malevolent, *harmful* magic. The diabolic concept of a heretical sect of witches gathering at the sabbat and being contracted to the Devil was not mentioned at all. On the other hand, the Carolina allowed the questioning of an alleged witch concerning his or her reputation and his or her gathering with other witches, and to ascertain from whom he or she had learned the art of *maleficium*. In this way the Carolina left the door open to the new cumulative concept of diabolic witchcraft.

The Imperial criminal law of the Carolina, moreover, included the *clausula salvatoria*, which sanctioned the perpetuation of the old legal customs found in the myriad territories, lordships, and cities in the empire. A witch-hunting territory could apply, under the auspices of the Carolina, to pursue a *processus extraordinarius* (a criminal procedure which ignored the ordinary rules of the law) when a crime of witchcraft was suspected, witchcraft being deemed an extraordinary offence. This permitted immediate prosecution, the rejection of a legal defence, and the use of torture. During the sixteenth and seventeenth centuries, various Imperial territories promulgated new laws concerning the conduct of witch trials. Such witchcraft laws were published in Protestant Saxony in 1572 and Catholic Bavaria in 1611/12, whereby these territorial lords and their legal bureaucracy attempted to establish overall standards to properly conduct a legal trial. This was especially pertinent to the handling of rumours, gossip, and slander, as well as to establishing clear definitions of witchcraft, sorcery, magic, necromancy, soothsaying, and other magical offences. It was also pertinent to the financing of witch trials in conjunction with the confiscation of the property of convicted witches.

In England, the first Witchcraft and Conjuration Act under Henry VIII (1542) was never put into practice as far as we know, and it was repealed in 1547. But in 1563, during the reign of Elizabeth I, a new Act was established. The offence of witchcraft was now defined as a felony. Hence, with few exceptions, hanging was the expected form of execution. One who committed the crime of killing a person with the help of *maleficium* was automatically sentenced to death. A year's imprisonment and four times at the pillory was the punishment for persons who caused damage by malevolent magic. A person already convicted once, who was charged a second time, faced the death penalty. For doing non-harmful magic, a witch received for the first offence the penalty of a year's imprisonment and four times at the pillory, whereas for a second offence they were sentenced to life imprisonment with the forfeiture of all their goods. In 1581, an Act also established the death penalty for any kind of prophesying and soothsaying regarding the Queen's reign with the help of occult practices and witchcraft. Fears of conspiracy against the security of the monarch and the realm, as well as human beings and livestock, were naturally rife in these years preceding the Spanish Armada.

Like the Carolina code, the 1563 Witchcraft Act did not explicitly mention the diabolic aspects of witchcraft—going to sabbats, making pacts, and the like. In 1604, however, the new King of England and Scotland, James I, ushered in a more severe Act. The death penalty was allowed for the first offence not only of murder but even of simply injuring humans, or for wasting, damaging, or impairing their belongings by witchcraft. Death was also allowed for the second offence of any kind of witchcraft. Moreover, the occult rituals of diabolic witchcraft were now incorporated, in that it became a capital offence to 'consult, covenant with, employ, feed or reward any evil and wicked spirit to or for any intent or purpose'. The Act also alluded to the 'familiars' or 'imps' which were thought to be the witches' helpful demonic companions, whom they were thought to feed with their blood through a teat found on the hidden parts of their bodies. Communicating with spirits and using magical arts involving parts of corpses were likewise judged a capital offence. A witchcraft Act was also launched in Scotland in 1563. Henceforth, the penal persecution of 'witchcraftis, sorsaries and necromancie' was labelled as pagan, popish, and erroneous 'superstition', and all kinds of sorcery and witchcraft were determined to be against the godly law and against the newly established reformed Kirk. In consequence, anyone practising the so-called supernatural arts and anyone who sought help by witches, sorcerers, or magicians would be sentenced to death. Here also we can find a strong, conspiratorial link between witchcraft, popish superstitions, and high treason against the ruling monarch. The latter element emerged during the notorious North Berwick witch-hunts in 1590/1.

Some of the European witchcraft legislation came in advance of the upsurge in witch trials. In the Spanish Netherlands, an ordinance published in 1592 by order of the Spanish King Philip II demanded a harsh, merciless prosecution of witchcraft, sorcery, heresy, learned and ritual magic, astrology, and soothsaying, thus targeting any alleged provider of magical arts. But obviously the Spanish King had little way of knowing about the devastating witch-hunts already underway in his realms, especially in Luxembourg, where hunts were orchestrated by the populace and local jurisdictions under the command of minor lords. Here, the provincial government, far from denouncing the belief in witchcraft, enacted several ordinances between 1563 and 1629 to gain greater control of the criminal proceedings against witchcraft and thereby restrain the freedom of manoeuvre of the various autonomous lordships under their official control. The issuing of laws against witchcraft was certainly not the only prelude to the increase in witch-hunts. But these laws showed clearly the emerging anxiety of the elite towards the new crime of witchcraft, a concern made particularly potent when joined with a dread of conspiracy.

Legal procedures differed widely across Europe. The majority of witch trials were conducted by secular criminal courts. But itinerant Franciscan and Dominican inquisitors, supported by the regional networks of their congregations, also launched witch trials during the fifteenth and early sixteenth centuries in parts of Switzerland, Burgundy, Luxembourg, and Italy. In Spain, Portugal, and the Papal State, where permanent institutionalized Inquisitions dealt with suspected witchcraft, death sentences for witchcraft were very infrequent. The inquisitorial criminal procedure had been 'invented' by inquisitors and the papacy to deal with clerical delinquents and heretical movements during the late twelfth and thirteenth centuries. From the late fifteenth century onwards secular criminal courts in continental Europe increasingly adopted the inquisitorial procedure together with a penal law code which followed Roman law. In this way a new form of inquisitorial procedure developed, one which was thought to bring greater accuracy to a system of criminal justice that was still pervaded with medieval accusatorial procedure, including ordeals, local customs, unlearned judges, orality, and arbitrariness.

The shift from accusatorial to inquisitorial criminal procedure brought significant changes both for the accusers and the accused.

The inquisitorial system was characterized by several principles. Officials such as judges initiated a criminal action against suspicious persons according to damaging rumours, eyewitnesses to a crime, or by the accusations of private persons. Witnesses and the accused were questioned to find evidence of criminal activity. These interrogations were held in secret. The depositions had to be written down for the records. Since Roman law defined torture as a valid judicial instrument to gain a confession from a highly suspect person, the inquisitorial procedure made questioning under pain of torture a vital element of criminal justice in general, especially with regard to capital offences. Only after an intensive examination of incriminating evidence, however, was the application of torture allowed.

But in dealing with the crime of witchcraft, clear evidence (for instance, two eyewitnesses) was hard to find. Dubious legal means of gaining evidence were allowed, therefore, such as the practice of 'swimming' or 'pricking' suspected witches. Swimming was essentially an ordeal by water. Suspected witches were placed in a pond or river, and if they floated it was a sign of their guilt, for God's baptismal waters had rejected them. Pricking concerned the search for insensitive Devil's marks on a suspected witch's body. Since the confession was judged to be the acme of evidence, torture appeared to be the best instrument for gaining this final and undoubted evidence of guilt. When the secular courts dealt with the crime of diabolic witchcraft, they were convinced that they struggled with Satan himself, who possessed the witch's body, helped it through the torments, and obstructed both her criminal and her spiritual confession. In that case, extracting a confession was nothing less than a sacred ritualized act with a deep religious significance, a mixture of torture, exorcism, and admission. The judge, whom demonology depicted as wise, unerring, and untouchable by demonic influences, gained the status of a father confessor with the sacred task of inspiring a contrite repentance in the accused witch and exhorting a confession of her sins. Only after a full confession was it possible to heal the damaged soul and regain her for Christendom. To overcome the Devil's hold, the accused witches had to be freed from their diabolic bonds by such practices as exorcism, by stripping off their clothes and dressing them in a new consecrated shirt, by washing them, making them drink holy water, fumigation with incense, and—if this failed to loosen the tongue of the unrepentant—the shaving or burning of every body hair, so that the executioners could search all over for hidden amulets and for the Devil's mark.

Even if these mortifying practices did not count as torture in a legal sense, they were effective in humiliating and disorienting the accused to prepare for their ultimate breakdown. We should avoid trying to establish a hierarchy of pain based on monstrous means of physical torment, though. 'Regular' methods of torture with the strappado, thumbscrews, and whipping were effective enough. 'Spanish boots' (wooden or iron instruments designed to cause crushing injuries to the shins or feet) were also used. In addition, we should not forget that torture in a wider context operated not only through humiliation and bodily suffering but in a more subtle, spiritual way. If an alleged witch showed herself or himself to be very stubborn and unrepentant, or if parts of their confession were revoked, the courts called for the help of father confessors, priests, and ministers, who were to tell the defendants that only a full confession would save them from eternal punishment. Obviously, even the strongest resistance was likely to break down after receiving such spiritual instruction. Additionally, both physical and mental torture was not limited to the interrogation room. It lingered on in the prison cells, conducted by the turnkeys, who could torment and rape the arrested persons at leisure. According to the records, some alleged witches confessed, not because of the authorized legal torture, but because of the harsh treatment at the hands of the turnkeys and the awful conditions of the gaols. For example, in 1598, a man from a small village in the Eifel region of western Germany confessed after several days in prison without any torture, only because he could not stand his mistreatment by the turnkeys anymore.

It was essential for the judges to extract a confession and to avert its revoking, because the penitent's confession contained the authentication for the subsequent trial and for the guilty verdict of the witch. In this way the judges and court members obtained a final affirmation that, without a doubt, they had not washed their hands in the blood of innocents. Instead they accomplished an honourable, blessed work of godly justice. Moreover, torture was an impressive demonstration of power. Even if the procedure was not conducted in public, everyone knew or at least heard rumours about it. This overt exchange gave witch-hunters a feared reputation. In consequence, torture and sub-sequent executions were instruments to authorize and to demonstrate domination, control, and sovereignty. The notion of torture as a remedy for a polluted soul was all part of a wider understanding of repentance and redemption culminating in execution.

Yet within the inquisitorial procedure, torture could be handled arbitrarily. Within the patchwork of territories of the Holy Roman Empire, cities and even minuscule lordships with the right to exercise high criminal justice conducted witch trials at leisure and in idiosyn-cratic fashion. Witchcraft was treated in a variety of juridical ways. Some courts clung to the *processus ordinarius*, prosecuted only harmful magic, and did not accept the notion of the sabbat. Only moderate torture was applied, which could be withstood, so that many accused were able to walk free. Other courts persecuted alleged diabolic sects of witches (rather than simply prosecuting harmful acts of magic) with the greatest zeal, believing that witchcraft was an exceptional crime, which allowed any procedure necessary to convict and destroy the wicked, Devil-worshipping accused. In these particular trials, both the lay and the learned judges seemingly believed in the existence of the sabbat gatherings, whose hidden members they had to detect by forcing the charged witches to name their accomplices through severe torment. In the electorate of Cologne, and in the prince bishoprics of Bamberg and Würzburg, only the intervention of the Imperial Cham-ber Court or the Imperial Aulic Council of the Holy Roman Empire could stop the further progress of brutal witch-hunts, but not before thousands of people had lost their lives at the stake, in prison, or under torture.

French courts also applied inquisitorial practices, with local courts of high justice first trying suspected witches by interrogating witnesses and applying torture to the accused, before then passing sentence. But, since the local courts were subject to the state control of superior appellate courts, the defendant had the right to appeal to one of the superior courts. Of these, the *parlement* of Paris covered about half of France (alongside the smaller districts of Rouen, Rennes, Bordeaux, Pau, Toulouse, Aix-en-Provence, Grenoble, and Dijon). In these cases of appeal, the accused and the records of the trial were moved to the legal seat of the *parlement*, where educated judges could modify, con-firm, or reject the local verdict. On the one hand, this legal practice resulted in very few confirmed verdicts and death penalties in cases of witchcraft. On the other hand, it sometimes resulted in the lynching of acquitted witches after their return home. The south-western Ardennes, which partly belonged to the kingdom of France, was characterized by numerous unofficial executions. Here, the *parlement* of Paris tried to assert its legal authority in the face of opposition from local officials. Because the *parlement* maintained a relatively restrained approach towards the legal treatment of witchcraft, the local inhabitants regularly resorted to lynching, stoning, and drowning suspected witches. Perhaps as many as 300 people were drowned or burned without proper trials in this part of the Ardennes and in the neighbouring French territory of Argonne from the 1580s through to the mid-seventeenth century. Notably, the French criminal justice procedure applied only to the early modern kingdom of France, not to still autonomous neighbouring territories such as Lorraine, Alsace, Franche-Comté, Savoy, Navarre, and parts of Luxembourg, which were inherited or gained by France through war and union in later years. Thus, neither the witch-hunts in Lorraine nor those in Franche-Comté should be added to the French account.

The courts of England and Scandinavia followed their own distinct systems of common law. Thus, criminal procedures in the British Isles, where the accusatorial criminal procedure of trial in front of a jury remained in use, differed from the legal practices in the Holy Roman Empire or in France. In Scotland, local kirk (church) sessions and presbyteries had no criminal jurisdiction, but they nevertheless assembled cases against suspected witches, heard witnesses, and compiled dossiers, which could be passed on to secular courts. Most Scottish witch trials were held at local criminal courts under a commission of justiciary, which had to be authorized by the Privy Council in Edinburgh. Nine-tenths of all Scottish witch trials were conducted by these local 'ad hoc' courts, which were manned with members of the local elite, clergymen, and maybe a lawyer. Likewise, circuit courts tried witches. The rest took place at the central justiciary court in Edinburgh. In Scotland an official warrant of the Privy Council or Parliament could allow torture, mostly in cases which were judged as conspiracy against the state (treason, rebellion, witchcraft). Nevertheless, especially in Scottish witch trials, at the local level, torture was applied by local investigators in many cases. It included beating, sleep deprivation, shaving of the head and body hair, and pricking for the Devil's mark. These methods of compulsion are rarely found in the records.

In English common law accused witches were usually tried by a jury. County quarter sessions, borough courts, but mostly assize tribunals dealt with witchcraft cases under secular law, whereas ecclesiastical courts were primarily occupied with the practices of cunning-folk and slanderous accusations of witchcraft. It is noteworthy that learned judges, trained in London, chaired the assize tribunals. It is likely that their growing scepticism about witch trials crept into the provincial courtrooms. Even if these judges only presided over a jury composed of local men who very often were deeply entangled in local conflicts and quarrels, they were still able to guide the sentencing of the alleged witch. Assize judges frequently showed themselves to be decidedly reluctant to pronounce a sentence of death in a number of cases of serious crimes like homicide, grand larceny, burglary, high-way robbery, rape, and witchcraft. In England, torture was only allowed by law in cases of high treason. Still, an accused person could be brought to confession by the use of leading questions, by unauthorized torture such as sleep deprivation, by threats, or by the miserable conditions in the gaols as he or she awaited trial. While the accused waited in the local gaols for the arrival of the biannual assizes, the responsible justices of the peace or bailiffs, helped by the turnkeys, had ample opportunity to provoke a confession. However, because a confession could not legally be obtained by torture, judge and jury often had to look for other signs of evidence. They found them in the alleged apparition of familiars, in spectral evidence, in the Devil's mark, and in the practices of 'pricking' and 'swimming' accused witches. Moreover, the jury could sentence a non-confessing witch by circumstantial evidence only. In Essex, the watching and walking of suspects, thereby keeping them in an exhausted nervous state, was practised in 1645–7 during England's largest witch-hunt under the inspiration of the 'Witch-finder General' Matthew Hopkins and his associate John Stearne. The accusatorial criminal process, though already diluted with inquisitorial elements in Scotland, Sweden, and Denmark, made it more difficult to launch massive witch-hunts. Yet, as the approximately 2,500 executions in Scotland show, there was no guarantee it would prevent witch trials in general.

What the Sources Tell Us

The obligation to record officially the verbal procedure of a trial gained ground in both criminal procedure systems. All over continental Europe, the British Isles, and Scandinavia, clerks, scribes, and notaries were employed to transform the oral proceedings into a written format, yet with great diversity. During the Salem witch-hunts in 1692, more than eighty different hands were involved in recording the trials. With few exceptions, these scribes had neither education nor profession as legal clerks, but were entangled personally in the Salem cases. In the courtrooms of the Holy Roman Empire or in the Habsburg provinces, trained and sworn notaries wrote up the records. Whatever type of scribe was used the legally transcribed text was expected to correspond with juridical requirements and to serve as part of the evidence against the accused. As such, the act of writing itself was an instrument of power and suppression, especially in the minds of the illiterate accused. The majority of sources providing us with information about witch trials and witch-hunts are characterized by a mixture of labelling, fabrication, construction, and embedded interpretation, a cocktail flavoured with fascinating details about occult acts. In delving into the records and reports about witchcraft, untrained readers very often lose their way in the phantasmal world of witches, sabbat orgies, werewolves, demons, fairies, familiars, and the occult, and thereby they fall prey to a highly seductive line of argument and reasoning *within* the trial records and reports.

Sources concerning the witch trials at different stages in the legal process can produce different, and sometimes contrasting, interpretations of the crime of witchcraft and its punishment. Four principles should be assiduously adhered to in decoding the records and reports of witch trials, and for understanding the information they contain in the correct historical context. First, the fact that the varying court procedures across Europe resulted in the unequal use of torture and in the production of a very diverse range of written sources. Secondly, these diverse sources can be divided into four distinct groups (leaving aside demonologies and images):

1. The legal codes, which defined the penal offence of witchcraft and enacted the procedural laws concerning witch trials.
2. The great collections of contemporaneous records which emerged from the actual legal proceedings against accused

witches (for example articles of indictment, examination of witnesses and the accused, interrogations, depositions, original notes taken during the trial, formalized transcripts, official correspondences, financial records).

3. Records and related material which stemmed from superior or appeal courts (such as petitions pro and contra witch trials, legal advice from universities / superior courts, nullity suits, libel suits, charges of misconduct against a local court and its assessors).

4. The reports produced in retrospect about witch trials and witch-hunts: pamphlets, newspapers, leaflets, chronicles, travelogues, diaries, images, tracts, or private correspondence.

Thirdly, these four groups of source material communicated with each other, so to speak. Very often we can detect a close relationship between the witchcraft stories in tracts, images, records, and reports. The acknowledged transmission of information and narratives between the different layers of construction, recording, and commenting upon witch trial proceedings and witchcraft crossed religious, social, regional, and territorial borders. Ideas, stereotypes, case studies, and examples started to disseminate all over Europe and its colonies. Thus, witchcraft is mentioned in nearly every early modern genre of source material. The fourth and final principle which should be adhered to in decoding the reports and records of witch trials is to critically evaluate the source, be it law record or trial report.

So while the written records of court procedures against suspected witches provide us with an abundance of source materials, the modern decipherer should be aware of the pitfalls. For instance, the spoken vernacular of the trial proceedings is unknown to us. The original narratives and stories, given in their colloquial speech, as well as the inflections in the speech of witnesses, the accused, the judges, the juries, and the lawyers are now all lost. Their distant voices arising from the preserved texts are faint, disguised, and formalized, and should be extracted with great care and discernment. And we should never forget that the narratives and stories within the trial records were preserved in a specific legally constructed and formalized way, which primarily served the juridical procedure of a witch trial.

Moreover, the majority of witch trial records are lost. In the electorate of Trier, for example, most trial records were destroyed when the ruling Elector forbade further witch trials in his territory after 1652. In France, the majority of local trial records are lost as well, perhaps because they were burned with the victims. Fortunately, a multitude of judgements of the appellate courts (especially from the Paris *parlement*) have survived. In England considerable numbers of trial records are missing from large parts of the country for much of the period of the witch trials, mostly because they were not routinely preserved as official records. The best surviving run of indictments is for the Home Circuit assizes, which provide accurate if basic information about witch trials between 1563 and 1712 in Essex, Hertfordshire, Kent, Surrey, and Sussex (785 indictments involving 474 alleged witches, 104 sentenced to be hanged). In Scotland, a database survey calculated that at least 3,837 people were accused of witchcraft, though accurate information about executions exists in only 205 recorded cases.

In the Holy Roman Empire clusters of trial records survive mainly in very small ecclesiastical or temporal jurisdictions. In the independent territory of St Maximin near Trier, for instance, about 280 trial records together with lists of denunciations and executions have survived. One can assume that these highly formalized contemporary copies of the original records were written down so carefully for two main reasons. First, to present them as written evidence for the zealous practice of high criminal justice, the heart of independent territorial superiority. Secondly, to hide the manipulative and cruel procedures in the St Maximin court chambers where hundreds of women and men were brought to confession and denounced long lists of their fellows in only a few days. To give another example, Schmidtheim, a jurisdiction in the northern Eifel, western Germany, included only one village with about fifty households. Yet between 1597 and 1635 about sixty-one women and men were executed as witches: in 1630–1 alone, forty-eight people perished. Thus, the death toll of the adult population peaked at 50 per cent. With about sixty trial records in the private archive of the noble family of the lord responsible, an almost complete sample of the Schmidtheim records has survived. It seems likely that certain private archives of noble families within the former frontiers of the Holy Roman Empire, but probably also in France, still contain the records of witch trials that no one yet has explored. This corresponds with the already well-known fact that in proportion to their size and population, small territories and lordships all over continental Europe experienced the worst witch-hunts. To give two further examples: in the small village of Gollion in Switzerland, which contained only fifty households, between 1615 and 1631 the lordly court condemned more than twenty-four people to be executed as alleged witches. In the Ban de la Roch in the Vosge Mountains (about 1,200 inhabitants) 174 people were accused of witchcraft between 1607 and 1630, with a minimum of eighty-three of them being executed.

Given the only patchy survival of records, we have to resort to a speculative estimation of the numbers of witch trials in Europe and its colonies, although the process of extrapolation obviously itself creates new challenges and potential misunderstandings. Over the last two centuries or so, estimates of the number of executions and trials have varied wildly. In the eighteenth century Voltaire proposed that around 100,000 died as a result of witch trials. In 1793 a Protestant German archivist calculated that the number of victims was over nine million. The radical feminist movement of the mid-twentieth century posited the genocide of thirteen million women executed as witches. The figure of twenty million burned witches circulates around the internet. In his global best-selling novel *The Da Vinci Code* (2003) Dan Brown perpetuated such inflated claims by suggesting that five million female victims were burned as witches. He portrayed this as being orchestrated by 'the Inquisition' to exterminate wise women, pagan priestesses, midwives, herbalists, and gypsies. Figures for individual countries or states have also fluctuated wildly. There is no common consensus about the geographical framework in which trials and executions should be considered. Sometimes, the statistics are based on the early modern territories, sometimes on modern national borders, sometimes on a singular stock of trial records randomly sampled in a regional archive. Thus, comparing regionally focused witchcraft research may provide us with incompatible data. Additionally, there is no proper delineation between the number of trials, the number of executions, and the number of acquittals.

So, most of these made-up extrapolations which continue to float around the internet are not trustworthy. They are for the most part based on supposition and misinformation, and often ideologically misused. Nevertheless, careful estimation by recent historians has led to the approximate figure of 40,000 to 60,000 executions for witchcraft in Europe and its colonies, and of those 20,000 to 25,000 occurred within the territories of the Holy Roman Empire. It is noteworthy that, even in this purported 'heartland' of the witch-hunts, some states like the Palatinate in south-western Germany saw not one execution. Truly accurate numbers of witch trials and executions may never be attained because of several obstacles apart from the disappearance of trial records. While popular pamphlet accounts of trials and executions are an important source, particularly for England, for example, one should avoid using the numbers of witch trials and executions found in pamphlets, chronicles, or other retrospective reports. For the most part they are not reliable unless they are verified with the help of other source material. Beyond the trial records and the reports, there are however often further genres of sources to consult like financial records, records of ecclesiastical courts, or records of local justice, where only cases of witchcraft slander were heard. Here, more traces of trials, executions, or acquittals can be found. But sometimes these records do not provide us with names, life, career, or other information vital for a statistical analysis. Another dilemma is presented by the undefined term 'victim'. Whom shall we count in our statistics? Only the burned and the hanged? Should we not take the acquitted and banished into account, who very often had been mutilated by torture and were doomed to live an outcast life? Furthermore, alleged witches who were lynched, drowned, stoned, and burned by their neighbours, committed suicide, or died of torture or during imprisonment very seldom left traces in the records.

Those studying the witch trials also have to be aware of the fabrication and falsification of trial records and reports. For example, in 1829 the French author Étienne-Léon Lamothe-Langon composed a three-volume history of the Inquisition in France (which never actually existed as an institution). Allegedly, he based his work on an in-depth analysis of archival source material. He claimed he had discovered documentary evidence of a witches' sabbat as early as 1275 and of massive witch-hunts in southern France between 1300 and 1350, organized by the Inquisition. Learned nineteenth-century witchcraft scholars like Wilhelm Gottlieb Soldan and Joseph Hansen included these 'new' results in their own respective surveys of source material concerning European witch-hunts. In this way, this apparent proof for medieval witch-hunts conducted by the Inquisition sneaked into modern witchcraft historiography. Only in the 1970s did the historians Norman Cohn and Richard Kieckhefer unmask Lamothe-Langon as an impostor who had invented his sources.

Moreover, some early modern pamphlets and leaflets deliberately created sensational news about witch trials or exaggerated the numbers of witches and their evildoings. These overt manipulations send us a warning. Most of the sources concerning witchcraft emerged from the hands of those who either were concerned with the criminalization and extirpation of reputed witches or who profited by publishing pamphlets and reports about the trials. These sources obviously provide the reader with a biased viewpoint, designed to influence events, not necessarily to document reliably the goings-on in the courtrooms.

The Witch in the Records

From the evidence we have, the vast majority of people across Europe who were accused of being witches never attempted to conduct harmful magic against their accusers. Only a small minority of those executed were of the benign variety: healers, midwives, sorcerers, and cunning-folk, etc. There were, of course, significant regional variations to this wider pattern. In parts of Hungary and Finland, for example, significant numbers of cunning-folk, diviners, and healers of various types were prosecuted as witches. It is important to bear in mind here that witch trial records have the tendency to convey the impression that the accusations of *maleficium* and witchcraft were rooted in a long-standing career of the person as a malign witch. Denunciations included in the list of charges and witness depositions might date back many years, during which time the accused person comes across as having been a notorious nuisance to the community.

Increasing numbers of defamation actions can also be found where people who had been libelled or slandered as witches tried to restore their reputation and their tainted honour. In the logic of the accusers, it was held as an admission of guilt if a defamed person did not take every step to clear their reputation. Suits concerning witchcraft defamation occurred at every level of the court hierarchy throughout Europe, from the lowest and ecclesiastical courts to the top of the appeal courts. But the decision to summon a slanderer into court was often avoided. Along with the trial costs, the danger existed of losing the case and thereby actually validating the original accusation of witchcraft. Thus, in some European regions a lost libel suit could lead to a witchcraft trial. The rich source material concerning the witchcraft trials, conducted in districts along the upper Moselle and in the Hunsrück, shows that people defamed as witches often sought to salvage their reputation by recourse to the law. But in hearing the two parties and their witnesses, more witchcraft denunciations and defamations were uttered under oath, so that in the end those bringing the suit for defamation were often subsequently tried in a criminal suit and executed as witches.

Even the most meticulous trial records never provide a truly faithful documentation of the actual events in the magistrates' parlour, the gaol, the courtroom, and/or the torture chamber. The original trial records have mostly survived as fragments, where essential parts like the depositions, the questioning, and legal advice are missing. The original transcripts, notes, and documents were often lost when the clerks summarized several legal papers into one formalized and shortened copy and destroyed the original records. In some instances these copies were archived and preserved in case bundles. At times, clerks compiled book registers, in which they carefully copied the summarized trial records. Parts of this documentation are likewise often missing. A typical record generally contains the bill of indictment, the questioning of witnesses according to the charges in the indictment, the questioning of the accused (with or without torture), including comments about their demeanour during the examination, his or her confession, and finally the verdict and notes about the execution of sentence. In England, the indictment contained basic details about the charges, and quite often the plea of the suspect, the verdict, and the punishment. In France or the Holy Roman Empire the alleged offences were listed in a bill of indictment written on behalf of a private accuser, such as an official, or else a group of accusers in the form of a witch-hunting committee. Sometimes this was accompanied by a list of witnesses, who were willing to give information about certain items in the indictment. In territories of the Holy Roman Empire or in the duchy of Luxembourg, these directives were needed to advance from one procedural stage to the next, from questioning to torture and ultimately to the verdict. In territories like the electorate of Cologne, where legally trained supervisors or commissioners appointed by the authorities were involved, the records frequently included their legal advice. Some records also preserve personal documents of the accused such as an inventory of their possessions, their testaments, or even the secret messages they managed to smuggle out of prison, but which were intercepted by officials.

Witness depositions are particularly valuable documents for providing vital information about the social relations behind and the background to the accusations and those involved. But even if a putative eyewitness might have wanted to give a 'true' account, he or she might not have been able to do so, due to the often fallacious or partial nature of memory. Testimonies of witnesses and accused were modified through the complex process of memory, by the need to tell a plausible, coherent, and compatible story, by the pressure of trial processes and interrogations, and by the legal clerks' transformation of everyday vernacular speech and dialect into Latin or a standardized, legal language. Cases of manipulating and counterfeiting statements are also not unknown. The witch found in the records is consequently a constructed, stereotyped, distorted image in which the most evil characteristics are all merged together. On the one hand, in records of single trials under accusatorial procedure, where a long defamed person was charged with witchcraft, old conflicts between the charged person and their family, neighbourhood, and community were often dredged up. Once placed under suspicion of witchcraft, the suspect's past and current misbehaviour, mischief, and deviance were all interpreted as signs of witchcraft. Previous quarrels and disagreements were re-interpreted as symptoms of a malevolent character full of evil, envy, greed, or fornication. In the trial records of massive witch-hunts, however, individual depositions lost their importance as supposed diabolic conspiracies were uncovered under torture and numerous people were named who had never before had any reputation as witches in their communities.

The *confessions* of convicted witches must be treated with even more critical care. Apart from torture, even confessions that were apparently willingly given might have been induced by fear and threat. In some cases, accused witches confessed to their crimes as a form of suicide by proxy, because even an acquittal would deliver the accused to the life of an outcast destined to live and die without the support of family, neighbours, and the community. And some of those who confessed without torture showed signs of mental illness such as dementia and infirmity, which were indeed sometimes recognized at the time.

In general, the contents of confessions are usually the outcome of what we would today regard as 'brainwashing'. At the very least, they reveal the influence of the formalized interrogatories used in the questioning. In this way, amazingly uniform confessions were recorded, with similar-sounding narratives. Consider the questions compiled by judges in Colmar, a city in Alsace:

> How long have you been a witch? Why did you become a witch? How did you become a witch and what happened on that occasion? Who is the one you chose to be your incubus (demon lover)? What was his name? What was the name of your master among the evil demons? What was the oath you were forced to render him? How did you make this oath and what were the conditions? What fingers were you forced to raise? Where did you consummate your union with your incubus? What demons and what other humans participated (at the sabbat)? What food did you eat there? How was the sabbat banquet arranged? Were you seated at the banquet? What music was played and what dances did you dance? What did your incubus give you for your intercourse? What devil's mark did your incubus make on your body? What injury have you done to such and such a person, and how did you do it? Why did you inflict this injury? How can you relieve this injury? What herbs or other methods can you use to cure these injuries? Who are the children on whom you have cast a spell? And why have you done it? What animals have you bewitched to sickness or death and why did you commit such acts? Who are your accomplices in evil? Why does the devil give you blows in the night? What is the ointment with which you rub your broomstick made of? How are you able to fly through the air? What magic words do you utter then? What tempests have you raised and who helped you to produce them? What plagues of vermin and caterpillars have you created? What do you make these pernicious creatures out of and how do you do it? Has the devil assigned a limit to the duration of your evil-doing?

Sometimes the interrogatories are missing in the preserved trial records, but in looking at the uniformity of confessions, we can safely assume their existence. It was not only due to torture, threats, interrogatories, and suggestive questions that uniform confessions were created. Witches' confessions were read out loud, so every bystander would have heard the essential elements before the execution. Also, sermons, tracts, and pamphlets helped make the matter of witchcraft common knowledge. Within small face-to-face communities, narratives about mischievous witches were disseminated through imaginative gossip. Imprisoned suspects would have heard from outside as well as from each other about the questions they could expect as well as the requisite stories of confession. Thus, even seemingly individualistic elements in confessions need to be scrutinized carefully. In addition to this, many of the more imaginative scenarios in the confessions which dealt with the occult, with *maleficia*, *beneficia*, sabbats, flight, shape shifting, and coitus with the Devil predominantly arose from the fantasies of the interrogators, not from the accused.

Along with the necessary confession, the questioning officer or clerk in charge demanded the naming of alleged partners in crime. Based on the concept of the witches' sabbat, where hundreds and thousands of Devil worshippers supposedly met, the accused were expected to give a list of names of as many fellow witches as possible. Even if the reality of supposed sabbats was not accepted by the courts, there were questions about accomplices, pupils, and tutors of the supposed witch. This energized the witch-hunts by providing the court with new suspects. It is not surprising, given the cruelty and duration of torture, the use of suggestive questions, and the suggestion of named accomplices, that long lists of denunciations frequently emerged. In St Maximin, between 1586 and 1596, a register was compiled, in which roughly 1,400 people from the surrounding villages and the city of Trier were denounced as witches. In the massive witch-hunts in the Lutheran city of Lemgo (in the county of Lippe), with peaks around 1560, 1590, 1630, and 1660, approximately 250 people were killed at the stake. Witchcraft denunciations were systematically noted down in the town's notorious so-called 'black book', which was publicly burned at the marketplace in 1715, thus officially ending the witch-hunts there. In the small city of Molsheim (in Alsace) at least 159 people were executed as witches at the end of the sixteenth and the beginning of the seventeenth century. They were registered in two so-called 'Blood books'. Whereas the first one has not survived, the second one lists 113 victims, including thirty-three juveniles and children, executed as witches in 1629/30.

Financial records such as those from the duchy of Bar in Lorraine (now France) occasionally listed the names and dates of imprisoned, sentenced, and executed witches, but their marginal entries often provide no further information about the social background and detailed procedure of the trial. Even seemingly complete financial records which on first inspection appear to offer no hint of a witch trial can be misleading. Sometimes the officials did not register it because the sentenced person possessed nothing to confiscate. And local trial records, no matter how substantial they seem to be, still present primarily the specific perspective of the prosecutors. Witnesses, self-testimonies, and confessions (forced or not) are of course very appealing sources, not least because they are filled with apparently fascinating material about the times in which they were made. But on the whole they are neither trustworthy reports about the events that led to prosecutions and executions nor transparent documentaries of 'facts'.

With the records and related material from superior appeal courts we are confronted with new perspectives. Sometimes women and men charged as witches could withstand torture and had to be released until further evidence allowed a second accusation. On release, they then often brought forward nullity suits and petitions to the superior appeal courts (e.g. the Imperial Aulic Court, the Imperial Chamber Court, ducal chanceries in Germany, the French *parlements*, the provincial court in Luxembourg) accusing the local trial courts of abuse and the misuse of torture. Moreover, they would sue for the reduction of inflated trial costs, for nullification, rehabilitation, and restoration of their honour. In these documents, we are given, in fact, a look behind the curtains of the juridical theatre in the courtroom. Here, the victims, who had been questioned as alleged witches, are very revealing about what was going on in prisons, torture chambers, and courtrooms. Even if these documents have to be read with caution, they do, nevertheless, provide us with stories that are a useful counterpoint to the 'victor's perspective' presented in the official local court records.

The Spread of the Trials: The Influence of Reportage

News about diabolic witches and witch trials spread rapidly across social, religious, political, regional, and language borders through the expansion of print media. The proliferation of printing presses, trade routes, and postal services allowed for the speedy dissemination of broadsheets and pamphlets. The shape, length, topics, and illustrative detail of these publications varied across Europe. Some pamphlets and broadsheets recounted details of trials based upon access to trial records. Others told stories about possessions, *maleficium*, or tempests invoked by witchcraft that drew on hearsay and invention. Since these were often commercial products, publishers wanted to arouse curiosity, shock, and wonder with a cocktail of crime, sex, and horror. Some were also vehicles for pedagogic instruction, teaching their readers and listeners lessons concerning morals, religion, and honourable behaviour. The configuration of both differed depending on the respective political and religious environments in which they were sold and distributed. While cheap news-sheets and pamphlets about witch trials present a mix of fiction and facts, falsification, and manipulation, nevertheless, with their elements of propaganda and polemic, they offer deep insight into contemporary *perceptions* of witchcraft and witch trials. Thus, like trial records, these retrospective reports tell a story of multi-layered mentalities, fears, interpretations, and realities.

In France, fewer illustrated broadsheets about sensational witch trials have survived, though we do have a number of leaflets and pamphlets dealing with cases of diabolic possession and Jesuit exorcisms. The notorious case of the Catholic priest Urbain Grandier, who was burned at the stake for having bewitched the young members of a nunnery in 1634, was detailed in an influential, illustrated broadsheet. It should be remembered that sixteenth-century France was shaken by wars of religion, wherein the Protestant Huguenots were demonized by their Catholic adversaries, especially by fanatic Jesuits like the Spaniard Maldonado, whose sermons and tracts were consulted by Pierre de Lancre and Martin Del Rio. Religious conflict nourished the idea of godless conspiracies, a topic which could easily be linked to the idea of clandestine witches, even in high places. For the Holy Roman Empire we know of more than 120 broadsheets which dealt with spectacular single witch trials or massive witch-hunts. The authors are usually unknown, and in order to circumvent censorship, some of their statements, particularly in the context of confessional conflicts, are phrased enigmatically. The best example is a broadsheet dealing with the well-known hunts in the archbishopric of Trier (printed in 1593, 1594, and thereafter). Close reading shows that the author of the accompanying tract and the engraver were from a Protestant milieu. They used the example of a major Catholic hunt to explain witchcraft as a horrid crime related directly to popery, and performed mainly by weak women, Catholic priests, monks, nuns, and even members of the Catholic elite. The message was that Protestants, as the true Christians, should have no fear of devilish attacks through witchcraft. By telling the most appalling stories, illustrated leaflets and pamphlets concerning witchcraft helped to establish the fear of witches and to trigger further trials. News about successful witch-hunts also legitimized the ruling authorities, showing that they were godly soldiers, acting against the enemies of creation. At such times broadsheets give the impression of policy statements.

Each broadsheet not only tells the story of trials and executions, but shows us how ideas of witchcraft circulated between the assorted media, crossing from one publication to another over time. For example, the confession of an old midwife from Dillingen (in the bishopric of Augsburg), named Walburga Hausmännin, who was executed on 2 September 1587, was transferred into the hands of a printer. The old woman was forced to confess under torture to the most horrid crimes, such as killing forty-four children by witchcraft, the attempted murder of the Bishop, the invoking of tempests, carnal coitus with the Devil, and desecration of the sacred host. Published as a leaflet, the confession gained great publicity because of its spectacular nature. Copies from her confession were found in the correspondence of neighbouring Lutheran princes as well as in the Fugger newsletters, which were digests of business information and other items of interest produced by the Fugger family, who were wealthy southern German merchants.

The case of the supposed werewolf Peter Stump in the Rhineland demonstrates quite clearly how regions in Europe could share a common interest in witchcraft belief that spanned religious and social borders. In 1589 several broadsheets appeared in the Holy Roman Empire and the Netherlands, which told the story of Stump, a notorious sorcerer and werewolf who had apparently been executed near Cologne in the same year. No official trial records have survived, although there are of course the pamphlet reports (as well as some short contemporary diary and chronicle references). However, the case gained great publicity all over Europe. Pamphlets concerning the execution of Peter Stump were published in London (1590) and Copenhagen (1591). The case appealed to Protestant propaganda. Witchcraft and popery were portrayed as two sides of the same coin of superstition and pagan lore. Thus, the story of Peter Stump from Catholic Cologne with its details of sodomy, fornication, incest, rape, and cannibalism presented the ugly distorted face of popery.

In 1599/1600, Martin Del Rio likewise included the confessional narratives of a monk from the Ardennes named Jean del Vaulx in his *Investigations into Magic*. Del Vaulx, who was executed for witchcraft in 1597, had referred to the famous witch-hunts in Trier and to the 'new Faustus', Dr Dietrich Flade. As vice-rector of the University of Trier, Flade was one of the highest-ranking victims of the witch-hunts, having confessed and been executed in 1589. Del Vaulx fabricated having been under the diabolic tutorship of Flade in Trier. The cases of Jean Del Vaulx and Dietrich Flade became key cases for Del Rio. Del Vaulx's sabbath narratives were used in the spectacular and widely reported witch trial in 1600 of a family of vagrants, the Pappenheimers. In Munich, some Bavarian privy counsellors were eager to trigger a new witch-hunt through the Pappenheimer denunciations. Applying brutal torture, confessions were gained which partly resembled the confession of Del Vaulx. Bavarian Jesuits reported the case to Del Rio, who included a report about the Pappenheimer trial as an outstanding proof for the existence of the witches' crimes in a new edition of his handbook. Simultaneously, a leaflet was published with detailed illustrations, which showed the different steps of the extremely cruel execution of the six suspects. A Dutch and an English translation appeared soon after, which transmitted the story about the Pappenheimers across Protestant Europe.

About one hundred pamphlets concerned with witch trials were published in England from the 1550s through to the early eighteenth century. Because of the loss of the majority of trial records, these pamphlets, some of which contain more than a hundred pages, provide much of the detailed information we have about the English witch trials. They offered notably more text and relied less on illustrations than the broadsheets from the Holy Roman Empire. In their diversity of length and style they were also produced for a wider, more educated readership. One of the first pamphlets appeared in 1566 and dealt with witch trials in Chelmsford, Essex. It was supposedly based on the confessions of three women heard at the assizes. The quasi-devilish pact with familiars and the witch's mark (the teat to suckle the familiars) were mentioned, and a hint of a link between witchcraft and popery was given. This is significant in view of the fact that until the end of the sixteenth century, English indictments were concerned largely with simple *maleficium* in rural communities and not with the continental diabolic aspects of witchcraft. This first pamphlet was followed by two more dealing with witch trials in Chelmsford (1579 and 1589), which were apparently based on the trial records. Links between trial and pamphlet can easily be traced in the 1582 case of the St Osyth witches in Essex. The justice of the peace Brian Darcy, who examined the accused, seems to be the prototype of later English witch-hunters. Rumours existed that his father had died by witchcraft. Darcy showed himself acquainted with the details of dia-bolic witchcraft and slipped this knowledge into the questioning of the accused. In the aftermath, he published a 'true and just record' of the St Osyth trials.

The report of the famous Pendle witches at Lancaster 1612 was compiled and published in 1613 by the clerk in charge, Thomas Potts, although the gathering of evidence and the orchestration of the trials had rested in the hands of the justice of the peace, Roger Nowell. The influence of King James's *Demonology* on the report of the Lancaster witches is obvious. In his 1591 publication the Scottish King had employed ideas of diabolic witchcraft coming from continental demonologists. Subsequently, the pamphlet concerning the Pendle Witches was used in 1618 by Michael Dalton in his much printed handbook for justices of the peace, *The Country Justice*. Therein, relying on the Lancaster trials, he propagated the belief that the presence of familiars and the witch's mark were legitimate evidence to identify a witch. In 1627, Richard Bernard published his *Guide to Grand Jury Men*, likewise using English pamphlets as well as Del Rio's tract in con-structing the offence of witchcraft. Since Del Rio had written the definitive handbook on witchcraft, which included the previous ideas of Institoris, Bodin, Rémy, and Binsfeld, Bernard needed nothing more to become well acquainted with continental views of the witches' crimes and their prosecution. Clearly, these examples show how in England ideas about *maleficium* on the one hand and diabolic witchcraft on the other were blended in a cocktail which served as a resource for future witch-hunters.

Continental witchcraft ideologies entered the British Isles in other ways too. In 1584/5, for example, the Jesuit John Weston and some companions were sent to England in order to support English Catholics. By then, the Jesuits already had experience with children who needed exorcism because of bewitchment and possession. News about spectacular exorcisms and witch trials flowed via the annual reports given by each Jesuit settlement in Europe. Consequently, the eager missionaries started with exorcisms, once they set foot on English soil. A young Puritan divine, John Darrell, seemed to be inspired by this Catholic armoury against the Devil and started a career as a Puritan exorcist. He focused his activities on girls and boys who were apparently possessed and tormented by demons that wicked witches had sent into their bodies. Cases in 1586, 1596, and 1597 are known, in which Darrell played a crucial role. A commission by order of the Archbishop of Canterbury declared Darrell to be a fraud and had him imprisoned for a year. However, a battle of pamphlets followed the affair, in which Darrell defended his actions.

More pamphlets were published in which similar stories about the possession of children were told, possessions that could be cured only if the witch who had invoked the possession was detected and could be made to reverse his or her bane. The inflicted child could name his or her tormentor, as the witch appeared in a spectral apparition only visible to the child. In this way cases of apparent child possession led to witch trials and executions. Pamphlet stories influenced other cases, as when children and their instructors used the descriptions of the behaviour of the possessed they found in these publications to imitate their demeanour. In two notorious cases of simulated possession, that of William Somers, of Nottingham, in 1597, and of Anne Gunter of North Moreton, Oxfordshire, in 1604, it was found that both used an influential 1593 pamphlet on the trial of the witches of Warboys in Huntingdonshire to get more information on how to behave like a possessed person. Both were unmasked as frauds. In 1612, three women from the parish of Salmesbury were accused by Grace Sowerbutts, a 14-year-old girl. Her fantasies about meetings on a sabbat had been implanted by a Catholic seminary priest well acquainted with the concepts of diabolic witchcraft. Additionally, the very well-published affairs concerning the possessed 'Bilson Boy' in the 1620s have to be interpreted within confessional debates, since the boy came from a Catholic household and had been exorcized by recusant priests. In short, the network of Jesuit and seminary priests, even in England, may have strengthened the efficacy of using bewitched children to act as prominent witnesses against suspected witches. In England, the so-called 'possession pamphlets', followed by debates and by the detection of frauds, were giving rise to more and more scepticism among the legal and religious elite. However, pamphlets and tracts implanted a particular pattern of persecution via the accusations of children, in Scotland, Sweden, and New England. The case of the Goodwin children in Boston in 1688, for example, showed similar characteristics to the cases of possession told in the Warboys witches pamphlet. And memories of the Boston case, as well as the story of the great Swedish witch-hunts in Mora (1668–76), in which the accusations of children played a vital role, helped fuel the infamous Salem witch trials in 1692.

The End of the Witch Trials?

Most territories in western Europe saw the end of large-scale and massive witch-hunts during the mid-seventeenth century. Just as the interplay of many circumstances was necessary to trigger witch trials, likewise many factors contributed to their decline. Even during the peak of witch-hunting in western Europe, some Imperial cities and the Palatinate saw none or very few executions (see Table 5). In the Holy Roman Empire, the Imperial Chamber Court and the Imperial Aulic Court suspended witch-hunts in Franconia and elsewhere around the 1630s. Some kings, princes, magistrates, and authorities opposed witch trials because they caused discord, turmoil, and economic decline. Pragmatic decisions were taken. Some territories forbade the practice of reading confessions aloud in public, including accounts of sabbats and lists of accomplices. Around 1653, the new elector in Trier, Carl Caspar von der Leyen, issued a secret order to stop the witch trials. He also probably ordered the destruction of most of the witch trial records, and so suspended further investigations. The Imperial city of Rothenburg ob der Tauber forbade any kind of

Table 5 The absence of witch-hunts in the Holy Roman Empire (selection)

Territory / city state / prince-bishopric	Main phases	Known executions
Baden-Durlach, margravate	1560–1631	6
Frankfurt/Main, imperial city		0
Nürnberg, imperial city		6
Palatinate, electorate	1560–1622	0
Rothenburg ob der Tauber, imperial city		3
Schwäbisch Hall, imperial city		0
Ulm, imperial city		4

witchcraft slander, while Nuremberg suppressed the dissemination of a leaflet that called for ruthless witch-hunts. Limiting communications about witch confessions, and suppressing rumours, denunciations, and propaganda served well to end the trials.

In general, early modern state building ensured centralized and close supervision and control of local courts. State monopoly over jurisdiction meant that the violation of sovereign prerogatives by witch-hunting committees, local bailiffs, and minor lords could no longer be tolerated. Witchcraft laws were repealed or suppressed, for example in France (1682), Prussia (1714), England (1736), in the Habsburgian Lands (1755, 1766), in Poland (1776), and in Sweden (1779).

It is important to note that sceptical voices can be heard throughout the period of the witch trials, even if they were anonymous or under-cover. Witch trials as well as massive witch-hunts produced, along with their inherent scandals, a 'crisis of confidence'. In the long run, legal as well as intellectual scepticism concerning the effectiveness and legitimacy of witch trials grew. Popular demands for prosecutions were increasingly met with caution, deliberate inaction, and refusal.

But enlightened thought, religious tolerance, state control, and better welfare could not eradicate a magical belief system that labelled so-called evil people as the disorderly others, as witches. In eastern Europe, for example in Russia, Poland, and Hungary, the peak of witch-hunting largely occurred after 1650. With around 3,000 witch trials after 1700, Hungary experienced far more executions during the so-called Enlightenment than in previous centuries. Today, European courts no longer prosecute 'witches', but the belief in the power of magic and the fear of witchcraft continues, triggered once more by the influence of the media. And in a global perspective, the African period of witch trials seemingly has just begun.

5

The Witch and Magician in European Art

Charles Zika

Witchcraft represented a new and intriguing subject for artists around the turn of the sixteenth century. Belief in men and women who had the power to manipulate magical forces in order to harm individuals and society—men and women who went under the name of magicians, sorcerers, cunning-men and -women, crystal gazers, healers, and diviners—was widespread throughout Europe in the Middle Ages and found expression in different forms of literature and visual imagery. But from the third decade of the fifteenth century more intense and focused discussion developed about the basis of such magical and sorcery practices. Harmful forms of magic and sorcery in particular were thought to depend for their effectiveness on a pact carried out with the Devil, and involved particular rites and ceremonies attended by groups of individuals who agreed to carry out the Devil's work. Around the turn of the fifteenth century, an increasing number of works on the subject were published and circulated widely amongst a literate readership using the relatively new technology of print. Trials from the 1420s and 1430s in Switzerland, as well as a series of treatises targeting the activity of Waldensian heretics in the western Alps in the 1430s and in northern France in the 1460s, represent the origins of this new diabolically based view of witchcraft. But it was printing that was instrumental in circulating, promoting, and broadening the reception of such views. During the first decade of the sixteenth century, leading artists (primarily from southern Germany, and therefore closely linked to the burgeoning printing industry) picked up on these ideas and began to search for a visual language to give pictorial form to this mixture of folkloric, legal, and theological speculation and discourse.

The New Visual Imagery of Witchcraft, 1490–1590

The most influential art work for the representation of witchcraft over the next century and more was a woodcut created in 1510 by the south German artist Hans Baldung (nicknamed Grien), commonly called *Witches Preparing for the Sabbath Flight*. Created by a precocious artist in his late 20s, and using the new technique of chiaroscuro to heighten the eerie atmosphere of his scene, Baldung's woodcut depicted a trio of naked women symbolically united by a triangle of cooking sticks positioned around a seething pot. The thick vapours filled with animal shapes that escape from the pot mix with the billowing clouds of smoke and vapour above; and through it a naked witch rides a goat backwards, transporting a pot with her cooking stick. The central scene is clearly a ritual involving cooking and sacrifice, and its transgressive nature is highlighted by the naked female bodies, the contrasting animal forms, the skulls and bones that litter the forest floor, the numerous allusions to the inversion of Christian norms, and the eerie forest setting. Baldung's woodcut successfully established a visual model for witchcraft that defined it as the practices of a female group, linked both to the uncontrolled sexual nature of women and to malevolent and chthonic (underworld) powers. The salves and potions the witches prepared in their pots and cauldrons defined witchcraft as quintessentially women's work.

For this extremely influential woodcut, which survives in three chiaroscuro and many black and white copies, Hans Baldung drew on a 1506 chiaroscuro drawing created four years earlier by his fellow south German artist, Albrecht Altdorfer. Altdorfer's drawing also depicts a group of women, all but one of them naked, engaged in some sort of group ritual activity in the forest. In this case, however, their rituals are clearly linked not only to the large circular vessel and animal skull on the ground but also to a group of animal riders ascending through a trail of smoke above the trees. The scene appears to be a version of the night ride of witchcraft, for which the witches are preparing salves to smear on their bodies. It is also probably related to contemporary stories and depictions of the Furious Horde and Wild

Ride—the cavalcade of demonic spirits and the souls of the dead. Baldung may well have become familiar with Altdorfer's drawing in the workshop of his master, Albrecht Dürer, where Baldung had lived and worked as an apprentice from 1503 to 1507.

It was certainly in Dürer's workshop that Baldung would have also seen another work which helped fix the view of witchcraft he promoted in his 1510 woodcut, Dürer's own engraving, *Witch Riding Backwards on a Goat*. Created around 1500, the engraving represented a very complex view of witches and their power. The print drew on a combination of classical and Italian models, on humanist ideas, and on the popular iconography of carnival. While Aphrodite Pandemos, the earthly Venus and goddess of lust, may have been the model for the woman riding a goat, the winged putti (naked, chubby male children) referenced the cults of Priapus and Dionysius found in fifteenth-century Italian works, and the Capricornian goat alluded to the association of witches and the god Saturn in much late medieval planetary literature and illustration. Dürer's call on classical references and the humanist readings he accessed through the works of Renaissance scholars such as Willibald Pirckheimer (1470–1530) were here balanced and enriched with local south German traditions. His overt reference to a backward ride on a goat, represented in the reversal of his monogram signature, drew on cultural motifs and practices associated with the vices, carnival culture, and cuckoldry, to represent a wild and powerful woman who appropriates male power and reverses the proper gender order.

Hans Baldung combined these views of witchcraft as gendered, transgressive, and highly sexualized with allusions to the Wild Ride of witches and stories of the Furious Horde in his 1510 woodcut to create an image of witchcraft which would influence artists over the next century and more. By the time of his so-called Freiburg drawings in 1514 Baldung had also developed a highly sexualized view of witchcraft in which the powers of witches were reduced to the fiery vapours, gases, and lusts that emanated from their bodies. While these almost pornographic chiaroscuro images were clearly meant to represent the seductive attractions of female sexuality for male viewers, their existence as one-off drawings meant that access to them was quite limited. But artists in the region were certainly very aware of them, as is clear from the four surviving copies of one of Baldung's drawings of 1514, and also from the wild, entranced, and tangled bodies of witches in a contemporary chiaroscuro drawing by an artist signing himself as 'HF' (possibly the Basel artist Hans Frank).

The influence of Baldung's 1510 woodcut, with its witches grouped around a cauldron or cooking on a fire, survived well into the seventeenth century, and did so through the circulation of various prints as book illustrations. The first and most important of these was a quite crude print that probably originated in Baldung's Strasbourg workshop. It was used by the Strasbourg printer Johann Grüninger, to illustrate the 1509 sermons of the Strasbourg cathedral preacher Johann Geiler of Kaysersberg that were collected by the Franciscan Johann Pauli for a work first published in 1516 called *The Ants*. The print appeared again in the edition of 1517, and over the next twenty-five years in three additional works and five editions. By the mid-1540s it must have become one of the most widely recognized images of witchcraft for German book readers. The scene depicted a trio of witches in a landscape strewn with skulls and bones, two of them naked and holding up flaming vessels, and physically and symbolically linked to a third woman on a stool. Many details in the woodcut, and in the story on which Geiler's sermon was based, suggest that this was meant to represent a wild sexual ride, but one ultimately based on illusion.

Versions of the scene continued to be reproduced throughout the sixteenth century. One woodcut that was clearly modelled on it—except that it now also included a witch riding a goat through the sky, as in Baldung's woodcut of 1510—appeared as a title page in three publications of the 1570s and 1580s. It went on to appear in a newssheet of 1571 written by a Catholic priest from Alsace named Rheinhard Lutz; in a new 1575 German translation of Ulrich Molitor's work of 1489, *On Female Witches and Diviners*; and in a short 1583 treatise on witchcraft, *The Devil's Hoodwink*, written by a Lutheran pastor active in the state of Hesse, Paulus Frisius. A third version of the same subject served as the title-page woodcut to part one of the second German edition of Johann Weyer's *On the Tricks of Demons* (1566), and subsequently appeared in the vernacular German translations printed in 1575 and 1586. In 1582 it again served as a title-page woodcut in a pamphlet published by the Marburg lawyer Abraham Saur about the execution of a woman convicted of witchcraft in Marburg in the same year. Its longevity and significance is demonstrated by its influence on the Dutch painter Jacques de Gheyn II's depictions of witchcraft in the first decade of the seventeenth century (of which more below).

What must have been especially challenging and even shocking in this new iconography of witchcraft was the way it transformed the common depiction of the medieval magician. Commonly clothed in the manner of a scholar or priest, and reading from a book of magic within the protected space of a magic circle, the male magician and custodian of esoteric and learned knowledge was replaced with the naked bodies of female witches with their pots, sticks, and cooking utensils, riding goats and engaging in bodily, rather than mental or spiritual, activities. Another woodcut produced at about the same time as Baldung's woodcut bears witness to this transformation, and also to the manner in which the new crime of witchcraft conflated learned or ritual magic with various different forms of village sorcery and malefice. The creator of the woodcut was the Swabian artist Hans Schäufelein, who had also been an apprentice in Dürer's workshop in the same years as Baldung, and was commissioned to illustrate a revised edition of the law manual, *The New Layman's Guide*, written by a Bavarian administrative official, Ulrich Tengler, and his canon lawyer son, Christoff. Christoff had introduced a new section on the punishment of the magical arts, 'On heresy, divining, black magic, sorcery and witches', and Schäufelein's woodcut depicted these arts. Around a central male magician, dressed in ritual garb and standing within a magic circle with a book and sword in his hands, are different forms of sorcery or magic practised by village women. These include stealing milk, maiming men, conjuring storms and chiromancy (palmistry), activities designated as diabolical by virtue of the strategically positioned demons hovering above several of the women and also by their association with witches riding goats through the sky or engaged in sexual intercourse with a devil. The ultimate message of Schäufelein's image matches Tengler's text: all forms of sorcery, magic, and witchcraft are to be condemned, and their outcome, as the woodcut also illustrates, will be eternal punishment in the fires of Hell.

Another major change from medieval iconography that Baldung's 1510 woodcut registered was that the new scourge of witchcraft not only involved individual women and men but was a *group* activity, and one orchestrated by the Devil. While images of individual witches were depicted, they were more frequently represented as members of a group. This reflected the new view of witchcraft as a sect that met together on periodic occasions for what was sometimes called a sabbat, a view articulated by a growing number of theologians, jurists, and social commentators in the second half of the fifteenth and the early sixteenth century. It also rested on myths from popular folklore such as the 'Wild Ride' and the 'Furious Horde' (on which, more below). The series of melancholy paintings by the court painter to the Elector of Saxony, Lucas Cranach the Younger, give expression to such connections. In all four paintings in the series, completed between 1528 and 1533, Cranach included a complex scene above and behind the female and winged figure of Melancholy. Within a thick cloud in the sky above a craggy landscape, Cranach depicted a cavalcade of riders on a range of different wild beasts. In one case the riders appear as military standard bearers raising their banners on high. Others resemble a hunting party moving in for the kill. In two other cases they are shown escorting a male captive, decked out in the fashionable dress of the contemporary nobleman or mercenary, in stark contrast to the naked bodies of his female captors. In these paintings Cranach links melancholy to the imaginative phantasms and dark desires of the human psyche, and these are identified with the moral disorder represented by witchcraft. Witchcraft is clearly not an individual activity; it is portrayed as a group of women in concert, flaunting the sexuality of their female bodies as they ride wild animals across the night sky.

In the first half of the sixteenth century this new iconography of witchcraft became established in the cultural and printing centres of south-west Germany and Switzerland, under the impact of the treatises and pamphlets published in these centres and also through the close collaboration between authors, artists, publishers, and printers in cities like Nuremberg, Augsburg, Strasbourg, Bern, and Basel. From the 1560s, however, the iconography of witchcraft was enriched by elements found in earlier French and Dutch illustration. This reflected a new stage in witchcraft discourse after the massive disruptions of the Reformation, the publication of new treatises such as Johann Weyer's *On the Tricks of Demons* (1563) and the increase in witchcraft accusations in the south-west of the Holy Roman Empire and along the Rhine. It was above all Pieter Bruegel the Elder (*c*.1525/9–69) who depicted witches riding brooms—an instrument that appears in earlier French illustrations of the Waldensian heresy from the 1450s and in some French Dances of Death—rather than the cooking forks found in south German iconography. In Bruegel's drawing of *St James and the Magician Hermogenes* that survives in a 1565 engraving by Pieter van der Heyden, witches appear as part of the monstrous demonic forces over which the magician exercises control. One rides a broom over a cauldron and up a chimney, possibly to join others riding goats and dragons through the sky, while engaged in violent battles and wreaking physical destruction and shipwreck on the earthlings below. A broom-riding witch is also found in the companion image, *The Fall of the Magician Hermogenes*.

Paintings specifically depicting witches and magicians seldom appear before 1600, although there are notable exceptions to this rule such the Melancholia series of Lucas Cranach, a 1526 painting of the biblical witch of Endor by the north Netherlandish artist Jacob Cornelisz van Oostsanen, and a Dosso Dossi painting of *Circe and her Lovers in a Landscape* of *c*.1525. These exceptions aside, the iconography of witchcraft was gradually established throughout the sixteenth century by means of prints and became widely known through the republication of these prints and their copies as book title pages or illustrations. An indication of the establishment of this iconography is the illustration of classical witches such as Circe, Medea, Pamphile, and Meroe. From the 1530s they begin to adopt more of the new visual cues for witchcraft, such as nudity, dishevelled hair, and cauldrons. In the second half of the sixteenth century, moreover, the increased publication of pamphlets and broadsheets as part of the new interest in sensational news-reporting leads to a concomitant increase in images of witches being punished for their crimes. Through the visualization of such punishment viewers are able to participate symbolically in the struggles against witchcraft and the calls to purify cities and territories from their diabolical attacks. The so-called 'Wonder-Book', compiled by the Zurich pastor Johann Jakob Wick between 1560 and 1587, is one of the richest examples of the manner in which such images were produced and often recycled as part of this contemporary interest in news of terrible events. There are well over thirty hand-drawn illustrations of stories and reports involving witchcraft in Wick's collection, some of them copies of woodcuts found in near-contemporary broadsheets, others seemingly quite original, but all testifying to the manner in which witchcraft had become part of the literary and visual vocabulary of much of Europe over the previous seventy to eighty years.

Witchcraft as Religious and Social Threat, 1590–1640

From the early seventeenth century, as witchcraft gradually became more widely accepted as a subject for painting and the centre of gravity for the production of images of witchcraft moved decisively from southern Germany to Flemish and Dutch artistic centres, the iconography of witchcraft also began to take on new features. Jacques de Gheyn II in the northern Netherlands, Franz Francken II and David Teniers II in Antwerp, the Polish artist Jan Ziarnko working in Paris—these artists created images of witchcraft that were in some critical respects quite different from those of the previous century and more in line with the descriptions of witchcraft found in the demonologies of men like Jean Bodin, Nicholas Remy, Martin Del Rio, and Peter Binsfeld, as discussed in Chapter 3. A number of new emphases become evident in these images: first, the depiction of witchcraft as a mass phenomenon involving large numbers of women, practising a wide range of magical rituals and destructive activities with the overt support of diabolical powers; and secondly, an emphasis on the innate cruelty and murderous nature of witches and their rituals.

A number of prints from the 1590s prefigure these developments. These include a 1591 broadsheet published by a leading Augsburg *Briefmaler* (sheet-colourer) Georg Kress that reports the case of approximately 300 women in the territory of Jülich, western Germany, who transformed themselves into wolves after making a pact with the Devil and killed numerous people and cattle. Sections of the broadsheet woodcut show these transformed wolves attacking carriage drivers and cattle, tearing apart bodies and ripping out organs, consuming human flesh, and strewing body parts. Other sections depict a group of women clustered around a male devil who distributes the magic girdles that will transform them into wolves, while they profess their obedience to him. Kress's broadsheet woodcut was no doubt influenced by widely circulating reports and illustrations of the case of Peter Stump, mentioned in Chapter 4. Stump was a peasant from the Cologne area who in 1589 confessed he had killed sixteen people as a werewolf, a transformation he achieved by means of a girdle received from the Devil. Despite the similarities in the two cases, Kress's print stands out by virtue of the depiction of mass violence and group rituals presided over by the Devil. The widespread integration of the Devil into scenes depicting the activities of witches becomes prominent from the 1590s. This can be seen in the title-page woodcut created for the 1591 and 1592 German-language editions of *A Treatise concerning the Confessions of Sorcerers and Witches* by Peter Binsfeld, suffragan Bishop of Trier. The original Latin edition was published in Trier. The two German translations with the title-page woodcut, both published in Munich, were used to support a Bavarian campaign to eradicate witchcraft and to counter widespread scepticism. The woodcut depicted witches paying homage and making sexual advances to a horned devil, concluding a demonic pact with a stylishly dressed demonic lover, lowering a child into a cauldron to be cooked, as well as more traditional iconography such as riding a goat through the air and cooking up a storm. Just like the treatise itself, it emphasized the key role of the Devil in acts of witchcraft, and also highlighted its cruel treatment of children. Although only six witches are depicted in the print, their engagement in different activities gives the impression of the massive threat they pose for society.

Another print to demonstrate a quite decisive break with the traditional depiction of witchcraft in the sixteenth century is an etching inserted in the 1593 and 1594 editions of a pamphlet by Thomas Sigfridus, *A Correct Answer to the Question Whether Witches Themselves Can Cause Death or Illness with their Magic Powder*. The inscription below the print claimed that it depicted a witches' meeting that took place in the Electorate of Trier. In fact, the scene has little in common with the actual evidence produced in trials in the Trier region. But it did succeed in visualizing some new features of the witch-hunts that took place in the Trier region from the late 1580s, such as the mass trials in which hundreds of witches were denounced and executed. It also helped support the claim that such a drastic response on the part of a society considered vulnerable to the invasion of large numbers of witches was absolutely necessary. The etching depicts numerous witches engaged in activities associated with the sabbat. One group is shown feasting and drinking to excess. Another dances around an idol in the form of a toad seated on a tall column. A third moves in procession behind a witch mounted on a horse cadaver. A fourth is grouped around a cauldron under which lie human remains, while other witches prepare to ride their brooms up a chimney or prepare a woman's body for flight with a salve. Everywhere there are signs of lasciviousness, including a witch copulating with a devil; everywhere there is frantic activity, signs of death, and books of magic. A number of male and priest-like magicians teach their learned black arts; individual devils assist, encourage, and direct the rituals; and in the background one sees the storms and fire that witches unleash on communities. While we do not know the name of the artist who created this sensationalist depiction of witches' rituals, the indirect influence of Bruegel the Elder is quite evident in the visual elements drawn from his images of *Luxuria* and *St James and the Magician Hermogenes*. This print is certainly the first widely accessible visual depiction of activities associated with sixteenth-century demonologists' descriptions of the sabbat—if we discount the one earlier representation, a pen and ink drawing of *c*.1570 depicting a sabbat that supposedly occurred in the woods near Geneva, which was only available to those who had access to Johann Jakob Wick's document archive in Zurich. Yet the central element of the sabbat in most demonological accounts would still seem to be missing: the presiding role of the Devil and homage given him by the assembled witches. However, it has been suggested that the king represented in three different places in the print may well be a reference to Dietrich Flade, the then town bailiff and richest man in Trier. Flade was executed for witchcraft in 1589, and was known as the leader of the sabbat who sat on a golden throne. So this print might indeed represent a locally inflected version of the diabolical sabbat.

A print by an established artist that *did* meticulously follow a literary description of the sabbath and which introduced iconographical details that would influence artists' representation of witchcraft over the first half of the seventeenth century was Jan Ziarnko's large etching of a sabbat. Ziarnko, a Polish artist from Lwow who spent most of his career in Paris working at the courts of Henry IV and Louis XIII, created this etching to illustrate the description of the sabbat by the French magistrate Pierre de Lancre in his *Description of the Inconstancy of the Evil Angels* (1612). The work stemmed from de Lancre's four-month stay in 1609 in the Pays de Labourd, the Basque region of south-west France, following his appointment by Henry IV as head of a commission established to investigate the activities of witches there. It was also based on materials he collected in the Spanish Basque lands, which were described by the inquisitor Alonso de Salazar Frías. Ziarnko's etching, together with a detailed key, was included in a slightly revised 1613 edition of the *Description* and combined some of the traditional iconography of witchcraft with new imagery that illustrates the written text.

The central focus of the etching is a number of women grouped around a cauldron, cutting up a toad and snakes to throw into the seething potion that spews out dark smoke in which witches are shown riding their brooms together with demonic spirits, bones, and body parts. For these witch figures and demons cavorting in the smoke of the cauldron, as well as for some other motifs such as a salamander and a strange underworld figure emerging from a cave (a possible reference to the classical figure of Envy), Ziarnko drew heavily on the *Preparation for a Witches' Sabbath*, an engraving of 1610 by the Dutch painter and printmaker Jacques de Gheyn. Some elements originated with the iconography developed in the previous century by Bruegel and Baldung. Around a turbulent vertical shaft at the centre of the engraving (which included a cameo-like image of a wild, dishevelled witch riding a goat with two infants) Ziarnko inserted five different tableaux featuring sabbat activities. There is the presentation of a child by a witch and devil to Satan, in the shape of a goat and seated on a throne flanked by the Queen of the Sabbath and another consort; a back-to-back dance of naked witches and devils around a tree; a group of witches and their demonic paramours seated at table and feasting on the flesh of unbaptized children; a group of younger naked women dancing back to back in a ring to the music of a female consort; a large crowd of noble and wealthy men and women attended by devils; and in a scene peculiar to Basque witchcraft, a group of children securing within a small pond the toads to be used in cooking up the witches' poisons and ointments.

Most of the scenes in Ziarnko's large print reflect the literary sabbat and mark a clear shift from the iconography prior to 1590. As in the 1593 Trier sabbat, they emphasize the large numbers and frenetic activity of those engaged in these diabolical rituals. Ziarnko's etching is certainly an illustration of de Lancre's text, but it may have also been influenced by the large woodcut series by an unknown artist that illustrated the first 1608 edition of *A Summary of Witches* (*Compendium Maleficarum*) written by the Milanese Barnabite Brother Francesco Maria Guazzo. For these woodcuts also represent the Devil as a goat seated on a throne; they depict the participants in the sabbat as members of both genders and also as wealthy and privileged members of society; they lay considerable emphasis on children being offered up to the Devil at the sabbat and also being cooked up for the witches' ointment; and they also feature scenes of dancing, feasting, and riding goats. In the Ziarnko etching and the Guazzo woodcuts witches are represented as members of a large diabolical and conspiratorial society, a counter-church that transgresses the most basic societal norms and threatens society's ongoing survival. They complement de Lancre's understanding of Basque witchcraft as an anti-kingdom that threatens the good social order assured by the French King.

Similar scenarios were also being developed at approximately the same time in the fertile artistic environment of early seventeenth-century Antwerp by the highly successful painter Frans Francken II. Between 1606 and 1610, Francken created at least six paintings of witchcraft scenes, the most important of which are now in Vienna, London, and Munich, as well as many drawings. Together with David Teniers II, an Antwerp painter of the next generation, and the Neapolitan Salvator Rosa, Francken effectively created witchcraft as a subject suitable for paintings as well as prints. Unlike the far more controlled and hierarchical setting of Ziarnko's etching, Francken's works depict witchcraft as panoramas of criminal disorder and frenetic excess, more in the line of the Trier sabbat of 1593. The focus of his paintings are young and elegant noblewomen, some beginning to undress in order to be rubbed with the witches' salve by older crones, others already naked and engaged in various rituals, some stretched out as though in a trance, and others transported limp and totally vulnerable through the air. Francken uses these figures to create a voyeuristic eroticism that underpins the multiple scenes of diabolical ritual. His canvases are filled with magic circles and other paraphernalia such as bones, knives, candles, and incantations, skulls and severed heads, flasks, phials, sieves and shears, strange Boschian demons and hybrids, mandrake roots, and the infamous hands of glory made from the hands of executed criminals, the cooking up of salves in monstrous cauldrons, acts of homage and idolatry, references to lust, theft, avarice, and brutal murder. As with Bruegel's Hermogenes prints, the action no longer takes place in the wild, not even in the town square. Except for one of the paintings, all scenes are located fully or partly within domestic space—from where witches ride their brooms up and out from the hearth, or from where the viewer can observe their night flying and acts of destruction. Witchcraft has become a form of disorder and excess that has invaded urban households, even those of the nobility and wealthy burghers; it has infected women across all divisions of age and rank; it has become a conspiratorial association at the very heart of Christian society.

Francken's interest in witchcraft was possibly related to the strong attack on it in the southern Netherlands, first by Philip II in the 1590s, and then by the Habsburg regents, Archduke Albert and Archduchess Isabella, who attempted to establish centralized control over its prosecution as a religious and social threat in an edict of 1606. The 'visual hyperbole' of Francken's paintings, as one scholar has dubbed it, involved a detailed referencing of numerous magical and ritual practices: love magic, divination, necromancy, metamorphosis, invocation, and idolatry. This suggests the strong influence of writers like Jean Bodin and in particular Martin Del Rio, the Jesuit native of Antwerp and ex-Vice-Chancellor and Attorney General for Brabant, whose *Six Books on Investigations into Magic* was first published in 1599 and then translated and republished in numerous editions. As well as the prominence in these paintings of female bodies in various stages of undress and consciousness, being rubbed and caressed with unguents or carried through the air as though lifeless, there is also an unusually strong emphasis on magical invocation and script. Reading and leafing through magical books, writing out magic formulae on loose leaves, enchantments inscribed around the perimeters of magic circles, all these different markers of literate and learned magic combine with the knives, bones, skulls, animal, and human body parts to stress the universal nature of the witches' black arts, drawing in women from every social rank. Just as the mix of demonic and female bodies demonstrates a lack of control over the bodily desires of the senses, so the prominence of magical script and books signifies a lack of control over the desire to access prohibited knowledge. While intriguing and fascinating for the viewer in their intricate and exotic depictions of magical paraphernalia and ritual, Francken's paintings represent the fear of a lack of moral and intellectual discipline as a threat to the proper workings of the Counter-Reformation state. As Martin Del Rio argued, this threat became critical, for 'swarms of witches [are] laying waste the whole of the North, like locusts', and unlike earlier times different forms of magic have 'infected even the noble, the well-educated and the rich'.

A fellow artist who also played a key role in the establishment of witchcraft as a suitable subject for artists in the seventeenth century was the Antwerp painter David Teniers II. From 1637, a year after Teniers became dean of the Guild of St Luke in Antwerp, he was employed as a court artist and curator of collections by the Regent of the southern Netherlands, Archduke Leopold Wilhelm, who would within a few years own one of the most outstanding painting collections in all Europe. Teniers went on to enjoy the patronage of the most prominent art collectors in Europe, was ennobled in 1663, and founded the Antwerp Academy of Art a year later. Because of his status, the dozen or so paintings of witchcraft he created must have become reasonably well known, and this is also attested to by the engravings of his paintings made by such artists as Jacques Aliamet and Jasper Isaac. Although Teniers' 1633 painting of a witches' assembly, as well as the content of other paintings, was strongly influenced by Francken, most of Teniers' paintings focused on one or two magical rituals or scenarios such as demonic invocation, the brewing of potions, the collection of mandrake roots and other herbs, and most especially the rubbing of ointment onto the bodies of those preparing to ride their broomsticks up the chimney. So while Teniers takes up very similar themes to those of Francken, he does not present witches as part of a frenetic assembly, and he also gives little exposure to the terrible crimes of witchcraft. Teniers's witches certainly do not represent the same threat as those in the large canvases by Francken. They are less exotic and more domestic. The exoticism that does pervade a number of Teniers' works is one that rests less on the practices of his witches than on the strange, wild demonic beasts— flying fish, frogs, bats, strange hybrids—that populate his witch paintings, as well as his many paintings of *The Temptation of St Anthony*. Many of these hybrids, monstrous beasts, and demons are inherited from Bosch and Bruegel to create a fantastical, almost surreal world, which becomes a strong feature of a significant number of art works from the second third of the seventeenth century.

An early seventeenth-century artist whose work articulates a more complex image of witchcraft that seems to align with a more nuanced set of attitudes than those of Frans Francken was the Dutch painter and printmaker Jacques de Gheyn II. As we have already seen in considering Ziarnko's 1613 sabbat, de Gheyn's imagery was taken up by many artists, even if (as in the case of Ziarnko) these artists might not have shared de Gheyn's more sceptical view concerning the reality claims of witchcraft. De Gheyn's fascinating drawing of 1610 (subsequently engraved, probably by Andries Stock) of *Preparations for the Witches' Sabbath* constitutes a kind of crossover point between the earlier sixteenth-century views of witchcraft represented by Hans Baldung Grien and his fellow south German artists and the new generation of Flemish and Dutch artists around the turn of the seventeenth century. The latter took inspiration from the tradition of Bosch and Bruegel to create an image of witchcraft that appeared far more threatening for society by virtue of the large number of its adherents, their widespread distribution through different social ranks, and the savage cruelty of their ritual practices and malefic acts. While artists such as Ziarnko and Francken emphasized the extent to which witchcraft was embedded within the social fabric of local communities, de Gheyn's imagery focused on the cruelty and inhumanity of witches' practices and, by implication, their terrible impact on human and social life. Yet we clearly need to be cautious in attributing such views to de Gheyn in any simple way. There are many signs from the social and intellectual circles in which he moved, as well as in his almost hyperrealist and fantastical imagery, that his witchcraft images depict acts of the imagination.

All de Gheyn's witchcraft images were created in the first decade of the seventeenth century, at approximately the same time that Francken was painting his witches' assemblies. Around 1601 de Gheyn had moved to The Hague, the location of the court of Maurice of Nassau, Stadtholder of Holland and Zeeland and later Prince of Orange, with whom de Gheyn had been connected socially and professionally for almost a decade before that. He had previously worked as an engraver in the Haarlem print-publishing business of his fellow artist Hendrik Goltzius, had set up his own print-publishing enterprise in Amsterdam, and in the mid-1590s had moved to Leiden, the intellectual centre of the Dutch Republic. During his time at Leiden and then at The Hague, de Gheyn gradually moved from engraving to drawing and then to painting, a sign of his growing self-consciousness as an inventive artist. This intellectual and emotional move also seemed to signify his increasing interest in the role of the fantastic, the world of the fertile imagination. This contrasted with and also supplemented the closely observed details of nature he created during this period, the natural world of flowers and insects to which de Gheyn was drawn through his close connection with scholars at the University of Leiden.

De Gheyn's 'demonological' works of the first decade of the seventeenth century would therefore seem to be as much about the powers of the human imagination as visual depictions of witchcraft beliefs. His 1603 drawing of *The Parable of the Devil Sowing Seeds*, for instance, has parallels with Lucas Cranach's *Melancholia* paintings, and points forward to Goya's *The Sleep of Reason*. The scene depicts the Devil as a farmer sowing his seeds. In the sky above the Devil, witches are riding spectral goats through the sky. Encircled by billowing clouds in the manner of religious visions, one of them with legs spread-eagled to reveal her genitals, these witches represent the tares or illusions that the Devil sows while one is asleep (a peasant is shown sleeping at the edge of the field). The message is clear: one should let the tares grow with the wheat, for it is God and not men who will uproot and burn them, in the time of harvest, that is, at the time of the Last Judgement (Matthew 13: 24–30).

De Gheyn's images of witchcraft are, however, quite enigmatic. On the one hand, he was almost certainly influenced by the view that claims of witchcraft were produced by the melancholic imagination of troubled minds. This strongly argued view of Johann Weyer was adopted by the English country gentleman and author of *The Discoverie of Witchcraft*, Reginald Scot, and Scot's work in turn was translated into Dutch just at the time de Gheyn was creating his witchcraft images in the first decade of the seventeenth century, and by none other than de Gheyn's brother-in-law Govert Basson and the latter's father Thomas Basson. Similar views were held by other Dutch scholars and jurists like Arnoldus Buchelius, who were well known to de Gheyn. So de Gheyn's highly atmospheric scenes with their brilliant light effects would seem to represent visual forms of imaginative illusion, phantasms of the mind. On the other hand, his drawings are filled with detailed objects and animals drawn from the world of closely observed nature, techniques very evident throughout his oeuvre, which endow his witchcraft scenes with physical reality. The introduction of elements of naturalism into his work provides his images with a credibility that ratchets up the viewer's horror at the strange and cruel world of witchcraft. But we are given to understand that this reality is one located in the imaginative phantasies of human subjects, not in the world of nature and social reality.

De Gheyn's carefully drawn skulls and severed heads, his rats and horse's head, or the frog nailed to the floor in the 1604 drawing *Witches in a Cellar* serve to emphasize the cruelty of witches as they set about their ghoulish work. A male cadaver stretched out as though on the anatomist's table to reveal the human skeletal and muscular structure forcefully suggests the murderous nature of witchcraft in its harvesting of human body parts. Similar effects are created by the skulls, cats, winged dragon, frogs, slithering salamander, and gnarled tree trunk in de Gheyn's engraving of *c*.1610, usually entitled *Preparations for a Witches' Sabbath*, not to mention the prominent bodies, coiffed heads and hair, and the expressive faces of the engraving's central female protagonists. The intense preoccupied gaze of these women on the ground contrasts with the frantic flight of other women and demonic beasts through the thickly clouded and turbulent skies. While figures of the human imagination, the witches are also—almost always in de Gheyn's images—figures engaged in most terrible and destructive human acts. In his drawings witches store human cadavers, they extract bodily substances from their mouths, they tip body parts into cauldrons and boil them up, they suck children dry in the manner of vampires. In *Preparations for a Witches' Sabbath*, which de Gheyn planned for a broader public, the destructive and violent work of the witches is seen as both more cosmically significant and more socially grounded than is the case in most of his drawings. The thick and heavy storm clouds and the lightning signify nature in disarray, and are a possible reference to the poisoning of wells, which was a common fear at the time linked to plague and witchcraft. In this his most public representation of witchcraft, and also his most inventive, de Gheyn refers us back to the imagery and compositions of Hans Baldung a century earlier, but he also marks the emergence of a new imagery, an imagery that emphasizes the broader cosmic dimensions of the threat of witchcraft.

Witchcraft and Imaginative Fantasy, 1620–1670

As the foregoing might suggest, one of the most significant characteristics of the representation of witchcraft throughout much of the seventeenth century was excess. This excess could be of two kinds. First, there was the excess associated with the activities of witches, as members of a mass movement or organization engaged in multifarious activities directed at harming individuals and the social order. Such excess defined witches as members of a counter-church or counter-society. This development is clear in the 1593 Trier sabbat etching, in the paintings of Frans Francken II, the Ziarnko sabbat, and, in a modified way, in the drawings of Jacques de Gheyn II. Secondly, there is the excess that concentrates on the demonic and spirit world within which witchcraft operates, the demons with which witches conclude their pacts and whom they sometimes worship, and the demonic hybrids and monstrous spirit-like beings who gather at locations where witches come together to ply their evil sorceries. Fascination with such beings is part of a Boschian tradition in northern Europe that is taken up by Bruegel in his Hermogenes drawings and prints. It is very evident in both the demonic animal and hybrid shapes depicted assisting, escorting, caressing, or cajoling witches and the diabolical idols that appear in Francken's depictions of sabbats. They also occur in the witch scenes of David Teniers, as well as in a related and well-established artistic subject that begins to include some witches in the seventeenth century: *The Temptations of St Anthony*. In the middle decades of the seventeenth century the excesses of witches' activities at the sabbat were further developed by artists such as Michael Herr and Matthäus Merian, and the unknown illustrator of a 1668 work, *Performance at the Blocksberg* by the prolific Baroque poet and author Hans Schulze, who has come to be known by his literary name Johannes Praetorius. The eerie and dark world of hybrid demons and skeletal shapes also becomes most prominent in the work of the Neapolitan artist Salvator Rosa in the 1640s.

Michael Herr, a south-west German artist active for the most part in Nuremberg, created a scene of witchcraft in the 1620s which would influence witchcraft iconography for much of the seventeenth century. Herr had made a number of preliminary sketches, one of which shows the influence of Ziarnko's sabbat, that seem to have been preparatory drawings for a 1626 broadsheet etched by Matthäus Merian the Elder and published with two different sets of accompanying verses. As in Ziarnko's sabbath, a cauldron that spews out black smoke and vapours takes centre stage and effectively divides the print. In this case the vapours are expelled with such force that they propel toads into the sky, and cause chaos among the witch riders: they dislodge one witch from either her broom or goat, spin another upside down, and force a male witch to hold desperately onto his hat. To the left and right of this central fuming column are two circular scenes, complementary yet distinct. On the left is the witches' dance in which masses of male and female witches swarm around and up the mountain. The mountain in question is the Blocksberg, the highest mountain in the Harz mountains of central Germany (also called the Brocken), and from the late sixteenth century well known as one of the most significant locations for witches' assemblies and dances. The witches follow their satyr-like leader, Satan, depicted with raised flaming arms. Interspersed among this winding and gyrating column, accompanied by a bagpiper and other musicians in the crowd, are individual devils, one of them in full frontal naked pose, with whom the female witches dance wildly and perform sexual acts.

The right side of the print depicts a male magician engaged in necromantic and invocatory magic amidst classical ruins. He stands nervously poised with his sword ready to strike in a large magic circle ringed with candles and magical talismans; while at its perimeter are all manner of ghost-like and demonic animal and hybrid shapes, some of them with mouths open and screaming, others beating drums or attempting to break the magic barrier with their weapons, and still others sweeping down from above ready to hurl their missiles. In the foreground of the print there is a cauldron surrounded by a number of female witches. One in particular stands out: a large, naked, and crowned witch with extremely long hair (whom the verses below identify as the queen of the sabbat). All around her are scenes of further decadence and immorality. A lewd devil gropes a drunken woman lying in front of a large tankard, his tongue sticking out as he draws near to her cheek and wraps one of his legs around her waist. An elderly winged devil defecates, breaks wind, and exhales at the same time, possibly overpowering a witch in a stupefied state nearby. And in the bottom right some witches are reading from magical books, guided by a male magician, while others gather around a barrel and perform various forms of ritual magic with skulls and other paraphernalia in the form of body parts, a sword, and a glass devil. In the background a procuress introduces a young witch to her male client.

Merian's print transmits extraordinary energy, frenetic movement, superabundant excess. It presents a scene of frenzied pandemonium. The focus is on moral disorder and excess, in particular lasciviousness, lewd dancing, and drunkenness. While there are hints of the destruction that witches wreak on society (with a burning church and gallows in the central background, and a dead child stored under a cover with human and animal skulls in the bottom right corner), it is sexual and moral disorder that is most prominent. The spewing cauldron in the centre of the print seems to have infected both the long line of lecherous conga dancers on the mountain as well as the raging monstrous spirits attempting to overcome the male ritual magician. In the foreground a witch with arms raised and shrieking invocations, a procuress, and a naked witch, seated with her back to the viewer, parallel the lewd and defecating devils on the left. This is truly the kingdom of darkness operating on earth. Yet it is a kingdom that takes shape through the blending of popular artistic themes and motifs rather than by following the literary accounts of the sabbat as elaborated by theologians and jurists. By contrast, the different accompanying texts below Merian's etching persuade the reader to look and draw more traditional messages from this 'terrifying, peculiar, chaotic and wild' scene and they make reference to Satan, the Devil's kingdom, and the ultimate damnation of these witches in the fires of Hell. The Merian etching presents witchcraft as a truly frenzied cult, an event almost beyond human experience involving innumerable adepts and numerous rampaging devils and spirits.

A similar expansion of an earlier visual representation of witchcraft can be seen in a German broadsheet of *c.*1625 that draws heavily on the composition and motifs developed by Jacques de Gheyn II in his 1610 drawing and later print, *Preparation for a Witches' Sabbath*. While most of the compositional elements are very similar to those in de Gheyn, the three witches in the earlier print are now replaced with a whole crowd. A group of witches in the foreground sit on the perimeter of a magical circle, and are clearly being tutored in the magical arts by a naked female witch; another group sits around a burning candle in a cave; a number of individual witches are being led by satyr-like devils through another cave to participate in the assembly; while in the background a large group of witches dance in a circle with their devils to the sounds of a lone bagpiping devil seated on a mound. Although not nearly as frenzied as the print engraved by Merian, the same impulse is quite evident to fill in the scene with large numbers of witches. And unlike Ziarnko's etching, this is not an illustration of an accompanying text. But the accompanying verses call on the reader to look at this 'devilish horde of witches' and their disgusting acts, which will ultimately send them to Hell.

This tendency to multiply the number of witches and thereby to emphasize their threat to the moral order of a well-regulated Christian society was also emphasized in the reworking of Merian's print by the anonymous artist who produced the frontispiece for Praetorius' 1668 *Performance at the Blocksberg*. Praetorius' work was immensely popular, and versions of this frontispiece print continued to be produced through the rest of the seventeenth, and well into the eighteenth century. By introducing into the centre of the woodcut the worship of the Devil by means of the ritual of the obscene kiss, the unknown artist succeeded in emphasizing the diabolical nature of witchcraft. He continued to link witches to the dancing and libidinous excess traditionally associated with the Blocksberg—introducing a trio of musicians to a prominent spot in the long line of cavorting figures. Indeed, almost all the dancers are now coupled with diabolical lovers in various animal and demonic forms. By the mid-seventeenth century the Blocksberg was coming to be well known as a location where spirits gathered and witches danced and performed their sabbat rituals. The illustrator has cashed in on these fantastic and entertaining stories, but at the same time ensures that the diabolical character of witchcraft is in no way weakened, forgotten, or dismissed.

The imaginative fantasies of witchcraft also featured prominently in the work of the Neapolitan artist Salvator Rosa. All the works that Salvator Rosa created on the subject of magic and witchcraft, except for his painting *Saul and the Witch of Endor*, were executed during the period he spent in Florence between 1640 and 1649. These works need to be understood in the context of the interests Rosa developed during this time as part of a network of poets, playwrights, scholars, and painters interested in serious philosophical themes, in particular those of classical Stoicism, concerned with vanity and death, as well as the satirical poetry of authors such as Juvenal and Horace. Rosa also combined this moral seriousness with a theatricality and sense of comic parody. In Rosa's depiction of witchcraft, the most common characteristic is his interest in the particular sorcery and magical techniques that witches claimed to use for different purposes— whether to gain love or wealth, to inflict injury or death, or to call up the dead so as to divine the future. In the four *tondi* (circular works of art) which Rosa probably created in the mid-1640s, scenes of witchcraft are connected to different times of the day: *Morning*, *Day*, *Evening*, and *Night*. The whole amounts to what one scholar has called 'a sort of anthology of all the mechanisms and ingredients of black magic'. This includes the transformation of humans into animals, the manufacture of putrid poisons and salves to inflict illness, the burning of wax tapers and images in love magic, crystal balls for divining the future, and priestly rituals of diabolical invocation and adoration. Rosa's best-known work, his painting of *c.*1646 that now hangs in the National Gallery, London, and is entitled *Witches at their Incantations*, also offers a sensational and grotesque compendium of witches' practices: acts of initiation, the fumigation of a hanging corpse for mummification, the use of the corpse's nail clippings and entrails for a salve, a wax manikin and mirror for love magic, a skeleton propped up in a coffin for necromantic communication, the use of swords and tapers by male magicians within a magic circle, seemingly to transfix hearts or wound unfaithful lovers. Everywhere there are skulls and skeletal animal shapes. This fascination with the entire range of magical, sorcery, and invocatory practices, together with the wide assortment of body parts and disgusting objects employed in these crafts, is typical of virtually all the witchcraft scenes created by Rosa.

A second important characteristic of Rosa's witchcraft iconography is the strong sense he creates of the world of infernal spirits and the dead. These are scenes set in dark, wild, and eerie landscapes, punctuated by flashes of light and fire, billowing clouds, and frenetic movement. In the air above, huge, often bird-like creatures and other bizarre skeletons hover, as though presiding over the activities below; while on the ground we see dragon-like skeletal beasts or weird skeletal monsters on which witches ride to the festivities. The scenes are frequently littered with signs of the dead, the skulls and bones of animals and humans, reinforcing the sense that witchcraft marks the borders of the realm of demons and the dead. While Rosa's scenes of witchcraft are truly original, the use of various human and animal skeletons is strong in Italian art of the later sixteenth and early seventeenth centuries through the work of artists such as Jacopo Ligozzi and Filippo Napoletano. They possibly also draw on the Italian tradition of associating witchcraft with the animal dead, as graphically displayed in the Venetian artist Agostino Veneziano's procession of dead animals in his early sixteenth-century print *The Carcass*. Details in Rosa's work would seem to echo some aspects of the earlier paintings of Frans Francken II and David Teniers; but among his fellow Italian artists only the 1742 painting of a witchcraft scene by Andrea Locatelli, with its hanging corpse, invocatory magic, human skeletons, and skeletal beasts, approximates the gruesome and horrifying atmosphere created by Rosa.

Rosa's painting of *Saul and the Witch of Endor*, completed in 1668, approximately twenty years after the witchcraft paintings, employed some of the motifs found in those earlier works but within a more constrained biblical narrative and setting. The biblical figure of the woman of Endor, the female necromancer who called up the ghost of the prophet Samuel at the request of King Saul (1 Samuel 28) so as to learn of his political future, was commonly regarded as a witch in the seventeenth century, and the ghost she called up was none other than the Devil. Rosa broke with iconographical tradition that generally located the biblical story in the witch's house or chamber. Instead, he located the events at Endor within a cemetery setting. In this way he clearly identified the witch as a necromancer who communes with the dead. Secondly, Rosa accentuated the woman's intense engagement by focusing on her magical techniques. He depicted her burning a cypress branch with a torch, a common practice in classical accounts of necromancy and also depicted in his other paintings. As she leans forward, her mouth is open and seemingly uttering her secret invocations, thereby creating an extraordinary emotional dynamic and contrasting demeanour to the immobile, almost statuesque figure of the prophet Samuel. Thirdly, and almost uniquely, he depicts fantastic, skeletal animal and human forms in the air above the woman, to represent the demons drawn to the scene through the woman's conjurations. Even though Rosa's painting does not specifically depict the woman of Endor with the typical attributes of a male ritual magician, he represents her powers as a witch as based on conjuration and invocatory magic.

Painted towards the end of Rosa's long career (he died in 1673), this marked the height of his artistic reputation. Soon after it was painted, it was the only work of a living artist chosen to be exhibited with the likes of Titian and Parmigianino for an exhibition held in Rome to celebrate the election to the papacy of Pope Clement IX by his family, the Rospigliosi. This popularity is significant for the later history of this subject, for Rosa's work influenced depictions of the biblical event through the seventeenth and also the eighteenth century among German, Dutch, and also French artists. These depictions concentrated far more than was the case previously on the magical paraphernalia that was thought to have been used by the woman of Endor in her acts of conjuration and necromancy, and also on the spirits of the dead and demons that her actions aroused. Even more significantly, Rosa's depiction of the subject indirectly influenced the way witchcraft would be visualized over coming decades in the face of growing scepticism about the reality of witchcraft.

The Defence of Witchcraft against Scepticism, 1670–1710

For the last three decades of the seventeenth century and the first decade of the eighteenth century witchcraft iconography seemed to play a critical role in the defence of witchcraft beliefs. The instrument used to mount this defence was none other than the biblical figure of the witch of Endor, which Rosa had succeeded in making such a popular subject for artists. It was probably the Swiss artist Joseph Werner II who introduced Rosa's work to German colleagues through the artistic circle that gathered around Johann Heinrich Schönfeld in Augsburg, where Werner lived and worked from 1667 to 1682. Both Werner and Schönfeld created versions of the scene, Schönfeld now representing the woman as a ritual magician with wand and magic circle, as did fellow artists in southern Germany such as Georg Andreas Wolfgang, Melchior Küsel, Johann Jakob Sandrart, Georg Christoph Eimmart the Younger, and Martin Engelbrecht. The leading European printmakers at the turn of the eighteenth century, the Dutch artists Caspar Luyken and Romeyn de Hooghe, were also soon portraying the woman of Endor in similar fashion. This strong interest among artists helped create the necessary context and stimulus for the adoption of this biblical figure as representative of witchcraft in general. This was particularly useful for those looking to defend the reality of witchcraft against the attacks of critics such as Balthasar Bekker and Christian Thomasius. For the next half century or so witchcraft would be in part visualized through the depiction of a single woman cooking up her potions in a cauldron, while also engaged in the invocatory magic that called on the assistance of demons.

Whereas the story of the woman of Endor and King Saul had been illustrated in all manner of bibles and historical chronicles from as early as the twelfth century, in the later seventeenth century it began to appear in treatises related to witchcraft. It is unsurprising perhaps that it appeared in William Faithorne's frontispiece to Joseph Glanvill's *Saducismus triumphatus* (Sadducism Conquered), a work in defence of the reality of witchcraft and of the spirit world that was published in several editions from 1681. When Glanvill's work was translated and published in German in 1701 it again featured a frontispiece engraving of the witch of Endor, this time by an unknown artist. It was a copy of a woodcut by the German engraver Georg Eimart, originally included in an Augsburg picture Bible of 1695. This is a very theatrical scene located in a large vault displaying human skulls and bats. It depicts the witch, with wand and magic circle, raising the figure of Samuel from his circular grave through columns of billowing smoke, to the shock of Saul and his attendants. One of the interesting characteristics of this and many of these seventeenth-century images of the witch of Endor is that she is endowed with the attributes of male ritual magicians—a wand, book, and magic circle—attributes not generally found in depictions of witchcraft prior to the seventeenth century. The attributes which immediately identify male ritual magicians—as in the most famous case of Thomas Marlowe's Dr Faustus—now become the attributes of this female witch.

Just such a female figure with the traditional attributes of a male ritual magician—book and circle—as well as those of a female witch—seething cauldron and goat—appeared in an Augsburg work of 1687 called *The Broken Power of Darkness*, written by the fervent Pietist pastor of that city, Gottlieb Spitzel. It was a popular image at least among printers. It was reproduced six years later in 1693 in a German translation of *Demonolatry*, the well-known work of the chief prosecutor of Lorraine, Nicholas Remy, originally published a century earlier; and then for a third time as the frontispiece to the work of a Lutheran pastor from Hollstein, Peter Goldschmidt, entitled *The Defender of Depraved Witches and Sorcerers* and published in Hamburg in 1705. In all these cases the female witch was not simply modelled on a witch of Endor figure in a general way; it was a precise copy of the witch of Endor that we find in a 1679 picture Bible created by the Augsburg engraver Melchior Küsel. Both the artist and his work must have been known to Gottlieb Spitzel. The three works in which this image was included all strongly defended belief in the reality of witchcraft, and it would seem that the choice of this figure was meant to bolster the claims for witchcraft as supported by biblical precedent.

The other significant feature of these three etchings was that the female witch/magician has been spliced with elements of the iconography developed by the anonymous illustrator of the Praetorius work of 1668 discussed above. This included a line of dancers following the satyr-like figure of the Devil with upraised arms and flaming paws around the side of a hill, to the rhythm of two musicians, as found in that print. But instead of the obscene kiss performed by a single woman as depicted in the Praetorius frontispiece, the creator of this print has now introduced a whole line of women and also children pushed forward by a devil to partake in the ritual. In this way the artist has been successful in giving the impression that the two lines of participants are related and the group obscene kiss of the sabbat ritual becomes a defining characteristic of witchcraft. The adoption of the obscene kiss ritual of the witches' sabbat into witchcraft iconography of the late seventeenth century is most likely related to witch trials that took place in Sweden, especially the famous Mora case, between 1668 and 1676. A characteristic of these trials was the involvement of children, supposedly abducted by adult witches and taken to sabbat celebrations on the legendary meadow of Blockula. Ultimately, well over seventy adults were convicted and executed on the testimony of children, all but one of them women. Fifteen children were also executed and many more were punished by whipping. A well-known woodcut of the execution containing other scenes of witches' activities was created to accompany the protocol of events, and was soon circulated with translated versions of the protocol in Dutch, German, and English. It was quickly included in contemporary news accounts of recent events as well as in pamphlets and treatises. A sensationalist account of the events made its way into later editions of Joseph Glanvill's *Saducismus triumphatus*, for instance, and Gottlieb Spitzel was instrumental in circulating news of it through his *Broken Power of Darkness*. The extent of the confessions and executions convinced many of the truth of such claims, and the events were used to stress the ongoing threat of witchcraft throughout Europe. In the case of the Spitzel illustration, then, biblical testimony was spliced with the evidence from near-contemporary and shocking events to construct a counter-argument against any attempt to diminish the threat of witchcraft and brand it either as sensationalist nonsense or as entertaining fable.

Attributes of male invocatory magic were also incorporated into the iconography of witchcraft in the second half of the seventeenth century. This development was stimulated by a general identification of all forms of magic with the witchcraft phenomenon. We have seen such a development occurring visually in the different representations of witchcraft by Frans Francken, for instance, and it can also be found in the paintings of David Teniers II. But it was above all the preoccupation with representing the witch of Endor's attempts to raise the ghost of Samuel from the dead that was responsible for introducing invocatory magic into the iconography of the Endor story from the beginning of the seventeenth century, especially through the increasing number of prints in illustrated German and Dutch bibles, as well as in paintings and drawings (by artists as varied as Benjamin Cuyp, Ferdinand Bol, Christoph Murer, Christoffel von Sichem II, Pieter Hendircksz. Schut, Jacob Savery, Romeyn de Hooghe, and Martin Engelbrecht). Given the witch of Endor's singular status as a biblical witch, it is unsurprising that she was seen as one of the most powerful visual (and historical) weapons one could use to stem attacks on the very notion of witchcraft and its supposed magical powers.

The Parodying of Witchcraft and Early Romanticism: 1710–1800

In much of eighteenth-century Europe witchcraft beliefs succumbed to the pressure of growing scepticism and critiques of the abuses of judicial process. The number of witch trials in Europe declined radically, except in parts of eastern Europe such as Hungary and Poland, and from the 1790s there were to be no more legal trials for witchcraft throughout the Continent. The imagery of witchcraft from the second decade of the eighteenth century reflected this educated scepticism and decline, as serious treatment of the subject increasingly gave way to parody and ridicule. In 1710 a highly successful Parisian author, the *abbé* Laurent Bordelon, published in both Paris and Amsterdam a novel entitled *The Story of the Extravagant Imaginations of Monsieur Oufle, Occasioned by his Reading of Books Treating Magic, the Demonic Arts, Demoniacs and Witches*. The lead character—whose name, Oufle, was an anagram for *le fou* (the fool)—was described as believing in every form of superstition, including the witches' sabbat. Both 1710 editions contained a fold-out etching depicting Monsieur Oufle visiting a witches' sabbat accompanied by a fool. The print was in fact a parody of Jan Ziarnko's etching produced almost a century earlier.

Virtually all the cameos of witchcraft activities and individual witches found in Ziarnko's print are included in the Bordelon illustration, with the exception of the crowd of noble men and women. Ziarnko's depictions of the musical consort and of the children minding the toads, however, are seriously reduced in size and significance. But the critical change in comparison to the earlier Ziarnko print occurs in the depiction of the rituals performed in front of the figure of Satan on his throne. The artist has moved Ziarnko's cameo to the centre of his print, which then serves to structure the meaning of surrounding scenes and the print as a whole. Satan appears as a horned human in the upper half of his body and as a goat in the lower half, rather than in the animal form of a goat as in the earlier illustration; and before his throne a group of four male figures perform backward somersaults. The backward somersaults are clearly a reference to the inverted rituals of the sabbat; but they also parody those rituals by movements very similar to the somersaulting fools in Pieter Bruegel's print *The Festival of Fools*. This is surely another joke by the artist concerning the true foolish nature of Monsieur Oufle—who is shown observing this ridiculous dance from the perimeter of the print in the company of a fool.

Bordelon's book, with further examples of such foolish imaginings illustrated throughout, was an immediate success. It was translated into English and German in the very next year, 1711, and new French editions appeared in 1754 and 1793. Artists also picked up the reference. For instance, when an unknown artist sought to parody the sabbat in the 1719 German translation of John Webster's *The Displaying of Supposed Witchcraft*, he included a number of images from the 1626 etchings by Merian and Herr: the crowned naked witch with her cauldron; the male magician performing his invocatory magic; two witches riding, one on a goat and another on a broom; and even the dog-like monster hurtling through the air about to launch a missile. In the foreground the artist placed a young woman in bed waking up startled and terrified as though from a nightmare, as a devil and a monstrous snake confronted her. In order to ensure that the meaning of this scene was not lost on readers, the artist included two lines of verse: 'Here one sees as clear as day [where we find] witches in the world; it's in the head of a dreamer that thousands of them reside.' In order to underscore this message concerning the illusions of dreams with a contemporary cultural reference, above the door of the dreamer's bedroom the artist hung a picture of Monsieur Oufle.

Witchcraft as illusion was also prominent in the work of the early eighteenth-century French artist Claude Gillot. A teacher of Watteau known for his rococo inventiveness and interest in the comic and the grotesque, Gillot created several etchings of sabbat-like scenes before his death in 1722: for example, the print usually entitled *Errant pendant la nuit dans un lieu solitaire* (Wandering at Night in a Solitary Place), which may have been influenced by the Bordelon illustration of Monsieur Oufle's visit to the sabbat. For in this case too, a Satanic goat, seated on what appears to be a kind of stage, links arms with a group of bizarre and terrifying human and animalistic figures that dance to the music of another goat playing a fiddle. The grotesque and incongruous nature of the spectral and animalistic figures, and such details as the demon that lights a taper from the fart of a monstrous horse, suggest that this is as much parody as critique. Indeed, the later appended inscription supports this too, as it speaks of the terrible fears that these figures elicit at night, only to evaporate as the sun reaches its height. Another Gillot etching, entitled *Est-ce enchantement, est-ce une illusion?* (Is It Bewitchment, Is It an Illusion?), also depicts skeletal animals and monstrous shapes, although here the artist adds cadavers and tortured bodies. But in spite of the pervading sense of gruesome horror and death, the accompanying verses again suggest Gillot's fundamental question: are these terrors anything more than a terrifying illusion?

As Gillot's etchings show, by the 1720s the iconography of witchcraft was beginning to move away from documenting and exploring the world of witches and magicians, the harm they inflict on their society, and their interaction with the Devil, demons, or the spirit world in general. Traditional images of witches continued, of course, and especially in the form adopted from the mid-seventeenth century, depicting witches as conjurors and necromancers, calling up demons through invocatory magic, boiling up salves and potions in cauldrons, and riding animals and all kinds of implements through the sky. But the new imagery created by artists such as Henry Fuseli and Francisco Goya in the second half of the eighteenth century, together with a number of other Romantic artists, had more to do with the nature of the human imagination, with the stuff of dreams and nightmares, inner psychic forces and drives, the dark sides of human nature, the irrational and the uncanny. A classic example of this is Goya's etching *The Sleep of Reason Produces Monsters*. Created as part of his *Capricho* series in 1799, towards the end of the period in which Goya created his first set of witchcraft images, the monsters and demons depicted here are clearly the product of the human mind rather than the result of demonic pacts or invocatory magic. The imagery of magic and witchcraft continued through the nineteenth century, in the hands of artists as varied as Eugène Delacroix, Louis Boulanger, Anton Wiertz, Carl Spitzweg, Félicien Rops, Arnold Böcklin, Hans Thoma, John William Waterhouse, Lovis Corinth, and Teresa Feodorowna Ries. As well as exploring the uncontrolled imagination, these artists now used witchcraft to investigate themes such as superstition and enlightenment, the female body and sexuality, nature and human destiny. By this time, widespread belief in the power of witches was in serious retreat amongst the literate population of Europe, and the days of active prosecution had come to an end. But the power of witchcraft as a cultural trope for exploring the human psyche and its social institutions continued to grow.

6

The World of Popular Magic

Owen Davies

Although it is not always evident from the history books, the various European laws against witchcraft introduced during the early modern period were as much concerned with punishing magic generally as witchcraft specifically. Types of magical practice considered helpful by the general populace, such as unwitching, identifying thieves, detecting the whereabouts of stolen property, and resolving matters of the heart were, as is noted in Chapter 3, considered pure evil by some theologians. While witches killed the godly on Satan's behalf they did not damn the souls of their victims. Good magicians, however, insidiously seduced their clients to put their faith in human false promises rather than to trust in God's judgement. This sinful path led to damnation. For the secular authorities, the popular influence of magicians and prophets also threatened to undermine the authority of the state, clergy, and medical profession.

In 1542, during the reign of Henry VIII, the first dedicated law against witchcraft and conjuration was introduced in England and Wales. As well as concern over witches, the statute punished those who resorted to 'fantastical practises' to find buried treasure, and those who took 'upon them to tell or declare where goodes stollen or lost shall become'. The 1542 Act was repealed a few years later, and then in 1563 Queen Elizabeth I's government introduced a more detailed law based on that of 1542, which included the crime of 'intent to provoke any person to unlawful love'. When the 1563 law was revised in 1604 further magical crimes were added, namely entertaining evil and wicked spirits, and using corpses for magical purposes. This was the statute under which suspected witches and magical practitioners were prosecuted in England's American colonies. In

Calvinist Scotland, a witchcraft Act of 1563, which was not the same as the English statute of that year, made no explicit difference between the capital crime of witchcraft and beneficial magic. It was concerned with 'the heavy and abominable superstition used by divers of the lieges of this realm'. The Scottish Act also criminalized those that sought 'any help, response or consultation from any such users or abusers foresaid of witchcraft, sorcery or necromancy under the pain of death, which is to be executed against the user and abuser as well as the seeker of the response or consultation'. This harshness was unusual, though in practice few of those who sought 'any help' found themselves in deep trouble with the secular courts. Consulting magical practitioners was not a secular offence under most legal systems, and those prosecuted for providing unlawful magical services were usually treated less severely than those convicted of harmful magic and pact-making. This was the case under the Carolina code in the Holy Roman Empire. So, in 1582, the blacksmith and cunning-man George Kissling, of Ergersheim, Germany, was flogged and banished for the slander and extortion he had committed through his magical activities. Banishment was a common punishment for such crimes on the Continent.

In western Europe, however, relatively few cunning-folk and other magical practitioners were prosecuted under the general laws against witchcraft and magic. An analysis of 380 witchcraft cases in the duchy of Lorraine, in eastern France, found just two prosecutions for magical healing alone, and only one of those found guilty was executed, primarily because he was charged with making a tacit pact with the Devil. When magical practitioners found themselves in grave trouble it was usually because they had been accused of practising witchcraft as well as benign magic. This was the case with Agnes Sampson, who was tried and executed in Scotland in 1591. Of the fifty-three charges brought against her, over half concerned healing and divination; one of them, for example, concerned 'the healing of the laird of Reidshill's son by witchcraft, whom the chirurgeons had given over', and another concerned the curing of a child by 'gripping him and speaking some words of charming'. One reason for the general lack of prosecutions is that there was less incentive for people to report cunning-folk. The authorities may have put laws into place to suppress popular magic, but, unlike witches, cunning-folk served a valuable role in communities, even if they were thought capable of *maleficium*. Besides, most popular magicians, diviners, and magical healers were prosecuted before ecclesiastical and not secular courts.

Across Catholic and Protestant Europe church courts meted out penances and fines as punishment for sinful and immoral behaviour, which included consulting magical practitioners as well as performing acts of magic. Take the early modern church court records of the English county of Essex, for example, which reveal two cases of people burning livestock alive to remove spells placed upon the herds. Another case involved a churchwarden who went to consult a cunning-man concerning the whereabouts of his landlord's lost horse. With regard to the practice of drawing blood 'above the brow' to counteract witchcraft, a Scottish synod warned in 1728 that it was 'a sort and degree of witchcraft, not to be tolerated in a reformed land'. Sometimes, however, the prosecutions stemmed not so much from the magical acts committed but because they were practised on a Sunday when people should have been in church or at pious rest. The records of these church courts provide some of the richest material we have for the diversity and prevalence of popular magical practices. They reveal that every villager or townsperson across Europe had good access to a range of magical practitioners, much to the chagrin of parish priests and licensed medical men who saw popular magicians as a threat to their authority and incomes.

The Inquisitions of Spain, Portugal, and Italy were also kept busy with popular magic from the sixteenth to the eighteenth centuries. Between 1700 and 1820, for example, the Spanish Inquisition dealt with over 1,300 cases of magic, while the Portuguese Inquisition investigated over 500 magical practitioners and healers between 1715 and 1770. Inquisition tribunals could impose death sentences for magical activities deemed heretical, handing the guilty over to the secular authorities to perform the executions, but, again, lesser punishments were the norm. When, in 1619, Gabriel Monteche confessed to the Saragossa tribunal that he had for many years pretended 'he had the virtue to cure the bites of rabid dogs, and to cure other sicknesses and to deliver villages from hailstorms', he was sentenced to a hundred lashes and was banished from the district for two years. He was not punished for practising magic per se, but for having knowingly defrauded his many clients.

Why People Performed Magic

A lot of popular magic was concerned with combating witchcraft. Even with draconian laws in place to exterminate witches, the resort to the courts was only one of several strategies that the populace employed against those they suspected or publicly accused of being witches. As the trial records show, many witch prosecutions were a last resort after other informal methods of preventing, punishing, or vanquishing suspected witches were deemed to have failed. Trials were expensive, and they required witnesses and accusers to take time away from their daily work and to undergo the anxiety and stress of participating in a trial or judicial investigation. There was no guarantee of a satisfactory outcome. Execution rates in some European states were very low. In Finland fewer than 20 per cent of those tried were executed, and in England the figure is roughly around 25 per cent. So the witch trials only represent the tip of the iceberg when it comes to actions taken against suspected witches, and bewitchment was far more frequently dealt with informally.

While witchcraft was largely an imaginary crime in terms of what those executed were accused of doing, there is ample evidence for the use of harmful magic in popular culture. The difference between witchcraft and harmful magic is blurred, but they were not necessarily the same crime. Aggressive spells used to punish witches or force them to revoke their spells are a case in point. The practice of drawing blood from the suspected witch has already been noted. This was a common technique in England. According to some it had to be 'drawn above the breath', in other words from the forehead. But in practice other parts of the suspects' bodies were slashed or scratched with knives, pins, and other sharp objects. When in 1702 Richard Hathaway was prosecuted for falsely accusing and abusing Sarah Morduck for being a witch, the court heard how, 'with force and Arms, [he did] scratch the said Sarah, and did draw the Blood of her ... affirming himself to be freed from the said Diseases, by drawing said blood'. Hathaway submitted to various tests to see if he was telling the truth about his bewitchment, and one of them, designed by the local clergyman, concerned his claim to have felt instantly better on scratching Morduck. It involved deceiving Hathaway as to who he was actually scratching.

If you think the scratching this Woman, meaning Morduck, the pretended Witch, will do you any good, hold up your Hand, which he did, then the Doctor put the other Woman's Hand into his, and although at that time, he pretended to be Blind and Dumb, . . . yet he was apprehensive of what he did, and so jealous lest he should be imposed upon, and thereby his Imposture discovered, that he felt several times from the Wrist to the Elbow, to discover whether it was the Arm of the pretended Witch or no, before he would begin scratching, and being told he had fetched Blood, his Eyes were immediately opened, and his Speech restored.

There are numerous instances of people who used harmful charms and spells to influence rivals or to afflict others out of revenge and spite. But such people often had no reputation for witchcraft and never accrued suspicions of being witches. In the Mediterranean region, for instance, the 'ligature' spell was used to make men impotent. This usually involved tying a knot in a piece of string accompanied by some oral charm or other ritual. Such aggressive magic was often offered as a commercial service to others—witchcraft by proxy in a sense. The intermediary, a cunning-person, for example, was technically not a witch in the sense that he or she had no personal motivation for bewitching other than as a commercial transaction. The client might be motivated by 'witch-like' malice and envy, but had no power. So, when Antonia Donatino of Francavilla, Italy, wanted to cause the death of a man named Nicola Corvino, she went to an Albanian woman, who for a sum of money gave her a powder to throw in his fireplace.

In the world of popular magic most magical practices concerning witchcraft were defensive and not aggressive. It was better to ward off witchcraft from the body and the home than deal with its consequences. There was an array of charms, amulets, and apotropaic ('warding off') objects from which to choose. Certain plants, such as rowan, hazel, and angelica, were widely thought to keep witches at bay. In Poland, the leaves of the plant known as southern wormwood or European sage, which has a pungent, camphor-like smell, were kept as a protective amulet against witches. Then there were potent everyday agricultural items made of iron. The notion that witches and fairies were averse to the metal was widespread. Bits of broken iron implements, such as sickle blades and ploughshares, have been found secreted in the structure of historic buildings by archaeologists and builders, and they were clearly placed there for protection from witches and other spirits. The most obvious expression of this tradition was the nailing of horseshoes above doors. In the late seventeenth century it was observed that most houses in the west end of London had horseshoes on their threshold, and over a century later an antiquarian counted seventeen in one street alone. Not only was the horseshoe made of iron, but its crescent shape had magical significance. While the fear of witchcraft was a major incentive for resorting to such protective magic, there were numerous other external threats to people, their homes, and possessions. There were undesirable neighbours such as gossips and thieves, supernatural intruders such as devils, fairies, and ghosts. Then there were pests such as fleas, lice, and vermin, and also destructive natural forces such as lightning and hail. Through much of the historic period, prehistoric stone tools were kept to protect homes from lightning, for example, and they were known as thunder stones due to the common belief that they were formed by lightning strikes.

The predations of thieves were a perennial problem, second only to witches in their pestilential attacks on neighbours. There were two questions that magic could solve. First, who was the thief? If the culprit could be identified then they could either be reported to the authorities, or harmful and coercive magic could be employed to make them return their ill-gotten gains. One mid-sixteenth-century English conjuror gave his clients charms written on parchment that he instructed they sleep with under their heads. While they slept, he told them, 'thou shalt have a vision and knowledge who hath thy thing'. Alternatively, the victim of crime could bypass the ordeal of dealing with the thief, and see if magic could locate where their stolen goods had been deposited. Cotton Mather (1663–1728), the New England minister, scientist, and supporter of the Salem witch trials, wrote of someone he knew, 'who missing anything, would use to sit down and mutter a certain Charm, and then immediately, by an Invisible Hand be discretely led unto the place where the Thing was to be found'. When it came to thief magic even some of those authoritarian voices critical of popular magic recognized that, however erroneous the practices, the threat of magical investigation had a beneficial deterrent effect against the crime.

Affairs of the heart were another major concern that generated myriad rituals, charms, and spells. As we have seen, love magic was explicitly mentioned in the English 1563 Witchcraft Act, and it was also one of the most common magical offences dealt with by the Mediterranean inquisitions. Love magic is often seen as a female activity, but it was not fundamentally gendered in the sense that both men and women sought its influence. But its employment was shaped by gendered fears, social double standards, and unequal sexual power relationships. Male use of love magic was particularly concerned with sexual desire and potency. Women's resort to love magic was more concerned with relationships—marrying a good husband, reforming bad ones, and averting social shame. Many of the practices were not about protection or creating deterrents, but about attracting and provoking others. A sad but not infrequent problem was pregnancy out of wedlock—a disastrous situation for women at the time, with servant girls particularly vulnerable. So, in 1767, a Swedish court heard how a servant named Kirstin Gabrielsdotter became pregnant by a farmhand named Sven Andersson. Desperate to make him marry her, she resorted to magic. She was told that if she obtained a special sort of grass in the possession of a soldier named Dunckman and secretly placed it in Andersson's clothing she would win him over. In seventeenth-century Spain one popular service was concerned with giving males a *mala noche* or sleepless night through magical means. One prosecuted practitioner was accused of standing at a window, between eleven and twelve, casting spells to induce sleepless nights. These included the words, 'the bed in which you lie shall be made of thorns, your sheets made of nettles, from below the bed you shall hear a thousand whistling creatures'. These were intended 'to make a man go to a particular woman'. Another Spanish woman brought to trial for the practice was accused of promising that 'when she cast the spell the man would be raging all night long, thinking of her [the client] and craving the sight of her'. Such actions to provoke love could easily be interpreted as witchcraft—putting a spell over someone and making them act against their will or intent. But a lot of love magic was not about such aggravating coercion, but a matter of divination. A venerable example of the latter concerned the collection of fern seeds on Midsummer Eve. This had to be done just before midnight. The seeds were then taken home. All the doors were left open, and the seeds were placed on a cloth. Various different rituals then ensued depending on regions, but the main purpose was to draw the man or woman that would come to be their future spouse.

Treasure hunting was another popular magical crime that frequently came before religious and secular courts down to the nineteenth century. While at least some knowledge of literary magic was usually required to locate treasure, or to disable the spirits that were often thought to guard treasure, such hunts were usually group activities, with one person, sometimes a renegade clergyman, possessing the necessary magic books or knowledge, and the others providing assistance. As one German mayor observed in 1679, most treasure hunters 'had no knowledge whatsoever... they just dug with shovels and pick-axes on the spot where the treasure was supposed to be hidden'. Financial fortune could also be achieved through magically enhancing one's chances at gambling. Rituals for creating magic rings for this purpose could be found in grimoires (textbooks of magic), but for the general populace there were less arcane objects. The possession of bones from a dead criminal or pieces of a hangman's rope were widely thought to bring luck with the cards. Magical strategies for winning lotteries were numerous. In 1749 an Italian ecclesiastical court heard the case of one Vito Cavallo, who had instructed an apothecary on how he might divine successful lottery numbers. He was to go to confession wearing two lists of lottery numbers inside his shoes. Nine days after, he would feel a trembling in his arm, and this would be confirmation that the numbers he had written down were winning ones. Fifty years later, the London fortune-teller Joseph Powell made a good living selling 'lucky' lottery numbers. One of his disappointed clients wrote to him to explain, 'I was so very unfortunate in the two last Lotiaries [*sic*] that I never more will have any thing to do with it, as I was so much hurt by it.'

Much popular magic was concerned with general health problems. Not every illness was immediately attributed to witches or evil spirits. It was usually only lingering complaints or strange and unexpected symptoms that led to suspicion of supernatural causation. So epilepsy was often interpreted in this way. Internal cancers, where there was no visible sign of ailment, can also be identified from the archives. The trial records from all periods show over and over again how people would go to their local licensed doctors for treatment, and only when they repeatedly failed to cure them did suspicions of witchcraft develop; then the search for a magical cure began. There were numerous minor ailments and medical conditions that people dealt with through natural or simple charms. Let us examine these further by considering how such cures were thought to work.

The Practice of Popular Magic

To understand better the nature of popular magic it is necessary to consider *how* magic operated as well as *why* it was employed so pervasively. In predominantly illiterate societies, accounts of popular explanations for how magic worked are few and far between. Prosecutions involving the use of scratching, for example, rarely mention the conception behind the practice—other than that it was usually thought to work. We gain one rare insight from a mid-seventeenth-century Yorkshire case where a suspected witch, Elizabeth Lambe, was accused of magically stealing blood from the heart of her victim, Richard Brown. He came to the conclusion that to get better he must also draw blood from her to break the spell. This could reflect notions of *humoral theory*. Much popular and orthodox medicine at the time was based on the ancient Greek notion that health was governed by the balance of four substances or humours in the human body, namely yellow bile, black bile, blood, and phlegm. Imbalance between these substances in terms of quantity and quality led to ill health. In this context some witches' spells were thought to work by upsetting their victims' humoral equilibrium. The cure could be natural, through using herbal remedies or medical procedures to increase or reduce one or more of the humours, for instance, or it could be magical in terms of countering the witchcraft that was thought to have caused the imbalances.

To stick with the Yorkshire case for a moment, Brown's conception could also have been based on the widespread principle of *limited good*. This near universal popular belief was based on the notion that everything is finite within a community—goods, crops, health, prosperity, luck, beauty, fertility, and so on. If, say, one woman produced lots of babies then that explained why another woman was unable to conceive. Someone or something is always to blame if there is an imbalance in a world of limited good. In Brown's case the witch drew his blood and took it for herself, and the only way to restore the balance, and so break the spell, was to reduce the surplus blood in the witch's body, which would magically restore the blood back to his heart. There are more clear examples of limited good in other aspects of popular magic, such as the crime of magical milk stealing. There was a limited supply of possible milk in a community and so if a farmer's cows mysteriously stopped lactating then somewhere a neighbour's cows would be producing an obvious abundance. This led to suspicions of witchery. Such instances were quite common in Polish witchcraft trials. In 1613 one complainant said of the accused, 'she has plenty of butter from just one cow'. In a case from 1688, a husband defended his wife from accusations of witchery by observing, 'I have nine cows, but I don't have even a drop of milk, and my wife always used to say, "they call me a witch, even though I have to buy cheese."' In several early modern Russian cases, tavern keepers accused their rivals of witchcraft because they had fewer and fewer clients and their rivals more and more. In all these cases the unfair imbalance could be restored in one's favour either through directly dealing with the witch through judicial prosecution or by non-confrontational counter-magic. So if a witch was believed to have collected dew from the fields early in the morning to reduce the yields of a neighbour's cow, the neighbour could restore the balance by restoring moisture through sprinkling holy water on the cows or fields, for example, or washing the cows at sunrise with water from a mill wheel.

A lot of magic was popular in the sense that anyone could perform it, the knowledge being widespread orally and transmitted through generations of families and neighbours. No special knowledge, materials, or powers were required, and ingredients were at hand in the domestic and natural environment. A good example is the cure of warts by rubbing them with some moist organic material, a steak or a snail for example, and then placing it somewhere where the material would decay and shrivel. Let us focus on the humble mollusc. In the case of snails they were pierced on a thorny tree after being rubbed on the wart. Then, by an act of *sympathetic magic*, as the snail employed to rub the wart shrivelled so too would the wart. The 'law of sympathy' explains that any two or more things that had been in contact with each other had an enduring invisible influence that could be detected and manipulated magically. Similarly, two very different substances that shared a resemblance or likeness had occult or hidden sympathies. So the root of the mandrake, which sometimes had a humanoid form, and was carved to enhance such a resemblance, accrued a huge amount of magical lore. It was kept for good luck, bestowed divinatory powers, was used in love magic rituals, enhanced one's chance of winning lawsuits, as well as having numerous uses in herbal medicine.

Various rituals for detecting witchcraft and the identity of witches concerned the sympathetic relationship between the bodily fluids of the victim, urine in the case of humans and milk in the case of cows. In a trial document from eastern France, urine was poured onto a hot iron and if it evaporated the condition was natural and if the liquid remained it was witchery. In the Netherlands, if the urine or milk did not boil over when heated on a fire then bewitchment was diagnosed. The late seventeenth-century astrologer-physician Joseph Blagrave explained that bodily liquids contained 'the vital spirit of the Witch', as the Devil would not 'suffer the Witch to infuse any poisonous matter into the body of man or beast, without some of the Witches blood mingled with it'. The English witch bottle tradition is one of the most elaborate examples of this genre of sympathetic magic. Evidently popular from the mid-seventeenth century onwards, I shall let Joseph Blagrave explain the procedure and effect:

> Stop the urine of the Patient, close up in a bottle, and put into it three nails, pins or needles, with a little white Salt, keeping the urine always warm: if you let it remain long in the bottle, it will endanger the witches life: for I have found by experience that they will be grievously tormented making their water with great difficulty, if any at all.

So there were two acts of sympathetic magic taking place in this ritual. One concerned the link between witch and victim, and the other concerned the vessel of urine that represented the witch's bladder. The archaeological evidence shows variations in the practice. Some bottles were merely buried rather than heated, suggesting they served a domestic protective function rather than a means of divination or aggressive magic.

The most obvious act of sympathetic magic was sticking sharp objects into images and likenesses. As we saw in the first chapter, this was practised back in antiquity, and is well known today in the use of voodoo dolls. There were other variations. During the renovation or demolition of buildings in England shrivelled hearts pierced with numerous pins and thorns have occasionally been found. When a pig, cow, horse, or sheep died and witchcraft was suspected, then one form of counter-magic was to take the heart from the carcass and pierce it. The sympathetic link between witch and victim meant that piercing it with sharp objects and then slowly roasting the heart would inflict great and lasting pain on the heart of the witch. Similar rituals were used to provoke desire, as evident in numerous examples from the early modern Spanish trial records. One person reported how she was instructed 'to take an orange...and place it among the burning embers and should say... "let his heart burn with love for me just as this orange is burning now"'. In another case a witness stated, 'so that certain persons would love them well...she threw the eggs into the fire and they burst. And they said that the heart of the person for whom they were blinded would burn as that egg had burned.'

Transference is an aspect of sympathetic magic that concerned the removal of a disease or affliction from an individual by passing it on to another living thing through unwitting contact. In the days before germ theory was popularly understood it was commonly believed that some diseases could not be eradicated, and to be relieved of them they had to be passed on. So warts might be rubbed with pebbles or beans, and the pebbles or beans then placed in a bag and thrown over the shoulder. The curious person who subsequently picked it up, perhaps thinking money lay within, would get the warts while those of the original sufferer would disappear. Disease could be similarly transferred to a corpse, as exemplified by a custom in Germany of placing the clothes and objects of the sick in the graves of the deceased before burial. For those with more of a conscience regarding other living things, diseases could be ritually banished to running water. In the early seventeenth century the Scottish cunning-woman and suspected witch Isobel Haldane attempted to cure a child by washing its clothing in water while calling upon the Holy Trinity. She then carried the water and shirt to a stream. On the way, however, she spilt some of the water and became concerned that if anyone walked over it they would accrue the child's disease rather than it being washed away in the stream.

Some popular magical healing worked in symbolic terms, most notably the act of *passing through* as a ritual of removal. The best example to explain this concerns the numerous traditions whereby a cure was affected by crawling through a holed stone or a narrow gap between stones, which were either formed by natural processes or were the remnants of prehistoric stone monuments. The most famous example is the Bronze Age Men-a-Toll holed stone in Cornwall, where until the nineteenth century it was believed that the act of crawling through it without the knees touching the ground would cure rheumatism, rickets, and other ailments. A more elaborate Swedish passing through ritual involved a *smöjträ*. This was a naturally formed piece of tree branch that had fused to form a hoop. Two examples in Swedish museums are inscribed with the dates 1696 and 1787 respectively. The latter also had a pentagram, swastika, half-moon, and other magical symbols carved into the wood. Children suffering from rickets were passed though the *smöjträ*. Across Europe, hernias were cured by ritually passing the patient through the split trunk of a young tree. The cure also involved sympathetic magic as the hernia would only disappear once the trunk was sealed together and the tree began to heal itself.

A related symbolic process concerned the action of *encircling* or *circumambulation*—a magical act that we saw in Chapter 1 was important in the ancient Egyptian world. This could be a matter of containment, a ritual restricting the spread of an ailment, condition, or malign influence, or it could be an act of protection—keeping unwanted things at bay. The key was physically delineating the necessary boundaries. Thus wart charmers often made a circular motion around warts while muttering their charms. The seventeenth-century Scottish church court records provide several other examples of the practice. One George Beir treated his scrofula (which causes swellings on the neck) by winding two black silk threads around the affected area. A couple of other cases concerned the requirement that the patient walk around their homes at midnight. The act of measurement was also an aspect of containment, with many recorded examples from the medieval to the present. The ailment could not spread once it had been measured, and the healing ritual often then proceeded according to contagious and sympathetic magic principles, with the measuring stick or thread being buried or cut.

Astrology continued to be an important part of popular magical practice in the early modern and modern era. Planetary influences were integral to understanding the power of herbs in healing and magic. The influential seventeenth-century book of herbal medicine by William Culpeper, which was still in print two centuries later, observed that, if gathered under the influence of the planet Mercury, woody nightshade was 'excellently good to remove witchcraft, both in men and beasts, as also all sudden diseases whatsoever'. The illiterate healer with no access to the detailed accounts of the relationships between different plants and planets discussed in herbal texts still knew well that plants should only be picked at certain propitious times. Much of the oral lore concerned the lunar cycle. The main rule of thumb was to gather plants during the waxing of the moon, for as the moon grew so too would the potency of the medicinal or magical herbs. Some rituals had to be conducted as the moon waned, particularly those concerning the cure of swellings, for obvious reasons. One early modern German healer named Hans Röcklin possessed a magical healing stone which he applied to people's bodies 'three days in a row after the [full] moon' to reduce pain, while muttering a charm that instructed that the afflicted part 'should wane as the moon wanes'.

These core magical processes usually accrued other secondary but essential rituals, such as repetitive actions or the utterance of charms a certain number of times, triple replication being the most common. In seventeenth-century Scotland a healer named Agnes Anderson was reported for curing infant nausea by turning children three times head over heels between the doors of a barn. A French charm for burns ran:

> While passing down the street of Sainte-Blaise, Saint John said to Our Lord, 'Lord, here is a child that burns itself—Saint John blow on this child three times with your breath saying in the name of the Father and of the Son, the child will be healed.'

The snail wart cure often had to be performed nine times with the same snail. In the tradition of such oral charms as that above, it was also quite common for the laws of contra-sexual transmission and healing to apply. So, in Sweden, snakebite charms were only efficacious if passed down from female to male and vice versa. In England, the cure of swellings through the stroke of recently dead people's hands was also often thought to work only by this contra-sexual rule. Some rituals had to be performed at specific moments of the day, such as at sunset, dawn, and midnight—in other words liminal or boundary moments in the changing cycle of daily time. All these ritual prescriptions were never universal nor necessarily hard and fast rules, but they were pervasive.

How magic was practised also depended on where it was conducted. While most popular magic was not restricted to specific places, there were some locations that had particular significance. The churchyard is the most obvious example. In England, in 1775, a young man was buried up to his head naked in a churchyard for two hours in order to cure his rheumatism. It is unclear why it was thought to work, but presumably it was believed that the affliction transferred to the dead who lay buried there. Churchyard earth also had healing and magical properties. The church itself was the location of numerous magical rituals. In the late seventeenth century, Jesuit missionaries were shocked to find that in the German town of Untergrombach people practised a healing ritual that required walking naked around the altar. In Finland we find the remarkable nineteenth-century practice of secreting in Lutheran churches miniature coffins containing frogs. The custom seems to have served primarily as a means of countering witchcraft. Numerous rituals were conducted at physical boundaries and crossing points such as bridges and rivers that also had symbolic and supernatural significance. Prehistoric monuments and burial mounds, popularly interpreted as the dwellings of fairies or the gateways to their world, were also a common site for treasure hunting expeditions and the magic rituals that were required. During a Danish trial for digging into an ancient burial mound in 1825, it was heard how the ritual involved bread, sewing thread, and a piece of willow tree. Crossroads were another human-made landscape feature where the boundary between the mundane and spiritual world was permeable. Suicides were buried at crossroads and so they were a place where the spirits of the dead were likely to appear. Crossroads were also, for obvious reasons, the ideal place to practise transference magic. Where better to leave stones which had been rubbed on warts! In Italian folk magic hepatitis, or the *mal d'arco* or 'rainbow illness', could be cured by the patient urinating for several nights in a pot containing the plant common rue. This was then poured at a crossroads at night while reciting a magical formula. The next person who passed the crossroad contracted the illness.

While some practices as well as concepts were widespread and of considerable antiquity we should not consider popular magic as a static body of knowledge, preserving rituals and spells unchanged from time immemorial. While the fundamentals of popular magic were familiar across Europe, there were regional variations based on a range of factors. Different environments, flora, and fauna determined distinct magical needs—or not. Snakebite charms were not required in Ireland as there were no snakes in the country. Likewise, the magic lore surrounding bears and wolves was irrelevant in Britain because the former became extinct in the early centuries AD and the latter by the fifteenth century. Olive oil was an important liquid in Mediterranean magic and medicine, but not popularly used in northern Europe for obvious reasons. But commerce, migration, colonization, and the spread of popular literature had an impact. There was a lively long-distance trade in herbs, spices, and other items of magical value that were used in popular magic, items that were either scarce or exotic. In the early modern period, bezoars, which were the hard gastric balls created in the digestive tracts of Persian goats and other exotic ruminants, were widely prized for their magical and medical power to expel poisons. In early modern Italy the horn of the elk, a mammal of northern Europe, was sold as a great cure-all. Apothecaries, chemists, and druggists were significant resources for such popular magical ingredients as well as medicines. They drove a thriving trade in Dragon's blood. This blood-red resin from various non-European trees had been used medicinally since ancient times, but in nineteenth-century England it was commonly purchased for use in love magic.

Different kingdoms subscribed to different religions, of course. The huge array of Orthodox and Catholic rituals, masses, prayers, exorcisms, pilgrimages, as well as sacramentals, such as holy water, consecrated wafers, rosaries, and blessed candles and herbs, were integral aspects of popular magic in Catholic and Orthodox countries. Indeed, one way of defining much popular magic is the inappropriate or blasphemous use of Catholic and Orthodox practices by the laity. That does not mean that people considered they were being blasphemous or perverting religion. After all, was not religion meant to be for furthering the general good? So, in Poland, for instance, dairying processes could be protected from witchcraft by pouring the milk over blessed herbs or blessed cheesecloths boiled during Easter mass. In parts of early modern Germany the water and wine used to wash out the chalice after mass was much prized for its healing properties. A series of prosecutions in witch-trial era France concerned shepherds stealing holy wafers to feed to their sheep in order to protect them from wolves and witches. A seventeenth-century French magician used candles that had been burned at three high masses on Christmas Day, and the love potions he sold contained holy water, salt, sulphur, and incense, which he said he concocted under the shadow of a crucifix that contained a piece of the true cross. Herbs gathered on certain saints' days, most notably rue picked on St John's Eve, were given magical potency.

The Catholic saints were widely invoked in simple oral and written healing charms. Many variations of a widespread charm against toothache involved St Apollonia (a third-century saint who had her teeth knocked out). One French example ran:

> Saint Apollonia, sat on a marble stone, Our Lord passing that way asked her: Apollonia what are you doing there?—I am here for my master, for my blood and for my toothache.—Apollonia, go back; if it is a drop of blood it will fall, and if it is a worm it will die.

This story reflects the importance of apocrypha in popular healing. Apocryphal stories were accounts of events and encounters involving New Testament saints and their relations that were not actually in the Bible. They began to circulate in the early centuries of Christianity. Some were recorded in texts that the church fathers decided not to include in the definitive New Testament; others were legends that continued to circulate in charm form through until the present day. It was their apocryphal but still holy nature that imbued them with power. When a nineteenth-century English clergyman told a toothache charmer, 'Well, but Dame Grey, I think I know my Bible, and I don't find any such verse in it', she replied, 'Yes your reverences, that is just the charm. It's in the Bible, but you can't find it!'

With the spread of the Reformation hundreds of thousands of people were no longer able to procure the services of a priest or use most of the sacramentals. Exorcism was banned. But this did not stop people in Protestant lands from continuing to resort to 'Catholic' forms of healing and using Catholic ritual and liturgy in spells and charms. Protestant church courts across Europe spent a lot of their time attempting to suppress the continued lay resort to what was denounced as Catholic 'superstition'. In areas where the boundaries between the two faiths were close, such as in the Netherlands or in parts of Germany, people could illicitly cross state and religious borders to consult Catholic priests. But even in the likes of Calvin's Scotland, far removed from Catholic countries, people continued to resort to old holy wells and appeal to the saints for protection and healing.

The various branches of Christianity were not the only religious influences on popular magic in Europe. In Spain, elements of Islamic magic continued to form part of the magical arsenal centuries after the Moors had been defeated in the late medieval period and Christianity re-imposed upon the country. In southern Spain Arabic magic texts, real and imagined, were sought after by treasure hunters. In 1597, the Saragossa tribunal investigated a *morisca* (a female descendant of the Spanish Moors converted to Christianity) named Cándida Gombal. She was from Valencia and was accused of invoking 'demons by speaking in Arabic and on other occasions—when she was heard by the witnesses—would call on Barabbas, Satan, Beelzebub and Maymon'. Maymon was a lord of the djinn or genies. Much to the annoyance of the Inquisition, protective charms known as *alherces*, which contained verses from the Koran, also circulated quite widely amongst the general population. Despite the many persecutions over the centuries, Jewish populations across Europe also expressed their distinctive traditions of popular magic and religion. The most obvious example of this was the *mezuzah*, which was a small container containing a scroll of parchment containing passages from Deuteronomy that was nailed to doorposts for protection. Unlike the *alherces*, though, these rarely percolated beyond the Jewish community. As a nineteenth-century Hebrew scholar observed, 'a *mezuzah* in the hands of a Christian may be considered a curiosity, because a Jew would not knowingly permit it'.

As well as the religious geography, there were other forces shaping regional magical traditions. Different execution customs generated different magical healing and protective rituals and charms. In England the employment of public hanging generated the tradition of seeking out the hangman shortly after an execution to have swellings, such as goitre and wens, stroked by the still warm hand of the criminal's corpse. The hanging rope was cut into pieces and sold for cure, protection, and good luck in gambling. The practice of behead-ing in countries such as Sweden and some German states led people to seek out the blood that spurted from the corpses' necks, dabbing handkerchiefs in it or collecting it in vessels to be drunk as a cure for epilepsy or for other healing and magical purposes. At the beheading of the murderer Alexander Breitfeld in Stockholm in 1843, for instance, several people rushed forward as the axe fell to catch some blood. One of them who suffered from epilepsy had an attack as he sought to drink the warm liquid spurting from the neck, and nearly fell into the grave prepared next to the execution site. Such execution practices continued into the nineteenth century until public execution was abolished in most countries.

The rise of popular printed literature also led to the generation of different national strains of popular magic. As we have seen in previ-ous chapters, written spells, charms, conjurations, and adjurations had been transmitted on clay, stone, lead, leather, and papyrus since the advent of writing. The widespread use of parchment (made from animal skins) in the medieval period enabled the creation of books as we know them today with pages and stitched spines. New learned magic texts appeared attributed to the likes of Solomon, which were copied and traded illicitly in the seats of learning across Europe. Then with the rise of the printing press in the fifteenth century and increas-ing literacy down the social scale, literary magic became increasingly 'popular' rather than the preserve of clergymen and other university-trained elites. At first we find schoolmasters and physicians with a smattering of Latin using vernacular magical manuscripts to provide charms and to perform conjurations for themselves and the paying public. Then Renaissance magical texts by the likes of Cornelius Agrippa began to be printed, first in Germany and Switzerland, but by the mid-seventeenth century there was a boom in printed vernacu-lar editions of these occult books elsewhere. Learned magic was being democratized and the boundary between elite and popular magic blurred. Through such intermediaries as cunning-folk, arcane magic rituals and texts were reinterpreted and adapted for popular needs. Written charms for protecting the home and farm were created by cunning-folk from the bricolage of symbols, occult words, and conjurations contained in printed and manuscript magic books. Even if the purchasers of such charms were literate, the contents were not meant to be read. They were usually folded and secreted above doors and windows, or buried in the ground.

During the eighteenth century, different genres of magic book and grimoire appeared in different parts of Europe. The nature of this popular magical literature, whether in print or manuscript form, influenced the sort of magic practised by and for the general populace. The preoccupation with treasure hunting was greater in continental Europe than in Britain during the eighteenth and nineteenth centuries because popular grimoires on the Continent contained treasure conjurations. In Scandinavia we find the *svartbok* or black book, which was often attributed to the semi-legendary sixteenth-century magician Dr Faust or the legendary St Cyprian of Antioch. Some of these black books contained instructions on how to make a pact with the Devil. A number of trials in eighteenth-century Denmark and Sweden involved soldiers who had used black books to seek promises from the Devil to give them protection from bullets.

During the eighteenth and nineteenth centuries tens of thousands of small, cheap books of spells, talismans, and conjurations were illegally printed and sold throughout France. With names such as the *Grand Grimoire*, the *Grimoire du Pape Honorius*, and the *Dragon rouge*, the French grimoires were popular in the sense that they were affordable, written for the basic reader, and were widely available. But that is not to say they were used by all. They inspired awe and terror, and it was generally thought that only those who already held magical powers or secret knowledge could use them effectively. The Mediterranean inquisitions were successful at supressing the printing of such grimoires in Italy, Spain, and Portugal until the early nineteenth century, but they were unable to control the widespread trade in manuscript versions, and we have accounts of numerous Spaniards and Italians travelling to southern France solely to purchase copies for treasure hunting purposes.

Who Performed Popular Magic?

Having outlined *why* and *how* popular magic was performed, we now need to explore in more detail *who* used magic in different contexts and for different reasons. As has already been mentioned, much magic could be conducted by anyone, but readers will have already noted some patterns. To begin with, it is important to understand that the ability to perform popular magic was sometimes determined by restricted access to certain materials or activities. This could relate to control over bodily substances, for example. So women had possession of their menstrual blood and breast milk for use in love spells and healing. The use of menstrual blood, in particular, caused masculine concern as in some Mediterranean cultures it was mixed with food and drink to provoke love or control abusive husbands. Then there were executioners whose access to criminal corpse body parts and blood made them central figures in facilitating certain types of popular magic and necromantic rituals. This reputation led some executioners to come under suspicion of magic even when corpse constituents such as human fat were thought to have natural medical benefits. In 1579 a carpenter named Georg Schott sought out the executioner of Schongau, Bavaria, to obtain the colon of a dead man which he intended to burn to ashes and to mix with gunpowder to give him a sure shot.

Much popular magic was associated with specific occupations. Midwifery was one such role. The act of birth and the protection of mother and child during the early days and months required a considerable degree of intimacy and reliance on other women. This could generate suspicions of witchcraft against midwives when the child or mother fell ill, but also led to the belief that they had more knowledge than most about how to keep harm at bay. In Mediterranean countries, prostitutes and procuresses were thought to have intimate knowledge of how to manipulate the urges of love and sex, and unsurprisingly these occupations make up a significant portion of those prosecuted for performing love magic. Dairy processing was another predominantly female sphere. Butter and cheese making was a common target of witchcraft. Accordingly, women were often involved in performing the necessary counter-spells and protective rituals. These domestic responsibilities, including the care of children, help explain why women made up two-thirds of those who violently scratched or abused suspected witches in nineteenth-century Somerset.

In agricultural communities men were more concerned with magic regarding horses and herding. In 1703 the Rouen *parlement* sentenced three shepherds to death for 'having broken down a church door at night and carried off some Hosts from the tabernacle as well as Holy Water from the baptismal fonts' to cure their sheep. Herders who spent the summer months in the high pastures, living with their animals under the night skies, were thought to garner special knowledge of the stars, herbs, and veterinary cures; they lived in closer contact with the spirits that roamed the dark hours: men such as the Bavarian herdsman Conrad Stöckhlin who was arrested and tortured in 1586. By this time he had been the horse herder for the village of Oberstdorf for nineteen years. He accrued a reputation for magic and soothsaying, he said he gained knowledge from a guardian angel and he rode with a spectral horde of wild huntsmen. Because in some parts of Europe the executioner doubled up as a torturer, they were also thought to have unusually good knowledge of human anatomy, and were sought out for their ability to find witch's marks. Blacksmiths with their ability to transform metals and intimate knowledge of horses were another group. A public exhortation against witches and magicians published in Bavaria in 1611 included a warning about 'those blacksmiths in the country as well as in the towns, who sometimes display and use strange arts'. Amongst those males found accused of witchcraft in early modern Normandy we find a preponderance of shepherds and blacksmiths.

Masculine magical spheres also included fishing boats and mines. There were specific genres of ritual and belief regarding both these livelihoods, much of it around the avoidance of misfortune. It was a widespread belief that seeing a pig on the way to one's boat was bad luck, and so some fishermen would refuse to go to sea until the following day. Even saying the word 'pig' on board was avoided. British sailors prized the protective power of a baby's caul (the amniotic membrane that occasionally remains around a baby's head and face at birth) against drowning or shipwreck. Money was to be made by selling cauls to sailors with advertisements appearing in newspapers, such as this from the *Morning Post* in 1814: 'To Captains of Ships, and others—To be sold, a child's caul. Price 30 guineas.' Such was the demand amongst sailors around this time that there was a lively trade in counterfeit cauls made from lamb's skin. Miners developed their own distinct magical observances and notions based around the propitiation of the supernatural denizens of the mines

known as knockers in some parts of Britain or the *Bergmännlein* or Little
Men of the Mountain by German miners.

The use of guns also generated predominantly masculine spheres of
magical practice. Numerous charms and spells existed to ensure a
good shot or protect guns from witchcraft. Hunting accrued a considerable amount of magical lore, though its importance varied with
the degree of gun ownership in different countries. In Britain, where
the possession of firearms was very restricted, gun magic was not a
strong element of popular magic. In colonial and republican America,
however, stories of bewitched shotguns and the use of counter-magic
spells were widespread, with numerous traditions deriving from German and Swiss popular magic. To remove witchcraft from a gun one
could put a crumb of communion wafer down the barrel, fire grains of
salt or a silver bullet, or ritually wash the barrel in a stream as an act of
transference. War generated concerns not only over the ability to
shoot straight, but to prevent being killed by enemy guns. The resort
to diabolic pacts by Scandinavian soldiers has already been mentioned. A Russian spell for protection began:

> In the lofty chamber, at the river mouth, beyond the river Volga, a fair
> maiden stands, stands and decks herself, commends herself to valorous
> folk, glories in deeds of war. In her right hand she holds bullets of lead,
> in her left bullets of copper, on her feet bullets of iron. Do thou, fair
> maiden, ward off the guns of the Turks, the Tatars, the Circassians, the
> Russians, the Mordvins, of all tribes and foes.

An early eighteenth-century Russian military law ordered severe
penalties for the practice of such gun magic. The wearing of protective
charms was also widespread amongst the soldiery. These were often
religious in nature, particularly in Catholic countries. Printed and
manuscript pieces of apocrypha, known as *Himmelsbriefe* (Heaven
Letters) in Germany, and similarly *Lettres du Ciel* in France, were
found on dead Catholic and Protestant soldiers during the Franco-
Prussian War and the First World War.

These gendered boundaries of activity and responsibility were not
hard and fast, nor were they necessarily strictly adhered to at the time
in popular culture. Men would seek out remedies for bewitched milk,
women purchased charms for their soldier or sailor husbands to carry
with them in battle, and women used the apparatus of masculine

trades such as the horseshoe or horse's harness in their domestic magic. Men performed love magic. In Russian folk magic, fishermen could ensure a good catch by using nets made at midnight by a pregnant woman. Cunning-women and cunning-men, furthermore, pretty much dealt with the same breadth of problems and issues irrespective of gender.

Distinct from those who made a petty income from, or charitably provided, their limited magical services were trades and crafts that had their own rituals and apotropaic traditions that they employed as part of their professional practice. Everyday building practices involved a range of rituals designed to protect homes and their occupants. Some of these practices have left little or no record in written sources and it is only through archaeology and finds revealed by the demolition and renovation of old houses that we have become aware of them. One widespread practice recorded across western Europe, and the former British colonies of Australia and North America, was the placement of old or worn shoes in wall cavities, usually just one in a location but sometimes in pairs or groups. They have been found in chimneys in particular, but also above windows and doors, under the floorboards, and in the ceiling. It is most likely they were deliberately concealed to ward off intruders from entrances to the home, and they were sometimes deposited along with other objects such as clothing and animal bones. Cats were also bricked or plastered into the fabric of houses, occasionally with their mouths open or even, in a few instances, posed with a dead mouse, rat, or bird. The practice seems to have been a form of sympathetic magic, with the mummified cats serving to keep buildings free of rodent infestations and other pests.

Across Europe there were ethnic or 'outsider' populations that accrued reputations for possessing beneficial as well as harmful magical knowledge. Regarding the latter, this could be completely unfounded, as with the Jews who were repeatedly persecuted for imaginary, heinous magical crimes, but other groups had more equivocal reputations. In the early modern period Swedes considered the Finns and the Saami as particularly skilled magical 'others' for good and bad. When the Swedish woman Maria Persdotter Lind was prosecuted for magical healing in the 1720s, she confessed she told people she was a Saami in order to attract more customers. In Spain the *moriscos* were thought to possess ancient Moorish knowledge inaccessible to other Spaniards. The Seville inquisition investigated a *morisca* woman who claimed a Moor had given her a book 'for remedies of her illnesses...and with [which she] would heal and take away all illnesses'. Overseas conquest and expansion led to encounters with new indigenous 'others'. In eighteenth-century Portugal, for instance, we find elements of the magical traditions of Africa and South America entering the domestic milieu through slaves and servants. 'Foreigners' more generally were able to arouse interest or suspicion in communities. Numerous treasure magicians were described as 'strangers', and fraudster-magicians played upon this status. Thus a seventeenth-century German treasure hunter claimed to have come from Turkey, and another said he was from the Balkans. No outsider group had a more pervasive reputation for good as well as malicious magic over the centuries, though, than the gypsies—or the 'Saracens' or 'Bohemians' as they were also known.

In 1679 the synod of Otranto, Italy, issued a warning to the laity that the gypsies 'easily deceive the simple and careless by means of their illusions and divinations'. Gypsies were a perennial target of the English vagrancy laws, which included a section referencing their reputation for divinatory powers. The mid-eighteenth-century vagrancy Act covered 'all persons pretending to be gypsies, or wandering in the habit or form of Egyptians, or pretending to have skill in physiognomy, palmistry, or like craft science, or pretending to tell fortunes, or using any subtil craft to deceive and impose on any of his majesty's subjects'. Not only were they considered inveterate fraudsters, they were also considered to be beyond the Christian pale, not bound by the conventions and strictures of piety. As a seventeenth-century Spanish author complained, 'they do not know what the Church is, and do not enter it except to commit sacrilege. They do not know any prayers...they eat meat all the time without respecting Fridays or Lent.' They were liminal people—that is, they seemed to exist on the boundaries of order and disorder, faith and irreligion, and the mundane and the occult world. At a more pragmatic level their marginality and itinerant lifestyle enabled them to trick and dupe people with more impunity than the many crooked, sedentary magical practitioners.

In Spain, the gypsies were reputed for their ability to locate Moorish treasure, and one of the characteristic gypsy magic frauds regarding the accrual of great wealth was the *hokkano baro* or 'great trick'. The gypsy magicians would arouse the avarice of clients with an account of how they could, through a simple ritual, obtain great wealth. This required the client to gather some of their valuables or their savings and deposit them in a certain place while the magician performed a magic ceremony—'gold calls forth gold, and silver calls forth silver'. The client was then told that they must return after a certain period of time, and they would find their valuables multiplied. In the meantime, the gypsy made off with the goods. In 1762 an Oxfordshire gentleman was defrauded of eleven guineas under the promise that two nights after handing over the cash three white doves would deposit 200 guineas and more under his pillow. Consulting the gypsies not only emptied the pockets but could arouse considerable suspicion as to one's intentions. After all, gypsies also had a great reputation for cursing as well as divination. In 1612, a Venetian woman named Felicità Greca paid a gypsy woman to tell her fortune by the method of tossing fava beans. This involved the gypsy inter-preting the pattern they made when they were thrown and fell to the ground. A neighbour and former friend of Greca's, who believed her mother had been crippled by witchery, witnessed the two together performing this ceremony. She stormed over, and, as she testified, 'began to scream that it was wrong to do such things because I suspected that the bad magic had been put upon my mother'.

Cunning-Folk

Cunning-folk have been mentioned here and there in previous chap-ters, but who were they? The term is obviously English, and it was one of several popular names for the same type of magical practitioner, including 'conjuror', 'wise-man' and 'wise-woman', and 'wizard'. Similar figures can be identified across Europe, known variously as *curanderos* in Spain, *kloge folk* in Denmark, *désenvoûteurs* in France, for example. These were all people who, rather than having just a little more knowledge than their neighbours in one or other form of magic, offered a complete package of magical and medical services including herbalism, astrology, love magic, theft magic, fortune-telling, charm-writing, and most important of all the protection from and cure of witchcraft. They were clearly identifiable and important figures in the world of popular magic from the early modern period through to the twentieth century.

The majority were men, but not overwhelmingly so. They accrued their reputations for magical power in a variety of ways. As already noted, foreignness and certain ethnic identities, assumed or real, were a good basis on which to build a reputation. Some derived reputations through birthright, such as being a seventh son of a seventh son or a seventh daughter of a seventh daughter, being born with a caul, or, as with some Hungarian cunning-folk, being born with teeth or an extra finger. Several seventeenth-century French cunning-women claimed their powers from having been born on Good Friday. Power could also be learned rather than inherited by birth. In several cases from early modern France and England, women built their reputations for magical knowledge from having been (or so they said) the wives or servants of licensed physicians and eminent astrologers, or even the concubines of Catholic priests. An aspiring cunning-person certainly had a better chance of succeeding in generating a successful career if they inherited the business and paraphernalia from a reputed father or mother. The possession of literacy and books of magic were powerful aids. Bear in mind that illiteracy was high in much of Europe until the nineteenth century, particularly amongst women in Catholic Mediterranean countries. As already noted, cunning-folk mined occult texts to produce written charms for their clients, but they also made great ornamental show of books to impress upon clients the source of their power. Some cunning-folk claimed to have received special magical knowledge or powers from the spirit world through contact with fairies, ghosts, and angels. This could be achieved through ritual conjurations contained in grimoires, but numerous cunning-folk, particularly women, claimed to have been singled out by the fairies to acquire their special knowledge of occult things. As a mid-seventeenth-century account of the activities and trial of a cunning-man in northern England records:

> What this man did was with a white powder which, he said, he received from the Fairies, and that going to a Hill he knocked three times, and the Hill opened, and he had access to, and conversed with a visible people; and offered, that if any Gentleman present would either go himself in person, or send his servant, he would conduct them thither, and shew them the place and persons from whom he had his skill.

Due to the importance of literacy in the formation of cunning-folk's reputations it is not surprising that we find that many in the magic business were from the professions, trades, and crafts. These were the sort of people who from the sixteenth century onwards were most likely to have gained an education of sorts. Such mundane jobs helped provide a front for illicit magical activities which often brought in significantly more income.

People often went to cunning-folk as a last resort, particularly in cases of illness caused by supposed witchcraft. The first move was to go to licensed physicians, seek their treatment, and then, if dissatisfied, to go to cunning-folk. Some physicians believed that witches caused natural illnesses and offered to cure such afflictions by natural means. In a book exploring this issue, *Daimonomageia* (1665), the seventeenth-century English physician William Drage suggested seven ways to deal with witchcraft illnesses:

1. To punish the Witch, and that two wayes, 1. Either her own Body, or 2. The thing bewitched.
2. Call upon GOD.
3. Use Specifical Medicines, antipathetical to Daemons, if there be any such.
4. Use, or make the Witch use the Ceremonies of ridding the Sickness.
5. Make her, if the other fail, either to take the Disease her self, or transfer it to some Dog, or Brute.
6. Search, if there be no Charmes, or things resembling the Sick, laid about the house.
7. If the Witch is imprisoned, she is void of hurt, and Satan leaves her.

But many of Drage's contemporaries were sceptical and resisted diagnosing supernatural causation. So when an ailment persisted or got worse despite formal medical treatment, people turned to those who would confirm suspicions of witchcraft, thereby opening up the full range of curative actions listed by Drage. In Catholic countries the priest might be the next port of call for the bewitched rather than a cunning-person. In southern Italy in 1723, for example, one Anna Sanasi, distraught that her newlywed son was apparently impotent through a ligature spell, sought out a Capuchin friar who on several occasions read out the Gospel over the afflicted couple. When this failed to cure him, they sought cure from local cunning-folk. While some clergymen railed at the activities of cunning-folk in their parishes and saw them as competition for spiritual authority in their communities, some, to all intents and purposes, practised as cunning-folk themselves. Catholic and Orthodox priests already had an edge over everyone else in having ordained power and authority to administer sacraments, liturgies, and exorcisms for the general well-being of the people. The minor clergy were amongst the most learned in any community; they also often lived on very measly stipends. It is no surprise, then, that some took the opportunity to supplement their incomes by offering services that extended beyond their parochial religious duties. This was sometimes restricted largely to blessings or to exorcisms, but when it extended to astrology, herbalism, and treasure hunting then the distinction between a priest and cunning-person became blurred—at least in the eyes of the laity.

As already noted, cunning-folk were as much popular figures in nineteenth-century Europe as they were in the sixteenth century. We know this from criminal records and the work of folklorists. While the laws against witchcraft were repealed across Europe from the late seventeenth century through to the early nineteenth century, the practice of popular magic for financial gain remained a criminal offence, redefined in terms of fraudulent activity rather than sinful 'superstition'. Louis XIV of France issued a royal edict in 1682 that targeted the 'so called' magic of 'diviners, magicians and enchanters'. In the Napoleonic era, article 405 of the penal code against fraud allowed for the heavy punishment of those who persuaded others of 'the existence of false undertakings, of a power or of an imaginary influence'. In Britain the 1736 Witchcraft and Conjuration Act punished those who

> pretend to exercise or use any kind of Witchcraft, Sorcery, Inchantment, or Conjuration, or undertake to tell Fortunes, or pretend, from his or her Skill or Knowledge in any occult or crafty Science, to discover where or in what manner any Goods or Chattels, supposed to have been stolen or lost, may be found.

Such laws had very little impact on the number of practising cunning-folk and fortune-tellers, though. Periodic prosecution became part of the calculated risk of the job, just as it had been under the often harsher laws against their business in the age of the witch trials. Some nineteenth-century English cunning-folk accumulated several years' worth of time in prison, but went back to providing magical services each time they were released.

One reason why the practice of popular magic remained pervasive is because the fear of witches remained widespread. The repeal of laws against witchcraft meant that the state no longer provided a legal mechanism for punishing or getting rid of them. People had to rely totally on cunning-folk or their own counter-measures. Examples of mob justice against suspected witches occurred periodically through the eighteenth and nineteenth centuries. In regions such as southern England, the Netherlands, north Germany, and Poland this sometimes took the form of swimming suspected witches: if they floated they were guilty, if they sank they were innocent. While swimming was meant to be a divine test of guilt, God's baptismal waters either embracing or rejecting the suspect, the act became a form of punishment and ostracism of suspected witches. In England a chimney sweep named Thomas Collet was executed in 1751 for orchestrating the swimming of a suspected pair of witches, Ruth and John Osborne, which led to Ruth's death. Thousands of people turned up to witness the dunking of the Osbornes. Over eighty years later, hundreds turned out at Hela, near Danzig, to see Christina Ceinowa, a mother of six, beaten and drowned during a swimming. Across Europe and America such collective acts of popular justice became increasingly rare during the nineteenth century, but hundreds of individual cases of the assault, murder, slander, and ostracism of suspected witches occurred right through into the mid-twentieth century. Such violent expressions of witch belief represent, furthermore, only a tiny portion of the myriad accusations, suspicions, and acts of counter-magic that occurred in villages, towns, and cities in the industrial age. The history of witchcraft and magic is not one that can be consigned to a distant past.

7

The Rise of Modern Magic

Owen Davies

Through the second half of the eighteenth century and into the nineteenth century the continued practice of magic was generally portrayed in the West as belonging to either the realms of the rural poor of Europe or those in the colonies often labelled 'heathens', 'savages', or 'primitives' by missionaries, officials, and early anthropologists. Several decades after the end of the witch trials there was a widespread conviction that the days of witchcraft and magic could be consigned to the distant past or to 'backward' races. By the end of the eighteenth century it was becoming increasingly common to read references to how the witch trials were a terrible episode of the Middle Ages rather than the sixteenth and seventeenth centuries. The vogue for Gothic literature helped cement the notion of a benighted, Catholic age of superstition and persecution. This distancing effect helped bolster the notion that the disenchantment of Europe was a consequence of the Enlightenment, that magic had long been purged from the educated mind. Twentieth-century historians helped perpetuate this notion of the disenchantment of the West, influenced by the theories of the sociologist Max Weber (1864–1920). He theorized that the 'age of magic' was fatally undermined by the intellectual, social, and religious changes wrought by the Protestant Reformation. Society became increasingly secularized, the Churches were forced to become more tolerant, science was liberated to question received wisdom about the world. European society was changing, for sure, but not in a simple, inexorable way that could or should be defined as 'progress'. The belief in magic was not a stage of human evolution.

Throughout the era of the witch trials, magic continued to be an important religious and scientific method for exploring the hidden or

occult properties of the world. With the spread of literacy and the rise
of the printing press, books of magic—the tools of the medieval and
Renaissance magicians—began to disseminate far beyond the monastic libraries of the medieval period. Circulating widely in print and
manuscript, *The Three Books of Occult Philosophy*, by the German Renaissance occult philosopher Heinrich Cornelius Agrippa von Nettesheim
(1486–1535), became one of the most important magic books of the
early modern era and shaped the future development of modern
western esotericism. Agrippa's work was hugely influential in several
ways. First, the *Three Books* promoted a Christian conception of the
Kabbalah. The Kabbalah was a medieval, Jewish mystical philosophy
that, in its practical aspect, espoused the secret powers of the letters of
the Hebraic alphabet and their numerical value; these were the
building blocks of God's cosmos and hence the keys to divine wisdom.
Agrippa's writings were also an important vehicle for expressing
another branch of Renaissance magic known as Hermeticism,
which, as we saw in Chapter 2, also played a significant role in
medieval magic. This was a body of occult wisdom attributed to the
legendary man-deity Hermes Trismegistus, who was identified as the
Egyptian god of wisdom Thoth, and the Greek god Hermes, as well as
the biblical figure of Enoch, son of Abraham. Purportedly the author
of thousands of works on religion, magic, and philosophy, and referenced repeatedly in medieval magic books, it was only in the fifteenth
century that Hermetic philosophy became a dominant influence on
western European occultism. This came about because the Italian
magician Marsilio Ficino (1433–99), to whom we were introduced at
the end of Chapter 2, published a Latin edition of a Greek manuscript, the *Corpus hermeticum*, which was believed to encapsulate the
great wisdom of Hermes. For Agrippa, who read Ficino's work,
Hermes Trismegistus was one of the first masters of magic. The
Hermetic writings were presented as a method for exploring the
mystical aspects of religion for the spiritual benefit of mind and
body through the intimate relationship between the microcosm
(the human organism) and the macrocosm (the universe). Agrippa's
reputation as a great mage led to the dissemination in print and
manuscript of a spurious *Fourth Book of Occult Philosophy*, which
became a valued manual for the practice of geomancy, in other
words the method of divining the occult meaning of seemingly

randomly generated points and marks, such as those produced with dice. The *Fourth Book* also contained, more importantly, valued information about the nature of the most powerful spirits and how to summon them.

Ficino and Agrippa were not the only major figures of their age to cast a lasting influence over western occult thought. Giambattista della Porta was another influential figure, best known for his book *Magia naturalis* (1558). As the title suggests, this was a book about natural magic and not a guide to spirit conjurations and spells. That did not stop the Italian Inquisition harassing him. Grounded in the writings of Ficino and Agrippa in terms of its theoretical basis, *Natural Magic* was an impressive attempt to explain, through scientific experimentation with mirrors, drugs, herbs, illusion, and the like, phenomena commonly attributed to the supernatural. 'Magic is nothing else but the survey of the whole course of Nature', he stated. Porta's *Natural Magic* was an important rational, scientific text, but it was also a demonstration of the Neoplatonic workings of the world, in other words the intimate, interconnectedness of all things. This included, for instance, the pervasive influence of 'the Heavens, the Stars, the Elements, how they are moved, and how they are changed'. 'The parts and members of this huge creature the World, I mean all the bodies that are in it, do in good neighbourhood as it were, lend and borrow each others Nature', he wrote; 'for by reason that they are linked in common bond, therefore they have love in common; and by force of this common love, there is amongst them a common attraction... And this indeed is Magick.'

Another approach to practical Hermeticism and Neoplatonism was pursued by the Swiss alchemist, physician, and occultist Paracelsus (1493–1541). He, like della Porta, was a great believer in the laws of signatures and sympathy, which as we have seen, governed much popular magic. More to the point, Paracelsus developed a set of astrological lamens or talismans for cure and protection that were repeatedly borrowed over the ensuing centuries. Diseases could be caused by the malign influence of certain stars and could likewise be cured through astrological sympathies. The elements were also governed by elemental spirits. By engraving planetary symbols and occult signs on certain types of metal at certain astrological times, the resulting lamens could, when worn, cure and protect against the likes of epilepsy and witchcraft. As Paracelsus explained, 'Characters, Letters and Signes have several virtues and operations, wherewith also the nature of Metals, the condition of Heaven, and the influence of the Planets, with their operations, and the significations and properties. . . . Who can object that these Signes and Seales have not their virtue and operations?'

The Age of Occult Enlightenment

Come the late eighteenth century, there continued a current of intellectual interest in the possibilities for using magic to illuminate the secrets of the physical and spiritual world. Largely hidden from public consciousness, there were erudite men who carried the flame of the old medieval and early modern occult philosophers. Some clung to astrology and pursued the secrets of alchemy that had eluded the seventeenth-century scientists; some juggled with the hidden powers of secret words and symbols; others attempted to communicate with angels and other celestial spirits. In short, there were those who continued to think in terms of a Neoplatonic world. New pseudo-scientific 'discoveries' such as animal magnetism invigorated the sense that the old occult philosophers had been on the right path all along.

Animal magnetism, or mesmerism as it came to be generally known, was a theory of invisible life forces devised by an Austrian physician, Franz Anton Mesmer (1734–1815). His doctoral medical thesis had concerned the application of the Newtonian conception of gravity to understanding the influence of the stars on the human body, resulting in the concept of 'animal gravity'. During the 1770s, Mesmer's experiments with the influence of magnets on human health led to some of his patients reporting the sensation that a liquid-like substance coursed through parts of their body during treatment. He conceived that the magnets were emanating and channelling an invisible fluid consisting of fire, air, and spirit that connected all matter. A further revelation was that the human body was the ultim-ate magnet and so certain individuals, Mesmer included, could be trained to channel the flow of this magnetic fluid in others through touch and concentrated will power. By this means, striking cures had apparently been achieved. Mesmer was an international sensation, and animal magnetism seemed to some a fundamental scientific breakthrough. It was not, but it became a theory and practice with a life of its own, that spiralled far beyond Mesmer's conception and usage of the supposed magnetic fluid.

The concept resonated with Neoplatonic ideas of a spiritually interconnected world. It was held up as an explanation *for* magic, and was used to explain some of the extraordinary supernatural manifestations contained in the old witch trial confessions. As was suggested in the 1840s, animal magnetism could be considered as the 'Philosophy of superstition; its object being to investigate the natural causes of many of those phenomena which have hitherto been entirely disbelieved against positive evidence of their reality, or held to be the effects of supernatural agency.' Mesmerism also came to be used as a technique to put people into mesmeric trance states and induce clairvoyance. As a consequence, the emphasis in mesmeric investigation shifted from the physiological implications of animal magnetism to its spiritual and mental significance.

Just as the world of science continued to throw up new occult possibilities, so too did religion as the authoritarian grip of the established Churches, particularly those in Protestant lands, began to weaken. In response to the sober, conservative, and rational impulses of the Churches, new manifestations of Christianity emerged that reengaged with the mystical and magical aspects of seventeenth-century spirituality and theology. These were expressed in small explosions of enthusiasm for prophets and visionaries. At one end of the prophetic spectrum was the Swedish scientist and theologian Emmanuel Swedenborg (1688–1772). In 1744 he began to experience a series of visions and dreams which he believed to be divine communications. He became convinced that God had allowed him to communicate with angels, devils, and the spirits of the dead in order to aid his mission to reform Christianity. In his trance states he believed he travelled to Heaven and Hell. Swedenborg's conversations with the spirit world formed the basis of numerous publications that attracted mostly derision but also serious interest amongst a few influential philosophers, particularly Immanuel Kant, and also the artist William Blake. Some fifteen years after Swedenborg's death in England, churches sprang up there and in America based around his revelations and teachings.

At the other end of the prophetic spectrum were figures such as Joanna Southcott, whose occult practices, pronouncements, and appeal were born of grass roots popular culture rather than sophisticated theology. Southcott (1750–1814) was the daughter of a Devon farmer, and grew up in a devoutly religious environment, albeit one rooted in local popular culture and belief. She was interested in the meaning of her dreams and those of her acquaintances. She believed in astrological influences, and thought that Satan dwelled on the moon, but denounced astrologers in line with the biblical sanction against such prognosticators. As to witchcraft, she stated: 'I am truly convinced it is practised by evil and wicked people, who are in league with the Devil.' In 1792 she began to have a series of divine visions, spirit conversations, and struggles with Satan. She came to believe that she was the woman spoken of in Revelation 67: 12 who appeared as a wondrous sign in heaven: 'a woman clothed with the sun, with the moon under her feet and a crown of twelve stars on her head.' She was to be the bride of Christ on his glorious return to earth. On a more mundane level, she also apparently successfully predicted the death of a local bishop in 1792 and also a poor harvest in 1800. While still resident in Devon, her prophetic communications marked her out as someone with special powers to cure and protect. She helped a local farmer who had suffered repeated loss of livestock because of witchcraft. Joanna communed with her spirit guide, who told her to write 'Holiness to the Lord' on a piece of parchment and put it inside the horses' bridles and halters.

But the continued interest in prophecy and the occult world also fed into much larger and more enduring religious developments. In Protestant German lands the Lutheran movement known as Pietism, which re-emphasized the paramount importance of individual piety and the emotional expression of Christianity, spawned various groups that drew upon occult inspiration. The writings of the early seventeenth-century theologian Jacob Boehme (1575–1624) were a particular influence on eighteenth-century Protestant mysticism. His notion of Christian cosmology was interwoven with alchemical, Kabbalistic, and Neoplatonic ideas drawn, in turn, from Renaissance occult philosophers such as Paracelsus and Cornelius Agrippa. Such strands of mystical Christianity that accepted there were divine secrets to be unlocked through visions, spirit communications, and symbols sometimes led individuals to explore the blurred boundaries between mystical thought and the practice of magic. In Britain, some members of the Philadelphian Society, who were enthused by the visionary angelic experiences of the Berkshire clergyman John Pordage (1607–81), were also interested in practical, ritual magic. We find similar groups amongst the German émigré Pietist communities in America. In Germantown, Philadelphia, the mystic Johannes Kelpius (d. 1708) attracted those interested in Kabbalah, prophecy, and astrology during the early decades of the eighteenth century. The library of one of his followers, the English physician and occultist Christopher Witt, contained books on natural magic. Another Pennsylvanian centre of esoteric interest was Ephrata, founded by the Pietist Conrad Beissel. One of his disciples, Conrad Weiser, sold alchemical medicines imported from Europe. Later in the century, the fusion of Christian mysticism and popular magic led to the birth of the home-grown American religion of Mormonism. Its founder Joseph Smith (1805–44) clearly had some knowledge of literary magic from old English occult sources, and practised treasure divination using what was called a seer or peep stone.

In eighteenth-century England, John Wesley, an Anglican clergyman who had been influenced by Pietist theology, and who cofounded the evangelical Methodist movement, became the British national figure most associated with the continued belief in witchcraft and magic. Wesley had no interest in exploring the mystical paths to Christian enlightenment, but his conception of the world was one alive with miracles and spirits; angels and devils intervened in people's everyday lives. For Wesley, witches, which he saw as satanic conspirators, were a continued threat to Christendom. Like the demonologists of the witch trial era he believed the practice of magic, whether to inflict suffering or for purportedly benign purposes, was sinful. In a providential world, there were numerous examples of how faith in God could reverse misfortune and combat evil influences without resorting to the snares of cunning-folk and astrologers. Although often portrayed as a lone voice crying in the face of the Enlightenment, Wesley expressed beliefs that were undoubtedly held by many educated people but which were only uttered in private discourse. His expressed belief in witchcraft, magic, and ghosts also resonated with the continued supernatural concerns of the common people at a time when the Anglican clergy were chiding their parishioners for being superstitious.

The Practising Occultists

Astrology was the occult science that had the greatest continued reach. Astrological almanacs remained very popular. *Moore's Almanac* was selling over 100,000 copies in Britain during the mid-eighteenth century, and as the population expanded so too did almanac sales. For those wanting to practise astrology the numerous guides produced by well-known seventeenth-century astrologers such as William Lilly and John Gadbury continued to have considerable second-hand value. While astrological practice was often an aspect of the physician's business, aiding prognoses and ensuring the potency of cures, it also led some to engage in other related aspects of the occult sciences.

In Britain, Ebenezer Sibly (1751–*c*.1799) was the most influential public practitioner and published author on the occult. A Freemason and astrologer with Swedenborgian sympathies, in the 1780s he published *A New and Complete Illustration of the Celestial Science of Astrology* and then a *Key to Physic and the Occult Sciences* in 1792. *A New and Complete Illustration* was a huge, multi-volume work that went through several editions. It was not only a manual of astrology but a discourse on various aspects of magical practice drawn from the raft of astrological and occult books published during the mid-seventeenth century. One of Sibly's aims was to demonstrate how Neoplatonic ideas and practices could be accommodated with the latest scientific and religious thought. Mesmerism was given particular prominence as proof, at last, of a world suffused with invisible vital forces. As an astrological healer, Sibly subscribed to natural magic, exploring the occult properties of animals, vegetables, and minerals, particularly in relation to the influence of the planets. As he observed:

> Hence it happens that old women, without education or experience, by the help of a simple herb gathered in the planetary hour, in which hour it imbibes its greatest degree of strength and specific virtue, will sometimes perform very extraordinary cures, in cases where gentlemen of the faculty are absolutely at a loss how to treat them.

While Sibly eschewed ceremonial magic and declared himself against spirit conjuration he went into some detail on the nature of the astral spirit realm, infernal spirits, and ghosts. Part Four of *A New and Complete Illustration* included 'the Methods used for raising and consulting Spirits . . . with various instances of their Compacts with wicked

Men'. Whatever his views on ritual magic, Sibly's tome contained enough description and examples to excite and provoke others to explore what he considered as infernal or blasphemous practices. It evidently inspired a miniature painter and enthusiastic balloonist named Francis Barrett.

In 1801, Barrett's own occult guide *The Magus: Or Celestial Intelligencer* appeared in print. It was heavily influenced by Sibly's works, and based on the same set of older published texts, particularly the English translations of Agrippa's *Three Books of Occult Philosophy*, the spurious *Fourth Book*, and Porta's *Natural Magic*. Barrett was much less interested in astrology, though, and focused mostly on natural magic, the creation of talismans, and the procedures of 'cabalistical or ceremonial magic'. Whereas Sibly preferred the term occult, Barrett was out and out proud about practising magic. Ritual magic encouraged a pure and temperate life, he stated, and his aim was 'to free the name of Magic from any scandalous imputation; seeing it is a word originally significative not of any evil, but of every good and laudable science, such as a man might profit by, and become wise and happy'. That said, Barrett warned of the dangers as well as the benefits of spirit conjuration. In his instructions 'on the method of raising evil or familiar spirits by a circle' he noted that leaving the circle without observing the necessary ritual was inadvisable, 'because instances have been known of the operator experiencing sudden death'. Barrett's book was a sales flop compared with Sibly's publications, but its influence woved subtly through the development of modern ritual magic over the next two centuries.

Barrett also offered personal training in the magical sciences, and at least one rural cunning-man claimed to have benefited from his tutorship. But there had already been and were several esoteric and mystic fraternities which, although not offering lessons in ritual magic, provided an environment and sources of knowledge to encourage the aspiring magician. One fraternal focus was Rosicrucianism. Barrett, for example, claimed he was a member of one such Brotherhood. Rosicrucianism had its origins in the early seventeenth century when several tracts appeared detailing the history and teachings of a legendary fifteenth-century mystical healing brotherhood led by a German knight named Christian Rosenkreutz (Rosycross). The Order of the Rosy Cross was an invention but the story was believed in and the mix of astrology, spiritual alchemy, and mysticism ascribed to its teachings appealed to various seventeenth-century occult philosophers and natural magicians. In eighteenth-century Germany interest was reinvigorated with new statements of the Rosicrucian teachings appearing. These had an increased focus on alchemical knowledge and a more heavy emphasis on Christian mysticism. During the second half of the century a system of grades and rituals was created as the German Rosicrucian movement adopted the structures and form of Freemasonry, becoming at the same time an enclave of political and social conservatism.

The reformulation of Freemasonry in the early eighteenth century, as signified by the founding of the London Grand Lodge in 1717, and its subsequent offshoots in America, was inspired by political and religious Enlightenment principles. But it took only a few decades for esoteric strands to appear in new branches of French and British Freemasonry. One such was inspired by a Scottish exile living in France named Andrew Michael Ramsey (d. 1743). He had engaged with various mystical Protestant groups before converting to Catholicism, and becoming a Freemason in 1729. He constructed a genealogy for masonry that incorporated the transmission of ancient masonic teachings, perhaps of pre-Christian origin, via the medieval crusader orders who were thought to have rediscovered their secrets during their time in the Holy Land. What Ramsey, and others, alluded to was the idea that Freemasonry was a legacy of a secret tradition of wisdom dating back to an Old Testament past, through either the pyramid builders of ancient Egypt or the great biblical temple builder King Solomon and his masons. Other alternative origins were put forward, including that the masons were descended from the druids, who, at the time, were thought to have built Stonehenge. These imagined histories then inspired the adoption of symbols and rituals that accrued around the various masonic fraternities. Some esoteric Freemasons were convinced that obscure terms handed down in Freemasonry had Kabbalistic origins.

During the latter half of the century France was vibrant with occultists, amongst the most notable being the *Ordre des Chevaliers Maçons Élus Cohen de L'Univers* (Order of Knight-Masons Elect Priests of the Universe). This masonic order was founded by Jacques Martinès de Pasqually (1727–74), and had lodges in Marseille,

Bordeaux, Toulouse, and Paris. Its highest degree taught rituals based on Kabbalah and theurgy (the invocation of and uniting with the divine spirit(s)). These enabled the Order's 'priests' to communicate with angels and perform the exorcism and control of evil spirits. The ultimate goal was to call down the beatific vision of Christ. After de Pasqually's death, the *Ordre des Chevaliers Maçons Élus Cohen* was guided by Louis-Claude de Saint-Martin (1743–1803). He tried to reduce the emphasis on ceremonial magic and reshape the Order around a more orthodox mystical Christian framework. The movement soon splintered and dwindled as a consequence, with the French Revolution also shaking the masonic movement to its core.

The notorious Count Cagliostro offered, perhaps, the most overtly magical and pagan expression of Freemasonry during the eighteenth century. Cagliostro, whose real name was Giuseppe Balsamo, was a swaggering charlatan, con-man, quack doctor, and dabbler in magic and alchemy who inveigled himself into high society and royal courts across Europe. During the 1770s and 1780s he and his wife Seraphina pitched up in London on several occasions. Cagliostro claimed he had discovered a unique manuscript revealing that the origins of Freemasonry could be traced through the rituals of an Egyptian high priest known as the Great Copt who, in turn, had worked under the inspiration of the prophets Enoch and Elias. Cagliostro said he had been charged to restore the original ritual purity of Egyptian Freemasonry. He assumed the title of the Great Copt and recruited followers to his lodges, while his wife led female initiates in this unusually inclusive branch of Freemasonry. At the heart of Cagliostro's Freemasonry was the Egyptian Rite, which was effectively a séance of his own devising to communicate with the angels and the spirits of the dead through a child scryer or medium. The rite was conducted in rooms decked with candles, hieroglyphs, statues of Egyptian gods, and other paraphernalia redolent of ritual magic.

During his 1786 visit to London, the Great Copt attempted to interest Swedenborgians in his Egyptian Rite. He attended, along with some French acolytes, a meeting of the Lodge of Antiquity, one of the oldest British masonic lodges, to explain his system of Egyptian rituals, apparently with the aim of taking over the leadership of the Lodge. His influence on the night was undermined, though, by one of those present who ridiculed the activities of the Count. This meeting was then used as the setting for a mocking print about Cagliostro by the famed satirist James Gillray. Cagliostro returned to the Continent and not long after was arrested by the Roman Inquisition and condemned to death for the heresy of spreading Freemasonry. His sentence was commuted to a life sentence, and the Great Copt died of a stroke in prison in 1795.

While, as we saw in an earlier chapter, the pictorial representation of witches in the eighteenth and nineteenth centuries was a mix of the satirical, the comedic, and the whimsical, there was an earnest artistic interest in esotericism and ancient magical rites. Louis-Claude de Saint-Martin enthused about the role of art and the artist, and influenced the symbolism used in French literary Romanticism. In Germany, some of Goethe's work was inspired by his interest in Freemasonry, Rosicrucianism, and grimoires. The English Platonist Thomas Taylor (1758–1835) was a lesser known figure, but his translation from the Greek of *Iamblichus on the Mysteries of the Egyptians, Chaldeans, and Assyrians* (1821), and other translations of esoteric works from antiquity, were an influence on some of the greatest creative minds of the period, Keats, Wordsworth, Shelley, Coleridge, and William Blake, amongst others. The writings of Iamblichus, a Syrian Neoplatonic philosopher who lived during the third and fourth centuries AD, were of particular interest to the Romantics. His discourse on theurgy concerned how the embodied soul could transcend the degraded material world and attain divine spiritual unity through rite and ritual, through physical expression, and not just through pious internal contemplation. The likes of Keats and Shelley took their classical religious interests further, being attracted to the pagan deities and the rustic natural settings for some Roman and Greek ritual practices. This seemed so much more soulfully uplifting than the sober joylessness of established religion. William Blake depicted this sense of liberation in his Shakespearian illustration of 'Oberon, Titania and Puck with Fairies Dancing'.

A New Golden Age

Mesmerism, Freemasonry, and mystical Christianity swirled around the scientific and religious fringes of the western world during the early decades of the nineteenth century, providing fertile ground from which new occult and magical shoots grew. A surviving scrapbook of letters, advertisements, and other ephemera known as the 'Wonderful Magical Scrapbook' reveals, for example, a loose network of London astrologers and occultists communicating with each other from the 1820s to the 1840s. The three most significant figures in the network were the bookseller John Denley, the astrologer Robert Cross Smith (1795–1832), and Frederick Hockley (1809–85). Denley's bookshop in Covent Garden contained a treasure trove of old and rare magic books and manuscripts. Francis Barrett no doubt owed a great debt to him for the sources included in *The Magus*. Coleridge borrowed some occult texts from the shop on one occasion. Denley also published Robert Cross Smith's *The Philosophical Merlin*, which was supposedly the translation of a mystical geomantic manuscript once used by Napoleon, but clearly borrowed heavily from *The Magus*. It was dedicated to the famed French diviner Mademoiselle Le Normand. Smith then put together a more overtly magical work entitled *The Astrologer of the Nineteenth Century*, which contained several magical talismans, incantations, and invocations, some of which he claimed derived from a manuscript possessed by a secret magic society known as the Mercurii. Frederick Hockley was the most significant of the network in this story. As a young man he had worked for John Denley making copies and compilations of old magic texts, talismans, and charms for sale across the country. As well as accumulating his own library of magical texts, Hockley spent much of his later life experimenting with angelic communication via crystal balls, mirrors, and trances.

America provided particularly fertile ground during this period. Numerous small prophetic cults and visionary groups sprang up, with more established denominations like the Shakers (which encouraged visions and trances) and Universalism (which preached the salvation of all people) providing a transitory home for more radical occultists. The 'Poughkeepsie Seer' Andrew Jackson Davis (1826–1910) was one such figure. Early in his adult life he had been attracted to the Baptist Prophet William Miller. He also acted as a mesmeric medium, diagnosing and suggesting treatments for illnesses while in his trance state. He became a significant figure in Universalism, and began to experience a series of mesmeric spirit communications, most notably conversations with the spirit of Emmanuel Swedenborg. These trance communications were written down and published as *The Principles of Nature, her Divine Revelation, and a Voice of Mankind* (1847). Davis wrote of the imminence of a new spiritual era:

> It is a truth that spirits commune with one another while one is in the body and the other in the higher spheres—and this, too, when the person in the body is unconscious of the influx, and hence cannot be convinced of the fact; and this truth will ere long present itself in the form of a living demonstration. And the world will hail with delight the ushering in of that era when the interiors of men will be opened, and the spiritual communion will be established.

The likes of Davis would have rejected that they were doing anything magical. But, as we have seen, in purpose and inspiration spirit communication lay across the porous boundary between evangelical, mystical Christianity and ritual magic—the ritual nature of the attempted communication being the key determinate between 'right and wrong' practices over the centuries. One of Davis's more remarkable contemporaries, the mixed-race, African-American trance medium Beverly Randolph (1825–75), moved across that boundary when he began to practise spirit communications through magic mirrors. These were imbued with the highest clairvoyant powers due to a 'mysterious process' that he had learned on his travels in the Near East, and which he only divulged to his mail-order correspondents and to the Fraternitas Rosae Crucis order he founded in America. His advice on the ritual care and maintenance of these precious mirrors included cleaning them with 'cologne, fresh beer, or liquor spurted from the mouth'. Randolph's most influential contribution to modern magic, though, was his use of ritual masturbation and heterosexual intercourse as a magic sacrament for achieving a higher plain of spiritual awareness; 'true Sex-power is God-power', he wrote.

Numerous occult explorers travelled to Paris in the mid-nineteenth century to meet the most influential magician of the era, Éliphas Lévi (1810–75). Born Alphonse Louis Constant, Lévi trained to be a Catholic priest in his youth but was never ordained, and while he became a critic of the Church his deep Catholic faith remained unshaken. This shaped his understanding of the practice and purpose of magic. He delved into the history of and literature on the subject, reading the work of the Renaissance occult philosophers, exploring alchemy and Rosicrucianism, perusing eighteenth-century grimoires, and studying animal magnetism. His reading of many of the grimoires led him to condemn 'the diabolical evocations and practices of Black Magic'. He declared that he wrote about them, 'not that they be used, but that they may be known and judged, and that such insanities may be put aside for ever'. As expressed in his influential books, starting with *Dogme et rituel de la haute magie* (1856), the two main elements of Lévi's conception of correct magical practice concerned the Kabbalah and the Tarot. Indeed, the Tarot was the ultimate key. Without it, he declared, 'the Magic of the ancients is a closed book, and it is impossible to penetrate any of the great mysteries of the Kabbalah'. Lévi's conviction was inspired by the claims of a late eighteenth-century French Freemason and archaeologist, Antoine Court de Gébelin (1725–84), that Tarot cards originated in ancient Egypt. The images on the cards were, furthermore, fragments of the book of wisdom of the Egyptian priesthood, or so Gébelin claimed. One of his followers, Baptiste Alliette (1738–91), then elaborated on this, specifying that the Tarot derived from the work of the ibis-headed Egyptian god of magic and alchemy, Thoth. As Thoth was equated with the fabled Hermes Trismegistus, this neatly brought the Tarot into the Hermetic tradition. It was Lévi who made the connection between the Tarot and the Kabbalah, and this was, perhaps, his most influential contribution to the development of modern magical practice.

Lévi gained prominence at a time when Christian mysticism was blown wide open by the spiritualist movement. Table-rapping spiritualism spread around the western world from a humble farmhouse in New York State. It was there, in 1848, that two teenage girls named Maggie and Kate Fox claimed they communicated with the troubled spirit of a murdered pedlar. Through a series of raps they asked questions and the ghost replied. A spiritual telegraph had apparently been established. The table rapping, table moving séance was soon born, and the great age of the spirit medium began. As we have seen, mediumistic spirit communication with the dead had actually been an integral aspect of magical practice and mysticism for centuries. What modern spiritualism did was to transform spirit communication into a mainstream public activity. It also reconnected orthodox established religion with aspects of its old, condemned, mystical offshoots. Some clergy were concerned spiritualism was a new form of necromantic Devil worship, others dismissed it as nonsense, but many saw in it revelatory and scientific proof of the afterlife, and hence a fundamental affirmation of Christianity.

Spiritualism also made it more acceptable to engage with and even practise the mystical dimensions of other global religions, principally those of Europe's eastern empires. The most influential expression of this was the creation of the Theosophical Society in New York in 1875. Its co-founder and leading inspiration, the charismatic Russian émigré Helena Petrovna Blavatsky (1831–91), claimed that during a stay in Tibet she had entered a special relationship with a group of Mahatmas, holy men who held the key to the secret wisdom of the ancients. They communicated this knowledge to her psychically wherever she was in the world. It was their arcane wisdom which she said she channelled in writing her theosophical tome *Isis Unveiled* (1877). As many have pointed out, though, the content of the book was far more influenced by the writings of Éliphas Lévi than by the 'Esoteric Buddhism' of the East. The Theosophical Society proved a popular breeding ground for those who wished to explore aspects of the occult in a respectable social milieu. Blavatsky was also the first major female 'leader' in modern esotericism, working outside the masculine world of Freemasonry, and this profile, along with the prominence of women in spiritualism, undoubtedly encouraged other women to explore further into the world of ritual magic.

It was the convergence of the ritual structures of the masonic movement, the mainstream occultism of spiritualism and theosophy, and the personal esoteric interests of several, individual British Freemasons that ultimately led to the first modern organization dedicated to the *practice* of ritual magic. Around 1865–6 two experienced British masons with occult interests, Robert Wentworth Little and the linguist Kenneth Mackenzie, founded the Societas Rosicruciana in Anglia (SRA), effectively a new masonic lodge, with Little assuming the title of 'Master Magus'. Mackenzie claimed to have been initiated into Rosicrucianism during his early years living in Austria. Details of the SRA's activities are sketchy, but they did not seem to extend much beyond an annual dinner and quarterly meetings at which talks on esoteric subjects were given and brief rituals explored. A periodical called *The Rosicrucian* was edited by one of the early members, a surgeon named William Robert Woodman (1828–91), who would become 'Supreme Magus' after Little's death. The main purpose was not the performance and development of esoteric rituals, though, but the exploration of the origins of Freemasonry and its Rosicrucian connections, as spelled out by the earlier German Rosicrucian movement. William Wynn Westcott, a London coroner who joined in 1880, explained in a talk given to the Society entitled 'The Rosicrucians: Past and Present, at Home and Abroad': 'The study of Rosicrucianism is now once more in the ascendant and our Society has made rapid strides in the past ten years. It is curious to note that waves of interest in occult and mystical subjects, seem to sweep over a nation at intervals.' For Westcott, Rosicrucianism was a 'lineal descendant' of the rites of the Chaldean magi, the Egyptian priesthood, the ancient Neoplatonists and Hermeticists, and the medieval Jewish and Christian Kabbalists. Christianity was the underpinning principle though, not ancient paganism.

The primary significance of the SRA in the history of modern magic is as the well-spring for the first modern organization truly dedicated to the practice of ritual magic—The Hermetic Order of the Golden Dawn. This society and school of magic was founded in 1888 by Woodman, Westcott, and another recent member of the SRA, the vegetarian Samuel Liddell Mathers. Westcott described years later that the Golden Dawn was formed 'to give instruction in the medieval occult sciences'. But it became a vehicle for much more than that. Woodman was significantly the oldest of the three founders and seems to have acted as an occult mentor, facilitating their introduction to a wider network. Woodman was also a living link with the fraternity of London occultists of the first half of the century. Hockley had jointed the SRA before his death, and it is clear that access to Hockley's manuscripts was a crucial source for the initial magical basis of the Golden Dawn. Woodman died in 1891, and as we see him stiff in his formal Freemason's regalia, one wonders what he would have made of how the Golden Dawn developed and divided under the auspices of his co-founders over the next decade or so.

The Golden Dawn's first order, the Isis-Urania temple, opened in London in 1888. Another four temples were founded around the country, and by 1896 the Golden Dawn had over 300 members.

In an echo of Cagliostro's Egyptian Freemasonry, and influenced by the gender equality demonstrated by the Theosophical Society, the Golden Dawn welcomed women as well as men, and several had an important influence over the movement and the development of its rituals. As a result, the practice of learned ritual magic began, for the first time since antiquity, to be defined by its female practitioners as much as by the archetype of the male magician. Two of the leading women in the Golden Dawn, the actress Florence Farr and the artist Moina Bergson (wife of Mathers), were influential in integrating a strong Egyptian theme in Golden Dawn ritual and symbolism. They were, in part, influenced by the growing body of archaeological discoveries that were providing valuable new insights regarding authentic ancient Egyptian beliefs and practices. In the process they enhanced the dramatic aspects of the Order's rituals. This reached its apotheosis when the Mathers moved to Paris in 1899, and created theatrical performances of the rites of the goddess Isis that attracted interest beyond occult circles. Moina, dressed in dramatic costume, represented the High Priestess Anari, while her husband played the High Priest Rameses. As described by a report in an American journal:

> The High Priestess Anari invoked the goddess in penetrating and passionate tones. Then followed the 'dance of the four elements' by a young Parisian lady, who, dressed in long white robes, had previously recited some verses in French in honour of Isis...Most of the ladies present in the fashionable Parisian audience brought offerings of flowers, whiles the gentlemen threw wheat on the altar. The ceremony was artistic in the extreme.

Back in England, meantime, the Golden Dawn was splintering into various factions. The turbulence initially centred on the American-born Londoner Arthur Edward Waite (1857–1942), who had joined the Golden Dawn in 1891. Waite wrote widely on occultism, the Tarot, magic, and Freemasonry. His publications included a digest of Eliphas Lévi's writings (1886), and later an edited translation of Lévi's *Dogme et rituel de la haute magie* published under the title *Transcendental Magic*. It is still in print. Waite's compilation of rituals, talismans, and spells culled from manuscript and print grimoires, the *Book of Black Magic and of Pacts*, demonstrated one of the key reasons for the divisions in the Golden Dawn. Waite produced the book in order to expose what he, like Lévi before him, saw as the pernicious futility of ceremonial magic as found in much of the grimoire archive. There was an easily identifiable, if implicit, criticism of Mathers as well. He had already published translations of two historic grimoires for the benefit of informing the development of magical rituals. So why was Waite in the Golden Dawn? A clue lies in the fact that he also joined the Freemasons in 1901 and the SRA the following year. In short, Waite was interested in Christian mysticism and not ancient, magical ceremonial practice, and attempted to orient the Golden Dawn towards a familiar Rosicrucian path. By contrast, the Mathers and their followers immersed themselves in their own conception of ancient, 'pagan' Egyptian religion and magic. The two paths became increasingly incompatible under a unifying Order.

Mathers and Waite did not get on, but the most striking and influential animosity within the Golden Dawn in the early twentieth century was between Mathers and a young member who had joined in 1898, Aleister Crowley (1875–1947). The son of a wealthy lay preacher in the fundamentalist Plymouth Brethren church, Crowley's interest in ritual magic had been piqued by reading Eliphas Lévi and Waite's *The Book of Black Magic and of Pacts*, though he probably did not read the latter as Waite intended. Crowley thirsted for practical knowledge of ceremonial magic, and at first Mathers took him under his wing. After several years, though, they became bitter foes, with Crowley accusing Mathers of using black magic against him.

In 1904 Crowley claimed he was visited by a messenger from the Egyptian god Horus who told him he was to be the prophet of a new age. Crowley wrote down these spirit communications, which became *The Book of the Law*. This would form the basis of Crowley's Thelemic religion, guided by the principle: 'Do what thou wilt shall be the whole of the law.' Crowley's thirst to be master rather than student now led him to set up his own magical order, the Astrum Argentum (A∴ A∴), in 1907, which pursued his mix of Buddhist and yogic techniques with Kabbalah and western ceremonial magic. As usual, he claimed it had a venerable secret history. The order's journal *The Equinox* bore the motto 'The Method of Science—The Aim of Religion', and the introduction to its first volume stated grandly: 'With the publication of this review begins a completely new adventure in the history of mankind.' Crowley subsequently used the spelling 'magick' to distinguish what he did from stage magic and contemporary expressions of ritual magic, as exemplified in the title of his book *Magick in Theory and Practice* (1929). This was an old variant spelling of magic that was most notably used in the English edition of Porta's *Magia Naturalis—Natural Magick* (1658), and Daniel Defoe's *A System of Magick* (1727). It was occasionally used in non-occult nineteenth-century literature, but it was interest in Crowley's work that led it to become a commonly adopted term by post-war ritual magicians.

A couple of years before the First World War, Crowley also became the head of the British branch of a German magical fraternity known as the Ordo Templi Orientis (OTO). Meanwhile, in a series of trances Crowley claimed it was revealed to him that he was an incarnation of Cagliostro and Lévi, amongst other notorious figures in the history of magic. Once in a position of power over small occult groups, Crowley was able to pursue his practical interests in the magical aspects of drugs, sadomasochism, and sex. It was his magical activities in this respect that brought him the notoriety that he relished. He embraced the name 'Beast 666'. Crowley was image conscious and self-mythologizing. He orchestrated numerous staged photographs to represent his ritual activities and ceremonial garb. He was the first modern magician to achieve widespread press recognition, and access to images of him was part of this process. One photograph achieved quite wide circulation in the international press. It shows Crowley with palms pressed against his cheeks, deliberately emphasizing his penetrating 'basilisk' stare—that of the mesmerist. On his head is the hood of his Astrum Argentum robe bearing the image of a radiating pyramid. The book next to him has a pentagram on its cover and the words 'Perdurabo magister' on its spine. This combined the Latin for Master and the motto 'I shall endure to the end'. It was the title Crowley adopted for his magical persona.

The Golden Dawn has drawn the most attention and had the most lasting influence on the development of modern magic, but it was not the only occult organization around at the time. In America the Hermetic Brotherhood of Luxor appeared in 1884—though it boasted a venerable lineage. It was inspired, in part, by Blavatsky's description of a mystical eastern 'Brotherhood of Luxor', but it went to considerable lengths to demonstrate that it followed the true path to ancient occult enlightenment in comparison with what its members considered the inferior, Far Eastern 'Buddhist' preoccupations of the Theosophical Society. Its purpose was the study of 'practical occultism' as well as the usual esoteric historical and theoretical explorations. Its materials were familiar to the modern European hermetic tradition, and it also drew upon the ideas of Beverly Randolph.

In France, occult activity focused around the Martinist Order. This was co-founded by a Parisian doctor, Gérard Encausse (1865–1916), who would achieve considerable public recognition under the name 'Papus'. He was briefly a member of the Theosophical Society, but preferred the western tradition of occultism and joined various small Hermetic groups as he sought to carve out a clear occult identity. The Martinist order claimed to base its structure and rites on those contained in the papers of Martines de Pasqually, which Papus claimed he had rediscovered. This dubious assertion aside, Papus was an admirer of Lévi, but he was more interested than the master in practical experimentation, and read widely on Kabbalah and talismanic magic. What Papus achieved that other occultists of the period did not (and had no interest in doing) was an engagement with the wider world of popular magic. This was achieved through his popular *Traité méthodique de magie pratique* (1893), which went through numerous editions during his lifetime. Readers could skip through all the theory and go straight to the many pages providing advice on and illustrations of talismans, charms, and conjurations culled from the old French print grimoires and the likes of the *Fourth Book of Occult Philosophy*. There was also a section on how to set up a 'magic laboratory', the instruments and substances that were needed, how the walls of the room should be covered, and what furniture it should contain. As Papus explained in the introduction, the book would be 'a powerful help to the independent researcher and he will avoid great expenditure of time and money'.

Meanwhile in Germany various familiar strands of esotericism continued and developed. The aforementioned OTO was co-founded and led by the Freemason, pharmacist, and journalist Theodore Reuss (1855–1923). Over the previous few decades he had been at the centre of several other mystical and magical organizations including a branch of the Martinist Order, and the German Theosophical

Society. Reuss was keen on women being initiated into the OTO, in part because of what he stated about the Order's *raison d'être*: 'Our Order possesses the key which opens up all Masonic and Hermetic secrets, namely, the teachings of sexual magic, and this teaching explains, without exception, all the secrets of Nature, all the symbolism of Freemasonry and all systems of religion.' Elsewhere, occultism and the growth of German nationalism inspired interest in the mystical and magical power of runes. This shift in occult interest from Egyptian and eastern antiquity to pre-Christian Teutonic myth and symbolism was most notably developed by the Austrian dramatist and businessman Guido von List (1848–1919), and his followers in the Guido von List Society founded in 1908. One of those he influenced was Siegfried Adolf Kummer, who, in 1927, created a magic summer school around the use of runes, which he believed harnessed and controlled ethereal cosmic waves. Students were taught to create protective magic circles on the floor inscribed with the names of Germanic gods, within which they practised rune-yodelling and a form of meditation involving forming the shape of runes with their hands and fingers.

By the time of the outbreak of the First World War, hundreds of books ranging from hypnotism to the Tarot, magic to yoga, had been published by members of the various occult orders and brotherhoods that had formed from the late nineteenth century onwards. Wider interest in ritual magic and the occult was also being sown through various periodicals. In Britain, the *Occult Review* began in 1905, publishing a wide variety of articles on ghosts, spiritualism, dreams, and much else besides. Articles included: 'Magical Metathesis (teleportation of living persons)', 'Spurious Ecstasy and Ceremonial Magic', and 'The Magic of a Symbol' by Florence Farr. In Germany, the topic of magic was discussed in the likes of the *Metaphysische Rundschau*, 'a monthly journal for the study of practical metaphysics, psychology, oriental philosophy, and general occultism'.

In his *Encyclopædia of Occultism*, published in 1920, the Scottish journalist and student of mythology Lewis Spence concluded his entry for 'modern magic' thus: 'We cannot say that the true line of magical adepts ended with Levi, as at no time in the world's history are these known to the vulgar; but we may be certain that the great art is practised in secret as sedulously as ever in the past.' If Spence had heard of Crowley he chose to ignore him. Through the 1920s and 1930s the Great Beast became a notorious international celebrity. Through the lens of the popular press, his activities and reputation helped shape a largely negative public perception of modern magic.

While Papus toiled in a military hospital during the First World War, dying of tuberculosis in October 1916, Crowley spent the war in America, where he attracted modest newspaper coverage as an artist for his portraits of the spirits of the dead, which he painted with his eyes closed. The early 1920s finds him presiding over a scandalous community of his adherents called the Abbey of Thelema in Sicily. In 1923 a disgruntled member made various lurid accusations about the magical goings on in the commune. These were reported in the international press and led to the Fascist Italian authorities deporting Crowley. Over the ensuing years, Crowley would begin to experience the tawdry downside of the celebrity he had initially relished. In 1929 a number of American newspapers featured full-page illustrated accounts of Crowley's return to Paris in that year. One feature ran, 'Aleister Crowley is back again, a fatter, balder, older, sadder but apparently no wiser man.' It continued: 'The most tragic thing that could happen to "the Beast of the Apocalypse" has happened—he has become old-fashioned, he is no longer feared.' The following year Crowley made the British 'news in brief' columns when a lecture on black magic he was due to give to the Oxford University Poetry Society was cancelled after the intervention of the university's Roman Catholic chaplain. The university, however, was at pains to say it was not interested in or responsible for such censorship. Crowley was in the British newspapers again in October 1932 with reports on his talk at the National Laboratory of Psychical Research, an organization run by the showman psychic investigator Harry Price. Referred to in the press as a 'well-known "magician" and occultist, and a member of the mysterious Cult of the Adepts', Crowley gave a talk on his experimentation with a magical elixir that reversed the ageing process.

Two years later, Crowley hit the national headlines when he unsuccessfully sued a former friend, the flamboyant artist Nina Hamnett, for libel because she imputed in her book *The Laughing Torso* that he practised black magic. The trial held him up to a level of public ridicule that he clearly found profoundly discomfiting. This led to some embarrassing exchanges such as when the defence lawyer demanded: 'You said you succeeded in rendering yourself invisible. Would you like to try that on now for, if you don't, I shall pronounce you an impostor?' And, 'Try your magic now on my learned friend.' To which Crowley replied, 'I would not attack anyone, I absolutely refuse.' It was downhill from here in terms of Crowley's finances, influence, and reputation. One critic who met him in 1937 dismissed the Great Beast as a 'gross old man in a kilt sponging drinks and babbling drivel about pentagrams and elementals'. He died in penury in 1947, but his influence on modern magic lives on in the magical orders he founded and led, and the re-publication of the books and journals he had originally privately published.

Modern Witchcraft

As Crowley's star waned, so another arose in the magic firmament. Gerald Gardner (1884–1964) spent much of his career as an administrator and customs official in the Asian colonies. He returned to Britain on retirement in 1936, and pursued in earnest his interests in archaeology, folklore, Freemasonry, spiritualism, and esotericism. He was fascinated by the history of witchcraft propounded by the respected Egyptologist Margaret Murray. Through a highly selective and misrepresentative reading of trial accounts and confessions, Murray believed she had identified a secret, pre-Christian fertility cult that had survived centuries of Christianity until the great witch persecutions of the early modern period. These 'witches' gathered to worship a horned god, usually personified by a man though sometimes by a woman or an animal. Their celebratory gatherings were, she argued, interpreted by the authorities as diabolic sabbats. She presented this thesis in two books read by Gardner, *The Witch Cult in Western Europe* (1921) and *The God of the Witches* (1931). Murray's notion was not new in essence, though. The idea that witches had been part of a benign, liberating pagan sect persecuted by an intolerant Church had been put forward over half a century before by the French historian Jules Michelet in his book *La sorcière* (1862). Neither was Murray the only popular historian at the time taking witch confessions, usually given under torture, at face value. A popular historian of the occult with a dubious past, the ardent Catholic Montague Summers, had, in his oft reprinted book *The History of Witchcraft and Demonology* (1926), suggested that the trial records confirmed 'the possibility of commerce with incarnate evil intelligences'. But had any adherents of the witch cult survived the era of persecution? Apparently so, according to a book written by an enterprising American folklorist called Charles Godfrey Leland. In *Aradia, or the Gospel of the Witches* (1899), Leland claimed to have stumbled across an ancient pagan fertility cult alive in Italy. Leland said one of its adherents lent him the cult's ritual book, the 'Vangelo', replete with spells and charms, which he copied and reproduced in *Aradia*—the name of the goddess he claimed they worshipped. Gardner had his crucial missing link.

Gardner's occult interests also led him to a meeting with Aleister Crowley in 1947 when he was initiated into the OTO. It would seem that some time after this meeting Gardner began work on inventing his own ancient magical manuscript, just as other aspiring magicians had done before him. Gardner's interpretation of the survival of a witch religion first appeared in his 1947 novel *High Magic's Aid*, and over the next few years he set about creating a new magical order. He said he had been initiated into a coven of the ancient witch cult in the New Forest, England, in 1939. It was they, he claimed, who gave him their sacred text—'Ye Bok of ye Art Magical', which would become the basis of the more famed Wiccan *Book of Shadows*. There is no concrete evidence to support Gardner's story of the existence of such a witch cult or the venerable history of 'Ye Bok'. Gardner was creating rather than discovering a pagan witchcraft religion from a patchwork of existing histories, traditions, and organizations—just as numerous other occult orders and religions had already done.

Gardner set about creating the initiation structure and ceremonial content of Wicca. These he based heavily on masonic models, the Golden Dawn, and Crowley's writings, with a dash of Leland's *Aradia* and other sources. Through his existing social circles he began to attract interest in his new, pagan magic order. The year 1951 proved the perfect springboard to widen the pool of adherents for two reasons. First, it was the year that the 1736 Witchcraft Act was repealed and replaced with the Fraudulent Mediums Act. The matter had been debated with some humour in the House of Commons the previous year. Spiritualist organizations had been campaigning for a while to have the Act repealed, though the new law still allowed for the prosecution of those who 'fraudulently purported to act as spiritualist mediums, or to exercise powers of telepathy, clairvoyance or other similar powers'. Any such act performed purely for entertainment was excluded from prosecution. The key point, though, is that the repeal of the 1736 legislation erased 'witchcraft' from the statute books after four centuries. Remember, the 1736 Act defined witchcraft as a fraudulent pretence not a reality, and had absolutely nothing whatsoever to do with witchcraft as a religion as devised by Gardner. There was no chance of him being prosecuted under it unless he started charging for magical services or performing séances for public audiences. Yet the repeal gave Gardner and his early Wiccan adherents the perfect opportunity to weave legal suppression into their historical narrative. After centuries of persecution, they were now free to openly practise witchcraft! Gardner could announce to the world that the witch cult had survived.

The same year, the Wiccan movement effectively got its own museum to reinforce the idea of the long heritage of witchcraft as a religion. The secret cult was opening up and educating the public about the 'Old Religion'. The Folklore Centre of Superstition and Witchcraft at the Witches Mill, Castletown, Isle of Man, was founded by a former film editor named Cecil Williamson. Gerald Gardner was involved as the 'resident witch'. Williamson also offered his services as a witchcraft consultant, using his library of magic books to provide charms and spells. It was through the Centre and Williamson that the new Wiccan movement received one of its first and most influential members, Doreen Valiente. The relationship between Gardner and Williamson broke down after a few years, and in 1954 Williamson sold the museum building and part of the collection to Gardner.

Gardner and Williamson gave various press interviews in the early 1950s explaining the witchcraft religion. A multi-page feature in the *Illustrated*, entitled 'Witchcraft in Britain', focused on Williamson 'in action' but also gave space to the fertility religion devised by Gardner, without actually naming him. 'In general, modern witches believe that they will achieve controlled power by ritual, some of which is primitive', wrote the journalist. 'They feel that their meetings bring them emotional stimulus and old-fashioned good luck. These are, of course, the "pure" practitioners, who base their ritual on instructions handed down from the elders, eked out with the *Clavicules of Solomon*.' He went on to say that there was a cabbalistic circle practising in a garage in Brighton, an erotic magic group in the Finchley Road, London, and another magic group that met in a churchyard in rural Yorkshire.

It was only in 1954, with the publication of Gardner's book *Witchcraft Today*, that the history, nature, and general ritual basis of Wicca was revealed. From then on, interest and adherents proliferated. By the early 1960s there were numerous Gardnerian covens and, inevitably, various Wiccan offshoots appeared. Doreen Valiente formed her own coven in 1957. Most notable in media terms were the Alexandrians led by Alex Sanders, who, after Gardner's death, was happy to foster the title 'King of the Witches'. Sanders drew upon a broader set of literature than that encompassed in the Gardnerian *Book of Shadows* and placed more emphasis on Lévi and Kabbalah. Sanders possessed a ring he claimed belonged to the French occultist.

The likes of Gardner, Alex Sanders, and Eleanor 'Ray' Bone—who claimed to have been initiated into a different coven from Gardner in 1941—loved publicity, and the press was valuable in terms of attracting new adherents. But others preferred to keep the Old Religion out of the limelight. What the press were interested in reporting was not necessarily representative or, indeed, accurate. So, while ceremonial dress was important to the self-imagery and rituals of the Golden Dawn, Wicca came to be identified with a lack of clothing. During the mid-twentieth century many press reports on the 'new' witchcraft religion were accompanied by photographs of Wiccans performing rituals in the nude or 'skyclad'—a term that Gardner said he borrowed from Indian ritual. Undressed female Wiccans were particularly good copy. This obviously appealed to tabloid sensationalism, and reinforced the inference that sexual ritual activity was at the core of Wiccan religion. One newspaper report on the Alexandrian Wiccan priestess Janet Farrar, who became a major public figure in the movement in the 1970s, bore the headline 'Queen of the Sex Cult'. Farrar got so fed up with such press emphasis on Wiccan nudity she ended up refusing to be photographed skyclad.

The performance of ritual nudity in Gardner's Wicca is hardly surprising. He had long been a committed naturist for health reasons, and was a member of a naturist club near St Albans, Hertfordshire. Comfortable with public nudity, he then needed to find a magical purpose for it. He found it in Leland's *Aradia*, where in one passage Aradia tells her witches:

> And as the sign that ye are truly free,
> Ye shall be naked in your rites, both men
> And women also: this shall last until
> The last of your oppressors shall be dead

Those seeking deeper historical evidence also pointed to the sixteenth-century depictions of witches by the likes of Grien and Dürer that showed them performing their magic naked (see Chapter 5). Modern practitioners have also come up with other explanations for perform-ing skyclad. Some are based on magical principles, such as the view that clothing inhibits the emanation and absorption of psychic energy, or that naked bodies repel evil spirits. Other justifications are con-cerned with social rather than ritual considerations, namely that it is an expression of freedom, and that nakedness generates a sense of equality within a coven. But from the early days the practice did not appeal to all modern witches. Doreen Valiente accepted the value of performing rituals in the nude but pragmatically felt it really was not suited to the British climate. The English witch and astrologer Sybil Leek dismissed the practice completely, stating: 'I can get enough power for occult healing with six fur coats on'. These days it is fair to say that most modern witches and magicians adopt ritual clothing rather than ritual nudity.

Nudity could be titillating but the more disturbing press coverage of modern witchcraft concerned claims and accusations that they were Satanists and Devil-worshippers. This was nothing new. In the mid-1890s a French journalist named Léo Taxil wrote a series of sensa-tional publications alleging that the Freemasons were conducting satanic rites, and denounced Encausse as 'the demon Papus'. Crowley did little to discourage the public perception that he was a Satanist, despite being vocal in denouncing black magic and black masses. Wiccans and other pagan witches faced a long and sustained press misrepresentation that periodically stoked public fear. Pagans, by definition, cannot be Satanists as they do not adhere to Christianity. As early as 1952, the Halloween edition of an illustrated magazine featured a piece entitled 'Witches Devil-Worship in London'. It reported that covens were practising animal sacrifices and ritual sex in and around the capital. A spate of church robberies and the desecration of graveyards spread fears of a rise in Satanism. In 1959, for example, ten crosses were smashed in North Cray churchyard, Kent. The caretaker was reported as saying, 'Something very strange is going on and I would not be at all surprised to learn it was devil worship.' Despite the likes of Sybil Leek and Alex Sanders telling the press that their covens were, through their rituals, actively engaged in *protecting* the public from black magic, alarm over the supposed increase in satanic ritual desecrations and animal sacrifice was easily conflated with the 'suspicious' emergence of Wicca. The popularity of Denis Wheatley's 'black magic' novels, most notably *The Devil Rides Out*, and the film version that came out in 1968, further represented the practice of magic as *black* magic, while the same year Roman Polanski's *Rosemary's Baby* reinforced the paranoid idea of secret satanic cults working evil and making blood offerings in contemporary society. In America during the 1970s several high-profile evangelists garnered much publicity for launching campaigns against witchcraft as part of a broader fight against the tens of thousands of Satanists they believed infested the United States. Even today the press and police sometimes point fingers at pagan witches when investigating periodic cases of horse mutilation. Of course, such reports generated further interest in the witch religion. As Doreen Valiente observed in 1978, 'Every time there is a big "exposure of the evils of witchcraft" in the sensational Press, it is followed by sackfuls of letters from people wanting to know how they can join a coven!'

Modern Witchcraft Moves Overseas

Through the 1960s and 1970s the pagan witch religion, in its various forms, spread overseas in a very modest way. It was in America that it really took root. Indeed, in the 1970s, American witchcraft started to develop its own home-grown trends and expressions. Before then, pagan witchcraft in the States was mostly identified in the press with British émigrés, the publicity-hungry, storytelling Sybil Leek being the pre-eminent witch in America during the 1960s. Ever ready with a newsworthy quote and outrageous claims about her powers, she was influential on public perception in terms of representing Wicca as a jolly, friendly, and benign religion, and the practice of magic as a perfectly normal aspect of modern society. Leek was an independent operator in Wiccan terms, but another British couple, Raymond and Rosemary Buckland, set up the first Gardnerian coven in America in 1962. Inspired by Gardner's Museum of Witchcraft on the Isle of Man, they also set up the first American museum of witchcraft in their Long Island home.

Other American museums also opened in the early 1970s. After Gardner's death in 1964, the Isle of Man Museum continued under the management of his heir, Monique Wilson. In 1971 she closed it down and a significant part of the collection was sold to Ripley's Believe it or Not, Inc. This was a franchise operation founded by Robert Ripley (1890–1949), who, since the 1930s, had published a series of books and syndicated newspaper features about bizarre events, amazing feats, strange objects, and curious people. His company expanded to broadcasting the same sort of material on radio, film, and television. With all the media interest in witches, two Ripley Museums of Witchcraft and Magic opened in 1972–3 in San Francisco and in Gatlinburg, Tennessee. With the purchase of the Gardner collection their names were changed to Dr Gardner's Museum of Magic and Superstition, with the San Francisco branch displaying a wax effigy of Gardner and a reconstruction of an altar prepared for a black mass. An advertisement for the Gatlinburg museum contained an image of Gardner's head, and announced it was 'the world's largest collection of artefacts dealing with the occult'. It boasted that, 'through the most modern and exciting methods of Sound, Light, and Display, it has been acclaimed the very finest presentation of its kind in existence today'. Meanwhile, after selling the Isle of Man museum to Gardner, Williamson set up briefly in Windsor before moving his Museum of Witchcraft to the village of Bourton-on-the-Water, Gloucestershire. Concerns were expressed in the local community about its presence, and so Williamson moved one last time to the museum's current site in Boscastle, Cornwall.

It was in America that the witchcraft religion became a significant aspect of the counter-culture phenomenon, expressed most cogently in the feminist movement. After all, the majority of executed witches during the witch trials had been women. With grossly misleading execution figures circulating widely in popular culture, the idea that the historic witch persecutions resulted in the deaths of millions of women understandably led to such provocative descriptions as 'gynocide'. Couple this with the Gardnerian notion that the Church had sought to exterminate a liberated witch fertility religion that expressed its sexuality, and the feminist interest in witchcraft was obvious. They rightly saw social parallels between the past and present in terms of patriarchy and misogyny. In 1968 one radical feminist movement, which was not Wiccan in inspiration, called themselves 'WITCH', the Women's International Terrorist Conspiracy from Hell. Members of WITCH organized public protests and street theatre events to highlight the dominance of patriarchal capitalism.

Various feminist voices soon appeared in the pagan witch community, rejecting the patriarchy expressed in the leadership of early Wiccan groups and some of the gender biases in their rituals. In 1971 the Hungarian-American pagan Zsuzsanna Budapest produced a pamphlet manual of Gardnerian rituals solely for women called the *Feminist Book of Lights and Shadows*. The most influential feminist Wiccan text of the 1970s, however, was *The Spiral Dance: A Rebirth of the Ancient Religion of the Great Goddess* (1979). Its author Miriam Simos, better known as Starhawk, took Wicca in a new direction with a strong emphasis on ecological concerns, feminist spirituality, and shamanism. She co-founded the activist witch movement 'Reclaim' to further press for the social, political, and environmental concerns that resonated with her conception of a goddess nature religion. By the year 2000, *Spiral Dance* had sold more than 300,000 copies, influencing many feminists within and beyond the Wiccan community, and it was one of the first significant American influences on British Wiccans. One downside of its popularity was that Starhawk repeated the old falsehood that nine million people had been executed as witches during the European witch-hunts. Modern American witchcraft also had its gay activists, who were motivated both by the global campaign for homosexual rights, and also prejudice within modern witchcraft. Despite being a religion inspired by the paganism of the ancient world and its diverse sexual expressions, in the early decades of Wicca the emphasis had been on the importance of the 'natural', fertile relationship between male and female. The gay New York witch Leo Martello, who founded the Witches' Liberation Movement and the Witches Anti-Defamation League, stirred up the debate during the early 1970s.

The likes of *Spiral Dance* had a substantial influence on a growing trend towards solitary practice in pagan witchcraft and other expressions of modern magic. From the Golden Dawn through to Gardnerian Wicca, modern magic had been imagined as a community with hierarchies, collective forms of worship, and initiations and rituals that involved at least two people. But as Wicca matured so the idea of the solitary practitioner grew. From being Gardner's High Priestess in the early days of Wicca, Doreen Valiente came to prefer solitary magical working. In 1978 she wrote *Witchcraft for Tomorrow* as a guide on how to initiate oneself into the witches' craft without needing to join a coven. 'Many people, I know, will question the idea of self-initiation, as given in this book', she wrote. 'To them I will address one simple question: who initiated the first witch?' Once the desire for modern magicians to form fraternities, orders, and covens based on notions of ancient secret societies ebbed, the impulse to diversify and innovate spread. One did not need to religiously follow some imposed set text or a set of rituals defined by someone else. The phrase 'believing without belonging', which sociologists of religion coined to describe the decline of Christian church attendance, also applied to the growth of modern paganism in the same era. Regional and local expressions of pagan witchcraft proliferated, drawing upon folk magic practices, for example. These days there are those who call themselves witches but who do not consider themselves pagan, but are inspired by the spells, charms, and remedies of the cunning-folk of the recent past. Away from pagan witchcraft, an array of solitary magicians have forged their own tailor-made rituals and practices, often influenced by the writings of the Golden Dawn members, the OTO, or Crowley and his followers, but drawing upon a range of other traditions from outside the western magical tradition, such as Siberian shamanism. To put all this in perspective, there are undoubtedly far more ritual magicians in the western world today than there were five centuries ago.

8

Witchcraft and Magic in the Age of Anthropology

Robert J. Wallis

Writing in 1535, after visiting 'Hispaniola' (Haiti and the Dominican Republic), the Spanish navigator Gonzalo Fernández de Oviedo described the witchcraft and magic he found in 'the new world':

> Among other vices, the Indians of this island had a very evil one which consists of taking a smoke they call *tabaco*, in order to get out of their minds... [T]hey do not know almighty God and they worship the Devil in diverse forms and images, as is the custom among these peoples in the Indies... [T]hey paint, engrave, or carve a demon they call *cemí* in many objects and places... These infernal images they had in their houses in specially assigned and dark places and spots that were reserved for their worship; and there they entered to pray and to ask for whatever they desired... And inside there was an old Indian who answered them according to their expectations or in accordance with a consultation addressed to him whose evil image was standing there; and it is to be thought that the Devil entered into him and spoke through him as his minister... and they did not undertake or carry out anything that might be of importance without considering the Devil's opinion in any way.

Almost five centuries later, in 2012, *The Guardian* newspaper reported that in London 'a man and woman' of Congolese descent 'who tortured and killed a 15-year-old boy because they believed he was a witch have been found guilty of murder'.

These two reports, from very different times and places, suggest that witchcraft and magic are consistent features of human societies across time. Anthropologists, who study human societies, have tried to understand these phenomena, but from the first European encounters with indigenous communities to the present, the way in which witchcraft and magic have been discussed inevitably tells us as much about our own western thinking as it does about indigenous people themselves; marking out 'us' and 'them'. De Oviedo's view was coloured by his Catholic beliefs and was set against the witch trials emerging in Europe, and as such he and his contemporaries made sense of what they saw in terms of the very real (to them) struggle between 'God' and the 'Devil'. Christian missionaries, from the Jesuits of the sixteenth century to the many denominations today, have attempted to convert 'heathen' souls to Christianity, often unsuccessfully.

In the 'Enlightenment' of the eighteenth century, as rational, humanist philosophy revised this religious thinking, witchcraft and magic, and other religious behaviour, were dismissed as superstitions in need of correction. Again, little attempt was made to try to understand these phenomena on their own terms, within the societies in question. As scientific anthropology developed in the late nineteenth century within the context of Darwin's theory of evolution, witchcraft and magic were viewed as mistaken beliefs, destined to die out but of interest to science as relics of primitive practices and therefore worthy of record and study. This culture of collecting also led to the founding of modern museums which today house countless 'artefacts' pertaining to witchcraft and magic. In the twentieth century, as anthropology became established as a discrete academic discipline, more careful attempts were made to understand magic and witchcraft, with such theories as functionalism, structuralism, and postmodernism all making their mark.

In the globalized twenty-first century, with witchcraft and magic making newspaper headlines in European cities, the onus is on anthropologists to make sense of these 'other' practices, aware that any such translation is always subjective and never complete. Today, anthropologists might not talk about magic as 'supernatural' but as agency embedded in daily life, and performed by many people, even unintentionally, not just by specialist 'magicians'. And in parts of Amazonia, indigenous sorcery has been theorized in terms of aggression and the consumption of another's power—cannibalism. Witchcraft and magic are things against which the West has defined itself for 500 years or more. They are labels loaded with baggage, 'discursive constructs', and problematic grounds on which to characterize indigenous ontologies (ways of being) and epistemologies (ways of knowing), or 'lifeways'. The history of anthropological thinking on witchcraft and magic, then, must be seen equally as one that is partial and of its time.

From First Contact to Enlightenment Thought

Gonzalo Fernández de Oviedo wrote about 'Devil worship' in the Caribbean in the past tense because by the time he was writing in 1535 the indigenous communities there had almost been eradicated. The Christian world view informing his description was reproduced in 1557 by the French Franciscan priest André Thévet who reported on the Tupinamba Indians living near Rio de Janeiro in Brazil:

> These people—being thus removed from the truth, beyond the perse-cutions they receive from the evil spirit and the errors of their dreams— are so outside of reason that they adore the Devil by means of his minister called *pagé*. These *pagé* or Caribs, are people of evil custom who have given themselves over to serve the Devil to deceive their neigh-bours . . . Sometimes, if it happens that these *pagé* do not tell the truth and that things turn out differently than forecast, people have no difficulty in putting them to death, as unworthy of the title and dignity of *pagé* . . . The Americans are not the first to practice abusive magic; before them, it was familiar to several nations, back to the time of Our Lord, who erased and abolished the power that Satan exercised over human kind. It is therefore not without reason that it is forbidden by the scriptures . . . and worthy of great punishment.

Fifty years later, in 1585, the English explorer and artist John White produced the earliest known representation of an American Indian medicine man, among the Algonquians of North Carolina. His water-colour is entitled 'The Flyer' and captures a moment of the medicine man's ritual dance. His hair is roached (spiked up) and without locks or crests; he wears instead a bird as his badge of office. A pouch, probably containing tobacco, the most commonly used hallucinogen in the Americas, hangs at the waist of his breechcloth. White's medi-cine man is fey and serene, despite his energetic dance, and his posture draws upon classical representations of the Greek god Hermes, the messenger of the gods.

Writing almost a century later in 1664 about the indigenous inhabitants of what is now French Guyana, the priest Antoine Biet records how the *piayés* endured a rigorous training for 'curing illnesses and evoking the Devil', including dancing to exhaustion, fasting, and being bitten by large black ants which cause 'much pain'. Biet concludes that 'These poor infidels are in such blindness! See what they suffer in this life for a vain honor; they are true penitents of the demon, who starts to make them feel the torments of Hell, while they are still alive.'

Early ethnographic accounts, such as these from the Americas, are important for the useful first-hand descriptions of the practices they witnessed, some of which would be familiar to today's anthropologists studying indigenous religious and healing practices labelled as 'witch-craft' or 'magic'. But they are of course coloured by the Christian background of the reporters who tried to fit indigenous practices into their own, established, European framework of reference. Some of them believed the indigenous people did not have souls and were little more than animals, or that they were superstitious, while others thought that as fellow humans with a soul they could be converted and saved. These early ethnographers all represent indigenous prac-tices as the same Devil worship they believed existed in Europe. Witchcraft and magic were not yet the generic, universal terms anthropologists use today for comparative purposes, but were seen as self-evident and real. With anthropological hindsight, it is obvious that the early commentators made little attempt to understand indi-genous witchcraft and magic on their own terms. Indeed, these accounts tell us more about the western reporters themselves than the practices of magic and witchcraft in these communities. A more sensitive anthropological approach would not emerge until the twen-tieth century.

The modern distinction between religion and magic emerges dur-ing the Reformation when the Catholic Church was attacked for its doctrine of transubstantiation as a magical act. It was thought that nothing could happen outside of God's purpose, so magical acts must be ineffective and blasphemous, and only prayer could effect change. The 'Enlightenment' or 'Age of Reason' that followed was an intel-lectual movement in eighteenth-century Europe promoting scientific investigation and rational thinking, and opposing 'superstition' and the established abuses of power within the established Church and state. This development of rational thought recast witches as impostors who did not really communicate with the Devil or spirits, or have any success with magic, but who duped their communities with tricks and sleight-of-hand for their own ends. Attempts were made to expose as tricksters shamans who produced a worm, small piece of down, or a piece of charcoal from a patient as the source of their illness. This rethinking of the nature of witchcraft and magic removed the justification for executing 'witches' as Devil-worshippers, but the Enlightenment project was not a wholesale switch to rationalism; a tension persisted between reason and its opposites: irrationality, the supernatural, and romanticism. Goethe's tragic play *Faust* (part 1, 1808) epitomizes this tension at the height of the Enlightenment in Germany, with Faust caught between the forward-looking thinking of the age and the infinite possibilities promised by the magic of Mephistopheles, the Devil, but who ultimately is redeemed and goes to Heaven. In France, dynamic exchanges between philosophers and other thinkers at the salons culminated in the publication of the *Encyclopédie* (1751–72), edited by the philosopher Denis Diderot, which rapidly disseminated Enlightenment thinking across Europe. Yet Diderot himself, educated by Jesuits but a self-identified atheist, took an ambivalent approach to the occult. He described Siberian shamans as 'imposters who claim they consult with the Devil', and 'jugglers' as 'magicians or enchanters much renowned among the savage nations of America', but whose practices also 'make one think that the supernatural occasionally enters into their operations' and that their pronouncements were sometimes 'quite close to the mark'. The German philosopher Johann Gottfried Herder, writing in 1785, thought that labelling 'magicians' as 'impostors' alone was insufficient, noting that they required a community of believers ('they belong to the people as well') and relied on the power of the human mind (in particular 'brain and nerves') and its 'strength of imagination'. While still certain that magic was hokum, and seeing indigenous beliefs and practices as things to be collected, as curiosities, these Enlightenment thinkers were at least starting to attempt to understand the practices they saw or wrote about, and this scientific rationalism—problematic though it was—laid the groundwork for the development of anthropology as a discipline in the nineteenth century.

Armchair Anthropology: The Intellectualists and Social Evolution

Anthropology as a discrete and recognized discipline, the study of humanity (*anthropos*, Greek, 'man'; *-ology*, 'the study of'), did not emerge until the second half of the nineteenth century, with the work of Sir Edward Burnett Tylor (1832–1917) and Sir James Frazer (1854–1941). Tylor wrote *Primitive Culture: Researches into the Development of Mythology, Philosophy, Religion, Language, Art and Custom* in 1871, was appointed as the first Reader in Anthropology at Oxford just over a decade later in 1884, and has come to be known (via his student and successor Robert Ranulph Marrett (1866–1943)) as the 'Father of Anthropology'. Frazer's more widely known work, *The Golden Bough*, first published in two volumes in 1890, offered a comparative examination of consistencies in mythology and religion across cultures, and is equally controversial in its commentary on witchcraft and magic.

In their work, both Tylor and Frazer used the categories of magic, science, and religion to organize their thinking. They both thought that belief in witchcraft and magic in 'primitive' societies were 'survivals' from prehistoric times, and that these fossils of 'superstition' evidenced a ladder of progress by which cultures develop from 'savagery' to 'civilization', with religions developing from animism through totemism and polytheism to monotheism. 'Magic', as a superstitious practice, was destined to die out, but remained of interest to science as a relic of primitive practices and therefore worthy of collection, record, and study. It is important to consider the context out of which these ideas emerged. The notion of an underlying psychic coherence linking all of humanity was influenced by developments in the understanding of geological time, and Darwin's new theory of evolution expressed in *The Origin of Species* in 1859, published only a decade or so before Tylor's book, was also an important influence on the idea of how cultures, and religions, evolved. The thinking is problematic, however, because: (1) it is ethnocentric, belittling the complex and sophisticated ontologies and epistemologies of indigenous communities, (2) ethnographic and archaeological evidence shows that cultures do not 'progress' along evolutionary lines, but do adapt to ongoing internal and external pressures, (3) the mechanism by which one stage succeeds another is not explained—for instance, how an animist becomes a totemist—unlike natural selection for the evolution of species. Neither technological determinism (improvements in technology, from stone to metal tools, for example) nor cultural Darwinism (that certain cultures are unable to progress and so will become extinct—a racist, incorrect, if still prevalent notion) offers a corrective.

Tylor thought that magic has its origin in logical thinking where scientific laws are as yet unknown: in 'primitive' communities unaware of the laws of science, magic fills in the gaps—magic is a pseudo-science. He went on to address why people believe that magic works, arguing that in many cases it appears to never fail; when it does, failure is due to the inadequacies of the magician. Magic also tends to bring about events that will naturally occur anyway as people do not ask impossible things of magic. When asked by the anthropologist Meyer Forte to perform a ceremony, for an attractive fee, one magician replied, 'Don't be a fool, whoever makes a rain-making ceremony in the dry season.' Tylor also thought that belief in magic required selective memory, in that believers tend to remember instances of success rather than failure.

While they agreed on the psychic unity of humankind and the evolution of religion, Frazer disagreed with Tylor in some respects and took a harder, less sensitive line against magic—for Frazer magic was not a pseudo-science but a 'bastard science': 'magic is a spurious system of natural law as well as a fallacious guide of conduct; it is a false science as well as an abortive art.' He proposed a 'Law of Sympathy', according to which magic depends on an apparent association or agreement between two things. There are two parts to this theory, a 'Law of Similarity' (imitative magic) which states that things that are alike are the same, and a 'Law of Contagion' (contagious magic) in which things that were once in contact continue to be connected after the connection is severed. We have seen instances of these principles in previous chapters. A classic example of both imitative and contagious magic in operation (an overlap Frazer recognized) is with 'hunting magic': a prehistoric hunter makes an image of a bison penetrated by a spear on a cave wall, which by imitation will affect a living bison, and then jabs at the image with his own spear which once killed a bison so that by contagion it will affect the living animal. Frazer saw these 'Laws' as incorrect: a rational, empirical, scientific approach to a world subject to natural laws insists that the similarity or former connection between two things cannot be causally related; inanimate objects do not have agency. Frazer's approach was less sophisticated than Tylor's and both were deeply flawed, but Tylor's insistence on magic as logical remains influential, and Frazer's ideas on contagion and similarity do usefully address 'how magical ideas are formed through associations'.

Some of the more interesting theorizing on witchcraft and magic of this period was set out at the interface of philosophy, sociology, and anthropology. In *The Elementary Forms of the Religious Life* (1912), the French sociologist Émile Durkheim (1858–1917) made a distinction between the sacred and the profane, grouping magic and religion as sacred and science as profane. In *A General Theory of Magic* (1903), Durkheim's student Marcel Mauss (1872–1950) similarly points to magic, science, and religion as overlapping but distinct categories of social phenomena. Magic is functional in seeking to acquire tangible results, and therefore resembles technology and science. But while science is based on experimentation, magic requires belief. While magic seems similar to religion, Mauss sees magic as the antithesis of religion because it is secretive and isolated, and rarely performed publicly so as to preserve occult knowledge. While magic might appear to resemble both religion and science, it is a distinct social phenomenon, with its own internal logic. Both Durkheim and Mauss see social relationships as primary, with belief systems, such as those involving witchcraft and magic, as simply reflections or expressions of society. Rather than illogical or incorrect and representative of an outmoded way of understanding the world, as Tylor and Frazer supposed, magic for Durkheim and Mauss is a 'social fact' with its own common sense.

The French philosopher and anthropologist Lucien Lévy-Bruhl (1857–1939), in *How Natives Think* (1926), similarly opposed the notion of an evolutionary ladder for culture, but he was less interested in the social and more interested in the psychological aspects of collective native thought. He contrasted speculative and logical western thinking with the concept of magic in 'the primitive mind' that is 'pre-logical' and uses 'participation mystique' to manipulate supernatural agencies. While 'mystical participation' might be sociologically derived, and while he was interested in the differences between 'western' and 'native' minds, Lévy-Bruhl proposed that pre-logical mentality was common to all humans, and westerners are not exempt because we too think this way in certain circumstances.

Such thinking on magic in anthropology's formative years inevitably had a major impact on anthropologists in the first half of the twentieth century. Significantly, though, few of these intellectual thinkers conducted sustained ethnographic fieldwork of their own. As 'armchair anthropologists' Tylor and Frazer in particular examined reports of non-western cultures from the comfortable position of being privileged, white, European men, writing at the height of British colonialism and empire. This no doubt facilitated a presumed detachment from indigenous communities and an assumption of superiority which fed into their ideas. In the early twentieth century, anthropologists began engaging with indigenous communities in sustained ethnographic (recording) work—the mainstay of anthropological fieldwork to this day because being embedded gives the best possible chance of understanding the culture. The resulting ethnographies of these engagements must be recognized as partial and subject to the vagaries of translation, however. As such, they tell us as much about how these anthropologists attempt(ed) to make sense of witchcraft and magic, as about witchcraft and magic themselves.

Coral Gardens and Their Magic: Functionalist Anthropology in the Trobriand Islands

The first generation of anthropologists in the twentieth century, based on their sustained fieldwork in indigenous communities, began to reconsider witchcraft and magic. Bronislaw Malinowski (1884–1942), an émigré from Poland to England, conducted fieldwork in the Trobriand Islands of Melanesia between 1915 and 1918. He coined the term 'participant-observation' for this sustained and engaged approach to fieldwork involving close interaction with the daily lives of the host community. Where Tylor and Frazer, having never lived among indigenous groups, dismissed witchcraft and magic as superstitious and mistaken, without trying to understand them within context, Malinowski, having actually lived among the people he studied, argued that all aspects of society including witchcraft and magic are meaningful and interrelated. This thinking on the social relevance of witchcraft and magic founded the 'social school' of anthropology in Britain.

Malinowski began to theorize on magic in his essay 'Magic, Science and Religion' (1925), and set out how Trobriand Islanders use magic and why he thinks they practise magic in his books *Coral Gardens and their Magic* (1935) and *Argonauts of the Western Pacific* (1922). For the Trobriand Islanders, a variety of practical and magical knowledge is needed to accomplish a range of daily tasks, from gardening to lagoon fishing and canoe building. Garden magic is comprised of a complex cycle of rituals which begins when a field is cleared of weeds. In preparation, the men dress, paint their bodies, and perform appropriate magic over their axes. The ritual specialist, who fasts for the ritual, carries his axe in his right hand, his hereditary wand of office in the left, then enters the garden, cuts a sapling, and recites a spell:

> This is our bad wood, O ancestral spirits! O bush-pig, who fightest, O bush-pig from the great stone in the rayboag, O bush-pig of the garden stakes, O bush-pig drawn by evil smells, O bush-pig of the narrow face, O bush-pig of the ugly countenance, O fierce bush-pig. Thy sail, O bush-pig, is in thy ear, thy steering-oar is in thy tail. I kick thee from behind, I despatch thee. Go away. Go to Ulawola. Return from whence you have come. It burns your eyes, it turns your stomach.

The sapling is then deposited in the forest and this magic repels the bush-pig and other forces which might damage the crop.

In another instance, the tree to be fashioned into a canoe is chosen from the inland forest, cut down, and made as light as possible for the journey back to the village. It is cut to the right length, the branches cut off, debarked, then spells are performed to make the tree even lighter. A piece of dried banana leaf is placed on the log and the log is beaten with a bunch of dried *lalang* grass accompanied by the words, 'Come down, come down, defilement by contact with excrement! Come down, come down heaviness! Come down rot! Come down fungus!' In this way, the heaviness is drawn out of the log and into the grass, which is then ritually thrown away. The log is then beaten again, this time with a bunch of seared-dry *lalang* grass, accompanied by the words, 'I lash you, O tree: the tree flies; the tree becomes like a breath of wind; the tree becomes like a butterfly; the tree becomes like a cotton seed fluff', and this action makes the log lighter and speedier.

For Tylor and Frazer, magic of this sort was incorrect, implausible, and bad science. But for Malinowski, who also used the terms magic, science, and religion to organize his thinking, magic is practically reasonable because it fills in where there are gaps in people's knowledge (explained by western science). Magic, thinks Malinowski, overlaps with science and religion, and is 'to be expected and generally to be found whenever man comes to an unbridgeable gap, a hiatus in his knowledge or in his powers of practical control, and yet has to continue in his pursuit'. Magic and magical thinking, therefore, have a useful function in society and are like science and scientific thinking because both assist 'human instincts, needs and pursuits'. So, Malinowski views magic as psychologically and functionally valid in that it offers catharsis in times of crisis, and confirms, supports, and maintains the complex social system in which the various parts function together to promote social stability and cohesion. Magic, he states, 'supplies primitive man with a number of ready-made rituals, acts and beliefs, with a definite mental and practical technique which serves to bridge over the dangerous gaps in every pursuit or critical situation'. So for Malinowski, magic has a useful psychological function because practitioners feel they are doing something to address a particular problem and this action alleviates the frustration and anxiety presented by the problem. As a result, magic has a broader social function in maintaining social solidarity.

This view was an important and influential development in its day because issues of 'belief' in magic and its effectiveness (whether it 'works') become less important than how magic operates to maintain psychological and social cohesion. For example, soon after Malinowski's fieldwork in Melanesia, in the early 1920s the American anthropologist Clyde Kluckhohn (1905–60) worked with the Navajo (*Diné*) in the south-west of the USA, offering a functionalist interpretation of their witchcraft. While most Navajos attempt to live in 'beauty' (harmony, order, health, goodness), using ceremonials including healing 'sings' or chants, witches harness the opposite 'evil' (ugly, destructive, chaotic, unhealthy) forces, using shape shifting to become 'skin-walkers', parts of corpses to inflict 'ghost sickness', and magical projectiles to attack other people. They also commit incest and murder. In *Navajo Witchcraft* (1944), Kluckhohn defines witchcraft as 'the influencing of events by super-natural techniques that are socially disapproved', but he suggests that witchcraft is integral to Navajo society nonetheless because it resolves tensions and maintains social equilibrium. A prosperous but ungenerous man, for instance, may be accused of using witchcraft to accumulate his wealth. The Navajo live mainly in a semi-arid, high, desert plateau which is poor in resources and over-grazed by livestock. Kluckhohn thought this created individual anxiety, family insecurity, and tension between groups, leading to aggressive behaviour including acts of sorcery, so that witchcraft emerges as a channel for dealing with personal and social anxiety, aggressiveness, and individual ambitions for power. Kluckhohn's functionalist interpretation resonates with Malinowski's because in both cases witchcraft/magic is seen as enabling people to deal with instability and so social cohesion is maintained.

Witchcraft and Magic among the Azande

English anthropologist Sir Edward Evan (E. E.) Evans-Pritchard (1902–73) conducted participant-observation fieldwork among the Azande in southern Sudan in the late 1920s. His volume *Witchcraft, Oracles and Magic Among the Azande* (1937) is considered a classic text on the anthropology of witchcraft and magic. His functionalist interpretation differs from Malinowski's in some respects. For the Azande, witchcraft and magic are an integral part of daily life and many unfortunate events are explained by witchcraft. Evans-Pritchard provides the example of a granary which collapses and kills the people sheltering in the shade beneath it, leading people to ask:

> why should these particular people have been sitting under this particular granary at the particular moment when it collapsed? That it should collapse is easily intelligible, but why should it have collapsed at that particular moment when these particular people were sitting beneath it? Through years it might have collapsed, so why should it fall just when certain people sought its kindly shelter?... To our minds the only relationship between these two independently caused facts is their coincidence in time and space... Zande philosophy can supply the missing link... It was due to the action of witchcraft. If there had been no witchcraft people would not have been sitting under the granary and it would not have fallen on them, or it would have collapsed but the people would not have been sheltering under it at the time. Witchcraft explains the coincidence of these two happenings.

One reason that witchcraft is so prominent in Azande life is because witchcraft attacks are largely unintentional. The source of witchcraft is understood as an inherited, impersonal substance located in the belly which exists independently of the host. This means that the witchcraft can act without the conscious knowledge of the individual, so that some witches may be unaware of their actions. The performance of various magic rituals in order to protect against and counteract witchcraft attacks is an ongoing part of daily life.

When witchcraft is suspected, the individual looks for the source of witchcraft among his enemies. The most reliable way to do this is through the use of oracles. The most commonly used of these is the rubbing-board or *iwa* oracle which is made of wood and consists of two parts: the 'female' base looks like a small round or oval three-legged stool or small table with a long 'tail' forming the third support; the 'male' part is a flat piece of wood which fits the table like a lid. When used, the operator sits on the ground and steadies the board by placing his right foot on the tail. The juices of a plant or fruit, and some water, are squeezed onto the table so that the mixture froths and bubbles, and the diviner then rubs the lid backwards and forwards across the table while questioning the oracle. Usually, if there is friction and the lid sticks, the answer is affirmative, while if the lid is smooth-sliding, the answer is negative, and if the lid is neither of these then it is refusing to give a verdict and the answer to the question is uncertain. The rubbing-board oracle may be used to establish which name of a list of enemies is the witch, but the veracity of this must be confirmed with a more reliable oracle and the most reliable of all is the poison or *benge* oracle.

The poison oracle is based around the death or survival of a fowl which has been forced to ingest a poison:

> The poison used is a red powder manufactured from a forest creeper and mixed with water to a paste. The liquid is squeezed out of the paste into the beaks of small domestic fowls which are compelled to swallow it. Generally violent spasms follow. The doses sometimes prove fatal, but as often the fowls recover. Sometimes they are even unaffected by the poison. From the behaviour of fowls under this ordeal, especially by their death or survival, Azande receive answers to the questions they place before the oracle.

As only married men can afford to keep fowls and purchase the costly poison, this oracle is used less often than the rubbing-board oracle, and poorer men must rely on another relative or official to perform the oracle on their behalf. Evans-Pritchard reports:

> It is particularly the province of married men with households of their own to consult the poison oracle and no occupation gives them greater pleasure. It is not merely that they are able to solve their personal problems; but also they are dealing with matters of public importance, witchcraft, sorcery, and adultery, in which their names will be associated as witnesses of the oracle's decisions. A middle-aged Zande is happy when he has some poison and a few fowls and the company of one or two trusted friends of his own age, and he can sit down to a long séance to discover all about the infidelities of his wives, his health and the health of his children, his marriage plans, his hunting and agricultural prospects, the advisability of changing his homestead, and so forth.

The poison oracle is used to address various issues, including the origin of witchcraft attacks. Once a witch is identified, the action taken varies, depending on the circumstances. In cases where the loss is irreparable, when witches have scared away game at the end of the hunting season, for instance, the injured party will do nothing—it is useless 'to pursue the matter further, since no compensation can be obtained for the loss, and a witch cannot undo what has already been done'. Further, if the sufferer were to attack the witch, a loss of prestige would result, damages might need to be paid, and the additional hatred of the witch would be incurred. Action is only required if potential misfortune is uncovered, or a situation caused by witchcraft might worsen, for example if someone is bitten by a snake and their condition deteriorates. But it would be antisocial if the relatives of the sick person then approached and insulted or injured the witch because witches are entitled to live unmolested unless they actually kill people.

If a witch has been identified, a public oration, *de kuba*, might be performed. Shortly after sunset or before dawn, the orator climbs a termite mound or tree, cries out to attract attention, then tells his listeners how he has been besieged by a neighbour's witchcraft despite being a good, law-abiding member of the community, but that he does not want to shame the witch by naming him, and instead requests him to recall his witchcraft. More often than a public oration, the practice is for a relation of the injured party to take a fowl's wing, prepared at the poison oracle ritual, to a prince or more usually a prince's deputy. The deputy is informed of the outcome of the oracle (s) and it is his duty to send a reliable messenger to visit the accused witch, lay the wing on the ground in front of him, and state that the deputy has sent him with this message. Evans-Pritchard conveys eloquently how a dutiful witch should respond:

> Almost invariably the witch replies courteously that he is unconscious of injuring anyone, that if it is true that he has injured the man in question he is very sorry, and that if it is he alone who is troubling him then he will surely recover, because from the bottom of his heart he wishes him health and happiness.

The witch then swills water in his mouth, sprays it over the wing, and says that he addresses the witchcraft in his belly and beseeches it to 'become cool' (inactive), 'and that he makes this appeal from his heart and not merely his lips'. Evans-Pritchard reports that the 'whole point of the procedure is to put the witch in a good temper by being polite to him. The witch, on his part, ought to feel grateful to the people who have warned him so politely of the danger in which he stands.' As a result, 'good behaviour on both sides is habitual' and, besides, it is 'to the interest of both parties that they should not become estranged through the incident. They have to live together as neighbours afterwards and to co-operate in the life of the community.'

Evans-Pritchard saw the major problem of anthropology as one of translation, and clearly Azande witchcraft, oracles, and magic present a contrast to western ways of daily living. As a result, he is careful to articulate Azande understandings as clearly and respectfully as possible. He did not 'believe' in what he heard about witchcraft, but he did attempt to understand the relevance of it to the social climate, and he did this by living among the Azande, using oracles himself:

> [T]he best way of gaining confidence was to enact the same procedure as Azande and to take oracular verdicts as seriously as they take them. I always kept a supply of poison for the use of my household and neighbours and we regulated our affairs in accordance with the oracles' decisions. I may remark that I found this as satisfactory a way of running my home and affairs as any other I know of.

Evans-Pritchard approached the Azande use of witchcraft, oracles, and magic in terms similar to Malinowski's functionalism. Evans-Pritchard knew Malinowski at the London School of Economics. He was also heavily influenced by the structural functionalism of Alfred Reginald Radcliffe-Brown (1881–1955), whom he knew at Oxford. Radcliffe-Brown studied the Andaman Islanders in the Bay of Bengal between 1906 and 1908 (see *The Andaman Islanders* (1922)), and Aborigines in western Australia between 1910 and 1912 (see *The Social Organisation of Australian Tribes* (1931)). Applying structural functionalism, Evans-Pritchard saw witchcraft, and magical methods for dealing with it, as important for maintaining social cohesion, and he argued that they made sense within the internal logic of Azande society. Nonetheless, taking account of historical and colonial processes, in the face of what he termed the 'break-down of tradition', Evans-Pritchard thought 'the advances of science and technology have rendered magic redundant'; thus, science would replace magic.

Anthropologists in the first half of the twentieth century conducted sustained fieldwork which enabled them to revise understanding away from the social evolution and primitivism described by the intellectualists, to consider society as a complex system whose parts work together to promote solidarity and stability. On this view, witchcraft and magic have a functional role in *all* societies which maintain social relationships and the broader social structure.

Myth, Magic, and the Unconscious

Structural functionalism proposes that witchcraft and magic are rational, logical, socially effective, and very human ways of engaging with the world. Building on this understanding of magic as a human universal, the structuralist school of thinkers were interested in examining the underlying patterns of thought across human societies. Drawing on the structural linguistics of Ferdinand de Saussure (1857–1913) and Carl Gustav Jung's (1875–1961) concept of myth as an expression of the collective unconscious, the anthropologist Claude Lévi-Strauss (1908–2009) conceived of culture as a system of symbolic communication. He examined myth as a coded language of the unconscious, attempting to uncover the underlying structures or universal laws of how myths work, across cultures.

In *Mythologiques* (published in four volumes, 1964–71), he examined consistencies in American Indian myths, pointing to the importance of oppositions, particularly the tension between life and death, and the role of the trickster figure (usually a coyote or raven) in their resolution. He wrote that in the 'intellectual condition of man', 'the universe is never charged with sufficient meaning' and 'the mind always has more meanings available than there are objects to which to relate them', so that 'magical thinking' stands in to provide 'a new system of reference' to reconcile this dualism. The magician is, therefore, a significant figure in many indigenous communities:

> The patient is all passivity and self-alienation, just as inexpressibility is the disease of the mind. The sorcerer is activity and self-projection, just as affectivity is the source of symbolism. The cure interrelates these opposite poles, and demonstrates, within a total experience, the coherence of the psychic universe, itself a projection of the social universe.

So Lévi-Strauss's structural approach to the success of magic, drawing on semiotics (the study of human communication and meaning-making) and psychoanalysis, engages with the dynamics of individual and group psychology and the underlying symbolic mode of the unconscious, and argues for the power of magical thinking as an example of the power of the human mind. Just as structural functionalism had its limitations, though, Lévi-Strauss's structuralism, by examining perceived broader, inherent, or underlying structures similarly does not account for such dynamic issues as social change, agency, and inequality.

Magic, Liminality, and *Communitas*

Victor Turner (1920–83), though influenced by structural functionalism, developed a more dynamic, 'interpretative' approach which addressed how conflict in society was resolved through ritual, with particular attention to the liminal state of those involved in the ritual process. Turner studied the Ndembu of north-west Zambia with his wife Edith in the early 1950s. The Ndembu are agriculturalists and hunters, and hunting is a highly regulated activity accompanied by complex ritual and etiquette involving the hunter's relationship with powerful tutelary hunter ancestors or 'shades'. Ndembu hunting rites involve initiation into grades of esoteric knowledge and require the adept to gain the assistance of a hunter ancestor and magical charms in order to propitiate the shades and seek out game animals in the bush, understood to be inhabited by witches, sorcerers, punitive ancestral shades, and other potentially dangerous beings. When hunting, certain hunters of the Ihamba cult carry a pouch containing an upper central incisor tooth (the *ihamba*) from a deceased ancestor hunter, accompanied by two cowrie shells as 'eyes' which enable the hunter's shade to 'see' game in the bush. The influence of punitive ancestral shades extends to all aspects of society, including the origin of sickness, as all deaths are attributed to sorcery, be it derived from shades or malicious sorcerers. Divination is used to ascertain the origin of the sorcery, involving a journey to consult a diviner, a consultation or séance, followed by remedial action such as the administration of medicines, the performance of ritual (involving rhythmic drumming) to propitiate offended spirits or to exorcize shades, or the expulsion of a witch. These rituals are performed by various 'cults', each devoted to a specific branch of ancestral shades, with the afflicted patient eligible for entry into the cult and becoming a cult-adept through its various rites.

In his earlier work, *Schism and Continuity in an African Society: A Study of Ndembu Ritual* (1957), Turner examined social conflicts and how they are resolved by these 'cults of affliction', but later focused specifically on the role of ritual, the work for which he is best known (e.g. *The Forest of Symbols: Aspects of Ndembu Ritual*, 1967; *The Ritual Process: Structure and Anti-Structure*, 1969). As such, where structuralist anthropologists had focused on presumed and stable underlying structures in society, Turner explored the anti- or non-structural components, particularly the dynamism of ritual. Turner used the concept of 'social dramas' to think about conflicts, and how these show a 'processional' or processual pattern of four phases: (1) a breach of normal social relationships (between persons or groups); (2) a crisis or extension of the breach if not resolved; (3) strategies taken by leaders to redress the breach; and (4) the restoration of normal sociality or recognition that the breach is irreparable.

Ritual, for Turner, is a form of social drama, and he theorized it by extending Arnold van Gennep's (1873–1957) threefold structure of 'rites of passage' as (1) 'pre-liminal' (separation), (2) 'liminal' (transition), and (3) 'post-liminal' (reincorporation), focusing on the liminal phase in which individuals are 'betwixt and between': not a part of the old society they are separated from nor yet reincorporated into the new society. He used the term 'communitas' to describe the liminal state, which is 'beyond all categories of manifestation, transcending divisible time and space, beyond words, where persons, objects, and relationships are endlessly transformed into one another'. Addressing social dynamism and change, Turner argued that *communitas* is the opposite of structure and that a person/community in a liminal phase is a 'kind of capsule or pocket which contains the germ of future social developments, of societal change'.

For Lévi-Strauss and the French school of structuralism, the symbols of ritual and the relationships between these symbols are examined in their expression through underlying structures of speech and mythology, and these structures function to uphold the social status quo. But for Turner, understanding symbols requires approaching the *performance* of ritual. Turner emphasized the 'multi-vocality' of each symbol, the way in which one symbol will have different meanings for different people, rather than the relationship between one symbol and another. This aspect of Turner's work was influential because it was some of the first to examine ritual—as performance, in action—on its own terms and as a social dynamic, rather than as part of a broader, stable social structure. Turner also acknowledged the psychological benefits of ritual and pointed to a problematic lack of liminal experiences in western cultures, identifying more diluted forms of 'liminoid' ritual in, for example, theatre performances.

In earlier work, Turner suggested that, 'stripped of its supernatural guise, Ndembu therapy may well offer lessons for Western clinical practice'. Nonetheless, his collaborator Edith Turner suggests Victor thought that Ndembu rituals were 'a mixture of moving poetry and undoubted hocus-pocus'. The intellectualists such as Tylor and Frazer dismissed the supernatural as incorrect in the light of rational thinking; the functionalists such as Malinowski and structural functionalists such as Radcliffe-Brown attributed beliefs in the supernatural to their function in society and reproduction of underlying social structures; and interpretative anthropologists such as Victor and Edith Turner focused on the agency of witchcraft and magic, and the valuable experience of ritual healing. The issue of 'the supernatural' aspects of witchcraft and magic, however, has continued to trouble the next generation of anthropologists.

Postmodern Approaches to Magic and Witchcraft

While anthropologists have, over almost one and a half centuries of
scholarship beginning with Tylor, moved from viewing witchcraft
practices and magical thinking as deluded, illogical, and incorrect,
to rational and logical within their own cultural framework, the
underlying issue of their veracity endures. Normally, anthropologists,
like historians, take their informants seriously, but do not 'believe' in
magic. But the anthropological method for examining witchcraft and
magic made a radical turn in the 1980s and 1990s, in tune with the
'postmodern' shift in thinking across the humanities and social sciences. An emphasis on participant-observation, on taking part in the
life of the culture but remaining neutral and objective in one's analysis, turned to experiential and reflexive methods—in other words,
taking seriously one's own extraordinary experiences while engaged in
witchcraft and magic 'in the field'. This change was precipitated by
the impact of feminism, which from the 1960s onwards offered a
corrective to the presumption of neutrality and objectivity by pointing
to the inherent biases in many ethnographic accounts (written largely
by white, middle-class, western men, about men in non-western
communities). It had been assumed that an anthropologist could
study a culture without his objectivity being compromised; he could
live among the culture without 'going native'. But if complete objectivity is an imperfect aim rather than a reliable result, then the divides
of objective–subjective and insider–outsider are compromised. As a
result, reflexive methodologies emerged, including auto-ethnography
and experiential anthropology.

In her ethnographic research on witchcraft in the Bocage, a rural
area of Normandy in north-western France in the late 1960s and early
1970s, the French ethnologist Jeanne Favret-Saada scrutinized the
terms of previous scholarship and popular accounts which had
described peasants as 'credulous', 'backward', unaware of 'cause and
effect', and as practising secret rituals 'which have no meaning' and
'come from another age'. Finding that of course the 'peasants' are
'neither credulous, nor backward', Favret-Saada defined a witchcraft
attack as follows:

> a set of words spoken in a crisis situation by someone who will later be
> designated a witch are afterwards interpreted as having taken effect on

the body and belongings of the person spoken to, who will on that ground say he is bewitched. The unwitcher takes on himself these words originally spoken to his client, and turns them back on to their original sender, the witch ... [T]he act, in witchcraft, is the word.

Attempting to understand this witchcraft on its own terms, Favret-Saada contrasted her case with that of Evans-Pritchard among the Azande. The Azande accorded Evans-Pritchard the status of 'Prince without portfolio', which meant that he could only be bewitched by another Prince, and given that he was working some distance from court life, the Azande were effectively excluding him from bewitchment by others in the local community; in short, he was safe. For Favret-Saada, the circumstances were quite different: she was an insider (a French ethnographer working in France). Her informants denied witchcraft ('I don't believe in all that rot') or rarely spoke of it ('Those who believe in it ... have to pretend they don't'). The witchcraft being studied involved questions, words, answers, gestures, which make the anthropologist a part of the 'social drama', to use Turner's terms, or 'caught' up in the 'discourse', to use Favret-Saada's terminology. She related how 'nobody ever talks about witchcraft to gain knowledge, but to gain power ... the more one knows, the more one is a threat and the more one is magically threatened'. She herself, then, might be bewitched, be a witch, or called on to act as an unwitcher. The most everyday of actions and events, words spoken and unspoken, might be integral to this discourse: 'In time of war, nothing so resembles the characteristic weapons of the magician (words, look and touch) as an innocent "how are you?" followed by a handshake'; and, 'No one talks to the alleged witch, but this very silence is in itself a whole discourse, the silent assertion of a fight to the death, which always has some effect.'

In these circumstances, the traditional ethnographic approaches of participant-observation, interviews with informants, or empathy would be ineffective. When not only participation but implication is required, the ethnographer becomes immersed in the events she is researching and neutral positioning is irrelevant: 'When total war is being waged with words, one must make up one's mind to engage in another kind of ethnography.' Such insider ethnography and experiential anthropology takes the researcher's experience as valid data and recognizes that her own standpoint is woven into the discourse. Deciding, then, to be led by her interlocutors, Favret-Saada first identified as an unwitcher herself, was then recognized as being bewitched, worked with an unwitcher, and finally was asked by several bewitched people to 'uncatch' them. Attempting to understand what she experienced (at one point her physical ailments were interpreted by her informants as the symptoms of witchcraft), Favret-Saada argued that 'unwitching' is a therapeutic mechanism rather than a mere metaphor or conceptual device.

By becoming an agent in witchcraft discourse, Favret-Saada's experiential approach facilitated a remarkable ethnography which would otherwise have been impossible. But in order to rationalize her experiences, she did not 'go native' in terms of belief but instead had recourse to an interpretation which makes sense to a westerner, that of 'therapy'. In a similar way, the American scholar Tanya Luhrmann's anthropology of contemporary ritual magic and witchcraft in England required her to be 'involved' in order to understand her experiences.

In the late 1980s, Luhrmann examined ritual magic and witchcraft practised in and around London for her doctoral research. Her interest was in how apparently superstitious beliefs that appear to be absent from Euro-American culture were yet held by a significant number of people in the West. In her ethnographic work, Luhrmann spent two years researching a number of witches' covens and ritual magicians' lodges by being initiated into their practices. She made clear to her informants that she was doing this as anthropological research, not because she wanted to be a witch or magician. Nonetheless, being embedded in participant-involvement in this way trod a fine line between gaining full access to ethnographic data and demonstrating sensitivity to the confidence and trust given by her informants who were by necessity cautious of public perceptions of what they did. As we saw in the previous chapter, Wicca is a nature-based religion, not black magic or Satanism; but to term oneself a 'witch' inevitably invites negative stereotypes among some people and particularly the tabloid press.

Like Evans-Pritchard, Luhrmann became immersed in magical thinking, observing that she 'had little difficulty running my life in accordance with magical techniques'. Like Favret-Saada, she had to be involved, and in this case had to be initiated, in order to gather ethnographic information which was otherwise secret and unobtainable from 'the outside'. But unlike Favret-Saada, Luhrmann argues that she did not 'go native': 'The only reason I continued to think of myself as an anthropologist, rather than as a witch, was that I had a strong disincentive against asserting that rituals had an effect upon the material world. The anthropologist is meant to become involved, but not native.' Luhrmann thinks that in getting so involved in witchcraft in the Bocage, Favret-Saada lost her objective judgement. By contrast, Luhrmann 'stood to gain nothing' by believing in magic, but, stood to lose credibility and career by adherence: 'Throughout my time in magic, whenever I felt magical power inside the circle or wanted to say that a ritual had "worked", I chalked up the event as an insight into the field.'

Luhrmann's thesis was published in 1989 as *Persuasions of the Witch's Craft: Ritual Magic in Contemporary England*. Interpreting her experiences, Luhrmann proposed that in order to believe in magic, the magicians and witches she studied showed 'interpretive drift': 'the once-non-magician begins to do what magicians do, and begins to find magical ideas persuasive because he begins to notice and respond to events in different ways.' Belief in the power of magic unfolds unintentionally over a period of successive apparently uncanny encounters with what seems to be the results of magic. Luhrmann's approach and interpretation upset some practitioners and subsequent scholars reported that they found access to and the trust of informants all the more difficult. When researching Wicca in the 1990s, the scholar of modern witchcraft Joanne Pearson was asked, 'You're not going to do another Tanya on us are you?'

One of the most interesting 'insider' and auto-ethnographies of western witchcraft and magic in recent years, strikingly different from Luhrmann in theory and method, is the work of the ethnographer Jenny Blain on the *seidr* (also spelled *seid* or *sejd*) practices of reconstructionist Heathens. Today's Heathens draw on the Icelandic sagas, Norse mythology, and archaeology of the 'old north' in order to reconstruct a spirituality relevant in the present. A particular focus is *seidr*, sorcery, witchcraft, or magic, sometimes interpreted as a form of shamanism, which is described negatively in the sagas, particular by Christians, as a form of sorcery, yet clearly had a more positive role in certain instances.

In the saga of Erik the Red (*Eiríks saga rauða*) (written down in the thirteenth century but describing events of around the tenth century), a seeress named Thorbiorg visits a community in Greenland suffering famine and is treated with great respect. Before the ritual she eats a porridge containing the hearts of various farm animals (i.e. a nutritious and expensive meal). For the ritual the next day she wears a black lambskin hood lined with cats' fur and white cat-skin gloves, she holds a long staff topped with a brass knob, and sits upon a ritual 'high-seat' with a cushion of hen-feathers beneath her. She proceeds to foretell a positive future for the farm. *Seidr*-workers today reconstruct elements of this ritual as a shamanic séance in which the seeress alters consciousness and communicates with ancestors and other supernatural beings in order to answer questions put to her by the people gathered for the rite.

Men who practise *seidr* are referred to consistently in the sources as being *ergi*, denoting 'unmanliness' or 'passive homosexuality'. In our collaborative work, Jenny Blain and I examine how some male *seidr*-workers today re-negotiate this terminology to refer to the 'open', passive state of trance required to contact the spirits, as well as to challenge conventional western perceptions of sexuality and stereotypes of being gendered male, including those insisted upon by right-wing, homophobic elements of contemporary Heathenry. We have also considered the way in which some Heathens and other animist pagans engage with sacred archaeological monuments within living landscapes enchanted by ancestors, elves, wights, and other beings. The magic performed in these cases varies from structured rituals invoking the ancestors who built West Kennet long barrow (a Neolithic burial chamber in Wiltshire), to simple, solitary, small acts of magic involving engaging with and relating to a circle of megaliths on an isolated moor, the spirit of a tree, or wildlife at a bubbling brook. Contemporary pagan witchcraft and magic are as varied as the indigenous and prehistoric examples upon which in some instances they draw.

In contrast to orthodox anthropologies of witchcraft and magic gained by 'outsiders' using participant-observation, Blain's work offers a sensitive treatment of how witchcraft and magic, when experienced as meaningful and embodied as practice, disrupt the insider/outsider, rational/irrational, superstition/science divides.

Magical Consciousness

A number of anthropologists have worked in this reflexive, experiential vein, leading to important insights into the nature of witchcraft and magic in modern western societies. Susan Greenwood researched magical practices among contemporary pagans in London and the surrounding counties in the 1990s. In contrast to Luhrmann's approach, which devalues the reality of magic for its practitioners, Greenwood's research was reflexive, experiential, and, as a magical practitioner herself, from 'the inside':

> I include my experiences of the otherworld within the fieldwork context as part of the process of understanding and analysing otherworldly knowledge. This type of methodology asks new questions of anthropology as a social science: it breaks down the conventional barriers set up between the anthropologist and the 'other', and it directly challenges the traditional approaches to anthropological knowledge that are framed by western notions of rationality.

For Greenwood, to approach and understand magic, one must not only analyse it but also *experience* it. In a sense, anthropologists have been doing this for a century—Evans-Pritchard's daily use of oracles with his Azande informants, for example, affirms this. But Greenwood's point is more penetrating. Magic is a form of consciousness which must be encountered not just studied. Evans-Pritchard recognized the internal logic and daily usefulness of oracle work partly because he wanted to fit in; he did not entertain the validity of oracle use in English society. Greenwood takes magic in the modern West seriously and demonstrates the validity of this approach for its practitioners, with the concept of 'magical consciousness'. More than a functional component of social life (Evans-Pritchard), a role in psychological and social catharsis (Malinowski), an expression of unconscious codes (Lévi Strauss), or something which can be examined scientifically (the success of magic cannot be measured with scientific instruments), magic for Greenwood is a holistic orientation to the world that is essentially relational and expansive; it is not irrational or confined to the thought of so-called primitives, nor is magic the preserve of non-western, exotic societies. Rather, it is an aspect of human consciousness, and therefore it is especially appropriate to study magic in modern, western societies, where it often manifests as an undercurrent.

On this view, magic is an aspect of human consciousness which is expressed in different ways across cultures. The idea is reminiscent of Lévy-Bruhl's 'pre-logical mentality' and 'mystical participation', terms which were problematic because they seemed to suggest an inferior way of thinking or even an evolutionary stage towards the 'rational thought' of Europeans. Where Lévy-Bruhl compared 'western' and 'native' thinking, contrasting the individualistic, rational logic of the former with collective 'mystical participation' in the other, Evans-Pritchard argued that like must be compared with like and that both westerners and natives have mystical experiences; Azande thinking is no less rational than European thinking. But Susan Greenwood has since argued that Lévy-Bruhl was more interested in *ways* of thinking than in social evolution, and that while anthropology has since focused on the *social* context of magic it has at the same time neglected 'specific processes of human thought' or 'magic as a process of mind'.

'Magical consciousness' might risk making concrete an unproblematic, singular concept of consciousness, with magic as an important element, in opposition to 'rational' consciousness. But Greenwood uses 'magical consciousness' as a working category, a way of approaching a subject, rather than as a discrete definition, to 'draw attention to a certain dimension of human experience'. Her aim is 'to highlight a part—or strand, or thread, or "expanded" awareness—that is an important component of the whole process of consciousness central to how many practitioners of nature spiritualities experience the world'.

The spectrum of magical consciousness is broad, encompassing her own life-threatening exposure to the elements on a Welsh mountain during an all-night shamanic vigil, 'shamanic journeying' with her university students, and one practitioner's experience of recognizing plants as 'other-than-human' persons while walking in a vegetable garden.

Greenwood makes a significant contribution to the study of witchcraft and magic in considering critically some interesting western ethnographic examples and theorizing a new approach to 'magical consciousness' rather than that tricky term, 'magic'. She attempts to reconcile the universal (a singular concept of magical consciousness as potentially applicable to all humans) and the particular (a concept of magical consciousness which is localized and multi-layered). Another theoretical strand which attempts to address the universal and local aspects of witchcraft and magic is animism, according to which the world is understood as interdependent, something pointed to by Greenwood as well: 'the essence of an understanding of the experience of magic is not to be found in abstraction or any notion of causality, but rather, through a sense of association and connectedness'. Animism brings our discussion full circle, back to the intellectualist anthropologists who saw animism, and its cognates witchcraft and magic, as superstitious thinking and the origin of religion. Recent anthropological theorizing of animism, however, offers a more nuanced understanding.

Living in a More-than-Human World

Tylor and Frazer cast animism as the mistaken belief among primitives that inanimate objects have souls, and saw this superstitious thinking as the origin of religion. Tylor's definition of religion and animism is 'the belief in Supernatural Beings'. According to Frazer, 'to the savage the world in general is animate, and trees and plants are no exception to the rule. He thinks they have souls like his own, and he treats them accordingly.' The history of anthropological thinking on witchcraft and magic since delivers a critique of this approach, so that witchcraft and magic might better be seen as rational within their cultural context, functioning to maintain social relationships, relieve anxiety, and promote cultural harmony. But a tension endures nonetheless between a 'rational' view which takes witchcraft and magic seriously only as social conventions which cannot be empirically proven; and an 'irrational', mythical, or relativist view which deconstructs rationalism as only one way of understanding the world.

Recent thinking on indigenous religions in Amazonia, in particular, has recast animism as recognizing that the world is filled with people, only some of whom are human. For human persons there are such 'other-than-human' persons as jaguar-persons and peccary-persons (jungle pigs), and for jaguar-persons there are such other-than-jaguar persons as human-persons and peccary-persons. Tylor's and Frazer's notions of animism become unhelpful and misleading in this context. Animists must relate to other persons on a daily basis, attempting to adopt proper social comportment so as to maintain harmonious relations. But offence might still be caused, whether by accident or intention. To kill, for example in order to eat, presents a problem of cannibalism, of having to murder another person (such as a peccary-person). This predator/prey relationship between persons is complicated by the fact that all persons are similar in possessing souls. It is their outward appearance, their body, that is different. Moreover, shamans can transform and take the outward experience of, for instance, a jaguar, so one can never be sure that a person's outward appearance is not a disguise, mask, or matter of magic.

This Amazonian indigenous perspective is significant in the broader anthropological study of witchcraft and magic, both of which are strategies for relating in a wider-than-human world. Animism makes shamans important and necessary because they are often the ones who can 'see as others do' in order to negotiate good relations. But an emphasis on Amazonian shamans as healers neglects the role of 'dark shamans', violent witchcraft, and injurious magic. The *hoaratu* of the Warao Indians of Venezuela, for instance, use magic to inflict pain and death, and the *manhene-iminali* are 'poison owners' among the Baniwa, while the *kanaimà* of the Patamuna and Makushi in the Guyana highlands are initiates in a system of ritual practice which includes assassination by assault sorcery, often followed by grave-robbing, anal and oral mutilations, and cannibalism. Cannibalism, the consumption of another's power, enables sorcerers to transform into predators including deities and jaguars—who are themselves ambiguous in relationship to humans and other persons. There is utmost secrecy among the Baniwa over who commits assault sorcery, and among the Parakanã, discussed by Carlos Fausto, no one admits to being a shaman but only to being a dreamer, because even though the former can heal people from the intrusions of *karowara* ('spirits'), to admit to having seen *karowara* is to admit the possibility of being a witch. Whereas, the *hoaratu* and *kanaimà* are often well-known individuals and the *kanaimà* even brag of their deeds. Magic is a grey area; where sorcery and witchcraft end and healing begins is a fine line, and ambiguity is a defining theme of Amazonian and many other indigenous cosmologies.

I opened this chapter by contrasting one of the earliest reports on overseas 'Devil Worship' from Gonzalo Fernández de Oviedo in the mid-sixteenth century, with the contemporary case in London 2012 of Kristy Bamu, the teenage boy who was tortured to death by his sister and her boyfriend because they believed he was a witch. In her article for the *Guardian* newspaper, anthropologist Jean La Fontaine looks at this case within the context of the contemporary trend for 'divine mission' churches in Africa, which encourage and profit from beliefs in witchcraft: the pastors of these churches identify witches and exorcize the evil spirits for a fee. Children are often the focus of these accusations and the exorcisms, involving starvation and sleep deprivation, and can be so violent as to 'beat the spirit out'. But the sort of child abuse which resulted in the death of Kristy Bamu is not limited to Africa, nor to witchcraft.

Today's anthropologists are charged with making sense of witchcraft and magic without sensationalizing what appears to be incredible and in some cases abhorrent, while remaining aware that any such mediation is always subjective, standpoint specific, and never complete. Dealing with 'dark shamanism' in the Amazon, for instance, raises ethical questions: anthropologists do not want to be seen to demonize the people they study and reinforce long-held negative stereotypes and prejudices. Just as La Fontaine points to child abuse as a human problem rather than a culture-specific one, so anthropologists in Amazonia assert that:

> If the *Ashàninka* identify 'child sorcerers', against whom violent acts are then carried out to preserve community harmony, then it is well to remember, lest we judge the Amuesha to be Hobbesian brutes, that we similarly demonise our children as 'gang-bangers' and 'school shooters' ... [W]e may not assail our children with anti-sorcery measures, but the disruptive and different are no less condemned among ourselves.

Witchcraft and magic were contrived as 'other' things against which western modernity defined itself, right from the earliest encounters between Europeans and indigenous witches and magicians. This in turn had ramifications for how indigenous cultures negotiated the colonial disruption. 'Witchcraft' and 'magic' started out as imperfect European terms used to translate and understand indigenous ways of being and ways of knowing. Consequently, they rarely grasped them properly. When attempting to reveal magic as 'fraudulent', anthropologists ironically often only heightened interest in the reality of magic: science thereby failed to triumph over magic and the 'science' of anthropology often simply reiterated the apparent power of magic.

The Australian anthropologist Michael Taussig addresses how the insistence on magic as a fraud (albeit one with social relevance, as in the instance of Evans-Pritchard among the Azande) actually led to the anthropologist engaging in 'magic' himself and revealing, ironically, his own technique of trickery. In what was seemingly a dextrous instance of sleight-of-hand, a medicine man was in the process of extracting a piece of charcoal from a patient by wiping a sponge over his abdomen. Evans-Prichard interrupted the healing at a crucial moment, and secretly removed the charcoal from the sponge, so that when the witch doctor continued the operation, the offending piece of charcoal was absent and his action was witnessed as ineffective. Evans-Pritchard proceeded to show the witch-doctor the charcoal and extract a confession of trickery. The ethics of such intervention and assumed colonial superiority of the anthropologist aside, Evans-Pritchard had, ironically, himself resorted to 'trickery' in order to reveal the 'trick'.

Taussig also addresses the dynamics between indigenous scepticism and magic in the Winter Ceremonial of the Kwakiutl, a people of the north-west Pacific coast of North America, for whom the ancestral totemic spirits of 'Wolf', 'Thunderbird', 'Man Eater', and others emerge to take over the life of the village from November. The visually rich and complex performances of this ceremonial involve imitating the movement and 'flow' of the spirits, 'a fluidity of performance with identities . . . the trick is one of continuous movement and metamorphosis in, through, and between bodies, carrying power one jump ahead of its interpretation.' The English language, our translation, is inadequate to do justice to this magic; it is 'peculiarly inept', perhaps 'deliberately so'. Taussig explains that 'mimetic simulation is a way of keeping hidden things hidden while at the same time revealing them, of keeping secret things secret while displaying them'.

The history of the anthropology of witchcraft and magic demonstrates the problem of 'translating' the complexities of other cultures into our own cultural idiom. Early explorers and missionaries viewed indigenous shamans and magicians through a biblical lens and either persecuted them or attempted to convert them to Christianity. The rationalists of the Enlightenment thought witchcraft was ignorant superstition and that magicians duped their communities. The Victorian intellectualists saw animism and magic as mistaken beliefs and the origin of religion, to be replaced in due course by science in a ladder of progress from primitivism to civilization. Anthropological thinking up to this point might be seen as the origin of what has been described as the 'academic tendency to mystify indigenous discourse as spiritual and pious rather than practical and social'. Early anthropologists of the functionalist and structural schools of thinking then recast witchcraft and magic as rational ways of thinking within their own culture's system of logic, and as a crucial contribution to the maintenance of social order, albeit ways of thinking soon to be eradicated by more 'enlightened' colonial processes. Interpretative anthropologists, on the other hand, looked at the *symbolic* elements of ritual and the effects of these on individuals and their communities.

More recently, anthropologists have conducted insider research, 'auto-ethnography', and 'experiential anthropology' in order to ascertain the importance of magic, its effects, its reality, and capacity for re-enchanting the lives of witches and ceremonial magicians in the modern West. And the recent study of animism has forced anthropologists to 'think through things' rather than 'about things', so as to appreciate the social complexity of witchcraft and magic in indigenous worlds. The social anthropologist Alfred Gell (1945–97) suggested that 'magic causes things to happen', and the widespread practice of witchcraft and magic across cultures demonstrates that these are very human ways of approaching our world. They are as prevalent and relevant today in the presumed secular West as they are in cultures elsewhere in the world.

9

Witches on Screen

Willem de Blécourt

When the children enter the great hall with its magical sky, they can see the teachers behind the table at the far end. Several of the men have beards and most wear an assortment of robes and headgear. The women all wear pointed hats. There is a giant and a dwarf. They are all wizards and witches. The variation between them is possible because the most familiar stereotypes, the old bearded wizard and the elderly female witch with the pointed hat, are included. Over the years the teachers change, their number dwindles, and there are fewer women. The series of eight *Harry Potter* films (USA 2001–11) about the school years of a young wizard, who together with his friends fights the evil wizard Voldemort, is undoubtedly the most famous present-day cinematic portrayal of witchcraft. It has become a phenomenon in its own right with record-breaking audiences, generating huge revenues in the process—and a considerable amount of scholarly criticism.

Based on the books by J. K. Rowling, the *Harry Potter* films contain a mixture of Eng-lish and American elements. Rowling did not create her world of wizards and witches out of the blue, but rather pieced it together from an enormous number of borrowings from various existing stories in different genres. As far as this chapter is concerned, amongst her main sources were contemporary witchcraft television series and cinema films. Whereas the figure of the male wizard's apprentice is predominantly British, one of the main contributors to the Potter universe was the American television series *Bewitched* (1964–72), centred on the young, blond, clever, and beautiful witch Samantha, who has chosen to spend at least some of her (presumably immortal) life as the wife of a human, the advertising executive Darrin

Ste-phens. Especially when it concerns the English ingredients, Rowling's work shows influences of stories which were popular in the 1970s and 1980s, such as T. H. White's *Once and Future King*, where a young Arthur is apprenticed to the wizard Merlin (made into a one-dimensional Disney film in 1963). A 'Hagatha's school of witchcraft' is mentioned in *Bewitched*, which Rowling amplified into Hogwarts school of witchcraft and wizardry, an institution of Gormenghastian proportions. Boarding school witches have been around since the *Worst Witch* series of books by Jill Murphy, which began in 1974 and were televised in 1986, and in Diana Wynne Jones's book *Witch Week* (1982). Before these examples non-magical boarding school books included those by Enid Blyton, another source of inspiration for the author of Potter. One of the main plot elements, the survival of a dark wizard's soul en-capsulated in a magical object, echoes Sauron's involvement with the One Ring in J. R. R. Tol-kien's trilogy *The Lord of the Rings*. The result of all this cutting and pasting has been described as: 'something new: a generic mosaic made up of numerous individual pieces com-bined in a way that allows them to keep their original shape while constantly changing their sig-nificance'.

Rowling stirred into this brew the biblical line 'father, why hast thou forsaken me' (Matthew 27: 46), as throughout the series Harry repeatedly suffers from broken relationships with father figures, first with his real father who was killed together with his mother when Harry (played by Daniel Radcliffe) was still a baby. As an orphan Harry Potter was raised by his mother's sister, her tyrant husband, and spoiled cousin. They were all non-magical and forbade Harry to prac-tise any magic. At the end of the third instalment Harry discovers that he has a godfather, only to lose him by the end of the fifth. Nor does his substitute father, the headmaster of Hogwarts, survive. These losses are aggravated by Harry's constant fear of becoming like the evil Volde-mort. In the end, Harry even has to undergo the process of sacrifice; a part of him dies but he himself returns to the living. Notwithstanding the Christian themes of redemption and resurrection, the books and films were vehemently attacked by fundamentalist Christian groups, who since the 1970s had become increasingly alarmed by 'witchcraft', or rather by anything they deemed to be occult.

In the parallel world of witchcraft, and at Hogwarts in particular, eccentricity becomes the norm as there are teachers for Care of Magical Creatures, Charms, Defence Against the Dark Arts, Divination, Herbology, History of Magic, Levitation, Magical Potions, and Transfiguration. The pupils have wands and spell books and they learn new spells and recipes, and how to con-centrate in order to create the desired effect. As the headmaster Dumbledore puts it: 'At Hog-warts you're not only taught how to use magic, but how to control it.' Wizardry demands inten-sive schooling and practice. In the films, the emphasis on the classroom is minimized and by the fifth film, *The Order of the Phoenix*, Harry has to take over as clandestine Defence teacher. In the ordinary world Harry is not recognizable as a wizard; he wears normal clothes and his hair hides the high-voltage scar on his forehead. In the parallel magical world he is at-tired in his wizard robes and frequently flies on a broomstick.

An essay on contemporary representations of witches cannot ignore the ubiquitous boy wiz-ard, but it also needs to look beyond it and relate Harry, his friends, and his teachers to their cousins and ancestors outside the *Potter* universe and ask how *Potter* is different compared to them. One of the distinguishing characteristics of *Harry Potter* is the ab-sence of any explicit references to religion or demonology; spells are performed without the aid of a higher being, such as Aza(za)el, Hecate, Lilith, or some other deity. The 'dementors' in *Potter*, who represent a cross between 'demon' and 'dementia', come closest to demons; they suck away will power and are reminiscent of Tolkien's ring wraiths. There are also no classes given in meditation, control of emotions, and discipline of one's own mind; Harry merely receives individual tutoring in that respect. Moreover, with its focus on male witches, the role of women is slightly understated.

Studying the Screen Witch

Witches are among western society's 'internal others'. In its essence, traditional as well as mod-ern witchcraft is gendered, with different connotations when it involves men or women. Histori-cally, and within a patriarchal order in the most general sense of the word, witches were under-stood as women deemed to harm others by their non-womanhood. Male witches were either defined in terms of possessing extraordinary power, or feminized through their association with female witches. Witchcraft, however, was usually ascribed: witches were named as such by other members of their community. Of course, some people will have tried out spells, but apart from the question of whether or not these resulted in the desired effects, identifying a witch was generally the privilege of those who counteracted what they perceived as a bewitchment. Witchcraft accusations operated within a fairly close witchcraft discourse in which every event associated with the suspected witch was open to a reinterpretation of whether it fulfilled the ex-pectations of witchcraft or not. Later, witchcraft was called a 'superstitious backwardness' by those outside the discourse. A history of the representation of witches and wizards in the cine-ma and on television, though, is quite different from a history of everyday witchcraft. It differs from a more conventional history of witch trials in their political and religious context, and in re-lation to judicial altercations and economic explanations. Several steps removed from any pre-sumed or (very occasionally) genuine practice of witchcraft, an analysis of visual representation concentrates on the image itself, rather than on what it may have symbolized. In this sense the image is not an illustration of a particular history, it constitutes the primary source of its own his-tory. Writing about screen witches thus becomes more reflective than straightforward history by the very nature of its subject and has to take account of different analyses and opinions.

Images of witches may occur within a film or a television series, but the medium is rarely centred on the image as such. It concerns storytelling through images and these interact with dialogue. Notwithstanding pervasive common strands, every author, director, or screen writer applies her (or his) own twist. A dynamic narrative also makes way for a different history from that of non-moving images. The historian Marion Gibson called attention to the cinematic witch and a shift 'from the contested facts of history to the realm of imagination', but the question is whether talking about witchcraft in a traditional everyday-life setting did not also usually include at least some stories. It should also be asked how the 'imagined witch' of today influences peo-ple's actions or becomes a part of their identity and thereby spills over into the 'reality' outside the cinema. This last question can only be tentatively answered here. Some practitioners of witchcraft as a form of modern religion, such as Wicca, view screen depictions as wildy inac-curate, and sometimes harmful since they promote dangerous practices, and are shaped by commercial forces and the sensationally glamorous. Some, nevertheless, admit that exposure to the images of strong, magical women may have set them on the way to exploring pagan reli-gions.

If screen witches have any historical ancestors, they are the witches in fairy tales or other lit-erary works. These witches were usually evil, just like those in everyday life; they also had the power to turn people into animals—a practice that was never ascribed to their traditional histori-cal counterparts, who were only deemed to turn into animal shapes themselves. Witches in fairy tales evolved as entertainment in social circles that had left the witchcraft discourse behind them. They belonged in the main to the movements of romanticism rather than to the staunch Christian congregations where vestiges of the witchcraft discourse lingered on. The cannibalis-tic tendencies of fairy tale witches, as for instance in the original German story Hansel and Gretel, stemmed from Italian narratives mediated by aristocratic French versions, and they cir-culated in printed form. Traditional German witches certainly bewitched little children to death, but they did not bake them in ovens and consume them, nor did they live in fancy houses in the wood far away from civilization. Next to all the different versions of Hansel and Gretel, including the composer Engelbert Humperdinck's successful opera (1893), traces of literary witches can be found in those films which present a Shakespearian trio of witches. These were originally not witches but 'wyrd' sisters, that is to say the classical fates who spun the paths of people's lives instead of disrupting it now and then.

Modern American researchers often frame screen representations of witches with the reli-gious Wiccan movement and apply Wicca as a measurement for defining which elements are genuine and which fabricated. Some even suggest a direct correlation between the presence of witches in the media during the last few years of the twentieth century and the rise of Wicca as a religion. They consider the screen as part of a process of 'commodification'. Interaction be-tween religion and screen narrative, while not absent, still needs to be better established and can certainly not be generalized. Which religious movement, for instance, led to a contemporaneous increase in the screening of mangled bodies in crime series, or the rise of the zombie and slasher movies? What is more, theories about the impact of pagan religions are littered with misconceptions about historical witchcraft and 'folklore witches'; their authors seem incapable of or are resistant to assessing studies by historians, relying instead on Wiccan writings and feminist writers who often have little or no knowledge of historical research. The Wiccan per-spective is merely one way of looking at screen versions, and modern witchcraft itself may very well be understood as subject to market forces. A more neutral way of studying screen witches is to concentrate on the recognition of specific, recurrent motifs within films and televi-sion series, and foremost to seek to establish influences and responses within the domain of cinematic witchcraft representations. This also helps explaining the popularity among viewers more firmly in the context of contemporary (popular) culture, rather than of decontextualized mythical 'human universals', as proposed in more psychoanalytic approaches to the subject. There is also very little substantial material on the reception of the screen witch in daily life. The popularity of films, as defined by attendance figures, does not tell us much in this respect.

At first glance, witchcraft films and television series, or perhaps more accurately films and series which feature witches, can be classified according to a number of different genres, ca-tering for different age groups, from juvenile puppetry, adolescent adventure, to adult enter-tainment. The genre variation may even be considered as one of the characteristics of the screen witch. Witches can be found in programmes as varied as cartoons and documentaries, sitcoms, soap operas, and fantasy films. Only since the 1960s, and primarily in the United Kingdom, have they turned up in horror films. Witches existed earlier in children's films and in relationship drama; not only did they retain these positions but they also expanded into the teenage franchise later in the century. However, only a few discernible pervasive themes ap-pear to occur in the different genres, and screen witches are, moreover, connected by a web of references that makes them part of contemporary culture; they communicate a limited number of expressions which are nevertheless open to many different interpretations.

The following exploration of these genres is certainly not exhaustive but includes the main contemporary, dominant witch images. Films which are entirely set in some kind of imagined past have been left out here as they demand a rather tedious juxtaposition with the recon-struc-tions made by historians, which as a rule have escaped the attention of film writers, directors, and producers. The occasional fictional film, too, contains debatable historical references; the notion that witches were midwives who were prosecuted because of a jealous medical profes-sion, for instance, as expressed in *The Witches of East-wick*, does not stand up to histor-ical scrutiny.

In the United States Salem has become the template for historical witchcraft, yet the Salem in the movies (and of the tourist experience) is not one that is easily recognized by historians of seventeenth-century witch trials. The main historical issue which will be briefly addressed here concerns the image of the witch on the broomstick. In films the two main themes are those of the domestication of the female witch and her self-control. Whereas gender issues have been present from the start, the witch's internal struggle between good and evil only appeared in the 1990s. The issue of the role of gender returns at the end of this chapter when the predominantly female schools for witches are discussed, both pre- and post-*Potter*, as well as the oth-erwise largely absent male wizard. This underrepresentation of the witch's male counterpart in cinematic depictions may have something to do with his portrayal as a fraud in the most influen-tial twentieth-century witch film, *The Wizard of Oz*.

An American Fairy Tale

The 1939 film *The Wizard of Oz* is a quest story in which the main characters are all searching for their heart's desire: the scarecrow for a brain, the tin man for a heart, the lion for courage, and the female lead Dorothy (Judy Garland) for home. In this, they are aided by a good witch and obstructed by a bad one. According to the American historian Carol Karlsen, the film has 'done more than any single witch to shape the popular stereotype in this country'. As one film critic observed: 'Anyone who grew up in the US has likely watched *Wizard* on television numerous times, as it was aired yearly beginning in 1956.' Karlsen argues that the witch in Oz has two forms:

> In her earthly form she resembles the most negative recent depictions of
> New England witches. Angry, aggressive, contentious, and vindictive,

she is given to unreasonable provocation of the decent folk who live around her, even innocent children, and shows callous indifference to the most basic human values. In her supernatural form, she is murderous.

In the film the transition from human to alien is made visible when Dorothy is transported by a cyclone from Kansas to Oz, farmhouse and all; objects and people pass her window which functions as a film screen within the film. Her neighbour Ms Gulch (Margaret Hamilton) is first seen on her bike but then the bike changes into a broomstick and she into a witch. The dual na-ture of the witch, natural and supernatural, is mirrored in the other main characters of the film, with a few notable exceptions. The men who inhabit Dorothy's world in Kansas have their fan-tasy equivalents in the land of Oz.

The Wizard of Oz contrasts the wicked witches of the East and the West with the good witch Glinda (Billy Burke), who actually looks more like a fairy. When Dorothy has just landed in Oz and more specifically in Munchkin country, accidentally killing the Wicked Witch of the East, she is welcomed by Glinda, the Good Witch of the North.

GLINDA: What the Munchkins want to know is, are you a good witch or a bad witch?
DOROTHY: But I've already told you, I am not a witch at all. Witches are old and ugly. What was that?
GLINDA: The Munchkins. They're laughing because I am a witch. I'm Glinda, the witch of the North.
DOROTHY: You are? I beg your pardon. But I've never heard of a beautiful witch before.
GLINDA: Only bad witches are ugly.

The 1939 film was just one cinematographic version of the 1900 book *The Wonderful Wizard of Oz* by L. Frank Baum (1856–1919). In the intervening years the material had been performed many times: in 1902 on stage as a musical, in 1908 and 1909 as a so-called 'fairylogue' (a combination of slides, narration, and pieces of film), in 1910 and 1925 as a silent film. In the late 1920s there were stage performances for children and even a puppet version. In 1933 an animated film appeared and a radio show later that year. In all these different manifestations of the story, the Wicked Witch was sometimes present, sometimes not. While she was part of the book, she was written out of the musical, made a comeback in the 1910 film as 'Momba the Witch', and disappeared again from the 1925 film. Momba was just a different name for the Witch of the West, derived from the sorceress Mombi in Baum's *The Marvellous Land of Oz* of 1904. By then Baum had replaced his original illustrator William Wallace Denslow with John R. Neill. Yet the film was, like the musical, mostly based on Denslow's design. The use of these two artists accounted for the differences in design of books and film. Neill's witches, for instance, were much more dynamic than those drawn by Denslow. Both were closely related to witches in the fairy tales which had inspired Baum. This is even apparent in the film, for in-stance when the Wicked Witch of the West hides behind an apple tree she resembles an illus-tration by Arthur Rackham for the story 'The Two Sisters' in the *English Fairy Tales*.

It has been argued that Dorothy's wish to return home to Kansas 'inhibits her status as a pro-totypical feminist'. That is certainly the case in the film; one of the scriptwriters was indeed in-structed to ensure that Kansas would win over Oz. Nevertheless, even within the film this cre-ated a dilemma, as dull sepia-toned Kansas is set against the colourful Oz. Dorothy expresses very vocally that she longed for a place 'over the rainbow'. As Salman Rushdie put it:

> Are we to believe that Dorothy has learned no more on her journey than that she didn't need to make such a journey in the first place? Must we accept that she now accepts the limitations of her home life, and agrees that the things she does not have there are no loss to her? '*Is that right?*' Well, excuse *me*, Glinda, but it is hell.

In the *Oz* series of books, eventually reaching fourteen volumes, Dorothy kept returning to Oz, however, and in the end brought her adoptive parents with her. Even if the influence of the film has been greater than the book, since 'the vast majority of those who come to Oz come to it . . . long before they encounter the book', the domesti-cation of Dorothy was already coun-teracted within the film.

The film obviously contributed to twentieth-century witch imagery. The Wicked Witch be-stowed her green face on subsequent witches, especially Halloween representations, and the green face occasionally turns up in the 1960s series *Bewitched*. The Wicked Witch has neither warts nor missing teeth, though. These unfortunate facial attributes derived from Oz's cinematic predecessor and competitor, Walt Disney's *Snow White* of 1937. In contrast, Halloween witches dressed up as Glinda are as rare as they are in films or television series (or are unrecognizable, because they are mistaken for fairies or princesses). Did the depiction of the good witch then pave the way for the unnoticeable witch? That is questionable in as far as the role of the highly visible Glinda is restricted to Oz. At least the unnoticeable witch offered an alternative to the good witch.

The wizard who gave his name to Baum's stories was himself a second-rate magician who after he is unveiled leaves the land of Oz, never to return. Oz is ruled by women and all the witches are female. L. Frank Baum, an actor and a jack-of-all-trades before he found his calling as a writer of children's books, was influenced by his mother-in-law Matilda Joslyn Gage (1826–98), who was an influential campaigner for the abolition of slavery and the emancipation of women. Her 1893 book *Woman, Church, and State*, written in haste in between political rallies, put all the blame for the witch persecutions on the Church, and more especially its sex-starved clergy. Today, Gage's passages on the witch-hunt read like a collection of clichés; they were also partly based on the unwitting use of falsified documents that have long since been discredited by historians. Her witches were pre-Christian priestesses, especially adept in healing, and were unjustly persecuted. As the Oz books were mostly set in a fantasy land, their underlying ideology was even more extreme than Gage's and rulers were nearly all female. The 'witches had almost overnight become liberal metaphors for political dissent and female self-empowerment'. That, of course, only applied to the good witches. Baum invented his own American version of fairy tale figures—and the good witches were part of this invention.

A Series of Witches

A crucial element of the 1960s television series *Bewitched* was only introduced at a late stage of its preparation. Its creator, Sol Saks, doubted whether his original version would make a good series,

> because this woman could do magic and solve all her problems. [But] that's what drama is made of: conflict, problems. And then I came up

with the idea, her husband doesn't want her to do it. She is trying to break the habit. And once I came up with that, I thought, now it could be a series.

It was perhaps no coincidence that Saks found his inspiration after the film *Night of the Ea-gle* had been released in 1962, in which a husband is extremely sceptical about his wife's witchcraft and destroys all her magical paraphernalia. The possible and actual relations between witches on the various screens makes them a part of western culture through the active in-volvement of screen writers, directors, and actors. This was certainly the case with *Bewitched* where actress Elizabeth Montgomery was married to director William Asher. Viewers, too, had a voice, as both their actual and expected reactions counted in decisions about styling and the continuation of the screen witch. It was always a matter of balancing ex-pectations and surprise. Nevertheless in the case of witches a certain amount of uncertainty also played its part. Screen monsters such as vampires, werewolves, or androids had their trusted slot within the horror genre. The Wicked Witch of the West would have fitted in there, too, had she not made her appearance in a family film. Fairy tales always had their own scary elements, although opinions vary about their influence—as is the case with the stories them-selves. At least the American screen witch stayed grounded in the fairy tale genre, both on tele-vision and on the big screen.

Bewitched referred to its predecessors: *The Wizard of Oz* and Hansel and Gretel. And film historians will immediately point to two earlier American films which informed *Bewitched*. One is *I Married a Witch* (1942) and the other *Bell, Book and Can-dle* (1958). It is usually over-looked that the crux of the series, the witchcraft-practising wife versus the husband who wants nothing to do with it, did not feature in these two films but in the British film *Night of the Eagle* (1962), released in the USA as *Burn Witch, Burn*. In its turn, the television show also presented a blueprint for the plot of the more recent *Harry Potter* books and films. Rowling was certainly inspired by the *Bewitched* universe, for a considerable number of similar concepts can be identified in her work, first and foremost the congruence between 'mortals' in the television show and 'muggles' in the film, and the con-tempt that some of the witches harbour towards them. *Bewitched* not only channelled past films, it also offered blueprints for future ones. Of course, with more than 250 episodes *Bewitched* had much more space to try out various concepts than a single film, or even a sequence of eight films like *Harry Potter*.

Both *Bell, Book and Candle* and *I Married a Witch* deal with the courtship be-tween witch and non-witch. *Night of the Eagle*, on the other hand, is much more about university politics and most of the action is taken up by the husband's attempts to save his wife. *Bell, Book and Candle* exhibits a subtle and stylish imagery; its main witch Gillian (Kim Novak) is an independent woman with a degree in anthropology and deals in primitive art. Here witches look like everybody else and are therefore 'unrecognizable', but they are incapable of blushing or crying. Although the marriage referenced in the title of the earlier *I Married a Witch* is only covered in the tail end of the film (like *Bell, Book and Candle* it would have been more appropriately named *How I was Snatched Away by a Witch on my Wed-ding Day*), the witch Jennifer is likewise young and beautiful. For the iconography, however, the promotional material is much more revealing than the film itself. On posters and in maga-zine shoots the actress (Veronica Lake) appears with exposed legs and a witches' hat, which are later referenced in Darrin's drawings in *Bewitched*. The pumpkins in the background signal the Halloween connection. In one image Lake even rides a broomstick. In the film she appears fully clad, without a pointed hat, and she only rides a broomstick in a non-material form as a whip of smoke. *I Married a Witch* was based on an unfinished manuscript, *The Passionate Witch*, by Thorne Smith (1892–1934), the author of several comedy supernatu-ral novels, who may very well have read the Oz books by L. Frank Baum.

In its turn, *Bell, Book and Candle* laid some of the groundwork for *The Witches of Eastwick* (USA 1987), adapted from a novel by John Updike (1932–2009), in which three witches perform a ritual to attract a handsome dark stranger. Only this time they did not lure a writer of the occult but the Devil himself, or at the very least a Devil. The Disney film *Hocus Pocus* (USA 1993) appropriated the theme of the awakened witch from *I Married a Witch* even to the extent of situating the story in Salem. It is packed with familiar refer-ences: it takes place on Halloween and features a trio of witches who live in the woods and seek to rejuvenate themselves by taking the life force out of children. They keep their spells in a voluminous grimoire, brew their potion in a big cauldron, and fly on broomsticks (and on a vac-uum cleaner). The resurrected witch from *I Married a Witch* also figured in a number of British horror films from the 1960s and 1970s, where she has a more vengeful character. The concept of the good witch hardly found resonance in Britain, probably because of the compet-ing existence of the benevolent wizard figure. Richard Carpenter's television series *Catweazle* of 1970 and 1971 with its time-travelling wizard was, again, aimed at children.

In the USA the television show *Bewitched* provided the paradigm and even sometimes the specific details for later witchcraft films and television series. It had its own re-make as a film in 2005 (with Nicole Kidman and Will Ferrell). The film version was only moder-ately succesful because it eschewed the basic plot structure of the television series which con-sisted of the dramatic tension between Samantha, her husband, and his mother-in-law. The in-fluence of *Bewitched* is also clearly visible in *Teen Witch* (USA 1989), which even employed the actor Dick Sargent as the lead character's father. Sargent had replaced York as Darrin in the sixth season of *Bewitched*. In *Halloween-town* (USA 1998) a suburban family is portrayed in which the mother tries to live without witchcraft, but is then in-terrupted by her mother who entices the children to come into their power; this mirrors the rela-tionship between Samantha, Endora, and Tabatha in *Bewitched*. More generally, the American series *Sabrina, the Teenage Witch* (1996–2003), a 'bubblegum tween version' of commodified witchcraft, would have been unthinkable without *Bewitched*. Both paved the way for another American show, *Charmed* (1998–2006), featuring three sisters with powers of telekinesis, the freezing of time, and foresight. The close links between the three se-ries can be seen by the way in which the *Bewitched* episode 'I confess' of 1968 clearly left a trace in *Sabrina*'s season two episode 'To Tell a Mortal' and reverberated in 'All Hell Breaks Loose', the last episode of season 3 of *Charmed*. Earlier, 'I confess' had inspired the children's movie *Escape to Witch Mountain* (USA 1975). The plots of all four revolve around a central theme: outsiders becoming aware of witches in a world that denies their exist-ence, followed by the consequences of this revelation.

It may also be possible to consider George Romero's film *Jack's Wife*, also known as *Season of the Witch* (USA 1972), within the param-eters of *Bewitched*: both are about a housewife; Joan in *Jack's Wife*, turns to witchcraft to liven up her drab existence in suburbia. Now the characteristics are enhanced and made explicit: Joan seduces her daugh-ter's lover and shoots her husband by mistake, which merely represents a darker interpretation of *Bewitched*. Even in a later film with little thematic overlap such as the teen-age-oriented *The Craft* (USA 1996), the impact of *Bewitched* is acknowledged in a brief quote. By then, the solitary witch had largely been replaced by the portrayal of a group of witches, in the first instance the Macbethian trio of witches as in *The Witches of East-wick* (1987), but soon afterwards also as a coven. As early as 1966 in the United Kingdom Cyril Frankel had in *The Witches* 'brought witchcraft "home" ', with its rural setting and its combination of pagan belief, esoteric 'expertise', and ceremonial sacrifice. Yet here the 'coven' is dominated by the high priestess who is in pursuit of rejuvenation (she dies instead and the group falls apart). British film directors imagined witches as evil; certainly they con-sidered the few then practising Wiccans unfit for dramatization unless it involved scenes which they thought were pornographic. Early American representations of witches' groups depicted less a coven than a group of Devil worshippers, like in Roman Polanski's *Rosemary's Baby* (1968) and the more teenage-oriented *Satan's School for Girls* (1973). *The Witches* (UK 1990), based on the eponymous book by Roald Dahl (1916–90), followed the then British tradi-tion of a coven of evil witches headed by the Grand High Witch. The witches in the later *Stardust* (UK 2007), based on Neil Gaiman's novel, were rooted in both Shakespeare and the French fairy tale *L'oiseau bleu* (the Blue Bird).

Finally, in this geneological survey, we return to the adolescent wizard Harry Potter. Harry belongs to a line of British wizards that starts with Merlin. Potter's creator Rowling also made reference to *Bewitched* for images and background setting. Both the *Bewitched* and the *Potter* universe, for instance, lack an overarching force; there is no religion or demonology. The opposition between witches and mortals (or 'muggles') has already been mentioned. In both the television series and the sequence of Potter films the discussion of 'mixed' marriages ensues from this opposition (in the case of *Potter*, between muggles and non-muggles). Samantha's stay in suburbia in *Bewitched* is echoed by Harry's up-bringing there, where his uncle Mr Dursley's patriarchal prohibition of magic is not unlike Dar-rin's strong dislike of it. Even the wizard Dumbledore who carried Harry as a baby to Privet Drive has an earlier equivalent in Samantha's warlock father Maurice; the latter kidnapped what he thought was his grandchild and took him to his club in London. The pranks of the Weasley brothers in *Potter* are direct successors to those practised by cousin Edgar and uncle Albert in *Bewitched*. The *Potter* spell 'Avada Kedavra' is a conflation of 'abraca-dabra' with the intermediate 'Abner Kada-bra' mentioned in the first *Bewitched* season. When two of Samantha's aunts walk through the wall but her other aunt Clara bumps into it, this is echoed by Rowling's similar device on platform $9^3/4$ at Kings Cross, especially in *The Chamber of Secrets*. There are certainly more examples to be found in *Harry Potter*: pictures which talk and move, trips through chimneys, the reference to a magical illness, a ghost who can take off his head, the notion of a large witch family, and, last but not least, the adage that 'the only thing stronger than witchcraft is love'. This last line also featured in *I Married a Witch* which also contains a flying car diving into a big tree, a scene which Rowl-ing turned into Harry's and Ron's landing in the Whomping Willow. Of course, to pick up bits and pieces from previous narratives and mould them into a new one has always been part of a sto-ryteller's craft.

'We Demand a New Image': The Persistence of the Ugly Witch

In one of the early episodes of *Bewitched*, entitled 'The Witches Are Out', first aired on 29 October 1964, Samantha (Elizabeth Mont-gomery) is having tea with her three aunts. Sa-mantha is a young newly-wed housewife, while her aunts all appear elderly. Although they look like ordinary women the four of them are all witches. They deplore the way witches are depict-ed at Halloween. Aunt Mary remarks: 'It's not the broomsticks I mind so much, it's the way they make us look... those ugly, horrid warts and those long, crooked noses.' Whereupon Saman-tha replies: 'I guess they just don't realize that we're like anybody else, almost.' And her aunt Bertha (who in season three would be rebaptized as Hagatha) suggests: 'Someone ought to re-write those fairy tales. Well, you know, show Hansel and Gretel for what they really are... a couple of pushy kids going around eating sweet old ladies' houses.'

At the same time, Samantha's husband Darrin, an advertising executive (then acted by Dick York), is meeting a client, Mr Brinkman, who has very firm ideas on how to design the cam-paign for his sweets. 'An ugly old crone, with a long nose, I mean long. And then warts on her chin and broken teeth, a lot of broken . . . A whole mouthful of broken teeth . . . and a tall black hat and a broomstick.'

A potential conflict looms, since Samantha has suggested that her aunts ask Darrin to help counteract the degrading image of witches. When Darrin comes home Samantha's aunts have exited through the wall apart from aunt Clara, who found it an obstruction. When he starts to work on his client's project and draws the head of an old crone, Samantha sees it and becomes upset. The following dialogue ensues:

SAMANTHA: Why did you do it?
DARRIN: Because that's the way most people think witches look.
SAMANTHA: Is that any reason to discriminate against a minority group?
DARRIN: What minority group?
SAMANTHA: Witches, of course.
DARRIN: Sam, people don't believe in witches.
SAMANTHA: What's that got to do with anything?
DARRIN: How can you discriminate against something you don't know exists?
SAMANTHA: Don't split hairs.

In the end, Samantha manages to convince Darrin that she had experienced every Halloween as a horrible event and that she has to leave the country with her mother to escape the wretched images of witches. The next day in his office Darrin has trouble persuading his client and his boss to adopt a more positive, even sexy portrayal of a witch, in fact just like the design used for the promotional material of *I Married a Witch*. Darrin mentions witches to his boss Larry and he responds:

LARRY: Witches? You mean with long noses, blacked-out teeth and warts?
DARRIN: No, of course not, they probably look more like [he thinks for a moment, obvi-ously does not want to mention his wife] . . . Glinda.
BOSS AND
BRINKMAN BOTH: Who?

DARRIN: Glinda. The Good Witch of the North in *The Wizard of Oz*. Oh,
    she's gorgeous.
LARRY: The Good Witch of the North?
BRINKMAN: He does not want to hurt her feelings.

Samantha and her aunts then decide to take action. They form a
picket line in Brinkman's bed-room (or in his dream), explain that they
are witches and that their looks do not conform to his prejudice. To
press their argument home, they change his face to look like the ugly
witch of his own imagination. Not just with a long nose and warts but
also green. That helps. The next day he opts for Darrin's design of a
scantily clad young witch with the slogan: 'Only the choicest witches
eat Witches' Brew candy.' This leads to a big boost in sales, because,
as it turned out, most customers of his sweets are male.

Although at first it appears that Samantha is a typical stay-at-home
wife, busy cleaning and cooking while her husband goes out to work,
over the course of the series it transpires that it is she who really wields
the power in their marriage. Darrin may have asked her not to
exercise any of her craft (which she does with the twitching of her
nose and upper lip), but she always finds a reason to make an
exception. Darrin also often falls victim to the wiles of his in-laws; he
is changed into a child, an old man, an old woman, an ape, a
werewolf, and even into his boss. *Bewitched* suggests that life in suburbia requires a little witchcraft now and then, to ma-nipulate inanimate
objects or living beings, and to demonstrate the benefits of instant
transporta-tion.

Bewitched offers a good introduction to the prevailing witch images
in 1960s America. First and foremost, a witch is unrecognizable,
because she is indistinguishable from everybody else. But when she
takes on her witch aspects, she is equipped with a robe, a hat, and a
broom. A few episodes later, Darrin imagines how their children
would look; although he no longer thinks of long noses and missing
teeth, in his mind, they still ride on broomsticks and wear black capes
and pointed hats. A little later, Samantha tries again to persuade
Michael, a boy who stays with them over Christmas, that she really
is a witch. She finds that her robe is not sufficient proof and so she has
to add the hat and the broom. This is just like the cartoon witch icon
with which each epi-sode opens. However, the evil witch is not
completely absent from this series. She appears in the role of

Samantha's mother Endora (Agnes Morehead), especially in her relationship with Darrin: for him, 'witch' is synonymous with 'mother-in-law'. When a witch is unrecognizable and her powers are innate the danger of exposure is minimized. Samantha and her relatives only operate within a very particular witchcraft discourse, in this case the one of the television show. It saves them from attacks within the series, and, at least in the 1960s and early 1970s, from the public, too. At the time, the show found it easier than other pro-grammes to raise a number of political issues because it was 'only about witchcraft'. Within the universe of the series witches are occa-sionally exposed; to avoid this, their identity is kept restricted to one person, in particu-lar Samantha's neighbour Gladys, who is fre-quently declared insane. Half way through the show's eight seasons Darrin has become fed up with all the witchcraft around him, and rather than struggling to contain it he wants to tell the world about it. But Samantha shows him in a dream what will happen: they will be put on display, persecuted, or used for military or com-mercial purposes.

A number of episodes in the series were remade. The episode 'The Witches are Out' of the first season was filmed again in season six under the title 'To Trick or Treat or Not to Trick or Treat?' (30 October 1969).

While crucial lines were kept, the theme of the witch's image is now more firmly positioned in the Halloween setting. Samantha's and Darrin's daughter Tabitha (originally Tabatha) has be-come old enough to collect sweets in the neighbourhood and this time everyone also canvasses for UNICEF. Samantha is helping with the costumes, among them some witch costumes with gruesome masks, which offend her mother Endora. To prove her point Endora puts a spell on Darrin (Sargent), who gradually changes into a Halloween witch, only with-out the green face. He uses his disguise to collect money and ends up a 'Halloween Hero'. As Samantha tells En-dora: 'Do you realise that you have given the witch's image that we hate more publicity than it's had since the Salem trials?' She suggests using an image of herself as the Good Witch of the North for an alternative advertising campaign. She does not in fact dress up as Glinda but merely puts on her witch aspect, with hat but without a broom. The message has therefore changed: even a popular television show should not attempt the impossible and alter the existing witch image. And it should certainly not try replacing it with one that degrades women; better to nudge it towards the good witch who looks like the model housewife.

Three decades later, the Halloween episode of the third season of *Charmed* reprised the issue. The Halliwell sisters are dressed up as witches: Piper (Holly Marie Combs) all in pink, whereupon Prue (Shannen Doherty) asks her: 'Hey, are you a good witch or a bad witch?' Her then boyfriend (and husband to be) Leo confirms: 'Glinda helped the innocent, didn't she?' Phoebe (Alyssa Milano) has disguised herself as 'the Mistress of the Dark', Elvira (also a 1988 USA film, among others), and declares it to be a 'protest statement', since she is 'offended by the representation of witches in popular culture'. Later in this time-shifting episode, however, a seventeenth-century witch and midwife explains to her that the 'broom's traditional purpose is to sweep evil from your path' and that the conical hat 'helps to channel' the magic. Eventually Phoebe, without her Elvira outfit, decides 'to embrace the cliché' and flies her broomstick against the full moon. The advantage of having three witches instead of one is that the various images can be shown together. The late-twentieth-century Wicca influence has now turned the wicked witch into a spiritual role model. It was unthinkable that any of the three Charmed Ones would hide their good looks behind a green face and a long nose; for a protest, heavy mascara and a cleavage sufficed. But without a specific target public in the episode, the protest was void.

The image of the witch on a broomstick is originally more typical. In early modern European trials the broom served primarily as a means of transportation to the sabbat. It was largely ab-sent in places where the idea of the sabbat was not transmitted. But on the Continent flying on a broom was only one way to reach a faraway witches' assembly. Oven forks and animals, such as goats, were also used. And when the meetings were nearby, witches simply walked. Hardly anyone ever claimed to actually witness a flying witch and the closest people got to one was the observation of a sleeping woman who later declared she had flown—unless she was just telling stories. The concept of flying witches also did not figure in everyday life. If the notion occured in a trial, usually in combination with the sabbat, it was imported through learned, demonological tracts. Even among the experts the concept of witch flight was most contested. One of the reasons why witch trials stopped was that the people in charge of them started to doubt their methods of obtaining proof. While the witch-craft discourse remained in place on an everyday level, intellectuals embarked on a process of distancing themselves from popular belief and experience. At the same time, the lack of verification served the depiction of witchcraft very well. When an artist drew a flying witch he could be certain that his wealthy, educated public would recognize her.

Although there is still research to be done here, it seems that part of the process of distancing from belief in the existence of witches and witchcraft included dressing up as a witch and put-ting her on stage. In this context, in England, for example, where witches had hardly been per-ceived as flying at all, the combination of pointed hat and broomstick turned up first. As Ian Bostridge wrote in *Witchcraft and its Tranformations*, it concerned 'a fossilized image of the plebeian coun-trywoman of the late seventeenth century, and a stereotype which has per-sisted into the children's books of the late twentieth century'. The tradition also continued, albeit with fluctuations, in masked balls and celebrations which called for dressing up. In the last quarter of the nineteenth century it was taken up in Halloween feasts and trans-ported to the USA. Illustrators of fairy tales were inspired by this public tradition. Later on, the film industry, hardly at the forefront of artistic innovation, needed a recognizable witch and opted for the tried and trusted hat and broomstick image. This image became so powerful that in the 1970s femi-nists appropriated it.

The Domestication of the Female Witch

In the seventy-eighth episode of the series *Charmed* (31 January 2002) Phoebe is fold-ing the laundry. She complains that she cannot do it magically by twitching her nose. As she explains to her fiancé Cole, this was how Samantha did it in Phoebe's favourite television show *Bewitched*. But although she looked up to Samantha, she never wanted to become like her.

> Phoebe: See, Samantha, she was married to a human, Darrin. Darrin completely repressed Samantha's magic. Completely denied who she was. And it wasn't because he didn't love her. It was just . . . That's the way it had to be. . . .

It's just, growing up, that was my only role model for a typical marriage. So that's all I knew. And he was able to meet people and leave the house and go to work and build his career. And she had to stay home. You know, and cook dinner and do the laundry. She went from being Samantha to being Mrs. Darrin Stephens overnight.

In the course of the episode Phoebe turns into the black-and-white version of Samantha, com-plete with hairspray; she is only interested in playing the housewife and has lost her ability to formulate spells. As it is summed up at the end: there is 'the loss of identity, the subjugation by a man, the focus on housework'.

A coherent theme links *The Wizard of Oz* to *Bewitched* and beyond: the ten-sion between the domestication of the witch figure as a result of male anxiety on the one hand and her liberating power on the other. Dorothy's magical slippers are mainly meant to bring her home to dull Kansas; in that respect she falls into the same category as Glinda and it is thus no coincidence that the wicked witch and Dorothy have been construed as 'polar opposites'. Jen-nifer, at the end of *I Married a Witch*, is portrayed as a knitting housewife, her loose hair contained in a tie. Her successor in *Bell, Book and Candle* has turned from a seductive femme fatale into a demure florist, dressed all in white. In Britain the theme was expressed in the figure of the vengeful witch who had escaped male authority, but in the USA it was primar-ily located in suburbia where a number of witches were attempting to run more or less normal households.

Samantha in *Bewitched* has made domesticity into a virtue, although she possesses an almost unlimited, godlike power. The depiction of her in *Charmed* is thus superficial: she is always capable of exercising her power (only on one occasion does she find herself out of practice, but the situation is remedied immediately). Her husband dislikes her practising witchcraft at home, a concern that she basically agrees with, but there is always a chance to do a little twitching. Although it provides the necessary dramatic tension, it is also possible to see the curb on witchcraft in *Bewitched* purely within the logic of the show. The main un-mentionable subject between Samantha and Darrin is not witchcraft but Samantha's age. Given her history, she should be at least be a few hundred years old; her aunt Clara let it slip that Sa-mantha was with her mother in Tibet when Clara was serving Queen

Victoria, and there is also a suggestion that Samantha personally knew Shakespeare. Playing the housewife thus only occupies a very small period in her presumably immortal life. And then there are at least two reasons for downplaying witchcraft that may have been compelling. She may seem to have a large family but given the long timespan the witches in *Bewitched* have produced re-markably few offspring. Samantha has no siblings and only one cousin. Marrying a mortal is thus a sensible policy for perpetuating the bloodline. Another rationale for living with as little magic as possible is to be prepared for old age. Her experience of the frequent blunders of aunt Clara, whose magic more often fails than succeeds, may have convinced her to be prepared to live without witchcraft.

In the context of 1960s America, however, *Bewitched* does not so much celebrate domesticity as perpetually ridicule and undermine patriarchal order. Darrin's boss Larry toadies to every client in sight but constantly bullies his main creative executive; over the course of the show his actions become less believable; the attentive viewer knows that Larry is too dependent on Darrin to actually fire him. Darrin is thus routinely the butt of criticism at work by his boss and at home by his mother-in-law. Samantha herself does not shy away from taking on male au-thorities, whether it is the city council which has to provide traffic lights, or a councillor with shady dealings, or a capitalist who wants to turn the park into a shopping mall. The director and actors associated the theme of hiding witchcraft from the outside world with the way many ho-mosexuals had to hide their true identity. On a different level, as befitted the 1960s, *Bewitched* was critical rather than supportive of current mores and rules. Whether this was also the case with *Charmed* has been the subject of some debate. Referred to by cast and crew as 'Charlie's Angels on Broomsticks', *Charmed* is said to have celebrated femininity; it offered 'possibilities for female pleasure and empowerment' and had a large fe-male following, including among slightly older viewers than the target group. On closer inspec-tion, however, the feminine sheen of *Charmed* is more superficial; perhaps less a sign of women's political empowerment than of their subjection by turn-of-the-century consumerism. As one film critic remarked, the glamour in these shows 'may well be both a sequinned corset and a glittering prison'.

In the *Charmed* episode Phoebe's loss of powers provides a counter-point to the dis-cussion between her sister Piper and her husband Leo about temporarily turning off ('binding') the powers of their (as yet unborn) children so that they could grow up in a 'normal' way and enjoy 'the gift of innocence'. That goes much further than in the case of Samantha's children. In *Bewitched* it first had to be established whether a child had magical powers or not and, if so, training was needed. Suppressing magic was not an option and although it would have ac-corded with Darrin's wishes, Samantha and her mother never contemplated it. As a matter of fact, the ultimate transformation of Phoebe into the black-and-white knitting housewife is not so much a reference to *Bewitched* as to the end of *I Married a Witch* of the 1940s, although even in the latter film the message is undermined by the entrance of a child playing with a broomstick. *Charmed* may have led the occasional viewer to pursue more mod-ern versions of witchcraft, but more often than not, the magic on offer was a simplistic solution for the twists of the plots.

How untouched the three sisters in *Charmed* were by the women's liberation move-ment can be seen when the series is contrasted with the 1987 film *The Witches of East-wick*, which in this respect differs markedly from the book it was based on. Three single women, Alex (Cher), Jane (Susan Sarandon). and Sukie (Michelle Pfeiffer), come to live to-gether in a big mansion where they fight a demon. One is widowed, one divorced, and one abandoned. All have 'creative' occupations. Instead of inviting boyfriends to join them and to create a semblance of 'family life', they throw out their demon lover Daryl van Horne (Jack Ni-cholson), with much more style than the com-bined expulsion of all the demons in *Charmed*. The three women move from being marginalized in their little town to the 'landmark' place, the mansion of Eastwick's founder, where they become mistresses of their own domain. Their magic is initially unconscious yet it influences nature itself. The counterpoint to the demonic in *The Witches of Eastwick* is provided in the figure of Felicia (Veronica Cartwright), who personi-fies small-town, religious America. At the beginning of the film she is seen singing the American national anthem. She is the first to recognize the threat to their community. During a church service she rants about the sexual debauchery that is going on in their midst. Meanwhile the two male characters are stereotypes of their sex: a hypocritical 'horny' schoolmaster and a spineless newspaper editor. The earlier scene in the church is mir-rored when Van Horne delivers a speech, also in the church, about God's mistake in creating women; he displays the same affliction as Felicia before him. It costs him dearly as he is now subject to the conscious power that the three witches exercise. For a mainstream American film such gender dynamics are radical, especially since everyone involved in the making of the film was male.

However, as in *The Wizard of Oz* only the good witches are shown as home makers. Are wicked witches beyond domestication? Or do they serve as warning examples to all wom-en who resist male rule? One of the ways to counteract this is to protest against the image of the wicked witch and the refusal to make her more sexy.

Out of Control

Visual representations of the act of bewitching rely overmuch on rituals. Of course, it is hard to convey an image of a witch by showing a man or woman without any witchy symbols. A mere glance, for instance, is hardly sufficient to identify a witch. In practice the method of showing at least one significant gesture is more efficient. For example, the subtle twitching of Samantha's 'nose' in *Bewitched*, usually accompanied by the appropriate sound effects, achieved the desired result with a minimal effort. Such a gesture is essential, even if viewers are aware that the seemingly normal woman on screen is actually a witch and capable of the most outra-geous manipulations. And in *Bewitched* the more complicated spells require the reciting of a formula, too. Yet specific rituals are rarely shown. One example occurs in *Bell, Book and Candle*, when Gillian, her brother, and her aunt conjure up the writer of the book *Magic in Mexico* to help the publisher Shep Henderson (James Stewart), in whom Gillian is interested (this scene is, incidentally, cited in the episode 'Gingerbread' of the television show *Buffy the Vampire Slayer* of early 1999). The love spell, which is central to the plot in *Bell, Book and Candle*, is cast through the cat familiar.

The most 'witchy' scene in this film is the one in which the spell on Shep is counteracted, but only by a solitary unwitcher, and the effect is anyway merely temporary. Rituals, however, usu-ally need more participants than this. When cults and covens *are* staged, they tend to belong to the horror genre. While the ritual in itself is neutral, it indicates that powers can be hard to control, more so than when they are inborn.

The Craft (USA 1996) tells the story of three teenage girls who are known at their local Catholic highschool as the 'bitches of Eastwick'. They come into their power when a new girl, Sarah (Robin Tunney), brings her magic to the mix. At first they ask for improvement in their personal standing at school; only Nancy (Fairuza Balk) wants the ultimate power, which she achieves after a second ritual. When Sarah protests and tries to bind Nancy's power the other three turn on her, haunting her with snakes and other vermin, which is reminiscent of Alex's greatest fear in *The Witches of Eastwick*. Sarah finally calls on the powers of 'Mother and Earth' to invoke the Spirit herself.

> SARAH: He wanted me to give you a message: you're in deep shit. He says you've abused what he's given you, and you'll have to pay the price.
> NANCY: Did he?
> SARAH: He did.

Upon this, Sarah's binding spell finally succeeds and Nancy, who is now prevented from 'doing harm against others and herself', ends up in an asylum.

The depiction of witchcraft in *Buffy the Vampire Slayer* (1997–2003) relates to *The Craft* but is also more complex. For some, its analysis may seem frustrating because crea-tor Joss Whedon poked fun at genuinely practising 'witches'; he showed them being more in-terested in bake sales and dance recitals than witchcraft, and thinking spells were not very em-powering. The occasional witchcraft references relate to Hansel and Gretel and mostly to cin-ematic witches. The main witchcraft strand, however, focuses on the struggles of Buffy's friend Willow (Alison Hannigan), whose magical power increases over the course of the series. The character of Willow signals a shift from female power which is contained by men to a power which is *self*-contained. Rather than struggling with opponents, although there were plenty of them, Willow struggles with herself. In season six (2001–2) Willow takes it upon herself to resurrect Buffy (who had sacrified herself at the end of the previous season). This boosts her power to such an extent that Buffy's mentor Rupert Giles (Anthony Head) is genuinely worried.

GILES: (over his shoulder) You're a very stupid girl.

WILLOW: What? Giles ...

GILES: (turns to face her) Do you have any idea what you've done? The forces you've harnessed, the lines you've crossed?

WILLOW: I thought you'd be ... impressed, or, or something.

GILES: Oh, don't worry, you've ... made a very deep impression. Of everyone here ... you were the one I trusted most to respect the forces of nature.

He goes on to explain the enormous risk she took, which endangered both the world and her-self.

GILES: Oh, there are others in this world who can do what you did. You just don't want to meet them. (turns away again)

WILLOW: No, probably not, but ... well, they're the bad guys. I'm not a bad guy. (upset) I brought Buffy back into this world, a-and maybe the word you should be looking for is 'congratulations.'

GILES: Having Buffy back in the world makes me feel ... indescribably wonderful, but I wouldn't congratulate you if you jumped off a cliff and happened to survive.

WILLOW: That's not what I did, Giles.

GILES: (angry) You were lucky.

WILLOW: I wasn't lucky. I was amazing. And how would you know? You weren't even there.

GILES: If I had been, I'd have bloody well stopped you. The magics you channelled are more ferocious and primal than anything you can hope to understand, (even more angry) and you are lucky to be alive, you rank, arrogant amateur!

The scene, aired in October 2001 and written by Whedon regulars Douglas Petrie and Jane Espenson, can also be read as a response to the film *Practical Magic* (1998), where Sally and Gillian Owens (Sandra Bullock and Nicole Kidman) give the latter's lover Jimmy too much belladonna when he becomes aggressive. As Jimmy continues his assault on Gillian the moment he regains some form of life, they immediately send him back to the afterlife with the help of a frying pan. The film's director Griffin Dunne learned how to combine horror with hu-mour while playing one of the leads in John Landis's *An American Werewolf in London*. *Practical Magic* discusses less the consequences of resurrection than of killing. Gillian be-comes possessed by Jimmy's spirit and they have to call a full witches' coven to exorcize him.

In contrast, over the course of season six *Buffy the Vampire Slayer* spins out the pro-cess of Willow's addiction to magic, her attempts to overcome it, and her final relapse when she loses her lover Tara through a stray bullet. As a fury on a rampage, she consumes as much magic as she can find and turns into 'black Willow', with black hair, black eyes, black lips, and visible veins on her still white face. Giles may have confronted Willow directly, but it was Tara, Willow's lover and fellow traveller in witchcraft, who constantly and carefully voiced her con-cerns about Willow using 'too much' magic, especially in everyday-life situations where physical action would have been equally effective. Battling supernatural forces with magic is acceptable, but using it simply to make life easier dehumanizes the witch. Willow is the mortal version of Samantha and has even more reasons to keep her power under control. As expressed in the vocabu-lary of *The Craft*, Willow turns from being posh Sarah into being goth Nancy and has to spend the opening episodes of season seven battling with the effects of her addiction. In the *Buffy* universe Willow com-municates with higher female powers and there is a clear feminist message about the empowerment of women. The figure of the witch is more ambigu-ous, however; even the good witch runs the danger of turning into the bad witch.

As the *Buffy* series is not primarily about witches, the group or coven aspect is tuned down. It is briefly mentioned in the fourth season (late 1999) when Willow joins a group of pa-gans only to be disillusioned with them. There is one other main witch, Amy, who is also solitary, and whose prime function is to encourage Willow in her addiction. A powerful English coven is only alluded to and serves as a retreat for Willow to overcome her habit. Notwithstanding the subordinate position of the witch in relation to the vampire slayers, Whedon still managed to ad-dress a major issue in the control of magical powers. Meanwhile, witch films went in another direction as witches turned up as a trio or a larger group. Consequently the problem of how an individual handles power dwindled.

Educating Witches and Wizards

Films involving a boarding school for witches existed some years before *Harry Potter* appeared on the scene. *Satan's School for Girls*

(1973, a USA film made for television) does not count because it focuses on a Satanic cult rather than on a witches' coven, although the dividing line can be blurred. The British children's television film *The Worst Witch* (1986), however, certainly qualifies. It featured potion mistress Hardbroom (Diana Rigg) as a prototype of Alan Rickman's Severus Snape and Tim Curry as the Grand Wizard in a rehearsal for Kenneth Branagh's Lockhart character in Potter's *Chamber of Secrets* (one of Cur-ry's later roles would be the wizard Trymon in *The Colour of Magic*, 2008). The lead role of Mildred Hubble was acted by Fairuza Balk, ten years younger than when she appeared in *The Craft*. With its lessons in broomstick flying and a broomstick out of control, *The Worst Witch* also possibly contains the roots of the classes of Madame Hooch in *Potter* as well as an early version of the accident-prone character of Neville Longbottom. Its story is relatively simple: the headmistress's evil sister Agatha wants to take over the acad-emy and 'turn all these good little witches into mean, horrible, cruel little witches'. Mildred, who stumbles on them while fleeing school after she was bullied, prevents it by turning the wicked witches into snails. She does this by reciting a spell. The more adolescent *Little Witches* (USA 1996), on the other hand, was set in a Catholic boarding school for girls. Six of them stay over during the Easter break and find the remnants of an old sect in the caves underneath the church, a spell book included. Here, as in the contemporaneous *The Craft*, the dichoto-my of temp-tation versus control is played out between the two female characters rather than within a single character. The power to evoke in *Little Witches* is demonic whereas in *The Craft* it is some kind of fictional spirit; apart from the lack of any teaching in the magic Arts, the main difference with the juvenile British boarding school films is that witchcraft in American films is secularized, as it is in most of the American series.

One could speculate whether or not a boarding school subgenre would have continued with-out *Potter*, but it is more relevant to look at the traces the *Potter* franchise left in later films. The distinction between the British boarding school for witches and the American boarding school teaching a normal curriculum to a number of witches needs to be considered, too. A third variant on the boarding school theme entails the school as a front for a group of dark witches. Most screen witches had no formal education in their magic skills:

Samantha's daugh-ter Tabitha was only old enough to attend school in the final season of *Bewitched* and she went to a mortal one. So did the later *Teen Witch* Louise and her younger screen sister Sabrina who merely needed to practise for her 'witch's licence'. Witchright Hall in *Sabrina*, the school for 'maladjusted young witches', only featured in one episode in 2001, and the Magic School in *Charmed* only emerged in season six (early 2004), both post-*Potter*; the Halliwell sisters in *Charmed* themselves were not trained at any magical institution either. Likewise, the academy at which the protagonists of *The Covenant* (USA 2006) study teaches American history rather than magical history. *The Woods* (an international co-production of 2006) has a predominantly female cast. Its pro-tagonist Heather displays the early signs of inborn witchcraft; she can manipulate a pencil tele-kinetically like Sarah and Willow before her. However, the staff of the boarding school prove a menace; again, there is no sign of any training in magic. At least *The Initiation of Sarah* (USA 1978; remade 2006), in which the tension regarding how to use innate powers again plays a central part, featured a class in European Mysticism, although the actual magic remains hid-den in the secret rituals of two rival sororities. The conclusion from all this must surely be that the magical boarding school generally served above all as a useful *setting* for teenage girl trouble rather than serving any more central plot function.

Rowling's contribution to the boarding school genre was to make Hogwarts a mixed-sex school. This, however, marginalized the gen-der issue. Hermione's Society for the Promotion of Elfish Welfare was obviously inspired by Samantha's political activism, but without the context of domesticity it somehow fell flat. With the stress on male wizards and the theme of domestica-tion relegated to Privet Drive, witchcraft ceased to be a force that especially empowered wom-en. Critics have voiced different reactions to the gender issue in *Potter*; some argued that it merely reflected contemporary society while others felt that 'women are still marginalized, stereotyped, and even mocked'. In this whole critical discussion the potential *subversiveness* of witchcraft was overlooked. In this sense the *Potter* films, and the response to them, reflect modern consumerism as much as the *Charmed* series. Nor is the other main modern witchcraft theme, self-control, much developed beyond the occasion-al sign of Harry's self-doubt. The dividing lines between good and evil are firmly drawn.

Further Reading

General Studies

Bengt Ankarloo and Stuart Clark (general eds), *The Athlone History of Witchcraft and Magic in Europe* (London, 1999–2002), 6 vols.

Michael D. Bailey, *Magic and Superstition in Europe: A Concise History from Antiquity to the Present* (Lanham, Md, 2007).

Jonathan Barry and Owen Davies (eds), *Witchcraft Historiography* (Basingstoke, 2007).

Wolfgang Behringer, *Witches and Witch-hunts: A Global History* (Cambridge, 2004).

Wolfgang Behringer et al. (eds), *Späte Hexenprozesse: Vom Umgang der Aufklärung mit dem Irrationalen* (Bielefeld, 2016).

Willem de Blécourt (ed.), *Werewolf Histories* (Basingstoke, 2015).

Dietrich Boschung and Jan Bremmer (eds), *The Materiality of Magic* (Paderborn, 2015).

Euan Cameron, *Enchanted Europe: Superstition, Reason, and Religion 1250–1750* (Oxford, 2010).

Derek J. Collins (ed.), *The Cambridge History of Magic and Witchcraft in the West: From Antiquity to the Present* (Cambridge, 2015).

Owen Davies, *Grimoires: A History of Magic Books* (Oxford, 2009).

Owen Davies, *Magic: A Very Short Introduction* (Oxford, 2012).

Johannes Dillinger, *Magical Treasure Hunting in Europe and North America* (Basingstoke, 2012).

Jonathan Durrant and Michael Bailey, *Historical Dictionary of Witchcraft*, 2nd edition (Lanham, Md, 2012).

Malcolm Gaskill, *Witchcraft: A Very Short Introduction* (Oxford, 2010).

Richard M. Golden (ed.), *Encyclopedia of Witchcraft: The Western Tradition* (Santa Barbara, Calif., 2006), 4 vols.

Peter Maxwell-Stuart, *Witchcraft: A History* (Stroud, 2000).

Peter Maxwell-Stuart, *Wizards: A History* (Stroud, 2004).

Darren Oldridge, *The Devil: A Very Short Introduction* (Oxford, 2012).

Christopher Partridge (ed.), *The Occult World* (Abingdon, 2015).

1. Magic in the Ancient World

Tzvi Abusch and Karel van der Toorn (eds), *Mesopotamian Magic: Textual, Historical, and Interpretative Perspectives (Ancient Magic & Divination)* (Groningen, 1999).

Hans Dieter Betz (ed.), *The Greek Magical Papyri in Translation; Including the Demotic Spells* (Chicago, 1986).

Gideon Bohak, *Ancient Jewish Magic: A History* (Cambridge, 2008).

Jan Bremmer and Jan R. Veenstra (eds), *The Metamorphosis of Magic from Late Antiquity to the Early Modern Period* (Leuven, 2002).

Charles Burnett and W. F. Ryan (eds), *Magic and the Classical Tradition* (London, 2006).

Leda Ciraolo and Jonathan Seidel (eds), *Magic and Divination in the Ancient World* (Leiden, 2002).

Derek Collins, *Magic in the Ancient Greek World* (Malden, Mass., 2008).

Matthew Dickie, *Magic and Magicians in the Greco-Roman World* (London, 2001).

Jacco Dieleman, *Priests, Tongues, and Rites: The London–Leiden Magical Manuscripts and Translation in Egyptian Ritual (100–300 CE)* (Leiden, 2005).

Christoper A. Faraone, *Ancient Greek Love Magic* (Cambridge, Mass., 1999).

Christoper A. Faraone and Dirk Obbink (eds), *Magika Hiera: Ancient Greek Magic & Religion* (Oxford, 1991).

John G. Gager, *Curse Tablets and Binding Spells from the Ancient World* (Oxford, 1992).

Fritz Graf, *Magic in the Ancient World* (Cambridge, Mass., 1997).

George Luck, *Arcana Mundi: Magic and the Occult in the Greek and Roman Worlds: A Collection of Ancient Texts*, 2nd edition (Baltimore, 2006).

Marvin W. Meyer and Paul A. Mirecki (eds), *Ancient Magic and Ritual Power* (Leiden, 1995).

Marvin Meyer and Richard Smith (eds), *Ancient Christian Magic: Coptic Texts of Ritual Power* (San Francisco, 1994).

Daniel Ogden, *Night's Black Agents: Witches, Wizards and the Dead in the Ancient World* (London, 2008).

Daniel Ogden, *Magic, Witchcraft, and Ghosts in the Greek and Roman Worlds: A Sourcebook* (Oxford, 2009).

Geraldine Pinch, *Magic in Ancient Egypt* (London, 1994).

Kimberly B. Stratton, *Naming the Witch: Magic, Ideology, and Stereotype in the Ancient World* (New York, 2007).

Kimberly B. Stratton and Dayna S. Kalleres (eds), *Daughters of Hecate: Women and Magic in the Ancient World* (New York, 2014).

Andrew Wilburn, *Materia Magica: The Archaeology of Magic in Roman Egypt, Cyprus, and Spain* (Ann Arbor, Mich., 2012).

2. Medieval Magic

Michael D. Bailey, *Fearful Spirits, Reasoned Follies: The Boundaries of Superstition in Late Medieval Europe* (Ithaca, NY, 2013).

Jean-Patrice Boudet, *Entre science et nigromance: astrologie, divination et magie dans l'Occident médiéval (XIIe–XVe siècle)* (Paris, 2006).

Charles Burnett, *Magic and Divination in the Middle Ages: Texts and Techniques in the Islamic and Christian Worlds* (Aldershot, 1996).

Claire Fanger (ed.), *Conjuring Spirits: Texts and Traditions of Medieval Ritual Magic* (University Park, Pa, 1998).

Claire Fanger (ed.), *Invoking Angels: Theurgic Ideas and Practices, Thirteenth to Sixteenth Centuries* (University Park, Pa, 2012).

Richard Kieckhefer, *Magic in the Middle Ages* (Cambridge, 1990).

Richard Kieckhefer, *Forbidden Rites: A Necromancer's Manual of the Fifteenth Century* (University Park, Pa, 1997).

Frank Klaassen, *The Transformations of Magic: Illicit Learned Magic in the Later Middle Ages and Renaissance* (University Park, Pa, 2013).

Benedek Láng, *Unlocked Books: Manuscripts of Learned Magic in the Medieval Libraries of Central Europe* (University Park, Pa, 2008).

Paul Magdalino and Maria Mavroudi (eds), *The Occult Sciences in Byzantium* (Geneva, 2006).

Stephen A. Mitchell, *Witchcraft and Magic in the Nordic Middle Ages* (Philadelphia, 2011).

Sophie Page, *Astrology in Medieval Manuscripts* (London, 2002).

Sophie Page, *Magic in Medieval Manuscripts* (London, 2004).

Sophie Page, *Magic in the Cloister: Pious Motives, Illicit Interests, and Occult Approaches to the Medieval Universe* (University Park, Pa, 2013).

Catherine Rider, *Magic and Impotence in the Middle Ages* (Oxford, 2006).

Catherine Rider, *Magic and Religion in Medieval England* (London, 2012).

Don C. Skemer, *Binding Words: Textual Amulets in the Middle Ages* (University Park, Pa, 2006).

3. The Demonologists

Philip Almond, *England's First Demonologist: Reginald Scot and 'The Discoverie of Witchcraft'* (London, 2011).

Michael D. Bailey, *Battling Demons: Witchcraft, Heresy, and Reform in the Late Middle Ages* (Philadelphia, 2003).

Jonathan Barry, *Witchcraft and Demonology in South-West England, 1640–1789* (Basingstoke, 2012).

Wolfgang Behringer, 'Demonology 1500–1660', in R. Po-chai Hsia (ed.), *The Cambridge History of Christianity, vol. 6, Reform and Expansion 1500–1660* (Cambridge, 2008).

Alain Boureau, 'Demons and the Christian Community', in Miri Rubin and Walters Simons (eds), *The Cambridge History of Christianity, vol. 4, Reform and Expansion c.1100–c.1500* (Cambridge, 2010).

Hans Peter Broedel, *The 'Malleus Maleficarum' and the Construction of Witchcraft: Theology and Popular Belief* (Manchester, 2003).

Stuart Clark, *Thinking with Demons: The Idea of Witchcraft in Early Modern Europe* (Oxford, 1997).

Nathan Johnstone, *The Devil and Demonism in Early Modern England* (Cambridge, 2006).

Richard Kieckhefer, *European Witch Trials: Their Foundations in Popular and Learned Culture, 1300–1500* (London, 1976).

Pierre de Lancre, *On the Inconstancy of Witches: Pierre de Lancre's Tableau de l'inconstance des mauvais anges et démons (1612)*, ed. Gerhild Scholz Williams (Tempe, Ariz., 2005).

Brian P. Levack (ed.), *The Oxford Handbook of Witchcraft in Early Modern Europe and Colonial America* (Oxford, 2013).

Brian P. Levack, *The Devil Within: Possession & Exorcism in the Christian West* (New Haven, 2013).

George Mora (ed.), *Witches, Devils, and Doctors in the Renaissance: Johann Weyer*, De praestigiis daemonum (Binghamton, NY, 1991).

James Sharpe, *Instruments of Darkness: Witchcraft in England 1550–1750* (London, 1996).

Walter Stephens, *Demon Lovers: Witchcraft, Sex, and the Crisis of Belief* (Chicago, 2002).

Gary K. Waite, *Heresy, Magic and Witchcraft in Early Modern Europe* (Basingstoke, 2003).

Gerhild Scholz Williams, *Defining Dominion: The Discourses of Magic and Witchcraft in Early Modern France and Germany* (Ann Arbor, Mich., 1995).

4. The Witch Trials

Philip C. Almond, *Demonic Possession and Exorcism in Early Modern England: Contemporary Texts and their Cultural Contexts* (Cambridge, 2004).

Bengt Ankarloo and Gustav Henningsen (eds), *Early Modern European Witchcraft: Centres and Peripheries* (Oxford, 1990).

Wolfgang Behringer, *Witchcraft Persecutions in Bavaria: Popular Magic, Religious Zealotry, and Reason of State in Early Modern Europe* (Cambridge, 1997).

Willem de Blécourt (ed.), *Werewolf Histories* (Basingstoke, 2015).

Robin Briggs, *The Witches of Lorraine* (Oxford, 2007).

Stuart Clark (ed.), *Language of Witchcraft: Narrative, Ideology and Meaning in Early Modern Culture* (Basingstoke, 2002).

Kathleen L. Doty, 'Telling Tales: The Role of Scribes in Constructing the Discourse of the Salem Witchcraft Trials', *Journal of Historical Pragmatics* 8 (2007), 25–41.

Jonathan Durrant, *Witchcraft, Gender and Society in Early Modern Germany* (Leiden, 2007).

Malcolm Gaskill, *Witchfinders: A Seventeenth-Century English Tragedy* (London, 2005).

Marion Gibson, *Reading Witchcraft: Stories of Early English Witches* (London, 1999).

Julian Goodare (ed.), *Scottish Witches and Witch-Hunters* (Basingstoke, 2013).

Risto Hiltunen and Matti Peikola, 'Trial Discourse and Manuscript Context: Scribal Profiles in the Salem Witchcraft Records', *Journal of Historical Pragmatics* 8 (2007), 43–68.

Brian P. Levack, *The Witch-Hunt in Early Modern Europe*, 3rd edition (London, 2006).

Brian P. Levack (ed.), *The Oxford Handbook of Witchcraft in Early Modern Europe and Colonial America* (Oxford, 2013).

William Monter, *A Bewitched Duchy: Lorraine and its Dukes, 1477–1736* (Geneva, 2007).

Marko Nenonen and Raisa Maria Toivo (eds), *Writing Witch-Hunt Histories: Challenging the Paradigm* (Leiden, 2013).

Alison Rowlands, *Witchcraft Narratives in Germany: Rothenburg, 1561–1652* (Manchester, 2003).

Alison Rowlands (ed.), *Witchcraft and Masculinities in Early Modern Europe* (Basingstoke, 2009).

Walter Rummel and Rita Voltmer, *Hexen und Hexenverfolgung in der Frühen Neuzeit*, 2nd edition (Darmstadt, 2012).

Rolf Schulte, *Man as Witch: Male Witches in Central Europe* (Basingstoke, 2009).

James Sharpe, *Instruments of Darkness: Witchcraft in England 1550–1750* (London, 1996).

James Sharpe, *The Bewitching of Anne Gunter: A Horrible and True Story of Deception, Witchcraft, Murder, and the King of England* (London, 2000).

James Sharpe, *Witchcraft in Early Modern England* (Harlow, 2001).

Laura Stokes, *Demons of Urban Reform: Early European Witch Trials and Criminal Justice, 1430–1530* (Basingstoke, 2011).

Rita Voltmer (ed.), *Hexenprozesse und Herrschaftspraxis* (Trier, 2005).

Rita Voltmer, *Hexen: Wissen was stimmt* (Freiburg, 2008).

Rita Voltmer, ' "Hört an neu schrecklich abentheuer | von den unholden ungeheuer": Zur multimedialen Vermittlung des Fahndungsbildes "Hexerei" im Kontext konfessioneller Polemik', in Karl Härter, Gerhard Sälter, and Eva Wiebel (eds), *Repräsentationen von Kriminalität und öffentlicher Sicherheit. Bilder, Vorstellungen und Diskurse vom 16. bis zum 20. Jahrhundert* (Frankfurt am Main, 2010), 89–163.

Liv Helene Willumsen, *Witches of the North. Scotland and Finnmark* (Leiden and Boston 2013).

Wanda Wyporska, *Witchcraft in Early Modern Poland, 1500–1800* (Basingstoke, 2013).

5. The Witch and Magician in European Art

Rosemarie Beier-de Haan, Rita Voltmer, and Franz Irsigler (eds), *Hexenwahn: Ängste der Neuzeit*, exhibition catalogue, Deutsches Historisches Museum, Berlin (Berlin, 2002).

Linda C. Hults, *The Witch as Muse: Art, Gender, and Power in Early Modern Europe* (Philadelphia, 2005).

Maxime Préaud, *Les sorcières* (Paris, 1973)

Lyndal Roper, *The Witch in the Western Imagination* (Charlottesville, Va, 2012).

Claudia Swan, *Art, Science, and Witchcraft in Early Modern Holland: Jacques de Gheyn II (1565–1620)* (Cambridge, 2005).

Guy Tal, 'Witches on Top: Magic, Power, and Imagination in the Art of Early Modern Italy', Ph.D. thesis, Indiana University, 2006. Available to view at: <https://books.google.co.uk/books?id=Fu4ubXCyJMYC&printsec=frontcover&dq=witchcraft+art&hl=en&sa=X&ei=cycxVbvvCpHTaICvgZAN&ved=0CDEQ6AEwAw#v=onepage&q=witchcraft%20art&f=false>.

Renilde Vervoort, *'Vrouwen op den besem en derghelijck ghespoock': Pieter Bruegel en de traditie van hekserijvoorstellingen in de Nederlanden tussen 1450 en 1700* (Nijmegen, 2011).

Rita Voltmer, '"Hört an neu schrecklich abentheuer/von den unholden ungeheuer": Zur multimedialen Vermittlung des Fahndungsbildes "Hexerei" im Kontext konfessioneller Polemik', in Karl Härter, Gerhard Sälter, and Eva Wiebel (eds), *Repräsentationen von Kriminalität und öffentlicher Sicherheit: Bilder, Vorstellungen und Diskurse vom 16. bis zum 20. Jahrhundert* (Frankfurt, 2010), 89–163.

Charles Zika, *Exorcising our Demons: Magic, Witchcraft and Visual Culture in Early Modern Europe* (Leiden, 2003).

Charles Zika, *The Appearance of Witchcraft: Print and Visual Culture in Sixteenth-Century Europe* (London, 2007).

Charles Zika, 'Images and Witchcraft Studies: A Short History', in Marko Nenonen and Raisa Maria Toivo (eds), *Writing Witch-Hunt Histories: Challenging the Paradigm* (Leiden and Boston, 2014), 41–85.

6. The World of Popular Magic

Wolfgang Behringer, *Shaman of Oberstdorf: Chonrad Stoeckhlin and the Phantoms of the Night* (Charlottesville, Va, 1998).

Edward Bever, *The Realities of Witchcraft and Popular Magic in Early Modern Europe: Culture, Cognition, and Everyday Life* (Basingstoke, 2008).

Willem de Blécourt and Owen Davies (eds), *Witchcraft Continued: Popular Magic in Modern Europe* (Manchester, 2004).

Willem de Blécourt, Ronald Hutton, and J. S. La Fontaine, *The Athlone History of Witchcraft and Magic in Europe: Witchcraft and Magic in the Twentieth Century* (London, 1999).

Monica Chojnacka, *Working Women of Early Modern Venice* (Baltimore, 2001).

Owen Davies, *A People Bewitched: Witchcraft and Magic in Nineteenth-Century Somerset* (Bruton, 1999).

Owen Davies, *Witchcraft, Magic and Culture, 1736–1951* (Manchester, 1999).

Owen Davies, *Cunning-Folk: Popular Magic in English History* (London, 2003).

Owen Davies, *Grimoires: A History of Magic Books* (Oxford, 2009).

Owen Davies, *America Bewitched: The Story of Witchcraft after Salem* (Oxford, 2013).

Owen Davies and Willem de Blécourt (eds), *Beyond the Witch Trials: Witchcraft and Magic in Enlightenment Europe* (Manchester, 2004).

Judith Devlin, *The Superstitious Mind: French Peasants and the Supernatural in the Nineteenth Century* (New Haven, 1987).

Jacqueline Van Gent, *Magic, Body, and the Self in Eighteenth-Century Sweden* (Leiden, 2009).

David Gentilcore, *From Bishop to Witch: The System of the Sacred in Early Modern Terra d'Otranto* (Manchester, 1992).

Marijke Gijswijt-Hofstra, Brian P. Levack, and Roy Porter, *The Athlone History of Witchcraft and Magic in Europe: The Eighteenth and Nineteenth Centuries* (London, 1999).

Alan Macfarlane, *Witchcraft in Tudor and Stuart England: A Regional and Comparative Study* (London, 1970).

Joyce Miller, *Magic and Witchcraft in Scotland* (Musselburgh, 2004).

Valérie Molero, *Magie et sorcellerie en Espagne au siècle des lumières 1700–1820* (Paris, 2006).

Lynn Wood Mollenauer, *Strange Revelations: Magic, Poison, and Sacrilege in Louis XIV's France* (University Park, Pa, 2007).

Michael Ostling, *Between the Devil and the Host: Imagining Witchcraft in Early Modern Poland* (Oxford, 2011).

W. F. Ryan, *The Bathhouse at Midnight: An Historical Survey of Magic and Divination in Russia* (Stroud, 1999).

Laura Stark, *The Magical Self: Body, Society and the Supernatural in Early Modern Rural Finland* (Helsinki, 2006).

Mariá Tausiet, *Urban Magic in Early Modern Spain: Abracadabra Omnipotens* (Basingstoke, 2013).

Keith Thomas, *Religion and the Decline of Magic* (London, 1971).

Timothy Dale Walker, *Doctors, Folk Medicine and the Inquisition: The Repression of Magical Healing in Portugal during the Enlightenment* (Leiden, 2005).

Emma Wilby, *Cunning Folk and Familiar Spirits: Shamanistic Visionary Traditions in Early Modern British Witchcraft and Magic* (Brighton, 2005).

Stephen Wilson, *The Magical Universe: Everyday Ritual and Magic in Pre-Modern Europe* (London, 2000).

7. The Rise of Modern Magic

Jonathan Barry, *Raising Spirits: How a Conjuror's Tale was Transmitted across the Enlightenment* (Basingstoke, 2013).

Alison Butler, *Victorian Occultism and the Making of Modern Magic: Invoking Tradition* (Basingstoke, 2011).

Chas Clifton, *Her Hidden Children: The Rise of Wicca and Paganism in America* (Lanham, Md, 2006).

Owen Davies, *America Bewitched: The Story of Witchcraft after Salem* (Oxford, 2013).

Bill Ellis, *Raising the Devil: Satanism, New Religions, and the Media* (Lexington, Ky, 2000).

Dave Evans, *The History of British Magic after Crowley: Kenneth Grant, Amado Crowley, Chaos Magic, Satanism, Lovecraft, The Left Hand Path, Blasphemy and Magical Morality* (n.p., 2007).

John Fleming, *The Dark Side of the Enlightenment: Wizards, Alchemists, and Spiritual Seekers in the Age of Reason* (New York, 2013).

Joscelyn Godwin, *The Theosophical Enlightenment* (Albany, NY, 1994).

Joscelyn Godwin, Christian Chanel, and John P. Deveney, *The Hermetic Brotherhood of Luxor: Initiatic and Historical Documents of an Order of Practical Occultism* (York Beach, Me, 1995).

Kerriann Godwin (ed.), *The Museum of Witchcraft: A Magical History* (Boscastle, 2011).

Ronald Hutton, *The Triumph of the Moon: A History of Modern Pagan Witchcraft* (Oxford, 2000).

Ronald Hutton, *Witches, Druids and King Arthur* (London, 2003).

Richard Kaczynski, *Perdurabo: The Life of Aleister Crowley* (Berkeley, 2010).

Francis King, *Ritual Magic in England: 1887 to the Present Day* (London, 1970).

Sofie Lachapelle, *Investigating the Supernatural: From Spiritism and Occultism to Psychical Research and Metapsychics in France, 1853–1931* (Baltimore, 2011).

Gary Lachman, *A Dark Muse: A History of the Occult* (New York, 2005).

Christopher McIntosh, *Eliphas Lévi and the French Occult Revival* (London, 1972).

Christopher McIntosh, *The Rose Cross and the Age of Reason: Eighteenth-Century Rosicrucianism in Central Europe and its Relationship to the Enlightenment* (Albany, NY, 2011).

Sabina Magliocco, *Witching Culture: Folklore and Neo-Paganism in America* (Philadelphia, 2004).

H. C. Erik Midelfort, *Exorcism and Enlightenment: Johann Joseph Gassner and the Demons of Eighteenth-Century Germany* (New Haven, 2005).

Paul Monod, *Solomon's Secret Arts: The Occult in the Age of Enlightenment* (New Haven, 2013).

Alex Owen, *The Place of Enchantment: British Occultism and the Culture of the Modern* (Chicago, 2004).

Joanne Pearson, *Wicca and the Christian Heritage* (London, 2007).

William Ramsey, *Aleister Crowley: A Visual Study* (Kindle edition, 2014).

Jone Salomonsen, *Enchanted Feminism: The Reclaiming Witches of San Francisco* (London, 2002).

Corinna Treitel, *A Science for the Soul: Occultism and the Genesis of the German Modern* (Baltimore, 2004).

Websites: <http://geraldgardner.com/archive/index.php>.

8. Witchcraft and Magic in the Age of Anthropology

Jenny Blain, *Nine Worlds of Seidr-Magic: Ecstasy and Neo-Shamanism in North European Paganism* (London, 2001).

Jean Clottes and J. David Lewis-Williams, *The Shamans of Prehistory: Trance and Magic in the Painted Caves* (New York, 1998).

E. E. Evans-Pritchard, *Witchcraft, Oracles and Magic Among the Azande* (Oxford, 1937).

Carlos Fausto, *Warfare and Shamanism in Amazonia* (Cambridge, 2014).

Jeanne Favret-Saada, *Deadly Words: Witchcraft in the Bocage* (Cambridge, [1977], 1980).

A. Gell, *Art and Agency: An Anthropological Theory* (Oxford, 1998).

Susan Greenwood, *The Anthropology of Magic* (Oxford, 2009).

Graham Harvey (ed.), *Readings in Indigenous Religions* (London, 2002).

Graham Harvey, *Animism: Respecting the Living World* (London, 2005).

Graham Harvey and Robert J. Wallis, *Historical Dictionary of Shamanism* (Lanham, Md, 2015).

Amiria Henare, Martin Holbraad, and Sari Wastell (eds), *Thinking Through Things: Theorising Artefacts Ethnographically* (London, 2007).

Ronald Hutton, *Shamans: Siberian Spirituality and the Western Imagination* (London, 2001).

Ari Kiev, *Magic, Faith, and Healing* (New York, 1964).

Clyde Kluckhohn, *Navajo Witchcraft* (Cambridge, Mass., 1944).

Andrew Lattas, 'Sorcery and Colonialism: Illness, Dreams and Death as Political Language in West New Britain', *Man* 28 (1993), 51–77.

Shirley Lindenbaum, *Kuru Sorcery: Disease and Danger in the New Guinea Highlands* (Palo Alto, Calif., 1979).

Tanya Luhrmann, *Persuasions of the Witches Craft: Ritual Magic in Contemporary England* (Cambridge, Mass., 1989).

Bronislaw Malinowski, *Coral Gardens and their Magic* (London, 1935).

Birgit Meyer and Peter Pels (eds), *Magic and Modernity: Interfaces of Revelation and Concealment* (Stanford, Calif., 2003).

John Middleton, *Magic, Witchcraft and Curing* (Austin, Tex., and London, 1967).

Jeremy Narby and Francis Huxley (eds), *Shamans through Time: 500 Years on the Path to Knowledge* (London, 2001).

Joanne Pearson, 'Going Native in Reverse: The Insider as Researcher in British Wicca', *Nova Religio* 5 (2001), 52–63.

Fernando Santos-Granero (ed.), *The Occult Life of Things: Native Amazonian Theories of Materiality and Personhood* (Tucson, Ariz., 2009).

Michele Stephen (ed.), *Sorcerer and Witch in Melanesia* (New Brunswick, NJ, 1987).

Paul Stoller and Cheryl Olkes, *In Sorcery's Shadow* (Chicago, 1987).

Stanley Tambiah, *Magic, Science, Religion and the Scope of Rationality* (Cambridge, 1990).

Michael Taussig, *Shamanism, Colonialism, and the Wild Man: A Study in Terror and Healing* (Chicago, 1987).

Victor Turner, *The Forest of Symbols: Aspects of Ndembu Ritual* (Ithaca, NY, 1967).

Victor Turner, *The Ritual Process: Structure and Anti-Structure* (Chicago, 1969).

Robert J. Wallis, *Shamans/Neo-Shamans: Ecstasy, Alternative Archaeologies and Contemporary Pagans* (London, 2003).

Robert J. Wallis and Kenneth Lymer (eds), *A Permeability of Boundaries? New Approaches to the Archaeology of Art, Religion and Folklore* (Oxford, 2001).

Neal L. Whitehead, *In Darkness and Secrecy: The Anthropology of Assault Sorcery and Witchcraft and Amazonia* (Durham, 2004).

Johnnes Wilbert, 'The Order of Dark Shamans among the Warao', in Neil L. Whitehead and Robin Wright (eds), *In Darkness and Secrecy* (Durham, 2004), 21–50.

Robin Wright, *Cosmos, Self and History in Baniwa Religion* (Austin, Tex., 1998).

9. Witches on Screen

Note: the books and articles below should not be consulted for their accurate sense of the history of witchcraft.

Jes Battis (ed.), *Supernatural Youth: The Rise of the Teen Hero in Literature and Popular Culture* (Plymouth, 2011).

Karin Beeler and Stan Beeler, *Investigating Charmed* (London, 2007), glamour magic on television.

Helen A. Berger (ed.), *Witchcraft and Magic: Contemporary North America* (Philadelphia, 2005).

Andrew Blake, *The Irresistible Rise of Harry Potter* (London, 2002), critical view.

Emily D. Edwards, *Metaphysical Media: The Occult Experience in Popular Culture* (Carbondale, Ill., 2005).

Rebecca Feasy, 'Watching Charmed: Why Teen Television Appeals to Women', *Journal of Popular Film and Television* 34 (2006), 2–9.

Tanice G. Foltz, 'The Commodification of Witchcraft', in Helen A. Berger (ed.), *Witchcraft and Magic: Contemporary North America* (Philadelphia, 2005), 137–68.

Katherine A. Fowkes, *The Fantasy Film* (Chichester, 2010).

Carrol L. Fry, *Cinema of the Occult: New Age, Satanism, Wicca, and Spiritualism in Film* (Cranbury, NJ, 2008).

Marion Gibson, *Witchcraft Myths in American Culture* (New York, 2007).

Elizabeth E. Heilman (ed.), *Critical Perspectives on Harry Potter* (New York, 2003).

Hannah E. Johnston and Peg Aloi (eds), *The New Generation of Witches: Teenage Witchcraft in Contemporary Culture* (Aldershot, 2007).

Roz Kaveney (ed.), *Reading the Vampire Slayer* (London, 2002).

Tanya Krzywinska, *A Skin for Dancing In: Possession, Witchcraft and Voodoo in Film* (Trowbridge, 2000).

Walter Metz, *Bewitched* (Detroit, 2007).

Rachel Moseley, 'Glamorous Witchcraft: Gender and Magic in Teen Film and Television', *Screen* 43 (2002), 403–22.

Salman Rushdie, *The Wizard of Oz* (London, 1992).

Mark Evan Swartz, *Oz before the Rainbow* (Baltimore, 2000).

Rhonda V. Wilcox and David Lavery (eds), *Fighting the Forces: What's at Stake in Buffy the Vampire Slayer?* (Lanham, Md, 2002).

Dominique Wilson, 'Willow and Which Craft? The Portrayal of Witchcraft in Joss Whedon's *Buffy: The Vampire Slayer*', *Sydney Studies in Religion* (2005), 146–58. The article is available on open access: <http://ses.library.usyd.edu.au/handle/2123/1268>.

Index

Aaron (biblical figure) 8, 14
Abbey of Thelema 217
aboriginal/indigenous people ix,
    228–31, 235
Abraham (biblical figure) 196
Abraham's eye 55
Abrasax 24
actions x, 30, 36, 261
Adam (biblical figure) 34, 45
Adelard of Bath 33, 54
adultery 24
Aegean Sea 18
Africa 133, 189, 244–5, 255
afterlife, the 10, 210, 283
Agrippa, Henry Cornelius 79, 183,
    196, 200
   Fourth Book of Occult Philosophy 196,
     203, 215
   The Three Books of Occult Philosophy
     196, 203
Aix-en-Provence 112
Akhenaten (Pharaoh) 9
Akkadian 2
Albania 169
Albert (Archduke of the Spanish
    Netherlands) 146
Albertus Magnus 40
alchemy 35, 41, 198, 204, 208–9
Alexander IV (Pope) 53
Alexander the Great 27
Alexandrians 221
Alfonso X (King of Castile) 34, 42, 43,
    45, 49
   Cantigas de Santa Maria 49
   Libro de astromagia 42
Algonquians 229
alherces 182
Aliamet, Jacques 147
Alliette, Baptiste 209
Almandel 45
Alsace 96, 100, 107–8, 113, 123–4,
    137–8
Altdorfer, Albrecht 135
Amazonia 228, 253

American Werewolf in London (film) 283
Amiens 60
Amsterdam 90, 149, 161
Amuesha, the 255
amulets 5, 8, 9–11, 14–16, 20, 27–8, 54
Anari, High Priestess 212
Anatolia 19
anatomy 36, 186
Anaxilaus of Larisa 26
ancient world, the 9, 35, 206, 214, 216,
    226 *see also* Greece (ancient) *and*
    Rome (ancient)
al-Andalus 33
Andaman Islands 242
Anderson, Agnes 178
Andersson, Sven 171
Andrew (Apostle) 27
angelology 34
angels 15–16, 32, 41, 44–5, 47, 50,
    191, 198–9, 207
Anglo-Saxons, the 32
animal magnetism 198–9, 209
animals 17, 31, 34, 36, 77, 146, 150,
    154–5, 162–3, 186, 202, 218,
    233, 244, 253–5, 262, 276
    see also familiars
  bears and wolves 180
  beetles 9
  frogs 179
  goats 159, 180, 276
  magical 34, 51
  parts of 55
  sacrifice of 42, 223
  slugs and snails 178
  snakes 180, 240
animism 232, 253–6, 257
ankh, the 9
Anne (Queen of Denmark) 66
anthropology 9, 195, 227–38, 241–47,
    249, 250–7, 269
Antwerp 77, 141, 145–6 ·
  Academy of Art 147
  Guild of St Luke 147
Anubis (god) 9

Aphrodite 20
apples 20
Aquinas, Thomas 40, 69–70
    Summa theologiae 48
Arabic world 33, 41
    culture/ideas of the 33–6, 37, 40, 58
    and magic 31, 35, 40, 42, 58
Aragon 70
archaeology 8, 14, 16, 188, 218, 249
Ardennes, the 113, 128
Argonne 113
Aristophanes 20
Aristotle 36, 37, 48, 69, 82
Ars notoria 44, 46
Artisson, Robin 56
artists 134, 147, 151, 154–7, 163, 206,
        217, 229, 266
Artois 101
d'Ascoli, Cecco 59
    Sphere of Sacrobosco 59
Ascymor 43
ashaf 14
Ashàninka, the 255
Asher, William 263, 268
Asia 218
āšipu 3
astrologers 49, 79, 191, 200, 207
astrology 33–4, 41, 79, 109, 177,
        190, 197–8, 201–2
astronomy 33, 41 *see also* stars and
        planets, the
Astrum Argentum 213
Atalanta 20
atheism 89, 91, 231
Athens 18–24, 24
Augsburg 83, 102, 127, 139, 141,
        158, 159
Augustine of Hippo 38, 48, 76
    City of God 68
Augustus (Roman Emperor) 26
Australia 188, 242, 256
Austria 58, 101, 198, 210, 216
authorities 41, 95, 99, 105, 166, 218, 278
    religious 30, 50, 52–3, 75, 94, 172
    secular 30, 35, 61, 72, 73, 75, 100, 172
Autun, Burgundy 72
Azande, the 238–42, 247, 256

Babylonians, the 2
Baden-Baden 102

Baden Durlach 102
Baghdad 41
Baldung, Hans (Grien) 135–7, 138,
        144, 148, 151, 222
    *Witches Preparing for the Sabbath
        Flight* 135
Balk, Fairuza 282, 285
Balkans, the 189
Balsamo, Guiseppe *see* Cagliostro, Count
Balsamo, Seraphina 205
Bamberg 99, 102, 112
Bamu, Kirsty 254
Ban de la Roch 118
Baniwa, the 254
Baphomet 71
Bar, Duchy of 101, 125
Barrett, Francis 203, 207
    The Magus: Or Celestial Intelligencer
        203, 207
Basel 137, 139
Basque Country 76, 96, 100, 144, 145
Basson, Govert 149
Basson, Thomas 149
Batcombe (Somerset) 64
Baum, L. Frank 265–7, 269
    The Marvellous Land of Oz 265–7
Bavaria 95, 102, 107, 128, 185–6
beauty 237
Behringer, Wolfgang 95
Beir, George 177
Beissel, Conrad 201
Bekker, Balthasar 90
    De betoverde Weereld 90
Belgium 80
beliefs 3, 7, 86–7, 149, 228, 231, 237,
        245, 277 *see also* witchcraft,
            beliefs
Bell, Book and Candle (film) 268–9,
        278, 281
Bergmännlein 187
Bergson, Mina *see* Mathers, Moina
Berkshire 201
Bern 139
Bernard, Richard 64, 82
    Guide to Grand Iury Men 64, 65, 129
Bewitched (film) 269
Bewitched (television series) 258,
        266–81, 286
Bible, the 15, 17, 82, 88, 90, 158,
        159–60, 181

apocrypha/pseudipigrapha
  Enoch 15
  Jubilees 15
  Maccabees 12: 39 15
  Tobit 6: 8 14
books of
  Exodus
    6: 8–12 8
    22: 18 14
    39: 25 14
  Leviticus
    16: 8–10 13
    20: 27 14
  Numbers
    15: 37–8 13
    27: 21 12
  Deuteronomy
    15: 9 13
    18: 10–11 14
  I Samuel 158, 160
    15: 23 67
    28 156
    28: 8–19 13
  I Kings 14
  Nehemiah 10: 34 13
  Job 64, 67
  Psalms 121: 8 27
  Proverbs 23: 6 13
  Isaiah 34: 17 13
  Jonah 1: 7 13
  Matthew
    10: 1 82
    10: 8 82
    13: 24–30 149
    27: 46 259
  Acts
    8: 9 26
    19: 11–20 26
  Revelation 67: 12 200
  King James version 66
  New Testament, the 14, 63, 67,
    82, 181
  Old Testament, the 2, 12, 14, 64,
    67, 204
Biet, Antoine 230
'Bilson Boy', the 131
Binsfeld, Peter 79, 82, 100, 129, 141
  Tractatus de confessionibus maleficorum et
    sagaram 79, 141
Black Sea, the 19

Blagrave, Joseph 175
Blain, Jenny 249, 250
Blake, William 199, 206
  'Oberon, Titania and Puck with
    Fairies Dancing' 206
Blankenheim 103
Blavatsky, Helena Petrovna 210, 214
  Isis Unveiled 210
Blécourt, Willem de v, vii
Blocksberg 151, 154
Blockula 160
blood 168, 173, 175, 180, 183, 185
'Blood Books' 124
Blyton, Enid 259
boats 186
Bocage 246, 249
Böcklin, Arnold 163
Bodin, Jean 64, 65, 75–6, 82, 89, 129,
  141, 146
  De la démonomanie des sorciers 75
  The Six Books of the Commonwealth 75
Boehme, Jacob 200
Bohemia 101
Bol, Ferdinand 160
Bolingbroke, Roger 58
Bolos of Mendes 26
Bone, Eleanor 'Ray' 221
Book of the Dead 6, 11
Book of Shadows 219, 221
Bordeaux 65, 112, 205
  parlement of 76, 86
Bordelon, Laurent 161–2
  The Story of the Extravagant Imaginations
    of Monsieur Oufle . . . 161–2
Boscastle (Cornwall) 220
Bosch, Hieronymus 145, 148, 151
Boston 131
Bostridge, Ian
  Witchcraft and its Transformations 277
Boulanger, Louis 163
Bourton-on-the-Water
    (Gloucestershire) 224–5
Brabant 101, 146
brainwashing 123
Branagh, Kenneth 285
Brazil 229
Breitfeld, Alexander 183
Brenz, Johann 85
  Homilia de grandine 85
Briefmaler 141

Brighton 221
Brigue, Jeanne de 56
Britain 180, 184, 187, 193, 200, 218,
      235–6 *see also* England *and* Wales
  Freemasonry in 204, 206, 210–12
  magic in 216, 220, 222
  people of/from 186–7, 223
British Isles 94, 113, 115, 130 *see also*
      Britain *and* England *and* Ireland
      and Scotland
Brown, Dan
  The Da Vinci Code 118
Brown, Richard 173
Bruegel the Elder, Peter 140, 143–4,
      148, 151
  The Fall of the Magician Hermogenes 140,
      146, 151
  The Festival of Fools 162
  Luxuria 143
  St James and the Magician Hermogenes
      140–1, 143, 146, 151
Buchelius, Arnoldus 150
Buckland, Raymond 224
Buckland, Rosemary 223
Budapest, Zsuzsanna 225
  Feminist Book of Lights and Shadows 225
Buddhism 209 *see also* Esoteric Buddhism
Buffy the Vampire Slayer (television
      series) 291–84
bullae 9
Bullock, Sandra 283
Burchard of Worms, Bishop 32
Burgundian Penitential 31
Burgundy 98, 109
Burke, Billy 265
Burn Witch, Burn (film) 268
Byzantium 35

Caesarius of Heisterbach, Abbot
  Dialogus miraculorum 51
Cagliostro, Count 205–6, 212, 214
Calcagnini 79
Cambridge University
  Christ's College 64
Canterbury
  Archbishop of 130
  St Augustine's 60
capitalism 225
Caraphzebiz 37
Caribbean 229

carmina 23
Carpenter, Richard 270
Carpzov, Benedict 82
  Practica nova imperialis saxonica verum
      criminaliam 82
Cartwright, Veronica 280
Castile and León 34, 43
Castletown (Isle of Man) 220
Catalonia 96, 105
Cathars, the 53, 64
Cato 23
Catweazle (television series) 270
cause and effect 3, 39, 48, 85, 192, 246,
      253, 257
Cavallo, Vito 172
Ceinowa, Christina 194
celestial bodies *see* astronomy *and* stars and
      planets
Celsus 27
Chaldeans 211
Champollion, Jean-François 6
Charlemagne 30
  Admonitio generali 30
Charles V (Habsburg Emperor) 106
Charmed (television series) 270,
      276–80, 286
charms 27, 31, 54, 169–70, 178–83,
      187–8, 207, 215
Chelmsford 129
Cher 280
children 3, 9, 11, 93, 124, 130, 144, 150
  Mora case 131, 159
Christian society 16 *see also* communities,
      Christian
Christianity 29, 42, 63, 68, 86, 92, 135,
      146, 154, 181, 189, 196, 199,
      205, 228, 256, 259, 267
  and conception of witchcraft viii, 86,
      92, 227, 260, 282
  doctrines/notions espoused by 35, 43–4,
      47–8, 53, 63, 67, 196, 229, 259
  evangelical 208, 223, 259
  and magic 43, 58, 76, 182, 205–10,
      210, 217–18
    attitudes towards 26–30, 33, 41,
      260, 280 *see also* Church, the,
      attitudes towards magic
  opposition to 26, 58, 146
  and paganism 30, 35 *see also* paganism,
      and Christianity

reform of 72
spread of 25, 33
types of
   Catholicism 41, 67–8, 73, 74–5,
      79–84, 93, 96, 97, 107, 126–8,
      130, 167, 181, 187, 191, 192,
      195, 204, 208, 228, 285
   Protestantism 81, 88, 90, 92, 93, 96,
      104, 107, 118, 126–7, 128, 167,
      181, 195, 199–200, 204
     Anglican 201
     Baptist 207
     Calvinist 166
     Dutch Reformed 90, 90
     Lutheran 83–4, 124, 127, 137,
      159, 179, 200
     Methodist 201
     Mormon 201
     Pietist 159, 201
     Puritanical 64, 82, 84, 130
Christians viii, 25–7, 34, 40–1, 43–4, 72,
   76, 127, 249
  Catholics 70, 80, 93, 96, 126–7,
    130–1, 137, 187, 191, 208,
    217–18
  Protestants 93, 96, 127, 187
Church, the 66, 68, 82, 189, 195, 199,
   218, 225, 230, 267 *see also*
   authorities, religious
  Catholic 72, 180, 208, 230
   actions of 53, 73
   attitudes towards magic 28, 31, 58
   concerns of 46
   opinions contrary to those of 27
   rules of *see* penitentials
  Orthodox 35, 180, 193
  Protestant 113, 177
churches 179, 186, 195, 199, 213, 223,
   255, 281
Cicero 25
cinema ix *see also* films
Circe 19, 25, 140
circles 8, 155, 250
  magical 42, 138, 146, 153, 161, 177
  protective 8, 182
clairvoyants 208
Clark, Stuart 62
Clavicules of Solomon 221
Clement IX (Pope) 157
clothing 221

Cobham, Eleanor, Duchess of
   Gloucester 58
Coffin Texts 6–7, 8, 11
Cohn, Norman 120
Colchis 19
Coleridge, Samuel Taylor 206
Collet, Thomas 194
Colmar 123
Cologne 103, 112, 122, 127 8
colonialism ix, 235, 255
The Colour of Magic (film) 285
Columella 25
Combs, Holly Marie 276
commercial/financial matters 172–3,
   180, 183, 189, 193
communication 243–5, 250
communities 19, 104, 120, 122–3, 129,
   148, 166, 173–4, 193, 224, 226,
   228, 230, 232, 235, 240, 243–4,
   250, 257
  Christian 30, 50, 57, 76
  threats from within 93, 280
complexion 37
connectedness (of everything) 2
consciousness 251–3
conservatism 238
Constant, Alphonse Louis *see* Lévi,
   Éliphas
Constantinople 35
  Council of 27
consumerism 279, 286
cooking 135, 137, 138
Copenhagen 128
Coral gardens, the 235
Corby, Abbot of 55
Corinth, Lovis 163
Cornwall 177
Corvino, Nicola 169
cosmology 33, 43, 254
cosmos, the 30–1, 35, 36, 196
  conceptions of 2, 35, 42, 86 *see also*
   nature, understanding of
counter-culture 224
Counter-Reformation, the 65, 75, 83,
   104, 147
The Covenant (film) 286
The Craft (film) 271, 282, 284–5
Cranach the Younger, Lucas 139, 140
  Melancholia 140, 149
creation 7

Crépy, Jean
  A Description of the Witches' Assembly called
    the Sabbath 143
criminality 18, 22, 82, 88, 93, 99, 104–9,
    112, 114, 139, 145, 166, 172,
    193–4
Crowley, Aleister 213, 214, 217, 219
  The Book of the Law 213
  Magick in Theory and Practice 214
Crusades, the 71, 204
crystal balls 207
Culpepper, William 178
cults 244, 281
cultural phenomena vii
culture viii–xi, 28–9, 35, 96, 97, 136,
    139, 185, 187, 224, 228, 232,
    245, 248, 252–5, 257, 263
    see also counter-culture
  understanding 234, 242, 252
cuneiform 2–3
cunning-folk 70, 84, 166, 169, 176,
    190–4, 226
curanderos 190
Curry, Tim 285
curse-tablets 23
curses 4, 14–16, 20, 23
Cuyp, Benjamin 160

Dahl, Roald
  The Witches 271
Dalton, Michael 65
  The Country Justice 129
Damigeron 34
dance 152, 162
Dance of Death, the 140
Daniel of Morley 47
Dante 49
Danzig 194
Darwin, Charles 228, 232
  The Origin of Species 232
Darwinism 233
Dauphiné 98
Davis, Andrew Jackson 207
  The Principles of Nature, her Divine Revelation,
    and a Voice of Mankind 208
the dead 3, 11, 179, 187
  communing with 199
  raising 19
  realm of 19, 156
  spirits of 5, 156, 205

Dead Sea Scrolls, the 15
death 11, 14, 85, 156 *see also* the dead
  ·causing 27, 30, 224, 239 *see also*
    murder
  sentences of 107–8, 112–13, 167, 185
Defoe, Daniel
  A System of Magick 214
Deguileville, Guillaume de 55
  Pèlerinage de vie humaine 47–8, 55
Deir el-Medina (Egypt) 10
Del Rio, Martin 77–86, 126–7, 129,
    141, 146
  Disquisitiones magicae libri sex 77–80, 146
  Investigations into Magic 128
Delacroix, Eugène 163
demonologists 64, 67–8, 77, 80–7,
    92, 201
demonology 63, 64–5, 76–7, 81–7, 89,
    90, 91–2, 260, 271
  Catholic 80–4
  issues surrounding 77
  Protestant 80–4
  roots of 68
  systems of 67–8, 77, 83, 87, 90, 104
  works of x, 64–5, 74, 75–9, 115, 129,
    141, 149, 159, 276
demons 8, 26, 50, 62–3, 83, 91, 151,
    156, 260
  activity of 30, 38
  controlling/combatting 8, 50, 55,
    67, 280
  depictions of/ideas about 52, 56, 68,
    71, 146–7, 150–4
  exorcism/casting out of 26, 49, 82–3
    see exorcism
  as facilitators of magic 28, 38
  harm caused by 10–11, 72
  hierarchy of 68
  nature of 47, 50
  possession by 52, 62, 82, 130 *see also*
    possession
  power of 40, 48, 52, 57, 72
  relations/being in league with 15,
    30, 33, 40, 46, 47–50, 52–3,
    56, 59, 62, 69–71, 72, 75,
    77, 85, 89, 91, 108, 110,
    142, 182 *see also* women,
    and demons
  summoning/conjuring of 35, 47, 51,
    61, 158, 163

types of
  incubi 69
  Lamaštu 3
  succubi 69
and women *see* women, and demons
Dendera (Egypt) 9
Dendur (Egypt) 10
Denley, John 207
Denmark 98, 114, 184, 190
Denslow, William Wallace 266
depression 87
Descartes, René 86, 90
  Discourse on Method 86
désenvoûteurs 190
desire 49, 57, 146, 176 *see also*
  sex/sexual acts
  pursuit of viii
Devil, the 53, 56, 63–4, 67–8, 71, 78,
  83–4, 89, 91, 93–4, 97, 110,
  138, 153, 166, 170, 175, 199,
  227, 231
  association/pacts with 29, 63, 67–8,
  75, 79–80, 84–6, 91, 93–4, 97,
  124, 127, 134, 138, 141, 144,
  152, 184, 231
  depictions/images of 145, 148, 152–4,
  155, 158, 161
  ideas about 67, 91
  mark of 110, 114, 114
  minions of 104
  names for 182
  power from 84, 87
  worship of 72, 76, 124, 154, 217, 222,
  229–31, 254 *see also* satanism
Devon 200
Diana (goddess) 68
Diderot, Denis 231
Dijon 112
Dillingen 127
Dionysus 136
disease/illness 4, 10, 20, 104, 178, 185, 197
  causes of 14, 30, 192
  curing of/combatting 20, 24, 78,
  176–80, 183, 192, 197, 230
  see also healing
  protection from 28, 32
Disney 259, 267, 269
diviners/divination 5, 85, 206, 244
djed pillar 9
Dodona 20

dogmatism 95
Doherty, Shannon 276
domesticity 278–9
Dominican Republic 227
Donatino, Antonia 169
Dormiel 32
Dossi, Dosso
  Circe and her Lovers in a Landscape 140
Douai 77
Drage, William
  Daimonomageia 192
Dragon Rouge 184
dreams x, 199, 216, 275
  interpretation of 14, 35, 78
Dr Gardner's Museum of Magic and
  Superstition 224
drugs 214
druids, the 204
dualism 63–4, 243
Dürer, Albrecht 136, 138, 222
  Freiburg drawings 136
  Witch Riding Backwards on a Goat 136
  workshop of 138
Durkheim, Émile 234
  *The Elementary Forms of the Religious
  Life* 234

Earth, the 32, 47
economics 2, 97, 97, 104, 105, 261 *see also*
  commercial/financial matters
Edinburgh 113
education 106, 115, 192, 284–5
Egypt 5, 20–1, 28, 204–5, 209, 216
  culture/ideas of 7, 10, 14, 41, 196,
  204–5, 211–12
  magic in 5–12, 24
  religion in 7, 10–11, 209–10, 213
Eichstätt 99, 102
Eiffel 111, 117
Eimmart the Younger, Georg
  Christoph 158
Eleazar 12
elements, the 30
Elias (biblical figure) 205
Elizabeth I (Queen of England) 78,
  107–8, 165
Ellwangen (imperial abbey) 99, 102
emotions x, 5, 38, 200
Encausse, Gérard 215, 222
  Traité méthodique de magie practique 215

Encyclopédie, the 231
Engelbrecht, Martin 158, 160
England 47, 58, 70, 80, 83, 108, 176,
    182, 191, 199, 212, 235
  Civil War 64, 104
  culture/ideas of 258, 284
  magic in 53, 179–82, 200, 219, 221,
    248–9, 251–2
  people of/from 62, 65, 70, 149, 190, 229
  treatment of witches in vii, 65, 69, 87,
    96–7, 107–8, 113–14, 115,
    117–18, 121, 128–30, 132,
    165–8, 193
'enlightenment' 91, 132, 163, 201, 257
Enlightenment, the 195, 198, 201,
    221–3, 256
Enoch (biblical figure) 196, 205
environment, the x, 99, 225
Ephesia grammata 21
Ephesus 26
Ephrata 201
equality 212, 222
equilibrium/balance 5
The Equinox 213
Ergersheim 166
Erik the Red 250
erotic, the 20, 57, 145
Escape to Witch Mountain (film) 270
Esoteric Buddhism 210
Espenson, Jane 283
Essex 65, 114, 117, 129–30, 167
Estonia 94, 98
ethics 17, 256
ethnocentricity 232
ethnography 246–8, 249, 257
Euclid
  Elements 33
Europe 2, 43, 91, 94–8, 105, 116,
    118–19, 128–9, 183, 194–6,
    215, 225, 228, 230
  central ix
  colonies of 97, 116, 118–19, 188,
    195, 218 *see also* colonialism
  culture/traditions of ix, 248, 252,
    256, 286
  eastern 132, 161, 210
  northern 151
  people of/from 86, 164
  western ix, 29, 34–5, 131, 206, 228,
    246, 257, 260

Evans-Pritchard, Sir Edward Evans
    238–42, 247–8, 251–2, 256
  *Witchcraft, Oracles and Magic Among the
    Azande* 238
Evax 34
everyday life 10
  magic and 2, 15, 31, 172, 180
evil 3–4, 30, 33, 63, 132, 165, 199,
    202, 237, 264, 286
  doing of 30, 64, 68, 94
  ideas about/perceptions of 33, 67, 237
'evil eye', the 3, 12
  casting 15, 30
  protection against/warding off of 12,
    14–15
execution 27, 56, 58, 80, 85, 94–5, 97,
    111, 132, 168, 185 *see also*
    witches, execution of
exorcism 5, 26, 48–9, 82–3, 126, 130,
    193, 255
exorcists 5, 14, 193
exotic, the 39, 147
experience 153, 245, 247, 250, 257, 277
  spiritual 45, 50, 51
eye of Horus, the 9
Eymeric, Nicholas 70
  Directorum Inquisitorum 78

fairies 169, 191
fairy tales 264, 266–7, 271
Faithorne, William 158
familiars 36, 37, 94, 108, 114, 129
family 272
fantasy 151
Farr, Florence 212, 216
Farrar, Janet 221
Faust 184
Favret-Saada, Jeanne 246–7, 249
fear 5, 11, 108
  of magic 29, 169, 224 *see also* magic,
    attitudes towards
feminism 224–5, 263, 266, 277–9, 284
Ferrell, Will 270
Ficino, Marsilio 60, 196
  Corpus hermeticum 196
figurines 4, 8, 10, 15, 20
Filmer, Sir Robert 88
  *An Advertisement to the Jury-Men of England
    touching Witches* 89
  Patriarcha 88

Finland 94–7, 120, 168, 179
  Saami people of 188
Finnmark 96–7, 105
Flade, Dietrich 128, 143
Flanders 96, 101
Florence 59, 155
folklore 218, 263
Folklore Centre of Superstition and
    Witchcraft 220
forbidden/taboo, the 17–18, 33
foreign, the 24, 35, 189–91
Förner, Friedrich 100
Forte, Meyer 233
Fournival, Richard de 60
Fox, Kate 209
Fox, Maggie 209
Francavilla 169
France 58, 71, 73, 76, 80, 91, 95, 100,
        112–13, 126, 143–4, 193, 246–7
  culture/ideas of 231, 263
  Freemasonry in 204, 205, 209, 215
  and magic 53, 177, 180, 184, 187,
        190, 206, 206–7
  people of/from 57, 62, 120, 190, 207,
        224, 229
  revolution in *see* French Revolution
  treatment of witches in 96–100,
        112–13, 117, 121, 125, 132,
        166, 175
Franche-Comté 100, 113
Francken II, Franz 141, 145–51,
        156, 160
Franco-Prussian War 187
Franconia 96, 99, 100, 131
Frank, Hans 137
Frankel, Cyril
  The Witches 271
Frankfurt 73
Fraternitas Rosae Crucis 208
fraud 23, 189, 219, 255
Frazer, Sir James 232–7, 245, 253
  The Golden Bough 232
Freemasonry 204–6, 208–13, 214
French Guyana 230, 254
French Revolution, the 205
Frisius, Paulus
  The Devil's Hoodwink 137
Fuggers, the 127
Fulda 102
functionalism 228, 235–6, 242–3, 257

'Furious Horde', the 135, 136
Fuseli, Henry 163

Gaar, Georg 91
Gabrielsdotter, Kirstin 171
Gadbury, John 202
Gage, Matilda Joslyn 267
  Woman, Church, and State 267
Gaiman, Neil 271
  Stardust 271
Ganell, Berengario
  Summa sacre magice 60
Gardner, Gerald 218–19, 220, 224
  High Magic's Aid 219
  Witchcraft Today 221
Gardnerianism 221, 224–5
Garland, Judy 264
Gatlinburg (Tennessee) 224
Gébelin, Antoine Court de 209
Geiler, Johann 137
Gell, Alfred 257
gender viii, 136, 171, 187, 225, 250, 260,
        281, 286 *see also* witches, and
        gender
Geneva 143
Gennep, Arnold van 244
geography viii, 97, 106, 118, 182–3
Georgia 19
Géraud, Hugues, Bishop of Cahors 54
Germanicus 24
Germantown (Pennsylvania) 201
Germany ix, 58, 67, 73, 82–3, 88, 91, 95,
        111, 134, 139, 141, 152, 158,
        176, 181, 216
  culture/ideas of 206, 231
  Freemasonry in 216
  magic in 187, 210, 214–16
  people of/from 24, 88, 90, 117, 127,
        135, 137, 157, 158, 166, 178,
        187, 189, 196
  treatment of witches in 93, 96, 97, 111,
        117 18, 125, 128, 132, 193
Germany Theosophical Society, the 215
Gerolstein 103
Gheyn II, Jacques de 138, 141, 148,
        153–4
  The Parable of the Devil Sowing Seeds 149
  Preparation for a Witches' Sabbath 144,
        148, 150, 152, 154
  Witches in a Cellar 150

ghosts 10–11, 15, 19–20, 170, 191, 201, 216
Gibson, Marion 261
Gillot, Claude 162–3
　Errant pendant la nuit dans un lieu solitaire 162
　Est-ce enchantement, est-ce une illusion? 163
Gillray, James 206
Glanvill, Joseph
　Saducismus triumphatus 89, 158, 160
Glycas, Michael 79
God (Judaeo-Christian) 13, 15, 28, 38, 42, 44, 46, 52, 57, 63–4, 68–9, 79, 83, 85–6, 165, 192–3, 199, 230, 281
　calling upon 31, 40, 55, 192 *see also* prayers/requests
　denial of 91
　opposition to/enemies of 95, 104
　things derived from/ascribed to 45
gods, the 1, 4, 9, 12, 15, 19, 28, 68
goēs/goēteia 18
Goethe, Johann Wolfgang von
　Faust 231
Goldschmidt, Peter
　The Defender of Depraved Witches and Sorcerers 159
Gollion 118
Goltzius, Hendrik 149
Gombal, Cándida 182
Gonzaga, Francesco, Marquis of Mantua 61
goodness 264, 286
Goodwin children, the 131
Goya, Francisco 163
　Capricho 163
　The Sleep of Reason 149, 163
Grand Grimoire 184
Grand Guignol 25
Grandier, Urbain 126
Gratian 48
Graz 77
Great Copt, the 205–6
Greca, Felicità 190
Greece (ancient) viii, 34, 41
　culture/ideas of 17–20, 24, 28, 33–5, 41, 45, 55, 59, 173, 196, 206
　deities of 27
　magic in 17–23, 24, 58
　society of 19, 22

Greenland 250
Greenwood, Susan 251–3
Grenoble 112
Grillandus, Paulus
　Tractatus de hereticis et sortilegiis 74
Grimoire du Pape Honorius 184
Grüninger, Johann 137
The Guardian 227, 255
Guazzo, Maria
　Compendium maleficarum 145
Gui, Bernard 70
　Practica inquisitionis heretice pravitatis 70
Guido von List Society 216
Gundissalinus, Dominicus
　De divisione philosophiae 37
Gunter, Anne 130
gynocide 225
gypsies 118, 189

Haarlem 149
Habsburg Kingdoms 101, 115, 132, 146
The Hague 148
Hainault 101
Haiti 227
Haldane, Isobel 176
Halle
　University of 91
Halloween 222, 266, 267, 269–70, 272, 275–7
Halloweentown (television series) 270
Hamburg 59
Hamilton, Margaret 265
Hamnett, Nina 217
　The Laughing Torso 217
Hannigan, Alison 282
Hansel and Gretel 262, 268, 272, 282
Hansen, Joseph 119
harm 3–4, 9, 72 *see also* pain
　seeking to cause viii, 13, 24, 27, 31, 55, 78, 151
Harry Potter (films) 258, 259, 260, 268, 269, 271–2, 284
　Harry Potter and the Philosopher's Stone 260
Harsnett, Samuel 83
hartumím 8
Harz mountains 152
Hathaway, Richard 168
Haussibut 56
Head, Anthony 282
healers 21, 178, 254

healing 4, 9, 21, 78, 166–7, 173–5, 176–7, 181, 185, 198, 230, 245, 256
health viii, 173–4
heathens 29, 228, 249, 259
Hecate 260
Heer, Michael 151
Heer, Michael and Matthäus Merian (the elder)
Zauberey 93
heka 6–8, 11–12
Hekate 19
Hela 194
Helios 45
Hell 47, 57, 154
Hendircksz, Pieter 160
Henry IV (King of France) 143–4
Henry VI (King of England) 58
Henry VIII (King of England) 107, 165
herbalists 118, 193
herbs 5, 15, 19, 30–1, 38, 178, 180, 190, 197 *see also* plants
Herder, Johann Gottfried 231
heresy 52–3, 58, 70, 76, 80, 109, 138, 140
Hermes (god) 20, 196, 230
Hermes Trimegistus 34, 41, 196
Hermetic Brotherhood of Luxor 214
The Hermetic Order of the Golden Dawn 211, 214
hermeticism 196, 209 10, 214 15 *see also* magic, types of, Hermetic
Herrad of Landsberg 36
Hortus deliciarum 36
Hertfordshire 117, 221
Hesiod 19
Hesse 102, 137
van der Heyden, Pieter 140
St James and the Magician Hermogenes 140
Hezekiah (King) 16
hieroglyphs 5, 9
Hispaniola 227
historians 97, 218, 246, 263, 267
historiography 120
history xi, 62, 262
Hittites, the 2
hoaratu 254
Hockley, Frederick 207, 211–12
Hocus Pocus (film) 269
Hohenburg Abbey, Alsace 36
holem 14
holism 251

Holland, Henry
A Treatise against Witchcraft 65
Hollstein 159
Holy Land, the 71, 204
Holy Roman Empire viii, 95, 100, 106, 127, 128, 131
Imperial Aulic Council 112, 125, 131
Imperial Chamber Court 125, 131
treatment of witches in 93, 105, 111, 114, 117, 121, 166
Homer 19
Odyssey 19
de Hooghe, Romeyn 158, 160
Hopkins, Matthew 114
Horace 25, 155
Epodes 25
Satires 25
Horapollo
Hieroglyphica 6
Horus (god) 213
human beings 5, 36, 42, 48, 50, 52, 60, 63, 70, 73, 82, 90, 150, 153, 164, 186, 227, 229, 235, 242–3, 251–2, 257, 265
affairs of 91
bodies of 198–9
and demons *see* demons, relations/being in league with
and the gods *see under* gods
and nature *see under* nature
nature of 163
psyche of viii, 164
relationships between viii, 234, 244, 253 4
temptation of 69
transformation of 77, 155
humanism 136, 228
humanities 246
humanity ix, 231–2, 243, 257, 284
Humperdinck, Engelbert 262
Hungary 97–8, 120, 132, 161, 191
Hunsrück 121
Hunt, Richard 65
Huntingdonshire 130
hymns 7
hypnotism 216

I Married a Witch (film) 268–9, 270, 272, 273
Iamblichus 206

Iamneia 15
Iao 24
Iceland 98, 249
ideology viii
illusion 37, 77, 162, 189, 197
Illustrated, the x *Illustrate* 7
image 214, 221
images xi, 15, 37, 39, 54, 57–8, 115,
        140–1, 148–9, 163, 233, 266,
        274, 277 *see also* media, visual
imprisonment 107, 108, 119, 124,
        125, 130
incantatores 30
incense 39
India ix, 41, 221
individuals vii, 1, 6, 23, 99, 104, 122,
        124, 139, 151, 198, 238–9,
        257, 284
information 24, 126
initiation 219, 226
The Initiation of Sarah (film) 286
Innocent VIII (Pope) 73
    Summis desiderantes affectibus 73
Innsbruck 74
inquisitions 59, 70, 109, 112,
        119–20, 184
    against the Cathars 53
    Florentine 59
    Italian 172, 184, 197
    Portugese 167, 184
    Spanish 75, 167–8, 176, 182, 184, 189
inquisitors 60, 70–1, 72, 109–10, 114
inspiration 36
Institoris, Henry 64, 72, 74, 129
    Malleus maleficarum 64, 72–3, 77,
        81–2, 87
intellectuals and scholars 28, 33–4, 60,
        64, 69, 86, 91, 91–2, 198,
        253, 256
Iraq 2
Ireland 96, 98, 180
Irenaeus 26
irrationality 1, 163, 241, 250, 251, 253
    see also rationality
Isaac, Jasper 147
Isabella (Archduchess of the Spanish
        Netherlands) 146
Isidore of Seville
    Etymologiae 30
Isis (god) 9

Islam 43, 96
    and magic 33, 40, 182
Isle of Man 220, 224
Israel-Judaea-Palestine 12, 16, 24 *see also*
        Palestine
Italy ix, 25, 44, 58, 60, 75, 91, 105, 109,
        167, 169, 180, 184, 189, 192
        see also inquistions, Italian
    culture/ideas of 262
    magic in 216, 219
    people of/from 169, 196

Jack's Wife (film) 270
James VI (of Scotland) and I (of England)
        (King) 66, 108
    Daemonologie 66
Jerusalem 71
Jesuits 6, 77, 79, 88, 91, 100, 106, 126–7,
        130, 146, 179, 228, 231
Jesus 15, 28, 82,
jewellery 37 *see also* amulets
Jewish society 12, 13–15
Jews viii, 13, 15, 22, 26, 33–4, 76, 182,
        188, 211
John XXII (Pope) 52–3, 71
    Super illius specula 71
John of Morigny 59
    Liber florum celestis doctrine 46
John of Salisbury
    Policraticus 57
John of Seville 40
Jones, Diana Wynne
    Witch Week 259
Joshua 12
Jourdemayne, Margery 58
Judaism 13, 42 *see also* Jewish society
        and Jews
    and magic 12, 13–17, 25, 32–3, 43,
        45, 65, 195, 210
judges 73, 82, 92, 105, 112–13, 123
Jülich 144
Julius Caesar 25
Jung, Carl Gustav 237
Justin Martyr 26
Juvenal 25, 155

Kaadmau 39
Kabbalah 196, 201, 201, 205, 209,
        213, 215
Kail 103

kanaimà 254
Kant, Immanuel 199
Karlsen, Carol 264
karowara 254
kaššapu/kaššaptu 3
Keats, John 206
Kelpius, Johannes 201
Kent 87–8, 117, 223
khartum 14
khober 14
Kidman, Nicole 270, 283
Kieckhefer, Richard 120
Kircher, Athanasius 6
Kissling, George 166
kloge folk 190
Kluckhohn, Clyde 237
    Navajo Witchcraft 237
Knights Templar, the 71
knowledge 40, 42–3, 47–8, 79, 82,
        170–1, 174, 185, 188, 190, 193,
        203, 234, 237, 239, 247
    esoteric 138, 201, 203, 206, 210, 215,
        218, 244
    magic as a branch of 33, 35, 37,
        40, 237
    practical 213
    quest for 34, 61, 195
Koran, the 182
Kress, Georg 141
Kummer, Siegfried Adolf 216
Küsel, Melchior 158, 159
Kwakiutl 256
Kyeser, Konrad
    Bellifortis 50
Kyteler, Lady Alice 56

La chanson de Maugis d'Aigremont 51
La Fontaine, Jean 255
Lake, Veronica 269
Lambe, Elizabeth 173
lamina/lamellae 21, 24
Lamothe-Langon, Étienne-Léon 119–20
Lancaster 129
Lancre, Pierre de 65, 76–7, 143, 144
    L'incrédulité et mécréance du sortilège 65
    *Tableau de l'inconstancie des mauvais anges
        et demons* 65, 76
Landis, John 277
landscape 250
language 97, 126, 134

spoken 7, 11, 14, 123 *see also* words
translation of 33–5, 37–8, 40–1, 47,
        54, 59, 62, 88, 89, 90, 92, 128,
        137, 142, 146, 149, 158, 159,
        160, 162, 203, 206, 207, 212,
        228, 235, 241
vernacular 34, 93, 122, 183
written 6, 9–11
languages 77, 93
    Arabic 32–5, 35–6, 41, 43, 46, 47, 182
    Aramaic 15
    Castilian 34
    Coptic 28
    Demotic 6
    Dutch 90, 128, 160
    Egyptian 28
    English 34, 78, 87–8, 90, 128, 160,
        162, 190, 203, 214
    French 34, 87, 162
    Gaelic Irish 62
    German 34, 75, 88, 90, 91, 93, 96, 99,
        111, 134, 141, 157, 158, 162
    Greek 6, 17–18, 23, 28, 40, 45, 206
    Hebrew 8, 14–15, 28, 33, 34, 45, 81,
        92, 182
    Hungarian 62
    Italian 34
    Latin 24–5, 33–5, 38–9, 40–1, 50, 72,
        79, 87, 119, 141, 183
    Zande 238
lapidaries 34
Lapidario 34
Larner, Christian 66
law 2, 56, 67, 75, 78, 82, 89, 91, 100,
        106, 109, 114–16, 137, 149,
        165, 174, 178, 187, 189, 193,
        194, 213, 242 *see also* criminality
        and judges *and* legislation
    codes of 106–9, 115
        Constitutio criminalis Carolina (Holy
            Roman Empire) 106–7
        Fraudulent Mediums Act (1951) 219
        Napoleonic 193
        Witchcraft Act (Scotland, 1563) 166
        Witchcraft and Conjuration Act
            (England, 1542) 107–8, 165
        Witchcraft and Conjuration Act
            (England, 1563) 165, 171
        Witchcraft and Conjuration Act
            (England, 1736) 219

law (*cont.*)
    courts of 53, 57, 76, 89, 104, 106,
        109–13, 115–16, 117, 125,
        131, 132, 143, 167, 171
        rulings of 119–21, 168
    natural 233
    processes of the 86, 89, 91, 106–7,
        115–19, 118, 161, 193
    Roman 110
'Law of Contagion' 233
'Law of Similarity' 233
'Law of Sympathy' 233
Leek, Sybil 222–4
legal clerks 115, 122
legislation 22, 30
Leiden 149
    University of 149
Leipzig University 82
Leland, Charles Godfrey 219
    Aradia, or the Gospel of the Witches
        219, 221
Lemgo 95, 103, 124
    'black book' of 124
Le Normand, Mademoiselle 207
Leo XIII (Pope) 70
Leopold Wilhelm (Archduke of the
        Spanish Netherlands) 147
Levack, Brian P. 95, 97
Levi (biblical figure) 12, 216
Lévi, Éliphas 208, 210, 212–13, 221
    Dogme et ritual de la haute magie 209, 212
Lévi-Bruhl, Lucien 234, 252
    How Natives Think 234
Lévi-Strauss, Claude 242–3, 245, 251
    Mythologiques 243
    von der Leyen, Carl Caspar 131
Liber Almandal 41
Liber de essentia spirituum 41, 45
Liber iuratus 47
Liber munditie et abstinentie 45
Liber Razielis 35, 44
Liber Sameyn 45
Liber de septem figuris septem planetarum 40
liberal arts, the 36, 44
Libro de astromagia 34
Libro de las formas et las ymagenes 4
Liège 77
life 10, 199, 238 *see also* the living
Ligozzi, Jacopo 156
Lilith 260

Lilly, William 202
liminality 243–5
'limited good' 173–4
Lind, Maria Persdotter 188
Lippe 103, 124
List, Guido von 216
literacy 7, 15, 55, 115, 164, 173, 178,
        191–2, 195
literature 2, 6, 17, 19, 24, 51–2, 60, 63,
        144, 180, 183, 195, 214, 262
Little, Robert Wentworth 210
'Little Ice Age', the 97, 104
Little Witches (film) 285
the living 3
    lives of 5
    relations with the dead 3
    souls of 24
Livonia 98
local areas 9
Locatelli, Andrea 156
locating objects 85
locations 179
Lodève, Bishop of 70
London 95, 114, 128, 145, 170, 172,
        205–7, 211, 212, 221, 251, 254
    Bishop of 83
    Grand Lodge in 204, 205
    Isis-Urania temple 211
    National Gallery 155
London Medical Papyrus 9
London School of Economics 242
Long Island 224
Lorraine, Duchy of 96, 100, 113, 125,
        159, 166
lottery, the 172
Louis XIII (King of France) 143
Louis XIV (King of France) 193
Louvain 77
love 49, 57, 171, 185–6, 272 *see also*
        magic, types of, love
Lucan 25
    Pharsalia 25
luck
    bad 5
    good 174, 183, 220
Luhrmann, Tanya 248–9, 251
    *Persuasions of the Witch's Craft: Ritual
        Magic in Contemporary
        England* 249
lunulae 9

Luther, Martin 83–4
Lutz, Rheinhard 137
Luxembourg 96, 101, 104, 109, 113, 121, 125
Luyken, Caspar 158
Lwow 143

Mackenzie, Kenneth 210
Madrid 95
mageia 18, 19, 21
magi 23
magic *see also* everyday life, magic in
    attitudes towards 29–30, 41, 50, 53, 54, 61, 108, 132, 138, 155, 165–7, 216, 224, 226, 227–8, 228, 266–7 *see also under* magical practices *and* magicians/ magical practioners
    belief in 14, 16, 23, 86–9, 99, 253, 277
    conceptions/perceptions of 21, 28, 56, 126, 217, 222, 223, 243, 248, 250, 261
    defence of 59
    definitions of 1, 17, 29–30, 107, 236
    expertise/literacy in 11
    as a fluid category 1, 256
    The Magic Square of Mercury 40
    origins of viii, 240
    purpose of 15, 34, 37, 43, 170–2, 195, 207, 234–43, 246, 250–1
    as a reflection of broader society x, 235–6, 242, 251, 257
    as shaped by broader society ix, 235–6, 242, 251, 257
    systems of belief in 95
    types of 13, 77, 183
        angel 43–4, 45, 50, 205
        benevolent 93
        black 138, 209, 212, 217, 222–3, 248
        cabalistical 203
        ceremonial 203, 212, 216, 219
        charm-writing 190
        defensive 169
        demonic 48–50, 71, 78, 91 *see also* demonologists *and* demonology *and* witchcraft, demonic
        divining 14, 17, 35, 46, 78, 146, 175, 189, 244 *see also* diviners/ divination
        domestic 188

enchanting 7, 14
exorcizing 7, 14, 48–9, 181, 193, 255, 283 *see also* exorcism *and* exorcists
fertility 10, 19, 32–3, 35, 218–20, 225
folk ix, 179, 188, 190, 263
garden 236
geomancy 196
harmful 3–4, 13, 21, 23, 24, 28, 30, 63, 78, 107–8, 112, 120, 134, 166, 168, 169, 170, 188, 262 *see also* curses *and* harm *and* disease/illness *and* witches, harm caused by
    countering/undoing 23, 24, 28, 30, 78, 166, 169 *see also* magic, types of, defensive
healing 4, 9, 17, 78, 166–7, 176–9, 181, 256
Hermetic 41, 60, 196–7, 209
hostile 17 *see also* magic, types of, harmful
hunting 233
idolatry 146
image 39, 39–1 *see also* images
invocation 19, 39, 54, 146, 156–7, 160, 163, 207
learned 33, 35, 36, 37, 41, 49, 52, 54, 55, 60, 183
love 10, 16, 17, 20, 56–7, 146, 171, 176, 180, 185, 190, 281
maleficent/malevolent 80, 93–5, 166
metamorphosis 146
modern 218, 225–6
natural 37–8, 60, 77, 93, 203
necromancy 14, 17, 18, 20, 37, 46, 47–51, 56, 58, 59, 61, 107, 146, 157, 166, *see also* necromancers
popular 84, 166–83, 184, 187, 190, 194, 215 *see also under* everyday life *and* magical practices, performable by everyone
protective 5–7, 8, 13–16, 17, 38, 54, 169, 175, 182–3, 185–6, 190, 197, 239–40 *see also* amulets, protective *and* circles, protective
ritual 60, 158, 203–4, 208, 210, 214, 220, 226, 248–9

Index

magic (*cont.*)
    Solomonic 60
    soothsaying 16, 107–8, 186
    sorcery 26, 30, 50, 52–6, 58, 59,
          69, 93, 97, 107, 108, 244,
          249, 254
    summoning/conjuring 8, 16, 18,
          26, 35, 42, 47, 61, 120, 197,
    sympathetic 3, 174–7, 188 *see also*
          transference
    talismanic 215
    theft 190
    treasure/money-related 172–3,
          184, 189–90
    weather 75
magical ideas/thinking 233, 236,
          247, 257
magical knowledge viii, 15, 31, 184, 186
    see also knowledge
magical places 52–3, 245–6
magical power of 10–11, 30–1, 41–2, 44,
          58, 61, 97, 184, 216, 276, 280
magical practices v–vi, 18, 20, 33, 97,
          134, 149, 157, 173, 195, 199,
          204–5, 207, 209, 227, 234,
          245–7 *see also* occult practices
    basis of 134, 234
    condemnation of/attempts to
          repress 18, 20–2, 26–8, 30–1,
          56, 61, 64, 68, 74, 80, 101, 140,
          169, 184, 249, 273 *see also*
          forbidden/taboo, the *and*
          legislation, against magic *and*
          magicians/magical
          practitioners, prosecution of *and*
          trials *and under* witches
    constituent parts of 3
    as illicit activities 40–1, 44, 49, 52, 56,
          80, 82–3, 184, 192, 254
    instructions for carrying out 16, 18,
          38, 41, 64, 179–80, 211, 217
    items used as part of 159, 161, 174,
          202 *see also* objects
    as licit activites 32, 41–2, 49, 82, 216
    nature of 7, 9–10, 34, 140, 163–4,
          168–70, 174, 179–82, 186, 195,
          205, 207, 213, 224, 232–3, 246
    performable by anyone 31, 87, 174,
          176–8, 181, 186, 232

    reasons for carrying out 23, 33, 40, 87,
          168, 170–81, 186, 191–5,
          232–3, 246
    types of 167–8, 170, 179
        bewitching 280
        charms/incantations/spells/
            prescriptions 3, 5–6, 8, 11, 17,
            264, 276
        encircling/circumambulation 179
        sticking pins vii, 15, 176 *see also*
            voodoo
        unwitching 165, 247–8
magical texts 7, 32–4, 36, 38, 40, 41, 42,
          59–60, 134, 183, 207, 217–18
          see also magical practices,
          instructions for carrying out *and*
          occult, the, texts of
    acceptability of 41, 58
    appeal of 44
    circulation of 31, 196
    content of 49
    interest in 35, 205, 217
    nature of 2, 35, 184
    presentation of magic in 36
    reading of 208
    types of 183
        angel magic 43, 44
        execration 8
        Hermetic 41
        Himmelsbriefe 187
        learned magic 41, 52, 55, 58
        Lettres du Ciel 187
        natural magic 37
        necromantic 46
        Solomonic 41
        spell books 184
        svartboks (black books) 184
        written charms 183
magicians/magical practitioners 10, 93,
          108, 166, 180, 185, 194, 254
          see also 'cunning-folk' *and*
          witches *and* wizards
    actions/activities of 54, 60, 171,
          247, 260
    attitudes towards 14, 23, 26, 31, 56,
          75, 80, 194, 220 *see also* magical
          practices, condemnation of/
          attempts to repress *and under*
          witches

background/identity of 50, 56, 174, 191, 215, 220, 241, 260, 275, 277–8, 280
consulting/seeking assistance from 165–6
depictions of 138, 155, 158, 261
descriptions/perceptions of 18, 28, 56, 104, 126, 217, 222, 223, 248, 250 *see also* witches, perceptions of
expectations of 18
female 19, 25, 28, 56, 60, 69, 73, 75, 118, 135–7, 138, 144, 146, 150, 152, 154, 156, 159, 169, 171, 178, 182, 185, 205, 210, 212, 221, 225, 239, 258, 261, 264, 267, 277, 279, 282, 284 *see also* witches
fraternities of 203, 204, 208, 211, 214, 226
fraudulent *see* fraud
instructions to/for 42
itinerant 21
male 185–6, 261, 264
number of 226
powers of 29–30, 79
'professional' 7, 19, 24, 193–4, 220
prosecution of 57–8, 71, 94, 165, 168, 172–4 *see also* witches, prosecution of
protection from/countering 15, 174
punishment of 27, 30, 138, 165–6, 227 *see also* execution *and* legislation, against magic *and* witches, punishment of
and spirits 45
training of 203, 260, 284–5
types of 13, 70, 86, 89, 162, 189, 191, 254
Mainz 77, 103
Makushi, the 254
mal d'arco 179
mala noche 171
Maldonado 126
malefici 30
maleficia 93, 124
maleficium 69, 72, 76, 79, 85, 94–5, 105, 107–8, 120, 126, 167
Malinowski, Bronislaw 235, 237–8, 242, 245, 251

Argonauts of the Western Pacific 236
Coral Gardens and their Magic 236
'Magic, Science and Religion' 236
Manderscheid 103
manheneiminali 254
Manichaeism 64
Maqlû 4
Marburg 137
Marlowe, Thomas
Dr Faustus 159 *see also* Faust
Marrett, Robert Ranulph 232
marriage 57, 84, 171, 268–9, 277, 279
Marseille 204
Martello, Leo 225
Martinist Order 215–16
marvels 37, 40, 48–9 see also *miracula and* wonders
masculinity 50, 95, 185
Maslama al Majrītī 36
maš-maš 5
material world, the 69, 83, 90, 91
materialism 90
mathematics 33
Mather, Cotton 90, 170
Christian Philosopher: a Collection of the Best Discoveries in Nature . . . 90
Memorable Providences, relating to Witchcrafts and Possessions 89
Wonders of the Invisible World 89
Mathers, Moina 211, 212
Mathers, Samuel Liddel 211
Maurice of Nassau 148
Mauss, Marcel 234
A General Theory of Magic 234
Maxwell-Stuart, Peter viii–x
Mazzolini da Prierio, Silvestro
Strigimagarum demonumque mirandis 74
mechanical philosophy, the 86, 89, 91
Mecklenburg-Schwerin 103, 104
Medea 19, 25, 140
media 133, 221–4, 255, 262
printed 126–9, 134, 139, 140, 142–8, 215–16 *see also* literature
sermons 106, 124, 137
visual x, 134–5, 140, 141, 143, 146, 149, 150, 153, 157, 158, 160, 161, 256, 262
film 223, 258–71, 272, 280–6
television 258, 261, 263–4, 267–86

medicine 1, 10, 87, 165, 192, 264
  and magic 10, 18, 33, 180, 184, 197
  practitioners of 34, 183, 190, 193, 200
    see also midwives/midwifery
  works of 7, 38, 66
meditation 216
Mediterranean area 25, 169–70, 180,
    184, 185–6, 191
mekashef 14
melancholy 139, 149 *see* depression
Melancholy (allegorical figure) 139, 140
Memphis (Egypt) 6
men 71, 81, 117, 138, 159, 171, 185,
    187, 240, 250, 260 *see also*
    magicians/magical
    practitioners, male *and*
    masculinity
  and women 55–6, 135, 187, 279, 281
Men-a-Toll stones 177
mental health 95–6, 123, 210 *see also*
    depression *and* melancholy
me'onen 14
Mercurii, the 207
Merian, Matthäus (the elder) 151–4, 162
Mergentheim 103
Merlin 271
Meroe 140
Mesmer, Franz Anton 198–9, 202, 206
Mesopotamia 2–5, 11, 12, 14, 20, 41
  magic in 3, 7, 24
Metaphysische Rundschau 213
mezuzah 182
Michelet, Jules
  La sorcière 218
Middle East, the 13, 20, 33, 208
Midelfort, H. C. Erik 95
midwives/midwifery 185
Milano, Alyssa 276
Miller, William 207
Minden 95
mines 186–7
miracula 25, 83–4
misogyny 73, 225
missionaries 195, 228
Mnesimakhos 20
Molitor, Ulrich 75, 137
  De lamiis et phitonicis mulieribus 75
  On Female Witches and Diviners 137
Molsheim 124
Momba the Witch 266

monks 47, 61
  Barnabites 145
  Capuchins 192
  Dominicans 70–1, 73, 109
  Franciscans 109, 137, 229
monotheism 232
monsters 52, 151–2
Monteche, Gabriel 167
Monter, William 95
Montgomery, Elizabeth 268, 272
Montolmo, Antonio de
  De occultis et manifestis 60
Montpellier
  University of 70
monuments and mounds 179, 250–6
Moore's Almanac 202
morality 51, 81, 105, 126, 139, 153
    see also virtue
Moravia 101
More, Henry 90
morisca 182, 189
Morning Post, the 186
Mors anime 47
Moselle 121
Moses 8, 12, 14, 16
mummies 9
Munich 128, 145
Münster 105
murder 24, 27, 59, 166, 229
Murer, Christoph 160
Murphy, Jill 259
  Worst Witch (books) 259
Murray, Margaret 218
  The God of the Witches 218
  The Witch Cult in Western Europe 218
Museum of Witchcraft (Bourton-on-the-
    Water) 224–5
Museum of Witchcraft (Isle of
    Man) 223–4
Muslims viii, 33–4, 182 *see also* Islam
mysticism ix, 44, 200, 203–4, 206–11,
    213, 215–16, 252, 286
myth 2, 214, 242, 245, 253
  Norse 244–5

names 11, 16, 24, 32, 47 *see also*
    words
Namur 101
Napoleon 193, 207
Napoletano, Filippo 156

National Laboratory of Psychical
    Research 217
natural disasters 85
natural materials 39, 55
natural philosophy 5, 36, 60, 89 *see also*
    science
natural powers 54
nature 38, 150, 164, 197, 207, 221, 248,
    281 *see also* natural materials
  manipulation of 34, 38, 60, 78
  operation of 21, 34, 62, 233
  relation of human beings to 35, 60,
    78, 250
  understanding of vii, 35, 37, 42, 48,
    79, 89, 216, 253 *see also* natural
    philosophy *and* science
Navajo, the 237–8
Navarre 100, 113
Ndembu, the 243–5
necromancers 18, 20, 48–9
  female 156, 163
Neill, John R. 266
Neoplatonism 197–9, 202, 206, 211
Nero (Emperor) 25
Netherlands, the 80, 90, 96, 98, 101,
    109, 127, 140, 141, 146. 147,
    175, 182 *see also* Spanish
    Netherlands
  people from 89, 139, 144, 147, 157
  treatment of witches in 97, 174, 194
New Forest (England) 219
New York (city) 225
New York (state) 209, 210
News from Scotland 66
Newton, Isaac 90, 92, 198
Nicholson, Jack 280
Nider, Johannes 72
  Formicarius 72
Night of the Eagle 268–9
Nigidius Figulus 26
Nile, the 9
'Nine-Herbs Charm' (manuscript) 29
non-human entities 1, 5, 253–4
  action of 14, 16
Normandy 94, 98, 186, 246
North America 188
  indigenous people of 229–30, 237–8,
    242, 255
North Carolina 229
North Cray (Kent) 223

North Moreton 130
Norway 96–7
Nottingham 130
Novak, Kim 269
Nowell, Roger 129
nudity 140, 221, 222
Nuremberg 132, 139, 152

objects 8, 12, 13, 20, 21, 24, 26, 29, 172,
    175–6 *see also* rituals, objects
    used in
  enchantment of 32
  everyday 32
  inanimate 253
  magical 40, 53, 171, 179, 206,
    209, 267
  magical properties of 34, 37–8, 179
    see also occult properties
  making 54
  natural 38 *see also* natural materials
  nature of 12, 37
  precious 39
  transformation of 31, 185
  types of *see* amulets *and* charms *and*
    figurines *and* phylacteries *and*
    talismans *and* wands *and*
    witch bottles
  use of 2, 13, 20, 38–9, 40, 172, 175,
    188
occult, the 17, 57, 61, 71, 80, 196–203,
    206–7, 210, 214–15
  disciplines of 22
  ideas about 86, 115, 201 2, 224,
    234, 260
  sciences of 33–4 *see also* alchemy *and*
    astrology *and* magic *and*
    divination
  texts about 33, 197, 207
occult powers/properties 38, 50, 93
occult practices 71, 78, 80, 108, 199
Occult Review, the 216
  'Magical Metathesis' 216
  'The Magic of a Symbol' 216
  'Spurious Ecstasy and Ceremonial
    Magic' 216
Odysseus 19
L'oiseau bleu (fairy tale) 271
van Oostsanen, Jacob Cornelisz 140
oracles 238–42, 251
Order of the Rosy Cross 203

Ordo Templi Orientis (OTO) 214–15, 219, 226
Ordre des Chevaliers Maçons Élus Cohen de L'Univers 204
Origen 27
Osborne, John 194
Osborne, Ruth 194
Osnabrück 95
other, the 260
Otranto 189
Ottoman Empire, the 96
Oviedo, Gonzalo Fernández de 227–8, 254
Oxford University 232, 242
  Poetry Society 217
Oxfordshire 130, 190

pagan society 16
paganism 30, 211, 222, 225–6, 262, 271
  and Christianity 33–4, 218
  and magic 31
pagans 15, 26–7, 29, 68, 118, 218, 222, 225, 226, 250, 284
Page, Sophie viii–ix
pain 176
Palatinate, the 119, 131
Palestine 27
Pamphile 140
Panchiel 32
Pandemos, Aphrodite 136
papacy, the 53, 58 *see also* 'popery'
Papal State, the 109
Pappenheimers, the 128
'Papus' *see* Encausse, Gérard
Papyrus Brooklyn 10
Papyrus Ebers 7
Paracelsus 197, 200
Paraig (river) 45
Paris 95, 141–2, 161, 204, 208, 212, 217
  parlement of 86, 112–13, 117
  University of 46, 70, 87
Paris, Matthew 39
Parmigianino 157
parody 155, 161–3
Pasqually, Jacques Martinès de 204, 215
Parakanã, the 254
Parma, Giorgio Anselme da
  Opus de magia disciplina 60
Pascalis Romanus 34
Patamuna, the 254

patriarchy 94
Pau 112
Pauli, Johann 137
  The Ants 137
Pays de Labourd 144
Pays de Vaud 94
Pearson, Joanne 249
peasants 65, 71, 86, 246
Pendle witches 129
penitentials 31
people 27, 51, 93, 100, 132, 245, 261
      see also aboriginal/indigenous
      people *and* public, the
  non-human *see* non-human entities
Perkins, William 62, 64, 81–4, 89
  Discourse of the damned Art of Witchcraft 81, 84
Persia 18, 22, 41, 180
Peru 79
Peter of Bern 72
Petrie, Douglas 283
Pfeiffer, Michelle 280
Pharaohs 6–7, 9, 14
pharmakeus/pharmakides 18–23, 27
Philadelphia (Pennsylvania) 201
Philadelphia (Turkey) 21
Philadelphian Society 201
Philip II (King of Spain) 109, 146
Philip IV (King of France) 71
philosophy 22, 33, 36–7, 40–1, 44, 48, 57–9, 62, 89, 196, 199, 206, 228, 234
Phoronis 19
Phrygia 19
phylacteries 21
physiology 199
Picatrix 34, 36, 42
Pirckheimer, Willibald 136
plants 38, 169, 179–80 *see also* herbs
  magical properties of 34, 169
  types of
      lunaria 38
Plato 18, 20, 36, 206 *see also* Neoplatonism
  Charmides 21
Pliny the Elder 1, 23, 26
Pluto (god) 57
Plymouth Brethren 213
poison/poisoning 19, 22–3, 239–40, 254
Poland 98, 132, 161, 169, 180, 194
  people of/from 141–2, 235

Polanski, Roman
  Rosemary's Baby 223, 271
political sorcery 58, 76
politics vii, 50, 57, 62, 71, 76, 94–6, 97,
    104, 105, 125, 156, 204, 225,
    275, 279, 286
polytheism 232
Pomerania 103
Pompey 25
'popery' 127–8
Pordage, John 201
della Porta, Giambattista 197
  Magia naturalis 197, 214
Portugal 22, 109, 189 *see also* inquisitions,
    Portugese
possession 52, 82, 130–1 *see also* demons,
    possession by
postmodernism 228, 246
potions 19, 158
Potts, Thomas 129
Powell, Joseph 172
Practical Magic (film) 283
practical skills 23
Praetorius, Johannes 151, 159
  Performance at the Blocksberg 151, 154–5
'prayer rolls' 54
prayers/requests 5, 16, 30, 40, 41, 45, 54
Priapus 136
Price, Harry 217
priests/clerics 6 7, 11, 12, 14, 25, 31 3,
    49, 52, 60–2, 93, 95, 97, 111,
    113, 121, 126–7, 131, 138, 140,
    167, 172, 182, 191, 193, 200,
    202, 205–8, 226–7, 262
primitivism 242, 257
Priscillian, Bishop of Ávila 27
progress vii
prophecy 200
Prussia 132, 187
Pseudo-Apuleius
  Herbarium 30
pseudo-Phocylides 15
pseudo-science 190
psychiatry 87
psychic, the 210, 217, 222, 232
psychoanalysis 243
psychology viii, 5, 10, 234, 237, 245, 251
public, the 112, 131, 220, 225, 240, 277
    see also culture, popular *and*
    people, the
  opinion of 73, 217, 223–4
Pyramid Texts 6

qosem 14

Ra (god) 6–7, 9
Rabanus Maurus 48
racism 233
Rackham, Arthur
  English Fairy Tales 266
Radcliffe, Daniel 259
Radcliffe-Brown, Alfred Reginald
    242, 245
  The Andaman Islanders 242
  *The Social Organisation of Australian
    Tribes* 242
Ramsey, Andrew Michael 204
Randolph, Beverly 208, 215
rationality 1, 92, 228–9, 233, 242, 245,
    250–2, 257 *see also* irrationality
    and reason
Raziel 45
reality 8, 157, 159–60, 251, 255
reason 35, 229, 237, 250 *see also*
    rationality
Reformation, the vii, 67, 75, 82, 104,
    139, 181, 195, 230 *see also*
    Counter-Reformation, the
Regino of Prüm
  Two Books of Synodal Causes 67
  Canon episcopi 67–70, 75
Reidshill, Laird of 166
relativism 253
relics 39
religion vii–x, 30, 32, 79, 80, 84, 97, 104,
    105, 126, 180, 182, 189, 196,
    199, 201, 206, 210, 213, 216,
    219, 220, 221, 223, 225, 226,
    230, 232–6, 247, 253, 257,
    260, 262, 263, 271 *see also*
    authorities, religious
  comparative 232
  crises in 104, 126
  fallacies of 62
  and magic 1, 7, 10–12, 17, 20, 23, 28,
    79, 80, 84, 97, 104, 105, 126,
    180, 182, 189, 196, 199, 201,
    206, 210, 213, 216, 219, 220,
    221, 280
  monotheistic 16
  nature-based 248
  orthodox 44, 48, 54, 60, 64, 73, 77, 205
  practice of 7, 30
  threats to 141, 146
  transformation of vii

religious practices 18
remedium 24
Rémy, Nicholas 77, 79, 82, 129, 141
   Demonolatry 159
Renata, Maria 91
Rennes 112
reportage 125
Reuss, Theodore 215
Rhine-Meuse 105
Rhineland 127
Rickman, Alan 285
Ries, Teresa Feodorowna 163
rights 225
Rio de Janeiro 229
Ripley Museums of Witchcraft and
     Magic 224
Ripley, Robert 224
ritual 1, 18, 82, 108, 158, 203, 206–7,
    220–1, 226, 244–5, 248,
    249–50
rituals 141, 146–7, 175, 182, 185, 188,
    205, 221–2, 226–7, 254, 281,
    286 *see also* magic, types of,
    ritual
  Christianization of 43, 58, 181
  development of 212
  diabolic 145, 209
  instructions for carrying out 16, 31,
    40–2, 177–8, 219
  nature of 40, 43, 50, 55, 172, 175, 178,
    181, 210, 220, 221, 225, 244–5
  objects used in 5, 10, 41, 171, 177,
    185, 204, 212, 221–2, 250
    see also objects
  'passing through' 176
  performance of 39, 47, 59, 61, 145–6,
    154, 175–8, 206, 210, 221, 236,
    244–5, 250
  sacred 29–30, 82
    inappropriate 29
  stages of 4
Röcklin, Hans 178
Roermond 101
Rojas, Fernando de
  Celestina 56–7
romanticism 161, 163, 206, 231, 262
Rome 74, 76, 157
Rome (ancient) 15, 24–8, 35, 39
  culture/ideas of 22–4, 28, 35, 38, 59,
    109, 206

  deities of 27
  magic in 22–3, 25–6, 28, 58
  people of/from 2, 22
Romero, George 270
Rops, Félicien 163
Rosa, Salvator 145, 152, 155–7
  Day 155
  Evening 155
  Morning 155
  Night 155
  Saul and the Witch of Endor 155–6
  Witches at their Incantations 155
Rosenkreutz, Christian 203
Rosetta Stone, the 6
The Rosicrucian 211
Rosicrucianism 203, 206, 209, 210, 211
Rospigliosi family 157
Rothenburg ob der Tauber 131
Rottweil 95
Rouen 112
Rowling, J. K. 258–9, 268, 271–2
  Harry Potter (books) 258–9, 268, 271–2
    The Chamber of Secrets 272, 285
    The Order of the Phoenix 260
Royal Society, the 89
runes 216
Rushdie, Salman 266
Russia 94, 187–8, 210
  treatment of witches in 97–8, 132, 174

Sabrina, the Teenage Witch (television
    series) 270, 286
sacrifices 42, 135, 271
  to demons 30, 54
sadomasochism 214
St Albans 221
  Abbey 36, 39
St Apollonia 181
St Basil 27
St Blaise 178
St Cyprian 184
St John 26, 181
St John Chrysostom 27
St Joseph 28
Saint-Martin, Louis-Claude de 205–6
Saint Maximin (imperial abbey) 99, 103,
    117, 124
St Osyth witches 129
St Paul 26
St Peter 26

saints 30, 48, 181
Saks, Sol 267, 268
Salamanca
    University of 56
Salem 264 *see also* witch trials, Salem
Salmesbury 130
Samaria 26
Šamaš 4
Sampson, Agnes 166
Samuel (biblical figure) 158–9
San Francisco 224
Sanasi, Anna 192
Sanders, Alex 221, 223
Sandrart, Johann Jakob 158
Saragossa 167, 182
Sarandon, Susan 280
Sargent, Dick 270
Satan's School for Girls (film) 271, 284
satanism 63, 223, 242 *see also* Devil, the,
        worship of *and* witchcraft,
        satanic
Saul (biblical king) 14, 155–6, 158
Saur, Abraham 137
Saussure, Ferdinand de 242
Savery, Jacob 160
Savoy 96, 100, 113
Saxony 103, 107, 139
Scandinavia 94, 184, 187
    treatment of witches in 96, 113
scepticism 86–7, 89, 114, 132, 142,
        157, 256
Schäufelein, Hans 138
    *Magical and Sorcery Practices as Crimes of
        Diabolical Witchcraft* 134
Schleswig-Holstein 100
Schmidtheim 117
Schönfeld, Johann Heinrich 158
Schongau 185
Schott, Georg 185
Schulze, Hans *see* Praetorius, Johannes
Schut 160
Schwäbish Hall (Free Imperial City
        of) 075
science vii, x, 33, 35, 37, 40, 46, 48, 49,
        59, 62, 63, 67, 68, 69, 77, 82,
        86, 88, 176, 189, 193, 195, 199,
        202, 203, 211, 213, 232, 233,
        234, 236, 237, 242, 246, 250,
        251, 255, 257 *see also* natural
        philosophy *and* pseudo-science

and magic 1, 37, 195, 214, 237, 250
    see also occult, the, sciences of
Scientific Revolution, the 86, 89
Scot, Michael 49
Scot, Reginald 74, 87, 149
    'A Discourse upon Divels and
        Spirits' 88
    The Discoverie of Witchcraft 87, 149
Scotland 22, 66, 80, 108, 131, 178, 182
    people of/from 178, 216
    treatment of witches in 96–7, 110,
        113, 114, 117, 129–30, 165–6
séances 220, 250
Season of the Witch (film) 270
secrecy 60, 184, 204, 207, 213, 216, 226,
        246, 286
secularism 195, 257, 285 *see also*
        authorities, secular
seidr 249–50
Seneca 77, 79
sensus naturae 37
Sepher ha-Razim 16, 17
Seth (god) 8
Seville 189
sex/sexual acts 57, 72, 75, 77, 114,
        142, 152, 178, 185, 214,
        225, 273, 280
    engaging in 56, 69, 71, 94, 125,
        138, 152
    ritual 221–2
sexuality 136, 152, 164, 225, 225, 250
Shakers, the 207
Shakespeare, William 271, 279
shamanism 225, 226, 231, 249, 252–3
Sharpe, James vii, x
Shelley, Percy Bysshe 206
shoel ob 14
shoes 172
Siberia 226, 231
Sibly, Ebenezer 202
    Key to Physic and the Occult Sciences 202
    *A New and Complete Illustration of the
        Celestial Science of Astrology* 202
von Sichem II, Christoffel 160
Sicily 33, 217
Sigfridus, Thomas 142
    *A Correct Answer to the Question Whether
        Witches Themselves Can Cause
        Death…* 142
Sigismund, Count of Tyrol 75

Silesia 101, 105
Simon (Apostle) 26
Simos, Miriam *see* Starhawk
'skyclad' 221 *see also* nudity
slander 119, 132
Smith, Joseph 201
Smith, Robert Cross 207
    *The Astrologer of the Nineteenth
        Century* 207
    The Philosophical Merlin 207
Smith, Thorne
    The Passionate Witch 269
smöjträ 177
Snow White (film) 267
social relations x
social sciences 246
Societas Rosicruciana in Anglia
        (SRA) 210–11
society vii–viii, 66, 94, 116, 127, 134–5,
        146–50, 173, 225–8, 234,
        237–8, 241, 244, 251–2, 257
    contemporary vii, 251–2, 257, 260
    evolution/development of 232,
        234, 252
    ideas about 94, 138, 205, 232,
        234, 243
    institutions of 164
    magic and 235–6, 251, 257
    norms of 50, 135
    order of 91, 94, 132, 145–7, 151, 153,
        237–8, 248
    status within viii, 30, 50, 106, 147, 182
    threats to 140–1, 145–6, 151, 153–4,
        160, 162
sociology 195, 226, 234
Socrates 36
Soldan, Wilhelm Gottlieb 119
Solomon (King) 34, 41, 45, 183
Somers, William 130
Somerset 65, 185
sortilegium see magic, types of, sorcery
souls 22, 24, 44–5, 63, 165, 230, 253
South America 189, 229, 255
Southcott, Joanna 199, 200
Southwell, Thomas 58
Sowerbutts, Grace 130
Spain viii, 33–4, 100, 109, 167, 171,
        182, 184, 188, 189, 190 *see also*
        inquisitions, Spanish
    Muslim *see* al-Andalus

    people of/from 78, 172, 188, 227
    treatment of witches in 97
Spanish Armada 108
Spanish Netherlands 109
Speculum astronomiae 41, 47
Spee, Friedrich 88
    Cautio criminalis 88
Spence, Lewis 216
    Encyclopaedia of Occultism 216
Spina, Bartolomeo de
    Quaestio de strigibus 74
spirit 42, 45, 111, 196, 206, 209,
        225, 254
spirits 36, 39, 40, 42, 88, 151–2, 156–7,
        196, 245 *see also* the dead,
        spirits of
    commanding/compelling 41, 52
    communication/interaction with 20,
        45, 51, 78, 90, 91, 191, 197–8,
        205, 206–8, 213, 231, 250
    conjuring of 83
    of the earth 47
    evil 7, 19, 28, 36, 50, 222, 254
    good 50
    protection from 169, 223
    summoning 61, 197
spiritual activities 138, 206, 276
spiritual world 69, 90, 111, 151, 157,
        191, 200–1, 206
spiritualism 209, 216–19
spirituality 225, 257
Spitzel, Gottlieb 159–60
Spitzweg, Carl 163
spontaneous generation 37
Sprenger, Jacob 74
Stardust (film) 271
Starhawk 225
    *The Spiral Dance: A Rebirth of the Ancient
        Religion of the Great
        Goddess* 225–6
stars and planets, the 4–5, 31, 43, 177,
        197, 202 *see also* zodiac, the
        influence of 40
    Mercury 41–2, 178
    Moon, the 178, 200
state, the 59, 75–6, 108, 113, 132, 145–6,
        165, 230, 267 *see also*
        authorities, secular
    boundaries of *see* boundaries, between
        states

building of 33, 132
  and religion 66, 77
Stearne, John 114
Stewart, James 281
Stock, Andries 148
Stockholm 183
Stoicism 155
Stonehenge 204
Strasbourg 137, 139
structuralism 228, 243, 245
Stump, Peter 127–8, 141–2
Sudan 22
suffumigation 39
suicide 122, 179
Sumerians, the 2
Summers, Montague 218
  *The History of Witchcraft and
    Demonology* 218
sun, the 7
superstition 62, 78, 80, 84–5, 95, 108,
    161, 163, 182, 195, 199, 201,
    228, 235, 253
Surrey 117
suspicion 110, 169, 172, 185, 194
Sussex 117
Sweden 97, 99, 114, 131, 132, 159, 171,
    177, 178, 183, 188, 199
Swedenborg, Emmanuel 199, 202,
    205, 207
Switzerland 58, 95, 100, 105, 109, 118, 139
symbols 5, 177, 200, 212–13, 216–17,
    242, 244, 257
'sympathy' 2, 233
Syria 206

Tacitus
  Annals 24
talismans 31, 54–5, 152, 182, 184, 197,
    203, 215
Tanner, Adam 88
Tarot 209, 212, 216
Taussig, Michael 256
Taxil, Léo 222
Taylor, Thomas 206
  *Iamblichus on the Mysteries of the Egyptians,
    Chaldeans, and Assyrians* 206
technological determinism 233
Teen Witch (television series) 270, 286
Telchines 19
Tell el-Amarna 9

Tengler, Christoph 138
Tengler, Ulrich 138
  The New Layman's Guide 138–9
Teniers II, David 141, 145, 147, 160
  The Temptation of St Anthony 147, 151
Tertullian 27, 79
Teutonic Knights, the 103
Thābit ibn Qurra 41
  De imaginibus 41
Thelemic religion 213
theogonies 2
theologians 37, 38, 40, 42, 48, 50, 52, 62,
    67, 70, 72, 74, 77, 139, 153, 165
theology 7, 12, 44, 56, 59, 69, 82, 90, 95,
    135, 139 *see also* witchcraft,
    theology of
Theosophical Society, the 210–12, 214–15
Thessalus von Tralles 34
Thessaly 19
theurgy *see* magic, types of, angel
Thévet, André 229
Thirty Years War 104
Thoma, Hans 163
Thomasius, Christian 90
  De crimine magiae 91
  *Historische Untersuchung Vom Ursprung und
    Fortgang Des Inquisitions Processes
    Wieder die Hexen* 91
Thoth (god) 10, 209
Thummim 12
Tiberius (Emperor) 24
Tiberius Claudius Similis 24
Tibet 210, 278
Titian 157
Toledo 31
tolerance 87, 195
Tolkien, J. R. R. 260
  The Lord of the Rings 259
tondi 155
Torah, the 15
totemism 232, 256
Toulouse 70, 75, 112, 205
trances 250
transference 176, 179
treasure 50
trials 58, 65, 71, 88–91, 92, 94, 97–9,
    100, 104, 111–12, 116, 117,
    121, 125, 168, 171, 184 *see also*
    law, courts of, rulings of *and*
    witch trials

trials (*cont.*)
    political 58 *see also* political sorcery
    for sorcery 53, 69–70, 97
    of witches *see* witch trials
    of women 55, 87, 89
Trier 67, 77, 97–8, 116, 117, 124, 127,
        131, 142–4, 145, 151
Trobriand Islands 235
Tunney, Robin 282
Tupinamba Indians 229
Turkey 18, 189
Turner, Edith 245
Turner, Victor 243–7
    *The Forest of Symbols: Aspects of Ndembu
        Ritual* 244
    *The Ritual Process: Structure and Anti-
        Structure* 244
    *Schism and Continuity in an African
        Society...* 244
turnkeys 111, 114
Twelve Tables, the 23
Tylor, Sir Edward Burnett 232–5, 237
    *Primitive Culture: Researches into the
        Development of...* 232
Tyrol, the 64, 101

underworld, the 6
United Kingdom 256 *see also* Britain *and*
        England *and* Scotland *and* Wales
United States, the 187, 194, 199, 207,
        217, 223, 231, 248
    culture/ideas of 263–4, 268, 277–8,
        280, 285
    Freemasons in 202
    magic in 200, 208–9, 211, 224,
        225, 280
    New England 94, 188, 264
        treatment of witches in 130, 165, 265
    people of 207, 212, 219, 225, 237,
        248, 262
Universalism 207, 252
universities 74
Untergrombach 179
Updike, John
    The Witches of Eastwick 264, 269, 280
Urim 12

Valencia 182
Valiente, Doreen 220–3, 226
    Witchcraft for Tomorrow 226

vampires 150
Vaulx, Jean del 128
veneficia 23
Veneziano, Agostino 156
Venezuela 254
Venice 73, 190
Victoria (Queen of England) 256
Vienna 145
violence 55, 142, 194, 254
virtue 49
Visconti, Galeazzo 54
visionary groups 207
vitalism 202
vitality 6, 11
Voltaire 118
Voltmer, Rita v–viii
Vosge mountains 118

Waite, Arthur Edward 212
    Book of Black Magic and Pacts 212
    Transcendental Magic 212
Waldensians, the 53, 134
Wales 165
Wallis, Robert viii
wands 8, 11
Warao Indians 254
Warboys, witches of 130
Waterhouse, John William 163
Watteau, Jean-Antoine 162
wealth viii, 55, 144, 238
weapons 161, 247
Weber, Max 195
Webster, John
    The Displaying of Supposed Witchcraft 162
Weirtz, Anton 163
werewolves 142, 274
Werner II, Joseph 157
Wesley, John 201–2
West Kennet Long Barrow 250
Westcott, William Wynn 211
Weston, John 130
Weyer, Johann 87, 149
    De lamiis 87
    De praestigiis daemonum 87
    On the Tricks of Demons 137, 137
Wheatley, Denis
    The Devil Rides Out 223
Whedon, Joss 282–3
White, John 229
    'The Flyer' 229

White, T. H.
  Once and Future King 259
Wicca 215, 217–19, 222–3, 242, 244,
      256–8, 270
  adherents/practitioners of 220,
      221–2, 225, 271
Wick, Johann Jacob 143
  'Wonder-Book' 140
'Wild Ride', the 136, 139
William of Auvergne 37, 47
William V of Cleves-Jülich, Duke 87
Williamson, Cecil 220, 224
Wilson, Monique 224
Wiltshire 250
Windsor 224
wisdom viii, 204, 209
witch bottles 175–6
witchcraft 52, 93, 95–6, 97, 105–6,
      109–10, 112, 122, 146, 148,
      160, 168, 218, 220, 221, 229,
      249 *see also* wicca
  accusations of 72, 86, 91, 105, 110,
      114, 120–2, 125, 131, 139, 174,
      194, 217, 222, 255
  beliefs 157, 159–60, 164, 201
  cases of 35, 76, 82, 85–6, 89, 110, 168
  confessions of 74, 110, 114, 117, 121,
      122–3, 127, 131, 168
  defence of 157, 158–9, 220
  diabolic 95, 99, 100, 107, 108, 110,
      126, 129–30, 134, 141, 145,
      187, 218
  demonic 67–9, 70, 91, 110 *see also*
      magic, types of, demonic
  as a group activity 139, 141, 144, 145,
      154 *see also* witches, covens/
      sects of
  iconography of 138, 144, 156,
      159, 164
  ideas about 76, 79–89, 92, 95–6, 100,
      105–6, 109, 115–16, 126–7,
      130, 134, 179, 200, 204,
      218–20, 223, 224, 226,
      227–8, 236–42, 254–7, 260–6,
      275–81, 284–6
  investigations of 65, 71, 78, 85, 88,
      90, 170
  malevolent 94, 104, 107–8 *see also*
      magic, types of, maleficent/
      malevolent

  museums of 223–4
  rejection of 85
  as a religion 220 *see also* wicca
  satanic 73
  subversiveness of 286
  taming of 278–9
  theology of 56, 59, 65–6, 72, 77,
      139, 165
  women and 81–2, 135, 141–3, 146,
      159, 224–5, 262, 266–7,
      273, 274
'witch craze' or 'witch panic' 95–6
witch of Endor 14, 140, 155, 156, 158–9
witch-hunting 65, 74, 75, 76, 87, 88, 89,
      91, 93, 96, 104, 106, 107, 121,
      131, 132
'witch tax' 104
witch trials vii–viii, 72, 73, 74, 78, 80,
      88, 92, 93, 159, 161, 168, 170,
      194, 199, 201, 224, 228, 261,
      264, 277
  causes of 97, 100
  conduct of 105–9, 110, 122–3
  end of 131, 132, 160, 164
  Innsbruck 75
  nature of viii, 21, 93, 110–13, 168–9
  North Berwick (1591) 66, 108
  Mora case 131, 160
  pattern of viii, 100, 100, 127, 160
  records of 115–25, 128–9, 168, 176
  Salem 89, 115, 170
  types of 4
    by pricking/scratching 110, 155,
        173, 185
    by swimming 110, 194
    by water 78
witches
  actions/activities of 65, 75, 78, 144,
      165, 218, 280
  acquittal of 113, 122
  burning of *see* witches, execution of
  conviction of 65, 92, 110, 136, 158
  covens/sects of 74, 77, 97, 107, 112,
      218, 221–2, 225–6, 270,
      281, 285
  and demons 68, 72, 75, 108, 110
      see also under demons
  depictions of 137–8, 139–57, 158–63,
      206, 222–4, 258, 259–80,
      283–6

witches (*cont.*)
  detection of 174
  and the Devil 71–2, 93, 97, 110, 114
      see also Devil, the
  execution of vii– viii, 58, 78, 80, 91,
      93, 95, 98–100, 101, 102, 104,
      109, 114, 117–20, 124, 127,
      128, 130, 132, 133, 142, 143,
      155, 160, 166, 168, 182, 183,
      186, 194, 224, 225, 258,
      273, 279
  and gender 136, 145, 171, 187, 188,
      212, 225, 250, 264, 281, 286
  harm caused by 4, 142, 162, 168, 240,
      242 *see also* harm, causes of
      countering 4, 173–4, 175–6, 179,
      186, 189, 193, 198, 239–40,
      247–8, 282
  interrogation of 111, 122–3
  male 260
  origin of 83
  perceptions of 56, 57, 104, 126, 135,
      141, 143, 149, 155, 158, 217,
      222, 223, 248, 250 *see also*
      witches, depictions of
  persecution of viii, 59, 93–5, 97, 99,
      102, 108, 112, 131, 182, 188,
      195, 218, 219, 220, 224, 229
      see also witch-hunting
  prosecution of 28, 76, 87–8, 94–7, 99,
      105, 107–16, 117, 127, 129,
      132, 133, 164, 166, 168, 168,
      171, 174, 192 *see also* witch trials
  punishment of 73, 87, 107, 111, 115,
      121, 140, 160, 165, 166, 192
      see also witches, execution of
  relationships with 268–9, 277,
      279, 284
  sabbats 65–6, 72, 75, 83, 92, 94, 97,
      100, 107, 112, 115, 119, 124,
      128, 130, 139, 143–4, 145,
      150–1, 154, 159, 161–2,
      218, 276
  solitary 226
  stereotypes surrounding 91, 94, 106,
      158, 163, 222, 248, 269, 272,
      274–5
      animal sacrifice 222, 271
      cannibalism 98, 128, 228, 254
      cauldrons 152, 158–9, 163

  flying 68–70, 75, 84, 91, 94, 276
  goats 159, 162, 276
  having sex with demons / the
      Devil 94, 152
  possessing familiars 94, 108,
      114, 129
  shape shifting 75, 124, 144
  torture of viii, 88, 97, 105, 106–7,
      110–11, 114, 119, 124–8, 227
  types of 221, 222
      diabolic 125
      good 84, 169, 284, 286
      maleficent 78–9, 91, 94, 100,
      106–7, 111, 119, 125, 128–9
      see also *maleficium*
      wiccans *see* wicca
  as workers of harmful magic 5, 112,
      120, 142, 284, 286
  warding off / protection from
      169, 175
The Witches (film) 271
Witches' Anti-Defamation
      League 225
Witches of Eastwick (film) 263–4, 269–70,
      280, 282
Witches' Liberation Movement 225
Witt, Christopher 201
The Wizard of Oz (film) 264–8, 278, 281
wizards 190, 264, 271–2
Wodin (Odin) 29
Wolfgang, Georg Andreas 158
women 11, 19, 24–7, 30, 46, 51, 68, 87,
      93, 141, 171, 185, 187, 191,
      210–11, 216, 225, 261, 267,
      281, 286
  actions of 27, 56–7, 191, 225
  bodies of 135, 136, 138, 143, 146,
      163–4, 174
  and demons 33, 48, 55–6, 68, 71, 75
      see also sex/sexual acts,
      engaging in
  depictions of 19, 144, 145–6, 151,
      163, 262, 271, 277–81,
      284, 286
  emancipation of 267, 279–81, 286
  and men 55–6, 185, 187, 226, 277–80
  perceptions of 56, 81, 94, 222, 261,
      277–80, 281 *see also* feminism
      and misogyny
  power of 57, 135, 261, 267, 280, 284

a practitioners of the magical arts *see*
       magicians/magical
       practitioners, female
protection of 54
skill of 54, 193
treatment of 71, 87, 94, 117–18, 144,
       159, 224–5, 267, 279, 286
wise 118, 190
as witches *see* witchcraft, women and
Women's International Terrorist
       Conspiracy from Hell
       (WITCH) 225
'Wonderful Magical Scrapbook' 207
wonders 25, 83–4 *see also* marvels *and miracula*
   assisted by demons 26, 40, 74
Woodman, William Robert 210–11
The Woods (film) 286
words 7, 8–11, 14, 17–18, 30, 244–5,
       246 *see also* language *and* names
Wordsworth, William 206

World War I 187, 214, 216
The Worst Witch (film) 285
Würzburg 91, 99, 101, 112

'Ye Bok of ye Art Magical' 219
yid'on 14
York
   Archbishop of 83
Yorkshire 173, 221
Young, Robert 258

Zambia 243
Zeus 20
Ziarnko, Jan 141, 143, 144, 145,
       148, 151
   *Description and Depiction of the Witches'
       Sabbath* 148, 152
Zika, Charles x
zodiac, the 42
Zurich 140, 143